Equipped for Reading Success

EQUIPPED FOR READING SUCCESS

A Comprehensive, Step-By-Step Program for
Developing Phoneme Awareness and
Fluent Word Recognition

David A. Kilpatrick, Ph.D.

Professor of Psychology
State University of New York College at Cortland

EQUIPPED FOR READING SUCCESS:
A Comprehensive, Step by Step Program for
Developing Phoneme Awareness and Fluent Word Recognition

Copyright © 2016 by David A. Kilpatrick, Ph.D.

A previous edition was printed under the title:
WORD MAPPING AND PHONEME AWARENESS:
A Training Manual for Developing Fluent Word Identification (2002)
The present edition is expanded and fully revised

Original printing, October 2016
Reprinted with minor text changes and corrections, November 2023

All rights reserved. No part of this book may be reproduced or transmitted
in any form or by any means, electronic or mechanical, including
photocopying, or by any information storage or retrieval system
without permission in writing from the author.
The exception to this notice is that the owners of this manual can
photocopy Appendices A and C for individual classroom use.

Casey & Kirsch Publishers
P. O. Box 2413
Syracuse, NY 13220
800-331-5397

PRINTED IN THE UNITED STATES OF AMERICA

For Dr. Philip J. McInnis, Sr., Ed. D.

In memoriam

CONTENTS

Part I: What Needs to be Done

1	Fluent Word Recognition and Phoneme awareness	1
2	Understanding Phonological Awareness	13
3	Levels of Phonological Awareness	19
4	Orthographic Mapping and Sight Word Learning	27

Part II: How to Do It

5	Teaching Reading in Light of Orthographic Mapping	45
6	Word Study Activities that Promote Orthographic Mapping	53
7	*One Minute Activities* & Other Phonological Awareness Tasks	73
8	Becoming Proficient in Phonemic Awareness	77
9	How to Train Students in Phonological Awareness	85
10	How to Use the *One Minute Activities*	89
11	Assessment of Phonological Awareness	93
12	Letter–Sound Learning	101
13	Addressing Compensating Students	111
14	Remediation, Learning Disabilities, Dyslexia, and RTI	117

Part III: Training Exercises

One Minute Activities	125

Part IV: Appendices/Resources

Appendix A:	Phonological Awareness Development Chart	235
Appendix B:	Comparison of Program Levels with ARL & Rosner	236
Appendix C:	Phonological Awareness Screening Test (PAST)	237
Appendix D:	List of Word Study Activity for Lesson Planning	246
Appendix E:	Letter–Sound Helps	247
Appendix F:	Common Rime Units, Prefixes & Suffixes	249
Appendix G:	Look-Alike Words for Word Study	251
Appendix H:	Nonsense Words for Word Study	252
Appendix I:	Irregular Words for Word Study	258
Appendix J:	Glossary of Terms	260
Appendix K:	References	266
Index		279

TABLE OF ABBREVIATIONS AND CONVENTIONS

e. g.   *for example*

i.e.   *that is,* or *in other words*

/b/   letters in between slash marks refer to the *sound* made by that letter, not the letter itself

/a/   vowels in between slash marks and printed in lowercase refer to the "short" sound of the vowel (in this case, the /a/ sound as in c*a*t)

/A/   vowels in between slash marks and printed in uppercase refer to the "long" sound of the vowel (in this case, the /A/ sound as in c*a*ke)

(s)it   Letters in parentheses within a word represent the sound within the word that will be targeted for deletion or substitution.

A note about formatting:

I have chosen not to use standard citation format of the American Psychological Association (APA), which involves citing references in the text after facts and information are presented. Teachers and parents report that such in-text citations make reading cumbersome and difficult. Therefore, references from which I draw facts are not individually cited but are found in the References section in Appendix K. Another volume entitled *Essentials of Assessing, Preventing, and Overcoming Reading Difficulties* (Wiley, 2015) provides extensive citations from the scientific research literature to support the concepts and practices upon which this manual is based.

PREFACE

For the last few decades, researchers in psychology, linguistics, neurology, speech pathology, literacy education, and special education have been developing and fine-tuning our understanding of how children learn to read and why some children have reading problems. Their findings have been very encouraging. However, the fruits of their labors have not yet made their way into our school systems. The *American Federation of Teachers,* the *Journal of Learning Disabilities* and other sources have documented the gap between research and practice. The present manual is designed to provide a practical resource that focuses on the important discoveries regarding word-reading skills. One of the findings from hundreds of scientific studies is that a skill called *phonological awareness* is a key element in the development of word recognition skills. Most students with poor word-level reading skills display poor phonological awareness. To address this concern, *Equipped for Reading Success* is designed to be a comprehensive phonological awareness training program along with other resources to support word recognition skills.

In August 2001, Dr. Philip J. McInnis and I discussed a plan to co-author a phonological awareness training manual. Phonological awareness had been a part of his *Assured Readiness for Learning* (ARL) program since the 1970s. However, he recognized that many people could benefit from the phonological awareness training within the ARL program who would never have an opportunity to attend an ARL workshop. Not only was the ARL phonological awareness training based on research findings, but it had also been "field-tested" and improved for over three decades.

When he developed ARL, Dr. McInnis addressed phonological awareness by using the *Rosner Auditory-Motor Program.* Dr. McInnis and Dr. Jerome Rosner worked together in promoting phonological awareness training in the 1970s. When Dr. McInnis was president of the New York Association of School Psychologists, he asked Rosner to speak at conferences to promote phonological awareness assessment and training. At the time, this was met with indifference and even skepticism because phonological awareness was fairly unknown in education and psychology. Eventually, Dr. Rosner left education to return to his field of optometry. He told Dr. McInnis that he was free to further develop the phonological awareness program as newer research warranted. The copyright page of Rosner's 1973 program manual indicated that it became public domain in 1983. McInnis reworked the Rosner program to make it more effective. He did this based on 1) research published since Rosner's program appeared; 2) feedback from many teachers using the program, and 3) his conversations with Isabelle Liberman at reading conferences. Until her death in 1990, Liberman was unquestionably the leader in research on the relationship between phonological awareness and reading. McInnis readily admitted his indebtedness to the research of Liberman and her colleagues at the University of Connecticut and Yale University's Haskins Laboratory. Once the updates to the Rosner program were established, McInnis' phonological awareness training program continued to undergo incremental improvements based on research and clinical experience.

In the late 1990s, McInnis and I discussed further changes to the phonological awareness program within ARL based on the research advances in the 1990s. In the spring and summer of 2001, I began the task of assembling phonological awareness training exercises which form the basis of the present manual. My original goal was to provide a resource for parents so they could do phonological awareness training with their children at home. I routinely consulted with parents of children with reading problems and had found there was not much to recommend to parents for helping them train phonological awareness skills. By the time McInnis told me that he was planning on developing a "spin-off" manual that could reach a wider audience, I told him that my work on all the levels had nearly been completed. We agreed that I would send him the work I had done and from there, he would make his contributions resulting in a co-authored text. However, Dr. McInnis fell gravely ill in September 2001. After surviving a near-death bout with pneumonia and months of recovery, he fell ill again and died on March 14, 2002. He was not able to make his intended contributions to the present manual. However, we had the opportunity to discuss many of the changes and updates to the phonological awareness program. Even while he was confined to a rehabilitation center, McInnis and I discussed changes and further refinements by phone. He never saw the printed form of the first edition of this manual. Although he was unable to write any of this manual, he contributed to it in some very important ways. First, the term *One Minute Activities* is taken from his ARL program. Second, as mentioned, Dr. McInnis provided verbal input regarding the new elements I had incorporated into the training. Finally, and most significantly, he provided the inspiration for this entire endeavor. This project is modeled after Dr. McInnis' practice of promoting classroom teaching that is based on approaches that published research studies have demonstrated to be effective. Since the first edition of this manual (2002), many improvements have been made based upon teacher feedback and on updated research over the last 14 years.

Equipped for Reading Success was heavily influenced by the phonological awareness training portion of the McInnis/ARL program, which itself was based on the Rosner program. This means that the present program could be considered "third generation Rosner." Appendix B shows a comparison between the three programs. I am obviously indebted to those who laid the groundwork for the phonological awareness training portion of this manual. *Equipped for Reading Success* derives its research base from a large body of scientific studies combined with four decades of practical application from the Rosner and McInnis programs, along with earlier versions of this manual over the last 14 years.

The present program, however, goes well beyond Rosner and McInnis. When they developed their programs, neither Rosner nor McInnis had the opportunity to know about the discovery and development of *orthographic mapping,* which represents the process readers use to store words for instant retrieval. As it turns out, this process relies heavily on phoneme awareness (the most advanced form of phonological awareness), which helps explain the success of the earlier efforts by Rosner and McInnis. They knew phonological awareness was important for reading, but only in recent years has it become precisely clear as to why. This manual describes this current research and provides the reader with instructional information that will foster reading development in both typical readers and in students who struggle in reading.

ACKNOWLEDGEMENTS

There are many people I would like to thank for their help in preparing this manual. I would like to thank all of the teachers, parents, undergraduate students, and school psychologists who have provided me with feedback in presenting these materials over the last 15 years. I would also like to thank the reading teachers and resource teachers with whom I have worked as I prepared the original (2002) edition of this manual. These individuals include Linda Isler, Janelle Marciano, Norene Lavine, Carol Byrnes, Kathy Ruggeri, Diane Sidmore, Kathy Watters, and Marianne MacDonald. Their field-testing and feedback were very helpful. They also caught many typographical errors. Thanks to my wife, Andrea, for providing feedback on the manuscript. I would like to thank Janelle Marciano who proofread the thousands of words in the One Minute Activities. She caught many mistakes and I am very grateful to her for her efforts. I have since revised the manual, so only I am responsible for any typographical errors that remain. I would like to thank Judith Frumkin who not only encouraged the completion of the original version of this book in 2002, but also secured a grant to pay for the printing and distribution of the first edition of this manual to local teachers. For the revised edition, I want to thank Linda Isler, Janelle Marciano, Kathy Ruggeri, Norene Lavine, Melanie Kerwin, Denise Aaserud, Don Jackson, Darlene Randall, Rachelle Amo, and Lana Putnam for providing helpful suggestions and text corrections and/or for field testing portions of the revised manual. Particular thanks go to Luqman Michel, a reading disabilities tutor in Malaysia, and Shira Naftel a tutor in New York State, both of whom did extensive proofreading and caught numerous typographical errors. Also a special thanks goes to Dr. Linnea Ehri for providing helpful refinements to Chapter 4. Finally, many issues covered in this book draw heavily from the field of speech-language pathology. I have had the opportunity to consult with some excellent speech pathologists who have answered many, many language-related questions for me over the years and thus directly or indirectly contributed to this manual. These outstanding professionals include Floria Panels, Cheryl Lavigne, Sue Schiro, Rosemary Allmayer-Beck, Kathy Brown, Lynn Kells, and Kimberly Staniec-Pinkerton.

CHAPTER 1

FLUENT WORD RECOGNITION AND PHONEME AWARENESS

It is difficult to overestimate the importance of reading in our culture and in our educational system. Yet, according to U.S. Government statistics, nearly one third of fourth graders are substantially behind grade level in reading. In addition, the *National Research Council* reported in 1998 that 40% of adult Americans did not feel comfortable enough with their reading skills to read a whole book. These people are *not* illiterate. They can read. However, their reading skills are not strong enough for them to enjoy reading.

Reading is critical for *all* school subjects. Science and social studies require textbook reading. Many math tests now require reading. Students read word problems and explain their responses in writing. Poor reading virtually guarantees poor writing skills. Art, music, health, and physical education classes sometimes include background reading and written projects. As a result, reading skills affect a student's entire academic experience.

How well children succeed in school affects their future endeavors in life. While we all know of cases to the contrary, it is ordinarily the students who do well in school who are more likely to go to college and have greater career opportunities. Some children with high intelligence are unsuccessful in school because of weak reading skills. No matter how intelligent a student is, if he reads poorly, he will think of himself as "dumb."

Poor reading can also affect school behavior. Many children who display school behavior problems are poor readers. Because they cannot find reinforcement through academic success, they direct their attention and effort elsewhere, often resulting in behavioral problems. Also, a disproportionate number of poor readers become high school dropouts.

School districts and the federal government are fully aware of the impact reading has on students and on society. Each year, millions of dollars are spent on extra reading help, whether general educational help or special educational help. Rarely do weak readers "catch up." Normally they display slow, gradual progress and they hit a plateau well below grade level.

In education, our assumption that a substantial number of students will be poor readers has become "institutionalized." In other words, we expect it, we program for it, and we budget for it. It is time to challenge this institutionalized assumption. There is enough scientific information

Chapter 1

available to make such a challenge. Research over the last 30 years has indicated that most reading difficulties can be prevented, and among those that cannot be prevented, poor readers can make far greater progress than we have been experiencing in our schools.[1]

Bridging the Gap between Reading Research and the Classroom

For the last 30-40 years, researchers in psychology, education, special education, linguistics, speech pathology, pediatrics, and neurology have been studying the cognitive,[2] linguistic, and academic skills children need to be good readers. Unfortunately, very little of this has made its way into our schools. In 1999, the *American Federation of Teachers,*[3] the second largest teacher's union, noted the gap between scientific reading research and classroom practice. To illustrate this gap, consider the recent popularity of phonological awareness instruction in schools. It seems that phonological awareness began to gain attention in education following the National Reading Panel's report in 2000. It has nearly become an educational fad. Consider a quote from the *Journal of Educational Psychology:*

> The ability to perceive a spoken word as a sequence of individual sounds, which has been referred to recently as phoneme awareness, phonological awareness, and auditory analysis skill, is attracting increasing attention among reading researchers. The high correlation between this ability and success in reading is by now well established.

This quote seems to support the recent surge of interest in phonological awareness. However, this quote comes from 1980! It took nearly 20 years for this scientific finding to make its way into public schools. To be accurate, phonological awareness *was* popular in the 1970s and early 1980s via the Rosner and Lindamood programs. Unfortunately and ironically, such training fell out of favor shortly after this quote was made. Reading "philosophies" in schools began to change in the 1980s, but researchers continued to study the impact of phonological awareness on reading development and reading difficulties.

This twenty-year gap between research and classroom practice illustrates the point made by the *American Federation of Teachers,* mentioned above. Unfortunately, the push for more phonological awareness training since 2000 does not seem to have taken hold to a substantial degree. A 2009 special issue of the *Journal of Learning Disabilities* was devoted to this gap between research and classroom practice. Findings suggest that during their undergraduate and graduate training, teachers do not receive sufficient exposure to scientific research into reading, including the importance of phonological awareness instruction. I worked simultaneously in

---

[1] Not all studies get such impressive results. Studies that do not involve phoneme awareness training typically produce minimal results, even when they use explicit, systematic phonics and reading practice. Studies that involve phonics, reading practice and training in *basic* phoneme awareness instruction (segmentation and blending; see Chapter 7) show moderate results. Studies that use phonics instruction, reading practice, and phoneme awareness training using phonemic manipulation tasks (explained in Chapter 7) demonstrate the highest results.

[2] The term *cognitive* refers to one's thinking skills or mental skills, including perception, memory, retrieval, etc.

[3] See their publications listed in the bibliography. I will not be citing references for all of the facts presented. This volume is designed for teachers and parents, so for ease of reading, the standard APA in-text citation format is not used. The sources for the facts and research results presented in this manual are listed in Appendix M.

both a university setting and a public school setting from 1994 to 2016, so I am keenly aware of this "information gap." This book attempts to help bridge that gap.[4]

How Written Words are Stored in Memory: A Major Discovery in Reading Research

In recent years, there has been a breakthrough in our understanding of reading. Scientists have figured out how we store words for immediate and effortless retrieval. The ability to quickly store new words is the mark of a good reader. Most educators assume we store words by some sort of visual memory. This is not an accurate assumption (see Chapter 4). This book is designed to inform teachers, school administrators, and parents about what researchers have discovered about written word memory and retrieval. Chapter 4 describes this finding in detail. Chapters 5 to 14 will show how to use these findings to improve reading ability.

It is difficult to overestimate the significance of this finding. We've been teaching and remediating reading for many years, not knowing the precise details of how words are actually remembered in our long-term memory. We have had various beliefs and guesses about the process, typically assuming that we store words based on visual memory. We now know that this is definitely *not* the case (see Chapter 4). Without understanding the process by which words are efficiently remembered for later, instant recall, we will continue to "shoot in the dark" to find ways to help struggling readers. However, given that we now have a good understanding of how written words are remembered, we are in a great position to take a fresh look at both early reading instruction and reading remediation.

Learning From Good Readers

A common belief about reading is: "As long as the student gets the meaning, that's all that matters." Unfortunately, many children require great effort to get the meaning due to limited word recognition skills. By contrast, good readers quickly and effortlessly recognize all or almost all of the words they read. Weaker readers typically resort to compensating. We are not helping these children by letting them function that way. With each passing year, the reading vocabulary load increases, so compensation becomes more challenging. When word recognition is difficult, all school subjects suffer, and so does a student's motivation. Reading comprehension is our goal, and *the most direct route to good reading comprehension is to make the word recognition process automatic so a student can focus all of his or her mental energy on the meaning* (for more about compensators, see Chapter 13).

Good readers do not struggle over words—continually guessing or sounding them out. When they see words, they *immediately* recognize them. Table 1.1 provides some facts about good readers. For good readers, word reading is fluent. *Fluent* means fast *and* accurate, and includes proper expression. Fluent readers comprehend more of what they read because they can focus their attention on the *meaning,* not on figuring out the words. Meaning-focused reading approaches do not provide a way of overcoming poor word-level reading skills.

---

[4]See also Kilpatrick, D. A. (2015). *Essentials of assessing, preventing, and overcoming reading difficulties.* Hoboken, NJ: Wiley & Sons, for a thorough documentation of the reading research that supports this book.

Chapter 1

Good readers can recognize a word in 1/20th of a second.

Good readers can recognize a word flashed on a screen for 1/20th of a second.[5] They don't *respond* that quickly, but they only require *input* for 1/20th of a second to recognize a word. These experiments use words out of context, so *good readers do not require context for instant and accurate word recognition.*[6]

Good readers can read 150-250 words per minute.

When reading non-technical material, the average skilled reader can read rather quickly.

Good readers can immediately recognize tens of thousands of words.

Depending on the size of the reader's oral vocabulary and reading experience, the number of words that good readers can instantly recognize is huge (between 30,000 and 70,000 words, or more).

Good readers learn new words very quickly.

By second grade, average readers only require between one and four exposures to a new word before it becomes permanently stored for immediate retrieval. At first this seems hard to believe, but it has much experimental backing and fits with the growth rate in sight vocabulary we see in children.[7]

Good readers don't forget the words they learn.

Once good readers learn words, they don't forget them.[8] If a child keeps forgetting words he or she has learned, that indicates those words were not truly "learned," but had been previously identified through compensating strategies. They were not efficiently stored for later retrieval.

TABLE 1.1
KEY CHARACTERISTICS OF GOOD READERS

The point here is to emphasize the importance of efficient memory for written words (i.e., word storage). Researchers have discovered the mental process we use to efficiently store words for instant, effortless retrieval. It is called *orthographic mapping*. *Orthography* comes from the Greek words *orthos* (meaning "straight" or "correct") and *graphos* (meaning "writing"). Orthography refers to our knowledge of the correct way to write words. We develop a memory for the precise letter order of words. This is called *orthographic memory*. For example, when we see the word *pear* we think of a fruit yet when we see the word *pair* we think of a set of two things. Our memory for the precise order of the letters in those words activates the proper meaning, even though, in this case, the pronunciation is the same. Orthographic memory occurs at two levels of precision. First, we must have a precise enough orthographic memory to recognize the words we read. When we see the word *sent*, we do not confuse it with *set* or *send*. The second level of precision, which is often more difficult, allows us to correctly spell words.

---

[5] This happens even though the word is followed by characters (e.g., #####) to cancel out any retinal after-image.

[6] Context is needed to determine the meaning of words with multiple meanings, such as *match* or *ring*. However, no context is required to effortlessly recognize the pronunciations of words (except for *homographs,* which are printed words that have multiple pronunciations, like *bass, dove, lead,* and *wind*).

[7] The average child entering first grade can read 50-500 words. Two years later, entering third grade, they can instantly recognize several thousand words. Mathematically, for that to happen, students would have to remember new words after only a few exposures, rather than dozens of exposures per word.

[8] Notice we sometimes get "stuck" on the name of someone we have known for years or "stuck" on a word we are trying to say, yet we never get stuck on the *written* words we have already learned.

So, for example, most adult readers can instantly read words like *tongue, bouquet, colonel, license, rendezvous,* or *licorice,* yet far fewer adults can correctly spell them. For our purposes, we will be focusing on the first level of orthographic memory, that is, being able to remember a sequence of letters well enough to instantly trigger the word without sounding it out or guessing.

Chapter 4 explains how we remember the words we read via orthographic mapping. This memory process leads to effortless retrieval of familiar words. Orthographic mapping is thus the process we use to develop our *sight vocabularies*. A *sight vocabulary* (which scientists call the *orthographic lexicon),* refers to the pool of words we can immediately and effortlessly recognize regardless of whether they are phonetically "regular" or "irregular," so sight words are words we instantly recall from memory. Students who are good orthographic mappers have large sight vocabularies and read fluently. Students who are poor orthographic mappers have limited sight vocabularies and lack fluency. Thus, orthographic mapping is a major discovery that should dramatically affect how we understand and teach reading.

There are several mental skills associated with word reading. Phoneme awareness appears to be one of the most important of these skills. Phoneme awareness refers to the ability to notice that *spoken* words can be broken down into smaller parts called *phonemes.*[9] It may be surprising that an auditory-linguistic skill like phoneme awareness could affect word reading, but it most certainly does. Those with good phoneme awareness are usually good at remembering the words they read. They learn new words quickly and do not forget them. Those weak in phoneme awareness learn words slowly and often forget them. Studies show that as phoneme awareness improves, word reading typically improves as well.[10] While it has been known for decades that phoneme awareness is important for word-level reading, the discovery of orthographic mapping has helped us understand precisely *why* this is the case. Phoneme awareness is not the only skill that affects word reading. Yet it is very critical and it has not commonly been a part of our efforts at teaching reading. Chapter 4 explains why phoneme awareness is so important for remembering the words that we read.

Word Identification vs. Word Recognition

Someone may say to you "go into the meeting in the next room and tell the tall man with red hair and glasses that he has a phone call." Based on such cues, you could *identify* that man even if you have never seen him before. But sending you in the next room to tell your best friend she has a phone call is quite a different task. You already know your best friend. You don't need cues to *identify* her. Rather, you simply *recognize* her when you see her.

It is similar with reading words. We can distinguish between the terms *word identification* and *word recognition. Identification* is a broad term that means that a student correctly reads a word, regardless of whether he sounded it out, guessed, or retrieved it from memory.

---

[9] See Chapter 2 for the distinction between the terms *phonological awareness* and *phoneme awareness.*
[10] This depends on the age at which students develop phoneme awareness. Older students who develop these skills late may not automatically improve their reading. This is probably because he has spent a few years developing the habit of approaching reading in a compensating manner. Strategies for addressing this problem are found in Chapters 6 and 13.

Identification often takes effort. By contrast, word *recognition* refers to the retrieval of a *familiar* word from memory. There is no need to guess or sound out the word. *Recognition* is instant and effortless. It is based on whether or not that particular word is in a student's sight vocabulary (i.e., the words he can recall from memory). Word identification includes phonetic decoding, guessing, *and* word recognition (see Table 1.2). However, in this manual I will avoid the term *word identification* and use words more specific to how children read, such as *word recognition* (instant recognition of familiar words), *phonetic decoding* (sounding out an unfamiliar word), and *guessing* (using context or other cues to read an unfamiliar word).

Types of Word Identification		
Sounding-out unfamiliar words	Guessing unfamiliar words based on contextual, linguistic, or pictorial cues	**Word Recognition** instantly recognize familiar words

TABLE 1.2
TYPES OF WORD IDENTIFICATION

The term *decoding,* like the term word identification, is used in different ways. It can simply mean reading a word, regardless of whether the word was sounded out, guessed, or recognized from memory. This meaning of the word decoding is used to distinguish the word reading aspect of reading from the comprehension aspect of reading. Decoding is also commonly used in a narrower sense of figuring out an unfamiliar word. For clarity, I will avoid the term decoding except in the phrase *phonetic decoding.* Instead I will use the terms *word reading* or *word-level reading* to refer to reading words, regardless of whether the words are familiar or unfamiliar (i.e., read via phonetic decoding and/or guessing).

Identifying unfamiliar words requires effort. Word recognition is effortless and instant. Word recognition draws from a student's pool of known words. Because instant word recognition is effortless, it allows students to focus on comprehension. Orthographic mapping helps explain how words become familiar. If a word is "mapped" to permanent memory, it is a familiar word and instantly recognizable. No sounding-out or guessing is needed. If a word has not been "mapped," it is not familiar and needs to be identified in some other way. None of the classic reading approaches (phonics, whole word, or whole language) have done an adequate job with word *recognition*. The exciting news is that for the most part, scientists have pulled back the curtain on how words become familiar for instant recognition. This is why mapping needs to be a central focus of our teaching efforts (see more in Chapter 4).

The Skills Needed for Word Recognition and Phonetic Decoding

To recognize words quickly and accurately, or to sound-out new words, students need a combination of cognitive, linguistic, and academic skills. Table 1.3 lists the skills that contribute to instant word recognition and phonetic decoding. These skills affect who becomes a good reader and who does not. This list is a bird's-eye view of the components of the word-reading process. We must pay attention to these skills in order to *equip* students to be successful readers (hence the name of the program *Equipped for Reading Success*). Most of these skills will be addressed at various points throughout this manual (see also the Glossary). In Table 1.3, I have indicated which skills are primarily needed for phonetic decoding (PD), instant word recognition (WR), and which are needed for both. For clarity, this distinction regarding which skills affect PD vs. WR is somewhat oversimplified.

Oral vocabulary is a key component in reading comprehension, but also seems to play a minor role in word recognition.[11] Vocabulary is a *higher-level* language skill. Phoneme awareness, oral blending,[12] phonological working memory, rapid automatized naming, and verbal-visual paired-associate learning are *lower-level* linguistic skills. These latter skills have not received much attention in the teaching of reading, despite being examined in hundreds of studies. "Behind the scenes," these skills determine which students develop normal reading skills and which students do not. Looking at the skills in Table 1.3, it is clear that schools teach letter-sound skills and vocabulary. Yet to avoid reading problems, we must take account of *all* the key components that determine phonetic decoding and instant word recognition.

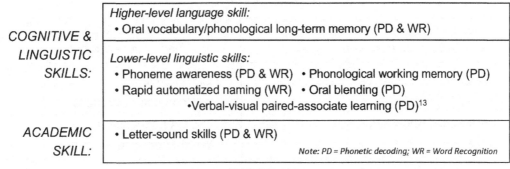

TABLE 1.3

SKILLS NEEDED FOR WORD IDENTIFICATION AND RECOGNITION

Understanding the Reading Process – The "Simple View" of Reading

Everyone agrees that the goal of reading is to comprehend what is read. What, then, are the skills required for reading comprehension? Philip Gough's "Simple View of Reading"[14] helps answer this question. The Simple View of Reading identifies the main ingredients of the reading process and has helped scientists understand both skilled reading as well as reading difficulties.

---

[11] Phonological long-term memory refers to words that are orally familiar, whether or not the meaning is known. Research shows that oral familiarity plays a central role in word reading. Meaning is obviously essential for comprehension but it is not as essential for word-level reading as might be expected. For example, I took Spanish in school and can still read it fluently, but I do not know what it means. The ability to read words at a level above your reading comprehension level is called *hyperlexia*.

[12] Some research suggests that phoneme awareness and oral blending reflect a single, *underlying* skill. But "on the surface," they pop up in different places in the reading process, so I have kept them separate here (see Chapter 7).

[13] The study of paired-associate learning has been around for over 100 years. Yet only in the last few years have researchers studied its relationship to other linguistic skills and to our emerging understanding of word storage. It appears that its primary role is in learning letter names and letter sounds.

[14] The *Simple View of Reading* was developed in the 1980s by Philip Gough and his colleagues. I have further developed it drawing from reading research over the last 25 years.

Chapter 1

For teachers, the Simple View of Reading is a very practical way to 1) understand the reading process, 2) make sense of reading difficulties, and 3) organize assessments, and 4) make instructional decisions (i.e., what to teach and how).

The *Simple View of Reading* divides reading into its most basic components. Reading comprehension is the product of two very broad skills, *language comprehension* and *word-level reading*. Gough argued that students do not struggle in reading if they have both good language comprehension (i.e., they understand material that is read *to* them) and good word-level reading skills. By contrast, students will struggle in reading if they are poor in language comprehension or word identification, or both. This is the most basic level of the *Simple View of Reading*. The Simple View breaks down language comprehension and word-level reading further into their component skills as seen in Table 1.4 (items with an asterisk have been added based on research since Gough's original version of the Simple View).

READING COMPREHENSION *is based on:*	
Language/Listening Comprehension, *which is based on:*	*Word-Level Reading,* *which is based on:*

• Vocabulary, grammar, verbal intelligence
• Inferencing*
• Background Knowledge*
• Attention*
	• Cipher Skills:
	  - Phoneme awareness
	  - Letter-sound skills
	• Word Specific Knowledge

Table 1.4

THE SIMPLE VIEW OF READING

Language Comprehension. Language comprehension is based upon vocabulary as well as knowledge of grammar, inferencing, and background knowledge. Consider the following simple passage (cited in Stuart, Stainthorp, & Snowling, 2008):

> Jane was invited to Jack's birthday. She wondered if he would like a kite. She went to her room and shook her piggy bank. It made no sound.

Most first graders would have no difficulty understanding this, but they would require inferencing skills to do so. Inferencing involves "filling in the blanks" of what a person meant without actually saying it. For example, we infer she will be buying a gift (thus the comment about a kite and her piggy bank). But one must have background knowledge to know what a piggy bank is and what it means that it made no sound when it was shaken. There is so much not actually stated that must be inferred, even in such a simple first grade level passage. In addition to inferences, *attention* is critical. Lapses in attention affect comprehension. If there is part of a story or of a set of instructions that a student did not fully hear because of a lapse of attention, he or she will have a difficult time understanding what was said (or read).

Word-Level Reading. Word-level reading is based on *cipher knowledge* and *word-specific knowledge*. A *cipher* is a type of code, and *cipher skills* refer to the abilities that are needed to deal with the "code" of written English. These skills are *letter-sound skills* and *phoneme awareness.* Both of these will be discussed in more detail later. *Word-specific knowledge* refers to a reader's pool of knowledge about specific words, based on past experience. For example, readers know they are not supposed to pronounce the *b* in *thumb* or the *s* in *island*, based on past experience with those words. However, word specific knowledge is not just for words with irregular spellings. Knowing that *save* is phonetically regular and is pronounced so that it rhymes with *gave,* and not like *have*, also represents word specific knowledge.

In recent years, *fluency* has received much attention. To develop fluency, a student must be skilled in all of the components of word recognition: automatic phoneme awareness, automatic letter-sound skills, and a large pool of known words. If all of the sub-processes of reading are fast and automatic, the student is almost certainly going to be a fluent word reader.

The Four Types of Reading Difficulty

The Simple View of Reading provides a basic yet powerful framework for understanding reading difficulties. Because reading comprehension can be affected by language difficulties or word reading difficulties (or both), the Simple View can alert us to the source of a reading problem. Based on the Simple View, reading difficulties can fall into one of four types:

1) Dyslexia   2) Hyperlexia   3) Combined/Mixed type   4) Compensator type

Dyslexia. Dyslexia is the most common type of reading problem. Unfortunately, in our societal consciousness it has been shrouded in 100-year-old misconceptions. The last 40 years of research into dyslexia have clearly shown that those with dyslexia do not see things backwards nor do they have any other sort of distortions in their visual skills. In fact, dyslexia is based upon what is called the *phonological-core deficit.* The problem is phonological/auditory, not visual. While those with dyslexia generally display normal visual skills, they display one or more deficiencies in *phoneme awareness, rapid automatized naming, phonological working memory, phonological blending,* or *phonetic decoding,* all of which are skills that are primarily phonological in nature, not visual (Chapter 14 discusses the phenomenon of reversing and transposing letters). Contrary to popular misconceptions, dyslexia is simply defined as poor word-level reading skills despite adequate effort, learning opportunities, and normal language skills. That's it. All else is based on popular lore.

Traditionally, the term dyslexia has not been used in schools. Recent state and federal initiatives have made dyslexia a specific category of educational disability, despite already being in the law under a different name. In the federal law, dyslexia has been referred to by two different terms: *Specific Learning Disability in Basic Reading* or *Specific Learning Disability in Reading Fluency* (see Chapter 14 for more on dyslexia).

Students with dyslexia usually have no difficulty understanding spoken language. Yet they display great difficulty learning to read words. This often affects reading comprehension because students with dyslexia (i.e., poor word-level readers) direct so much of their attention toward figuring out the words, little attention is left to focus on the meaning of what they read.

Hyperlexia. Students who can read words proficiently yet have difficulty comprehending what they read have a condition called *hyperlexia*. This name is derived from the fact that these students can read words at a level above and beyond (i.e., *hyper*) what they can understand. Hyperlexia involves a compromise in the ability to understand language generally, oral or written. This is called a *receptive language* difficulty. Such students should receive a language evaluation from a speech-language pathologist. This type of reading problem is actually a language problem that affects reading rather than a problem unique to reading. Hyperlexia should be addressed by remediating the language difficulties along with an emphasis on reading comprehension strategies. Teachers traditionally refer to students with hyperlexia as "word callers."[15] Students for whom English is not their first language often function like hyperlexics until their knowledge of the English language improves.

Mixed/Combined type. The third type refers to students with difficulties in both language comprehension and word-level reading. Such students are usually the weakest readers.

Compensator Type. Compensators are students whose reading comprehension is well below their language comprehension due to weaknesses in word reading. Compensators are often overlooked because they are very bright and compensate for their poor word reading. They may display average reading comprehension but would have stronger reading comprehension if not for their struggles with word reading (see Chapter 13 for more).

Notice how word-level reading difficulties are central to three of the four types of reading problems (dyslexia, mixed, compensator). Because phoneme awareness is the most common source of these word-level reading difficulties, it follows that phoneme awareness training can help the vast majority of students with reading difficulties.

It is generally easier for teachers to address word-level reading difficulties than language difficulties.[16] An important goal in dealing with the mixed/combined type of reading difficulty is to strengthen word reading skills. If these students struggle with comprehension, the last thing we want them to be doing is using mental effort and energy to figure out the words. As these students develop more automatic word recognition, they can place more focus on comprehension.

As mentioned, the most common source of reading difficulties is poor phoneme awareness. Hundreds of studies have highlighted its importance in reading development. Many studies have

---

[15] A mistaken notion has circulated in educational circles that "word callers" are the result of teaching phonics or not emphasizing meaning in reading instruction. On the contrary, students taught via phonics in first and second grade have better reading comprehension at the end of second grade than students taught with meaning-based approaches. This is because phonics-taught students can read more words and thus better understand what they read. By fourth grade, these reading comprehension differences usually even out. However, the point is that phonics does *not* produce "word callers." Rather, weak language skills are responsible for hyperlexia.

[16] Some excellent resources for teachers to help with language development include: 1) *Bringing Words to Life: Robust Vocabulary Instruction* (2013) by I. Beck, M. McKeown and L. Kucan; 2) *Developing Reading Comprehension* by Clarke, P. J., Truelove, E., Hulme, C., & Snowling, M. J. (2014); and *Developing Language and Literacy: Effective Interventions in the Early Years* by J. M. Carroll, C. Bowyer-Crane, C. Hulme, and M. J. Snowling (2011).

shown that training phoneme awareness can improve the reading progress of weak readers. More importantly, studies have shown time and time again that early training of phonological awareness in kindergarten and first grade prevents many reading difficulties from happening in the first place. The next two chapters will explore the nature of phonological and phoneme awareness. Chapter 4 will answer the question about why a phonological/auditory skill like phoneme awareness is so important to word recognition.

Summary and Looking Ahead

Far too many students are behind grade level in reading. In the last few decades, scientists have learned a great deal about how children learn to read and why some children have reading problems. Most of this information is found in inaccessible scientific research journals. One of the most significant findings is *orthographic mapping,* which is the process we use to efficiently store words for permanent retrieval. Phoneme awareness is one of the most important skills necessary for orthographic mapping (Chapter 4). There exists a staggering amount of research on reading acquisition and reading difficulties. In this manual, some of the most relevant aspects of this research are presented in an easy-to-understand manner. The second half of this manual is a comprehensive training program for phonological awareness skills and permanent word storage.

The next page illustrates the major components of the *Equipped for Reading Success* approach. Each of these will be presented in later chapters. The chapters and appendices that address each component are included in the illustration. Also included is an approximate timeline for each of the *Equipped for Reading Success* components. You may want to refer back to this graphic overview as you work your way through the manual.

Chapter 1

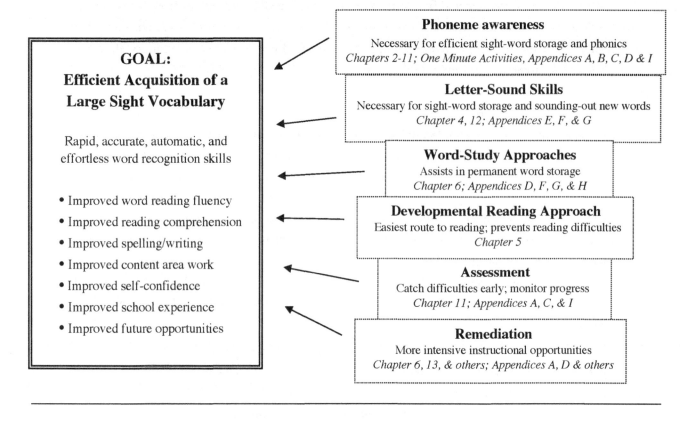

Equipped for Reading Success
– The Sequence –

General Education:

	Kindergarten	1st Grade	2nd Grade	3rd Grade	4th to 12th

- Developmental Reading
- Word-Study Techniques
- Letter-Sound Skills
- Phonological Awareness
- Assessment

Struggling Students (general education remediation or special education remediation):

- Developmental Reading — when ready
- Phonological Awareness — until mastered
- Letter-Sound Skills — until mastered
- Word-Study Techniques — until student is a skilled reader
- Assessment — until student is a skilled reader

— 12 —

CHAPTER 2

UNDERSTANDING PHONOLOGICAL AWARENESS

The findings from countless research studies have been consistent and clear: Students with good phonological awareness are in a great position to become good readers, while students with poor phonological awareness almost always struggle in reading. Poor phonological awareness is the most common cause of poor reading. Reading problems can be *prevented* if all students are trained in letter-sound skills and phonological awareness, starting in kindergarten. You may have heard there is a neurological/genetic basis for reading difficulties. This is accurate. This is apparently because phonological awareness difficulties often have a genetic basis. However, the good news is that despite their neuro-developmental origin, these difficulties are preventable and correctable.

Auditory Skills or Phonological Skills?

Some students with learning difficulties are described as having *auditory* problems. *Auditory* refers to *all* of the sounds we hear, while *phonological* refers only to the sounds of spoken language. Students with learning problems do not typically have auditory problems unrelated to speech sounds. They can understand and produce spoken language because their phonological issues relate to parts of words, not whole words. However, reading is a struggle for them because our alphabet is designed to encode parts of words, and they struggle to connect parts of spoken language to their alphabetic forms. In sum, such individuals have phonological difficulties, not general auditory difficulties.[1]

Phonological Awareness or Phoneme Awareness?

Phonological awareness is an umbrella category. *Phoneme awareness* is a specific skill under that umbrella. Phonological awareness includes all of the following:

- Word Awareness
- Rhyme awareness
- **Phoneme awareness**
- Syllable Awareness
- First Sound Awareness

The difference between the two can be defined as follows:

Phonological awareness: The ability to recognize and manipulate the sound properties of spoken words, such as syllables, initial sounds, rhyming parts, and phonemes.

Phoneme awareness: The ability to recognize and manipulate individual *phonemes* in spoken words.

---

[1] Thus, saying these students have "auditory difficulties" is somewhat imprecise.

Chapter 2

From this we see that *phoneme awareness* is a specific *type* of phonological awareness. In fact, it is the type of phonological awareness that is necessary for proficiency in reading. The other types of phonological awareness provide the foundation for phoneme awareness. *By themselves, these easier phonological skills do not result in skilled reading*. Many children with reading difficulties lack phoneme awareness, but they can demonstrate the easier phonological awareness skills.

What is a Phoneme?

The word *phoneme* comes from the Greek word *phonos* (meaning "sound" or "voice"). A phoneme is the smallest unit of sound in spoken words. Alphabet-based writing systems are designed to have written letters represent the phonemes used in spoken language. For example, the word *sat* has three phonemes (/s/ /a/ /t/).[2] It also has three letters. Each letter represents one phoneme. However, letters and phonemes are not the same thing. Phonemes are *oral* and letters are *written*. Phonemes are the smallest parts of *oral* words. Letters are the smallest parts of *written* words.

Quite often in English, phonemes and letters do not match up. For example, there are four letters in *bake*, but only three phonemes (/b/ /A/[3] /k/). In the printed word *shoe*, there are four letters, but the oral word has only two phonemes (i.e., two sounds). The *sh* represents one sound and the vowels *oe* team up to make one sound. Thus, four letters represent two phonemes. So *bake* and *shoe* do not have a one-to-one match between letters and phonemes. *Teachers and parents must understand the difference between phonemes and letters to successfully train phoneme awareness*. Remember: phonemes are *oral* and letters are *written*.

Many words have the same number of phonemes as letters (e.g., *van, red, Tom, sit, told, sprint*). However, in many words there is a different number of letters and phonemes (e.g., *bike, then, boat, tree*). Try this quiz. How many phonemes are in these words?

time ___   loose ___   new ___   guess ___   best ___   though ___   box ___

How did you do? See the footnote below for the answers.[4] Notice how the words *guess* and *loose* use five letters to represent only three phonemes. Also, *guess* and *yes* share the last two sounds, but represent those sounds with a different number of letters. Two words of interest are *though* and *box*. The word *though*[5] uses six letters to represent only two phonemes! *Box* has three letters but four sounds/phonemes. This is because the letter *x* is the only letter that has two sounds in it (/k/ /s/; consider that Boston's baseball team is named the Red *Sox*, not Red *Socks*, and *fax* rhymes with *snacks*). These examples illustrate the difference between letters and phonemes. Normally they match up, but in English, they often do not.

---

[2]Slash marks on each side of letters refer to the *sound* represented by that letter, not the letter itself.
[3]A capitalized vowel between slash marks (e.g., /A/) represents the vowel's "long" sound.
[4]*Time* = 3; *loose* = 3; *new* = 2; *guess* = 3; *best* = 4; *though* = 2; *box* = 4.
[5]Keep in mind that the digraphs *sh, th, ch, wh, ph,* and *gh* each represent a single phoneme.

What is the Difference Between Phonics and Phoneme Awareness?

Often confused, phonics and phoneme awareness are different. Phoneme awareness is an oral language skill, not discovered until the 1950s-1960s within the fields of linguistics and speech pathology. It deals with *spoken* language. Phonics has been around for hundreds of years and is an instructional approach for teaching *written* English.

- PHONICS is a method for teaching students to sound out unfamiliar *written* words via *phonetic decoding*. In phonetic decoding, letters are translated into the sounds associated with those letters, and then orally blended into spoken pronunciations. Phonics instruction is intended to develop skilled phonetic decoding but may also focus on spelling. Spelling and phonetic decoding are both based on letter-sound[6] knowledge.
- PHONEME AWARENESS has to do with noticing sounds in *spoken* words. It has nothing *directly* to do with letters.[7] It is an awareness of the sounds in *oral* language. It is a mental/linguistic skill. Chapter 4 will explain why phoneme awareness is important for *remembering* written words.

A way to remember the difference between phonemic awareness and phonics is that *you can do phoneme awareness with your eyes closed but you cannot do the phonic skill of sounding out words with your eyes closed*. Phoneme awareness deals with *oral* input, phonics/phonetic decoding deal with *visual* input. Table 2.1 presents the differences.

	Field of Origin	*Domain*	*Skill Type*	*Role in Reading*[8]
PHONICS	Education	Written Language	Academic	Teaches skills for sounding out new words
PHONEME AWARENESS	Linguistics/ Speech Pathology	Spoken Language	Linguistic	Supports memory for written words and spelling

TABLE 2.1
KEY DIFFERENCES BETWEEN PHONICS AND PHONEME AWARENESS

While they differ in various ways, phonetic decoding and phoneme awareness are both necessary for students to become successful readers (see Chapter 4).

What Does "Awareness" Mean in the Term *Phoneme Awareness*?

By age one, most children can tell the difference between two words that differ by only one phoneme. For example, they can distinguish between *us* and *up*, or *toy* and *boy*, or *came* and *game*. Each word in these word pairs differs by one phoneme. Speech pathologists call this

---

[6] The term *letter-sound knowledge* is commonly used by researchers and that is the term that will be used in this book. Others call it *sound-symbol knowledge* or *grapheme-phoneme knowledge*.

[7] Phoneme awareness is certainly *related* to reading but the connection to letters is *indirect*. For example, the oral sound /z/ can be represented by different letters, like *s* (*has, is*) or *z*. Phonological awareness is about understanding and being aware of the sounds we make when we say words. The minute you introduce letters, you have left the realm of phonological awareness and entered the realm of phonics.

[8] This is a slight oversimplification. The letter-sound aspect of phonetic decoding is critical for permanent word storage, but phonic rules are not. Also, phoneme blending assists with sounding out new words.

Chapter 2

phoneme discrimination. However, it is not until age 6 or 7 that children can understand *why* these words sound different from one other. Understanding why words sound different is phoneme awareness. One of the earliest reports on phoneme awareness was from 1963 in *The Journal of Soviet Psychology and Psychiatry*.[9] The report describes a dialog between a researcher and two school children. The first child was four-year-old Sasha:

Researcher:	What's your name?
Sasha:	Sasha
Researcher:	Nice to meet you Asha
Sasha:	But my name is Sasha.
Researcher:	That's what I said, 'Asha,' right?
Sasha:	No, you said 'Asha' but my name is 'Sasha'
Researcher:	But aren't those the same, 'Sasha' and 'Asha'?
Sasha:	No!
Researcher:	Then how are they different? They sound the same to me.
Sasha:	(no response).

Sasha could not say *why* the names were different. She knew the two names sounded different (discrimination), but had no idea why (awareness). Next, we are told of a first grade boy by the name of Igor.

Researcher:	What's your name?
Igor:	Igor.
Researcher:	Nice to meet you Gor.
Igor:	No, my name is 'Igor,' not 'Gor,' you forgot the *I* at the beginning.

Igor immediately knew *why* the names were different. This illustrates the *awareness* part of phoneme awareness. Both children had good phonemic *discrimination*—they immediately noticed the difference between their names and the names the researcher used. However, only the first grader knew *why* the names were different. Igor had phoneme awareness but Sasha did not. She was not aware of why the names sounded different. Being aware of the individual phonemes is not necessary to understand the flow of spoken language. But when oral language gets matched up with written letters, phoneme awareness becomes a necessity (see Chapter 4).

Important Note: If you suspect a student has difficulty with phonemic *discrimination*, refer that student to the school nurse and a speech pathologist. Impaired phonemic discrimination can affect both reading and general language development.

But Don't Most Children Read Well Without Phoneme Awareness Training?

Absolutely! About 60% to 70% of children develop phoneme awareness very naturally, without being taught. Other children will never develop those skills unless they are directly taught. Yet phoneme awareness is not "optional" if one wants to be a good reader. It's just that some students develop it naturally as they learn to read, while others do not.

---

[9] Russian speech pathologists discovered phoneme awareness in the 1950s. The connection between phoneme awareness and reading emerged in the late 1960s from the husband-wife team of Alvin Liberman, a linguistics professor at Yale, and Isabel Liberman, a cognitive psychologist at the University of Connecticut.

Phoneme Awareness and Intelligence

There is only a small correlation between phoneme awareness and IQ scores. Some children with low IQs develop good phoneme awareness and become good word readers. They often don't understand what they read, however. By contrast, there are many students with average to above average IQs who have poor phoneme awareness. These students represent the dyslexic or compensator type of poor readers mentioned in Chapter 1. Such students are puzzling to teachers and parents because of our intuitive assumption that if a student is "smart enough," he or she should be able to easily learn to read.

Which Children Should Receive Phonological Awareness Training?

Starting in kindergarten, *all* children should receive phonological awareness training. This is due to the fact that not every child who is destined to have phoneme awareness problems can be identified in kindergarten.[10] If *all* children are trained starting in kindergarten, potential reading difficulties can be prevented or minimized. This prevention effect has been demonstrated in many studies. By training *all* children starting in kindergarten, fewer children struggle later. This manual provides everything needed for such training.

Second, typical first and second graders can learn to read more quickly and efficiently when they are trained in phoneme awareness. All schools are interested in boosting the performance of their "average" students. Early phonological awareness training is a great way to do it. This would allow students to focus more on comprehension earlier in their reading careers because they can more quickly build a large sight vocabulary.

Finally, there are many bright students who never develop to their potential because teachers are not aware these students have phoneme awareness difficulties. These are the compensators mentioned in the previous chapter. With much effort and compensation, these bright children perform average to low average in word-level reading. But because their overall reading comprehension is average, they normally do not receive extra help. They simply underachieve relative to their potential. Training all students in phoneme awareness could prevent much of this type of problem (see Chapter 13).

Which Ages or Grades Should Receive Training?

Training the most basic phonological awareness skills (e.g., rhyming, first sound awareness, and syllable segmentation) can start in pre-school. This would involve reading stories that contain rhyming and alliteration and various word games. One British study demonstrated that children with exposure to the classic nursery rhymes in preschool were better readers by the end of second grade than children without such exposure. This was true even though the two groups were matched for socioeconomic status. Thus, reading stories with rhyming and alliteration may help develop early phonological skills. Other studies have also shown this link. Children who

---

[10]Most basic phonological awareness problems can be detected as early as the first half of kindergarten, before reading problems have a chance to develop. However, not *all* children with this problem can be detected early.

Chapter 2

are read to in preschool (and beyond) tend to have stronger letter knowledge and phonological awareness than children who were not.[11]

Formal approaches to training phonological awareness typically start in preschool or early kindergarten and often include rhyming activities and clapping out syllables. However, the goal is to help students develop phoneme-level skills because alphabetic writing systems are phoneme based. It is important that when children begin formal reading instruction, they have sufficient alphabet knowledge and phoneme skills so that the writing system makes sense.[12]

Phonological awareness continues to develop along with early reading skills. All students should get phonemic awareness training through the end of second grade. After second grade, students should be screened for phoneme awareness skills using phonemic manipulation activities (see Chapter 7). If a student seems to have mastered these skills and is doing a fine job reading, then further training is unnecessary. However, students who have not mastered these skills should get training. *There is no age where a student is "too old" for phoneme awareness training—if the skills have not been mastered, the student should get training.* Research has shown that older, struggling readers almost always have difficulties in phoneme awareness that were never addressed. Such individuals will continue to struggle with reading until this difficulty is corrected.

High school students and adults who are weak in phoneme awareness (and therefore weak readers) should get training. In our public middle schools, high schools and colleges, students who are weak readers are often provided with strategies to "work around" their weak reading skills. It is assumed that if they have not developed proficient reading by that point, they won't ever develop it. However, as mentioned, these students almost always have phoneme awareness difficulties that were never detected or trained. This is a perfectly correctable cause of their difficulties, and we are unknowingly letting them continue to struggle when they really do not need to. *There is no statute of limitations on training phoneme awareness skills when they are weak.* If students at any age are poor readers, check their phoneme awareness skills, and address them if they are inadequate.

Summary

Phoneme awareness is a linguistic skill that is essential for learning to read. It is different from phonics, though the two are both important for reading. Phoneme awareness works alongside phonetic decoding to allow children to master the skill of word recognition. Phoneme awareness is arguably the most common source of reading difficulties. The good news is that it is trainable. This manual provides everything needed for that training.

---

[11] For most children, phoneme awareness difficulties have a genetic basis. There are many children whose parents read to them in their early years yet they still struggle in reading. The good news is that even phonological awareness difficulties of genetic origin generally respond very well to direct phonological awareness training.

[12] This assumes the reading approach is developmentally appropriate (see Chapter 5).

CHAPTER 3

LEVELS OF PHONOLOGICAL AWARENESS

Children sit before they walk, and walk before they run. Similarly, phonological awareness shows a developmental pattern. Researchers have identified three general levels of increasing difficulty in phonological awareness skill development:[1] the *syllable level*, the *initial phoneme (onset-rime) level*, and the *phoneme level*. The chart below provides a general idea of when these levels normally develop in students *not* receiving phonological awareness instruction. When they receive such instruction, they do better than what is shown below. Importantly, low achieving readers can master all of these levels, which they would not do without instruction.

When Phonological Awareness Skills are Normally Acquired or Mastered When Not Directly Taught:

	Phonological Awareness Level	Typically Achieving Readers	Low Achieving Readers	Equipped for Reading Success Program Levels
1)	SYLLABLE LEVEL	Pre-K to Kindergarten	Pre-K to Second Grade	D, E
2)	ONSET-RIME LEVEL	Early Kindergarten to Early First Grade	Late Kindergarten to Second Grade	F, G
3)	BASIC PHONEME LEVEL	Mid First Grade to Early Second Grade	Early Second to Fourth or never	H, I, J, K, L, M, N
	ADVANCED PHONEME LEVEL	Late First Grade to Third Grade	Often Never	H, I, J, K, L, M, N

Syllable Level

Through word games, nursery rhymes or children's books, preschoolers learn word play, including rhyming and alliteration.[2] Also, children learn to separate (or "segment") syllables. For example, Kevin learns his name has two parts (Ke-vin).[3]

Syllable segmentation, rhyming, and alliteration developmentally come before phoneme-level awareness. These early activities are the first opportunities for children to focus on the sounds we make when we say words. When a young child hears a word like *table*, he or she thinks about what a table *is*, not about the *sound* we make when we say "table." When children are exposed to word play, such as alliteration and rhyming, they begin to focus attention on the

---

[1] In the last few years, some researchers have reopened the issue of the proper order of phonological awareness development. It has become a very complex issue but has little direct bearing on what I am presenting here.

[2] Alliteration uses words that begin with the same sound/letter (e.g., Dr. Seuss' "Aunt Annie's Alligator, A a a").

[3] No direct exercises for rhyming or alliteration are provided at this earliest level, but levels F & G tap into the same skills needed for alliteration and rhyming. Teachers can add supplemental rhyming and alliteration activities early on, but given the structure of this program, that is not necessary for phonological awareness development.

Chapter 3

oral properties of words. To rhyme, alliterate, or do syllable segmentation, children must think about the sounds we make when we say words, and not the meanings of the words. This is their entry into phonological awareness.

Onset-Rime/Initial Phoneme Level

The onset-rime level represents the first time children actually break apart a syllable. It is an important step on the way toward focusing on middle and ending phonemes, which is the next level. *Rime* is not a misspelling of the word *rhyme*. It is an alternative spelling of rhyme tucked away in Webster's dictionary and used by reading researchers in a specific way.

Onset. The onset of a syllable refers to any consonant sounds that come *before* the vowel in that syllable. For example, in *sat, them,* and *spring,* the onsets are *s–, th–,* and *spr–.* Some syllables/words have no onsets, such as *out, am,* and *ice* (there are no consonants before the vowel).

Rime. The rime is the part of the syllable that includes the vowel sound and any consonant sounds that follow the vowel sound, within that syllable. Let's consider again *sat, them,* and *spring.* The rimes are *–at, –em,* and *–ing.* Words like *we, go,* and *see* have only vowel sounds for rimes, *–e, –o,* and *–ee.* They have no consonant sounds in their rimes. The rime can involve more than one written vowel if it is part of the same syllable. For example, in *food, boat,* and *read,* the rime units are *–ood, –oat,* and *–ead.* In silent-e words such as *made, like* and *rope,* the *–ade, –ike,* and *–ope* are the rimes.

In printed words, the rime is equivalent to what is sometimes called a *phonogram.*[4] Researchers use the word *rime* to refer to both the oral rime and the printed rime. For clarity, I will use the word *rime* to refer to the *oral* rime, and *rime unit* to refer to the *printed* rime.

Written and oral rimes do not always match up. For example, the words *have* and *save* share the same rime unit (*–ave*), but they don't rhyme. *White* and *right* rhyme, but have different rime units (*–ite* and *–ight*). At the *onset-rime* level of phonological awareness, a rime is a rime regardless of the spelling pattern or whether it rhymes with anything else. Consider these examples of onsets and rimes:

Type of ONSET	WORD	ONSET	WORD	ONSET
Single phoneme onset	cat	c	sit	s
Two phoneme blend onset	clap	cl	flip	fl
Three phoneme blend onset	spring	spr	splash	spl
No onset	out	(none)	in	(none)
Type of RIME	WORD	RIME	WORD	RIME
Single vowel, single consonant rime	pen	en	sat	at
Rimes with phoneme blends	bent	ent	first	irst
Vowel digraph or silent e rime	boat	oat	make	ake
No consonant sound in rime	tree	ee	so	o

The onset-rime level of phonological awareness goes beyond the syllable level because the child has to break apart the syllable. For example, in the word *top,* a student can separate the syllable at the onset-rime juncture: *t-op.* Even though the *t* is a phoneme, attending to the first phoneme in a word is easier than attending to phonemes in the middle or at the end of a word, so researchers distinguish between the onset-rime and the phoneme level.

---

[4]In printed words, phonograms can represent any one of many word parts (prefixes, suffixes, roots), but this term has also been used for the rime unit. The ARL program used the term *Decoding Key.*

Onsets and rimes can only be understood *within* a given syllable. Not every syllable has an onset, but *every syllable has a rime*. This is because every syllable has a vowel.[5] Thus, two-syllable words have two rimes and three syllable words have three rimes, etc. For example, let's divide the word *carpenter* into onsets and rimes. The first syllable is /car/. The onset in this syllable is /k/, and the rime is /ar/. The second syllable in *carpenter* is /pen/. The onset is /p/, and the rime is /en/. The last syllable is /ter/. The onset is /t/, and the rime is /er/.

Phoneme Level

The third level of phonological awareness is the *phoneme level*, hence the term *phoneme awareness*. To be a good reader, students must master phoneme-level skills. It is not enough to master syllable-level and onset-rime level skills. Those levels are foundational to phoneme awareness. However, *unless students master the skills at the phoneme level, you will not see the desired effect on reading*. I have evaluated hundreds of students who had good syllable and onset-rime skills yet were weak readers because they had not mastered phoneme-level skills. Phoneme awareness is the most difficult type of the three broad levels of phonological awareness, and can be subdivided into basic and advanced phoneme levels (see Chapter 7).

How Much Phoneme Awareness is Necessary to Be a Fluent Reader?

To be a fluent reader, a student must be thoroughly competent at the phoneme level.[6] Average and above average readers demonstrate instant responses to phoneme-level manipulation tasks by second grade to fourth grade, even if they have never been trained in phoneme awareness. Students who struggle with reading tend to get "stuck" at the onset-rime level or the basic phoneme levels. This represents a mid first grade to early second grade level of phonological awareness development. These students are expected to progress through school with a first to second grade level of phonological awareness. To get "unstuck," these children will require direct, conscientious phoneme awareness training. Once they have mastered phoneme-level skills, these children may require ongoing reinforcement of their skills.

Many phonological awareness programs focus on phoneme *segmentation* tasks. Such tasks are easier than phoneme *manipulation* tasks. Phoneme segmentation is typically mastered by late first grade. But phonemic skills continue to grow after first grade and this additional growth is best measured via phoneme manipulation tasks (see Chapter 7). I have evaluated many poor readers who quickly and accurately respond to phoneme segmentation tasks but not to phoneme manipulation tasks. If we only use segmentation to assess phoneme awareness, the teacher or evaluator might mistakenly assume that a poor reader has sufficient phoneme skills for reading when he does not. In this situation, the teacher is left in the dark as to why the student is not progressing in reading and the child may not be given the phoneme awareness training he desperately needs. Many otherwise positive efforts at training phoneme awareness have relied too heavily on segmentation (see Chapter 7). This is why phoneme manipulation forms the basis of the assessment and training in this manual.

---

[5]Not every syllable has one of the usual five written vowels. For example, the words *by* and *sky* use *y* as a vowel.

[6]More precisely, one must display *phonemic proficiency*, which is best demonstrated via instant responses to phoneme deletion and/or substitution tasks (see Chapter 7).

Chapter 3

Program Levels of the *Equipped for Reading Success* Phonological Awareness Training Program

The labeling system for the levels in the *Equipped for Reading Success* program (Level D, Level E, etc.) is coordinated with the Rosner and the McInnis/ARL programs. Appendix B provides a chart that cross-references these three programs. Levels A through C are not typically needed and are not addressed here. They involve matching and one-to-one counting.

With years of experience in many school districts, McInnis's ARL Phonological Processing Program has refined the three research-based levels of syllable, onset-rime, and phoneme. Rosner and McInnis discovered that not all syllable level tasks are created equal. For example, it is far easier to delete the first syllable of a two syllable, compound word (e.g., *cowboy* to *boy;* Level D1) than it is to delete the first syllable from a three syllable word when that first syllable is the stressed syllable (e.g., *holiday* to *iday;* Level E4). Likewise, some phoneme-level tasks are more difficult than other phoneme tasks. For instance, *deleting* a phoneme from the end of a word (e.g., *seen* to *see;* Level I) is much easier than *substituting* a phoneme at the end of the word (e.g., *beat* to *beam;* Level L). Rosner and McInnis reasoned that lumping the difficult and easy items together created an unnecessary challenge for children, especially those with learning problems. They preferred a smooth transition from easiest types of words and manipulations to the most difficult. McInnis' ARL program, to my knowledge, was the only program to train phonological awareness in a more fine-grained and developmentally sequenced manner. This sequencing was based upon extensive field trials in dozens of school districts over three decades. *Equipped for Reading Success* smooths out McInnis' levels even further to create a program that has no big hurdles for students. As they move from one level to the next, there is no place for any student to "get stuck."[7]

Based upon 1) McInnis' three decades of phonological awareness training, 2) several years of field testing I have done, and 3) emerging research over the last 10-15 years, I have provided sub-groups within the syllable level and the phoneme level. The syllable level is divided into basic and advanced types of syllable manipulation. The phoneme level is likewise divided into basic and advanced. Recognizing that there are easier and harder tasks within the syllable and phoneme levels helps ensure that children's skills can develop without getting "stuck" at any level. If children ever seem to get stuck, Chapters 7 through 9 present ways to prepare students for the next level and are virtually guaranteed to get them "unstuck." Below is an overview of the program levels in the *Equipped for Reading Success* manual's comprehensive phonological

---

[7] An exception was made to maintain the three levels of syllable, onset-rime, and phoneme highlighted by the National Reading Panel. Some syllable-level tasks (E3, E4, & E5) are actually harder than onset-rime tasks (F, G). Appendix B indicates that McInnis' Level I got moved back to become E5 in this program to keep it within the syllable level. But E5 (McInnis' Level I) is more difficult than F and G so it belongs right where McInnis placed it (E4 is also more difficult than F and G). I feared that as more teachers became aware of the three research-based levels of syllable, onset-rime, and phoneme, they may assume I was not following the research because some syllable activities would be *after* onset-rime activities. Based on that potential "social pressure," E3-E5 are before F & G, even though they are harder than F & G. However, the introduction to the advanced syllable section (E3, E4 E5) indicates that those levels should be taught after or alongside the training of Levels F and G.

training program. Then the following two pages give a more extensive overview so you can readily see the entire program from a "bird's eye view." Also, Appendix A provides a similar overview in the form of a student progress chart for phonological awareness development.

Phonological Awareness Level	*Program Level*
SYLLABLE LEVELS (D and E)	
Basic Syllable Levels	D1, D2; E1, E2
Advanced Syllable Levels	E3, E4, E5
ONSET-RIME LEVELS (F and G)	
Onset-Rime Levels	F1, F2; G1, G2
PHONEME LEVELS (H through N)	
Basic Phoneme Levels	H1, H2; I1, I2
Advanced Phoneme Levels	J; K1, K2; L1, L2; M1, M2
Optional Advanced Phoneme Levels	N1, N2

Chapter 3

Description of Program Levels

I. SYLLABLE LEVEL

Basic Syllable Levels

Level D *Deletion of a syllable from a two syllable word*
- D1 Delete a syllable from a compound word   *sail(boat) → sail; (toy)box → box*
- D2 Delete a syllable   *sil(ver) → sil; (ham)per → per*

Level E *Deletion of a syllable from a three syllable word*
- E1 Delete a syllable from a compound word   *basket(ball) → basket; (pine)apple → apple*
- E2 Delete an unstressed syllable   *(im)provement → provement; (vol)cano → cano*

Advanced Syllable Levels

- E3 Delete a stressed first syllable; the second syllable is either 1) consonant-vowel-consonant; 2) consonant-vowel, or 3) vowel-consonant   *(won)derful → derful; (ar)chitect → chitect; (wil)derness → derness*
- E4 Delete a stressed first syllable; the second syllable is comprised of only a vowel   *(tel)escope → escope; (an)imal → imal*
- E5 Delete the last syllable; the second syllable is comprised of only a vowel   *clari(net) → clari; holi(day) → holi*

II. ONSET-RIME LEVEL

Level F *Deletion of an onset or a rime*
- F1 Delete an onset from a single syllable word   *(s)at → at; (c)ab → ab*
- F2 Delete a rime from a single syllable word   *m(an) → /m/; s(een) → /s/*

Level G *Substitution of an onset or a rime*
- G1 Substitute an onset in a single syllable word   *(wh)ite → (r)ight; (c)ub → (t)ub*
- G2 Substitute a rime in a single syllable word   *f(it) → f(or); t(ell) → t(ag)*

– 24 –

III. PHONEME LEVEL

Basic Phoneme Levels

Level H *Manipulate initial phoneme in an initial blend*

    H1   Delete the first sound in an initial blend   *(f)lip → lip; (s)nail → nail*

    H2   Substitute the first sound in an initial blend   *(c)rown → (f)rown; (f)lew → (g)lue*

Level I *Deletion of an ending phoneme*

    I1   Delete the final sound in a final blend   *car(t) → car; gras(p) → grass*

    I2   Delete the final sound from a word   *see(n) → see; rai(se) → ray*

Advanced Phoneme Levels

Level J *Substitution of a vowel phoneme*

    J   Substitute a medial vowel   *h(a)t → h(o)t; s(a)ck → s(i)ck*

Level K *Manipulation of the second phoneme in an initial blend*

    K1   Delete the second sound in an initial blend   *t(r)y → tie; t(r)ail → tail*

    K2   Substitute the second sound in an initial blend   *f(r)ee → f(l)ee; s(k)y → s(p)y*

Level L *Substitution of an ending phoneme*

    L1   Substitute the final sound   *ca(t) → ca(p); grea(t) → gra(pe)*

    L2   Substitute the final sound in a final blend   *war(n) → war(m); for(m) → for(k)*

Level M *Manipulation of the second to last (penultimate) phoneme in an ending blend*

    M1   Delete the second to last sound in a final blend   *ca(s)t → cat; le(n)d → led*

    M2   Substitute the second to last sound in final blend   *li(f)t → li(s)t; be(n)t → be(s)t*

Optional Advanced Phoneme Level

Level N *Reversal of phonemes*

    N1   Reverse the sounds in a single syllable word   *make → came; back → cab*

    N2   Reverse the sounds in a two syllable word   *midnight → tine dim; oat pit → tiptoe*

CHAPTER 4

ORTHOGRAPHIC MAPPING AND SIGHT WORD LEARNING:
WHY WE NEED PHONEME AWARENESS

Phoneme awareness is a critical cognitive/linguistic skill needed to store words in memory for immediate, effortless retrieval. The connection between phoneme awareness and permanent word storage is not the least bit obvious. Our intuitions ask, "Isn't phoneme awareness *auditory* and our memory for words *visual*?" In this chapter, you will learn what scientists have discovered about how written words are remembered and why phonological abilities are so important in this process. The focus will be on *phoneme awareness,* not *phonological* awareness. This is because storing words in permanent memory requires *phoneme*-level skills.

In education, the term *sight word* has at least four meanings.[1] We will use only one; the one that researchers use. A *sight word* is a familiar written word that is recognized instantly, automatically, and effortlessly, without sounding it out or guessing. It does not matter if the word is common or uncommon, phonetically regular or irregular. Its only defining feature it that it is stored in memory and it is instantly and effortlessly recognized. A *sight word vocabulary* (or *sight vocabulary*), refers to all the words a student knows and instantly recognizes. Phoneme awareness plays a central role in building a sight vocabulary. This may seem puzzling because most people assume that we store words based on visual memory. In the next section, we will learn why scientists have shown that this is not the case.

What Scientists Used to Think About How We Store Words

Until recently, almost everyone thought that we store words by having some type of visual image of every word we know. This assumption is based on strong intuitive evidence. It *feels* like we are rapidly accessing words from a visual storage bank of some sort. As soon as we see words, they *look* familiar so we recognize them as quickly as we recognize other visual input like objects or faces.[2] The process would look something like this:

---

[1] The term "sight word" is used by many to refer to irregular words that cannot be easily sounded-out. We will call those words "irregular" or "exception" words, not "sight" words. Also, the term "sight words" is used to refer to the high frequency words commonly taught in kindergarten and first grade. Finally, the term historically referred to a type of reading approach, the *sight word approach,* also called the *whole word, look-say,* or *basal approach.*

[2] Actually, good readers can recognize printed words faster than objects and colors! This speed difference was

Chapter 4

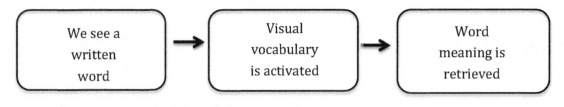

FIGURE 4.1

A TRADITIONAL VIEW OF SIGHT-WORD MEMORY AND RETRIEVAL

It was assumed this visual memory system contained all the familiar visual images of the words we know. Almost everyone believed in this theory, but there was one problem . . . everyone was wrong! Despite the strong intuitive appeal and widespread acceptance, scientific research has demonstrated that we do not remember words based upon visual memory.

Researchers had college students read words in mixed case; every other letter in each word was uppercase, so WoRdS lOoKeD lIkE this. The researchers reasoned that because mixed case words do not match a previously stored visual image, students would have to slow down to identify the words. Not surprisingly, the college students identified the mixed case words more slowly than normally printed words. At first, researchers thought this supported the "visual memory" theory. Later studies, however, showed that the slower reaction times were because the students were not accustomed to seeing words printed in this unusual manner.[3] So they trained the students using a set of mixed case words in order that they would get used to seeing words printed that way. After the training, students read a fresh pool of words they had *never seen* in mixed case. The students recognized this new batch of words in mixed case as fast as they recognized those same words in normal print! This convinced the researchers that these readers were not matching those words to stored visual images because they had never seen those specific test words printed that way before.[4] Something else was going on.

Years ago, I had an experience that illustrates this finding. By late second grade, my second son Kevin was a fluent reader. We had borrowed some *Calvin & Hobbes* comic strip books. Kevin had *no* previous exposure to comic strips. Yet with his first try, he read them aloud as quickly and fluently as he read anything else. This surprised me because comic strips are written in all capitals! Words in all capitals are visually different than in all lowercase. There was no way Kevin had seen all those words before in all capitals in order to store visual images of them. Something else was going on.

---

discovered and reported in a scientific journal about 130 years ago (Cattell, 1886). It was an early, unrecognized clue that word recognition does not use the same memory process as visually remembering objects.

[3] We have all experienced this when we get a wedding invitation or graduation announcement and it uses a very ornate font. It is difficult to read the first few words or sentences, but by the end we adjust and can read it just fine.

[4] In a different study, researchers flashed mixed-case words on a screen very quickly (1/20th of a second), just fast enough to be seen and processed. Students had no difficulty recognizing the words. Many students didn't even notice that the words were mixed case. A few students argued with the scientists, insisting the words were not mixed case! Thus, it was the *the specific order of the letters* that allowed them to identify the words. That letter order apparently registered in their brain faster than a conscious awareness of the physical way the letters were printed. So it was the letter order that was important for recognizing the word, not the visual look of the word.

– 28 –

One thing we know isn't going on when we read that quickly is phonetic decoding. There is no way Kevin (or those college students) could "sound-out" and blend words that quickly. If they were not sounding out these words, and they were not retrieving a visual image, then something entirely different was involved. It had to be something that was not very obvious at all. It was something that had escaped reading researchers for nearly a century. But one thing was certain. We are not simply retrieving a visual image of every word we read.

Challenging the Belief that Word Recognition is Based on Visual Memory

Most people assume that words are stored in visual memory. Many teaching approaches presume this. We assume that if students see the words enough, they will learn them. This is not true. Children with reading problems often cannot remember new words, even after many exposures. When they finally learn new words, they may forget them over school breaks or even long weekends. We mistakenly blame their visual memories. Meanwhile, average readers learn new words very quickly. Good readers only need one to five exposures to new words to learn them. Then, once learned, they don't forget them.

I believe this assumption that we store words based on visual memory is a major reason why we have widespread reading difficulties in our country. *Until we properly understand how to promote permanent word storage, we will continue to have many weak readers.* Listed below are several factors that demonstrate how scientists know that we do not remember words based on "visual memory." The list is not exhaustive, but should establish the point:

1) As described above, mixed case experiments have demonstrated that we are not retrieving words from a visual memory bank.

2) Closely related to the first is the everyday phenomenon of reading words fluently in various fonts and typestyles, all capitals (like comics), and a wide variety of people's personal handwriting, whether their handwriting is cursive or manuscript. It is difficult to believe that that we have a visual memory for all those variations in the look of each of the tens of thousands of words we know.

3) A footnote above indicated that about 130 years ago it was discovered that word recognition is faster than visual recognition of objects. Participants in the study said, "chair" faster when they saw the word *chair* than when they saw a picture of a chair. This provided an early hint that visual object recognition and word recognition may not involve the same mental process.

4) If word reading involves accessing visual memory, we would expect that children with reading problems would have poor visual memory. This is not the case. Research since the 1970s has shown that as a group, children with reading disabilities alone (i.e., they have no math or other learning difficulties) generally perform as well on visual memory tasks as children who are good readers.

5) There is only a very small statistical correlation between visual memory skills and sight vocabulary. By contrast, there is a large statistical correlation between phoneme awareness and sight vocabulary. If word reading were based upon visual memory, why would it correlate strongly with an auditory/phonological skill like phoneme awareness but not with visual memory skills? This finding suggests that visual memory is not a major component of word reading. While visual memory does not contribute much to word recognition, it does contribute to other aspects of reading (see below).

6) Studies using high-tech brain imaging techniques indicate that the regions of the brain activated when performing the visual memory task of naming objects (a chair, a house, a fork, etc.) differ from

the regions activated when naming familiar or unfamiliar written words. This finding is not consistent with the view that reading involves the retrieval of visual images of words.

7) Research on the deaf population is inconsistent with the visual memory theory of word reading. Most students who are deaf graduate high school with about a third grade reading level. If reading were based on visual memory, those who are deaf should not be so impaired in reading. There is no alternative "visual memory" approach the deaf population uses for efficient word recognition.[5]

8) Consider the fact that we all temporarily forget the names of common objects or familiar people. We "block" on them and it is frustrating. Consider how we occasionally block on the names of people we've known for years. By contrast, we do *not* forget the printed words we know. When a familiar word is sitting in front of us, we do not block on it like we do in other visual memory situations. Reading is not like visual memory – something different is going on.

9) Scientists who study visual memory (unrelated to reading) have shown that we do not have a precise enough visual memory for efficient word storage. Our *visual* memory system is not capable of storing 30,000 to 90,000 words for immediate retrieval. Consider the following examples:

> Here's a visual memory quiz: In what direction(s) are the presidents facing on a penny, nickel, dime, and quarter? Researchers have tested adults' visual memories for such things and find it is far weaker than people realize. We have been exposed to those coins hundreds of times, and most people cannot correctly guess the proper direction of all four of them! How can we expect to remember thousands of words—many that look very similar to each other (e.g., *black, block, blink, bleak, brick, brink, break, broke, brisk, brush, blush,* etc.)? Our visual memories are neither precise enough nor efficient enough for that type of visual information (strings of letters). Many types of visual-spatial experiments have demonstrated similar results. We overrate our visual memory, plain and simple.

> When you look up a phone number, it is a visual task. The number is visual and your response is visual-motor (touching the phone's keypad). If our visual memories were so good that we could remember 30,000 to 90,000 words for immediate retrieval, then remembering a visual image of a phone number for 15 seconds should be very easy. But it is not. We translate that visual number out of the visual realm and into the phonological realm (we repeat it out loud or in our heads). Then we translate it back into the visual realm as we dial the number. Our visual memory is relatively weak and imprecise for sequences of numbers and letters. So, we must translate out of the visual mode to remember the number.[6]

Does Visual Memory Play Any Role in Reading?

The section above demonstrates that we do not store words based upon visual memory. However, visual-perceptual skills, including visual memory, play important roles in other aspects of the reading process. The following are some of these aspects:

Alphabet recognition. Learning the alphabet letter names and letter sounds is based on visual-phonological memory. Children need to learn that the letter *m* makes the /m/ sound, and *s* makes the /s/ sound, etc. There is nothing about those little squiggly figures we call letters that would suggest any given sound—it is all a matter of visual-phonological memorization. Also, visual memory is required to distinguish the letters *b, d, q,* and *p*. So, *visual memory is absolutely essential for letter learning*. But notice the difference between letter learning and word learning. For good readers, it only takes one to five exposures to new words and they are remembered. However, with letters, it takes children hundreds of

---

[5] It is encouraging that some researchers have had recent success with developing phonological awareness in individuals with profound deafness. Interestingly, their innovative techniques are linguistically based, and use multisensory techniques to develop those linguistic abilities (e.g., finger spelling, attention to verbal articulation and segmenting of speech sounds). Also, students with cochlear implants who are able to perceive the phonemes in language often develop normal reading skills.

[6] The example of the phone number deals with our temporary working memory buffer, while remembering written words involves our long-term memory. However, similar results have been found with both types of memory.

exposures for a letter to become fully automatic in memory. Another interesting point is that this visual memory aspect of learning letters is almost never the culprit when children struggle remembering their letter names or sounds. Recent studies have shown that it is the phonological aspect of this visual-phonological learning that is the problem.

Reading comprehension. There is a correlation between visual memory and reading comprehension. Presumably, if you can create a good mental visual-spatial representation of what is going on in what you are reading, you are better able to understand and remember it.[7]

So, visual-spatial-perceptual memory *is* likely to be a contributor to at least two aspects of the reading process (letter learning and reading comprehension). However, it must be made clear that there is no evidence that visual memory directly contributes to word recognition or reading fluency, once the letters have been learned. As outlined above, we have enough evidence to dismiss the ingrained notion that we store words based upon visual memory. We need to stop teaching our children to read using methods based upon a faulty understanding of the reading process. However, this discredited view is still held by almost everyone in elementary and special education and it drives our teaching practices. *Adherence to this traditional view will guarantee that we will continue to have widespread reading failure. We will not improve the performance of poor readers until we adopt a proper understanding of how we store words.*

How then do we store words? We will now turn to this question.

The Discovery of Orthographic Mapping

Orthographic mapping is the mental process we use to permanently store words for immediate, effortless retrieval. Orthographic mapping is the process we use to take an unfamiliar printed word and turn it into an immediately recognizable sight word. Orthographic mapping occurs fairly naturally and "behind the scenes" for most students. Simply expose children to literacy activities and over time they will learn to "map" words to permanent memory. In the research, the concept of orthographic mapping has been referred to by different terms, such as *direct mapping, unitization, the bonding hypothesis, the amalgamation hypothesis,* or *the representation hypothesis.* However, the developer of the theory, Dr. Linnea Ehri, now calls it orthographic mapping.

Having a good understanding of how words are stored will determine *what* we teach, and *how* we teach it. When a student's orthographic mapping skills improve, his or her sight vocabulary grows. This leads to improvements in reading fluency and reading comprehension. So orthographic mapping is critical to reading fluency and comprehension.

---

[7]Several studies in the research suggest that visual-spatial-perceptual skills influence reading comprehension. However, most researchers agree that more study of this needs to occur before they reach any conclusions.

Chapter 4

When people talk, the words they say are represented by sequences of sounds. We immediately recognize those sound sequences as familiar words. It works lightning fast and looks something like this:

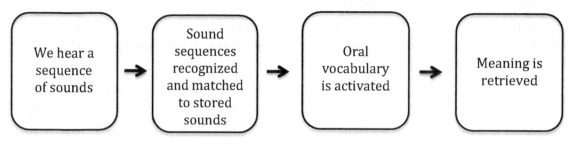

FIGURE 4.2

ACCESSING WORD MEANINGS IN LISTENING

We have a highly organized and efficient oral/mental filing system that allows us to instantly access the words that we hear. Our oral dictionaries are very fast. If they were not, we would struggle to understand spoken language. The stream of sounds that we hear activates our oral/mental dictionaries. If someone speaks in an unfamiliar language, that stream of syllables is meaningless to us. Those sounds find no matches in our oral filing system.

The big discovery regarding orthographic mapping is that this oral "filing system" is the foundation for the "filing system" we use for reading words. We have no separate "visual dictionary" that runs alongside our oral dictionary. This idea was not obvious to researchers over the last 100 years, perhaps because speech has to do with sound while reading has to do with sight. Because reading involves visual *input,* everyone presumed that it also involved visual *storage*. However, input and storage are not the same thing. When you buy a new vacuum cleaner, you "input" it into your house via the front door but store it in the front hall closet. Likewise, in the example earlier in the chapter, we may *input* a phone number visually, but we *store* it phonologically. Because written words are input visually, we must resist the strongly intuitive temptation to think they are stored visually.

Two concepts may be useful here, *meaningful letter strings* and *familiar letter strings*. A *meaningful letter string* is a sequence of letters in a meaningful order. For example, USA is a meaningful letter string because it is an acronym that stands for the United States of America. Those same letters are not meaningful if they are in a different order (UAS or SUA) because they are not in the order of the words they represent. Meaningful letter strings can be familiar or unfamiliar. A *familiar letter string* is immediately recognized, based on past experience while an unfamiliar string is not. Consider the following "letter strings":

Meaningful letter strings				**Random strings of letters**	
Familiar strings		Unfamiliar strings		(not meaningful or familiar)	
FBI	NFL	NASP	IEEE	QNZ	STE
SPCA	IRS	SSSR	SBE	BASM	RWR

TABLE 4.1

EXAMPLES OF TYPES OF LETTER STRINGS

For those who live in the United States, the first group of letter strings in Table 4.1 should be familiar.[8] They are acronyms for four organizations in the United States. These strings of letters are meaningful because each letter in the string stands for a word (e.g., FBI stands for *Federal Bureau of Investigation*). As acronyms, these letter strings gain their meaningfulness because the letters represent the first letters of each word in the organization's name.

The letter strings in the second column also represent organizations. These letter strings are probably *not* familiar to the reader because the reader is probably not familiar with these organizations (e.g., SSSR stands for the *Society for the Scientific Study of Reading*).[9] Because they are acronyms, these letter strings are *meaningful*. However, the letter sequences in the second column are not familiar letter strings to most readers. They are not familiar because the reader does not have past experience with them. The letter strings in the first and second columns are equally *meaningful* (they are all acronyms), but they are not equally *familiar*.

Once familiar, these letter strings become *unitized*. That is, we treat that sequence of letters like a unit. For example, when we see FBI, we do not say "Hmm, F – B – I . . . Oh, FBI!" No, we see the letter string FBI and instantly know what it is. It is familiar to us, while FBU, or MBI are not familiar. We no longer have to *consciously* focus on the "parts" of the FBI letter string. Rather, we recognize that sequence of letters as a unit. However, any change in that sequence throws us off, as the examples FBU or MBI illustrate. So, it is the *sequence of letters in that specific order* that becomes familiar to us, and that sequence is made up of a precise set of individual letters, in a precise order, regardless of the "look" of the sequence (i.e., in what font it is printed or in whose handwriting it is written).

The last column contains random letter strings. As far as I know, they don't mean anything. They are non-meaningful, so there is almost no chance they are familiar. Familiar letter strings are familiar because we have remembered them. We have remembered them because they are meaningful. *Sequences that are not meaningful are very difficult to remember*. Because they are meaningless, there is little or nothing we can use to anchor them in permanent memory. By contrast, acronyms are easy to remember because when we first learn them, we recognize that they match up with the first letter of words, which help make them familiar more quickly.

Because acronyms are not words, they only provide an *analogy* to word reading. Yet they provide a helpful way to illustrate the concepts of meaningful letter strings and familiar letter strings. We must now apply these concepts to words. We will seek to answer two questions:

1) What is meaningful about the letter strings that make up printed words?
2) How do the letter strings become so familiar that we can instantaneously and effortlessly recognize them?

---

[8]For those outside the United States: FBI = Federal Bureau of Investigation; NFL = National Football League; SPCA = Society for the Prevention of Cruelty to Animals; IRS = Internal Revenue Service.
[9]NASP is the National Association of School Psychologists, SBE is the Society of Broadcast Engineers, and IEEE is Institute of Electrical and Electronics Engineers.

Chapter 4

Why Written Words are Meaningful Letter Strings

The letter sequences in words are meaningful because the letter order is designed to match the order of the sounds in spoken words. For example, each letter in the word *stamp* is in the same order as its corresponding spoken phoneme. If the letter order used to represent the oral word *stamp* was different, say *smapt*, then that order does not meaningfully represent the phoneme sequence in that word. This is the whole idea behind alphabetic writing systems. The letters are designed to represent the *sounds* in oral words. While English has many "irregular" words (discussed later), the basic idea of alphabetic writing is that the letter order matches the phoneme order in the oral word. Thus, letter strings represent phoneme strings in a meaningful way. By their very nature, *written words are made up of letter strings in a meaningful order!*

Letter strings in a meaningful order (i.e., written words) can be anchored into permanent memory if the reader is able to recognize why those letter strings are meaningful and are in that order. As mentioned, the letter *sequence* is meaningful because it matches the stored phoneme sequence in the spoken word. If a student has phoneme awareness, he can recognize this connection. Without phoneme awareness, these letter strings are not meaningful to him, so it is very difficult to remember them and make them familiar. If words do not become familiar, reading is seriously compromised.

Consider an analogy. You have a room full of adults participating in a memory study. Half of the people are American sports fans. Half are Australians with no knowledge of American sports. Both groups have equal *command* of the English language. You give both groups the task of remembering random letter strings. They are told that the following strings of letters are random and should be committed to memory:

| NFL | NBA | LPGA | MLB |
| WNBA | PGA | NHL | NCAA |

Later, those in our imaginary study are asked to recall as many of the letter strings as they can. You can bet that the American sports fans would do far better than the Australians who had no exposure to American sports. All of the above letter strings are acronyms for American sports leagues. These are meaningful strings to *American* sports fans, and not meaningful to the Australian non-sports fans. The Australians were *not aware that these letter strings are meaningful,* so they would have a very hard time remembering them. To them, they were memorizing random strings of letters, which is very difficult.

It is roughly similar with orthographic mapping. First graders with basic phoneme awareness and good letter-sound skills are like the American sports fans. They immediately recognize that letter sequences in printed words have a meaningful relationship with the phonemes they hear in a spoken word. This is how they anchor words into permanent memory. They associate the string of phonemes in the word's pronunciation with the letter order in the written word. By contrast, children who are weak in phoneme awareness or letter-sound skills are like the Australians from our example. Because they lack one or both of these skills, *they do not recognize the meaningfulness of the letter strings that make up printed words.* For these students, remembering letter strings is very difficult because they do not have a reliable way to do it. It is as if they were trying to remember random letter sequences. They have an uphill battle trying to make those letter strings "familiar" and instantly recognizable. They therefore cannot remember words efficiently, so they struggle in reading.

This is the basic difficulty in reading acquisition. Children who struggle with phoneme awareness struggle in reading. Why? Because they do not notice the logical/meaningful relationship between the word's pronunciation and the letters used to represent that pronunciation in print. This makes words extremely difficult to remember. Until phonemic proficiency is developed, a student will not have an efficient way to make letter strings familiar. Students with good phonemic proficiency naturally associate the phonemes in spoken pronunciations with the letter strings used to represent those pronunciations in print. As a result, they easily remember the words they read. Phonemic proficiency allows the student to make effective use of the lightning-fast oral dictionary we use for spoken language.

While phoneme awareness and letter-sound skills are equally important for mapping, phoneme awareness difficulties are more commonly the problem. The vast majority of students with word recognition difficulties lack sufficient phoneme awareness. Students with problems in both struggle the most.

In recent years, a greater emphasis has been placed on phonics or letter-sound skills due to the research supporting its importance. But research has also supported the importance of phoneme awareness in learning to read. Yet while many teachers have heard phoneme awareness is important, there is not much clarity as to *why* it is important. As teachers learn more about the mapping process, it should become clear why both phoneme awareness and basic phonics (i.e., letter-sound skills) are critical for remembering words as sight words.

To illustrate, consider two students in late first grade. For the first time, they see the word *sent*. They both have the letter-sound skills needed to sound it out. The first student has phoneme awareness while the second does not. The first student immediately notices that the spelling of *sent* aligns perfectly with the phonemes in the spoken word *sent* (/s/ /e/ /n/ /t/). For this student, it will be easy to remember that sequence and distinguish it from other, similar looking sequences (e.g., *set, send, scent,* or *cent*). However, the student with weak phoneme awareness skills will not be aware of the sounds in *sent*. He will not notice the meaningful relationship between the spelling *s-e-n-t* and the phoneme sequence in the spoken word. To him, *s-e-n-t* is no more meaningful of a way to represent *sent* than *s-n-e-t, s-t-e-n,* or *s-e-t-n*. Why would *s-e-n-t* be a more suitable way to represent the spoken word *sent* than those other ways if the student has no way of noticing the sounds within the spoken word *sent*? There is really *no* reason that *s-e-n-t* is more meaningful than those other letter orders (e.g., *s-n-e-t*) *unless* you have an awareness of the individual sounds within the spoken word *sent*. But that is precisely what students with poor phoneme awareness do not have. They are not aware of the oral sequences within spoken words, as a result it is difficult for them to see the meaningfulness of the letter order in the printed words they see.[10] If there is nothing meaningful about the letter order, then

---

[10] The exception to this is with the first letter and first sound in a word. Even most students with reading disabilities can notice the first sound in spoken words and they can match first sound to the first letter.

only inefficient, raw memorization is possible, and sight vocabulary growth is dramatically hindered.

This is the essence of what researchers call the *alphabetic principle*. The alphabetic principle is the idea that at some point, it dawns on children that the written letters match up to the phonemes in spoken words. This may seem obvious to us, but to a beginning reader, it is not. They gain this insight through early literacy activities and/or instruction in phonics. Without the combination of good phoneme awareness and good letter-sound skills it is very difficult for students to develop the insight we call the alphabetic principle.

Making Letter Strings Familiar: How We Map

Letter strings are considered *familiar* if we can immediately recognize them. In fact, the concept of "familiar letter strings" is another way of saying "words in our sight vocabulary." You will recall that a *sight word vocabulary* refers to the pool of words we can instantly recognize, without guessing or sounding them out. How do we make letter strings familiar? It is a multi-step process that begins with the letters. Without automatic letter-sound skills, orthographic mapping is inefficient or impossible. This cannot be emphasized enough. Letter-sound skills are not optional for the efficient permanent storage of words—they are essential.[11]

When a student learns a letter/sound combination to the automatic level, the sight of that letter immediately and effortlessly activates the sound associated with it.[12] When the student sees the letter *t*, the /t/ sound is instantly activated in the temporal lobes (the area of the brain that stores auditory/phonological information). Letter-sound associations are learned during preschool, kindergarten, and first grade for most students. Children typically require hundreds of exposures to letters before they are mastered to the point of automaticity.[13] Once automatic, the sight of the letter will activate the sound in memory just as quickly and efficiently as if the student heard someone produce the sound orally. In other words, whether they see the letter *t* or hear the /t/ sound, the memory for that sound is activated in the temporal lobes of the brain. This is probably why the areas of our brains that interpret speech are active even during *silent* reading. Whether sound information involves visual input (written letters) or auditory input (oral phonemes), similar memory centers in the brain are activated.

As letter-sound knowledge and phoneme awareness develop, strings of two or more letters "unitize" to activate the sounds associated with those groups of letters. When we see *ip* in a word, we do not need to sound it out. Rather, that letter combination *as a unit* activates the pronunciation of /ip/. This means *ip* has become a familiar letter string, just like words become familiar letter strings. Common words parts such as rime units (*–et, –ig, –ap, –ot, –ut*, etc.), blends (*tr, bl, sn, cr, str,* etc.), suffixes (*–ing, –ed, –tion*) and prefixes (*re–, con–, un–, dis–*) work this way. When we see common word parts within words, their pronunciations are activated. We treat familiar letter combinations as units without consciously treating each letter-sound separately. If you identify *ip* by sounding it out one letter at time, that is phonetic

---

[11] See Chapter 12 for more on letter-sound learning.

[12] Technically, it can activate more than one sound, if the letter has more than one sound associated with it. The context of that letter allows us to determine the correct sound and the others get "discarded." This happens so quickly that cognitive scientists call it "pre-cognitive," meaning it happens before we have time to think about it.

[13] As mentioned earlier, *letter* recognition is based partially on visual memory, even though *word* recognition is not.

decoding. But if you instantly recognize *ip* based on past experience, that means *ip* has become a familiar letter string. You no longer need to break it apart letter by letter.

But how do words or parts of words become familiar if not visually? Here is where phoneme awareness comes into play. Word parts, such as /ip/, are not words, yet they are still part of our existing oral language system. While /ip/ never appears by itself in our language, the sound /ip/ is familiar to a student with phoneme awareness. That student has /ip/ filed away in his oral dictionary as a *familiar part* of words such as *dip, hip, lip, rip, sip, zip, chip, clip, drip, flip, grip, snip, trip, whip,* etc.[14] If a student does not have phoneme awareness, the simple two-letter string *ip* will not anchor to anything in particular in memory. For that student, *ip* represents two random letters that must be memorized—he does not have the awareness that /ip/ is a common part of a whole bunch of words he already knows. By contrast, if a student *has* phoneme awareness, he can notice parts of oral words. Such awareness allows him to participate in a connection-forming process between the letter combination and its pronunciation. This is the essence of phoneme awareness—being aware of the sound structure of spoken words. The letters of our printed language are supposed to represent the sounds of our spoken language. Therefore, we need to be aware of those spoken phonemes in order to anchor their printed forms in permanent memory. The oral form of the word is already stored in memory. When we map, the letters of the printed form of the word piggyback onto the phonemes in our existing rapid oral filing system, which we use to understand spoken language. *If a student is not attuned to the sounds within oral words, there is no efficient way for printed words to become familiar letter strings.* There is nothing to which they can efficiently connect the strings of letters for later retrieval.

Some readers may think I'm suggesting that when we read we are doing "phonics" very quickly. This is not the case. I had the same first impression when I began to read the research on mapping back in 1997. What I am describing here is immediate sight word recognition, not sounding out words. Sounding out words takes longer than instant recognition. Phonetic decoding focuses on one or two letters at a time. Immediate word recognition involves processing all of the letters at once. All of the letters in the word can be seen with a glance of the eye, and the entire letter string is recognized as a familiar. How is this?

Clues from Eye Movement Research

When we read, we process virtually every letter of every word we read. Various types of clever experiments have demonstrated this. If our brains did not register and make use of every letter of the words we read, we could not instantly recognize words that differ from one another by only one letter.[15] Second, when we read, we experience the illusion that our eyes sweep evenly across the page. However, eye movement research has demonstrated that our eyes move across a line of text in little jumps. We stop and fixate on a spot briefly, and then jump to the next spot.[16] Our eyes jump so quickly that during the jump, we take in no useful information—

---

[14] Not to mention the multisyllabic words that contain *ip* (e.g., *tulip, zipper, eclipse*)

[15] There has been a notion promoted by some in educational circles that we do not process every letter of every word we read. This may be true for weak readers, or good readers who are skimming. It is not true for typical reading. There is a popular e-mail "forward" circulating that purports to prove this. But that e-mail demonstrates a phenomenon called *contextual facilitation* and does not represent our normal word recognition processes.

[16] You don't need experimental equipment to see this for yourself. Have someone read the top lines of a book. Watch

Chapter 4

just an extremely quick blur. But during each fixation, we take a very brief "picture" of what we see. The perceptual system within our brain then "stitches together" these little visual "photographs" so that we feel like our eyes are moving smoothly across the page.

When our eyes fixate on a spot, we take in about 7-8 letters to the right of the fixation, and about 4-5 to the left.[17] This perceptual span of 11-13 letters allows us to take in all the letters of a big word, or all of the letters of a few small words. Those letters are taken in simultaneously, not in a sequence like when we sound out words phonetically. When a reader encounters a string of letters, he or she immediately recognizes it as a familiar letter string, which in turn activates the oral word and its meaning. This does not occur one letter at a time from left to right, as is the case with phonetic decoding. Rather, the visual span takes in *all* the letters at once; so all the letters simultaneously activate the oral word (just like we instantly perceive all the letters in acronyms like USA, NFL, and FBI). This simultaneous perception of all of the letters is why it feels like we read words as whole units. In one sense, we are reading them as whole visual units, given that all of the letters are activated at the same time. Yet it is not visual memory that activates the word, as was mentioned earlier in the chapter. The activation occurs at the letter-phoneme level. *We recognize a letter string as familiar,* which in turn activates the word it represents. If activation did not occur at the letter level, we would constantly confuse look-alike words. The word's pronunciation and meaning are all activated together because they are all connected in memory, once the word is permanently mapped.

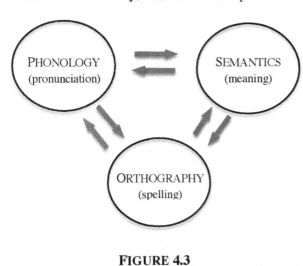

FIGURE 4.3

ACCESSING WORD MEANING IN READING

Earlier in the chapter, Figure 4.2 illustrated the processing of oral language. Figure 4.3 shows the interaction between the visual input of familiar letter strings (or orthography) and the instant activation of both the word's pronunciation and meaning. Whether we hear a word spoken or see a familiar, mapped letter string, the word gets activated in our brains. Oral words are made up of sequences of oral sounds. Written words are strings of letters designed to represent those sounds. A word's pronunciation (phonology) and meaning (semantics) is connected in memory with the word's spelling (orthography), so when the printed word is seen, the pronunciation and meaning are instantly accessed. There is no guessing or sounding out the word. The word just effortlessly pops into your mind.

---

his or her eyes closely because it happens very quickly. You may see this jump-fixate-jump-fixate pattern.

[17] Readers of modern Hebrew and Arabic show the opposite pattern, with a perception of 7-8 letters to the left and 4-5 to the right. This is because Hebrew and Arabic are read from right to left rather than left to right.

Notice this recognition process is not simply a matter of visual memory. Researchers prefer to use the term "orthographic memory" because it is a memory *for a specific sequence of letters,* not a visual-spatial memory for the "look" of the word based on its visual properties. It does not matter if the letters are all uppercase, lowercase, handwritten, or in differing fonts. The visual look of the word is not important as long as the letters are legible. Once the word's letters enter the visual system, orthographic memory takes over. Rather than visual memory, it is a memory for a specific letter string. That particular letter string has become familiar and unitized in the memory system.

Consider when you type a web address into a web browser (e.g., Internet Explorer, Safari, Firefox). It tries to "guess" the address you are typing based upon what is in the browser's memory. So when I type in *www.a,* I get *www.apple.com,* because I have an Apple computer. The Apple address is in my browser's memory. Regardless of what site I try to visit that starts with the letter *a*, I still get that Apple address after typing the letter *a*. That is because the computer is limited to one letter at a time for its "guess." If I follow the letter *a* with the letter *d*, then *www.adobe.com* comes up automatically. That is a software company in my browser's memory. Again, the browser is simply making the best guess given the limited information it has available so far. It appears that our brains work in a similar way, except much more efficiently. Unlike our browsers, our brain has access to *all* of the letters of a word at the same time. While the web browser has only one letter at a time available to make its best guess, and narrows the choices as it goes along, our brains get all the letters at once to activate the word! This is a far more efficient system. It is not like phonics, sounding out one letter at a time. Rather, it is a whole letter string rapidly accessing a stored word based upon the previous association between that letter string and the phonemes in the word's pronunciation. *The letter string becomes familiar because the person had the phoneme awareness to connect the oral phonemes in the word to the letters used to represent that word in print.* This process informs us about what a sight vocabulary actually represents. Words mapped in memory have bonded the oral sounds (which are already stored in our oral/mental dictionary) to the written letter strings that are designed to represent those oral words. When words have been completely mapped, those familiar letter strings activate the oral words instantly.

Once a letter string becomes familiar, it becomes *unitized*. We treat the letter sequence as a unit. For example, when we see *spend,* we don't say, "Hmm, s – p – e – n – d, Oh, *spend*!" Rather, we see that letter string *spend* and instantly recognize it as familiar. *Spend* is familiar to us, while *stend* or *slend* are not. And, we don't confuse the letter order in *spend* with words like *send,* or *spent,* because those are different strings of letters that have been unitized in their own right. Thus, we no longer have to *consciously* focus on the "parts" of the letter string, but recognize the whole letter sequence as a unit. However, any change in that sequence throws us off, as the examples of *stend* or *slend* illustrate. It is thus the *sequence* of letters that becomes familiar to us, and that sequence is made up of a precise set of individual letters, in a precise order, that is, the word's orthography. It is familiar regardless of font or case. The unitization phenomenon is why it *feels* holistic as we read words.

Chapter 4

Going back to our analogy of acronyms from earlier in the chapter, we feel like we "holistically" process acronyms like NFL, NHL, and NBA[18]. However, this instant recognition only occurs by correctly perceiving the actual sequence of letters that distinguish them from any other sequence. NLF or FNL do not make us think of pro football, but NFL does.

The Relationship Between Orthographic Mapping and Phonetic Decoding

Mapping must not be confused with phonics. Mapping and phonics differ in some very important ways. The biggest reason they seem similar is that both require letter-sound skills and phonological. However, mapping and phonetic decoding use these skills differently. Phonetic decoding starts with an unfamiliar printed word. The letters are translated into sounds, which are then blended together to identify the spoken word. By contrast, mapping is a two-way process that requires an awareness of the phonemes in the spoken word (i.e., phoneme awareness). When a student encounters an unfamiliar word and sounds it out via phonetic decoding (text to brain), behind the scenes, unconsciously, our brains naturally attach the phonemes in the pronunciation to the letters in the printed word (brain to text). This cannot happen efficiently unless a student has very proficient phoneme skills to the point that they can segment words without even thinking about it (explained in more detail in Chapter 7). Being proficient with the sounds in the spoken language and the letter-sound relationships in the printed language assists the student in anchoring the sequence of phonemes in the word's pronunciation to the letter string used to represent that particular oral word. The word's pronunciation is already stored in long-term memory, and mapping helps the printed letter string anchor to that pronunciation in long-term memory, making it familiar. The key is to go from pronunciation to letters (mapping) rather than letters to pronunciation (phonetic decoding). After a few exposures, the process of mapping is complete. The word is "mapped," so it is now a familiar letter string, and seeing that familiar letter string instantly activates that word's pronunciation. For that word, phonetic decoding or guessing are no longer needed.

Another way to see the difference between phonetic decoding and mapping is that phonetic decoding uses the letter-to-sound relations to *activate* oral words from an unfamiliar letter string. By contrast, orthographic mapping uses sound-to-letter relationships to *anchor* phonemes in a word's pronunciation to the printed letter strings into long-term memory for future retrieval. Phonetic decoding uses letter-sound skills to *identify* words while orthographic mapping uses letter-sound skills to *establish a memory* of printed words. Mapping does not involve identifying unfamiliar words; it involves a connection-forming process that turns unfamiliar printed words into familiar printed words. These are different processes; both essential to reading. Yet both rely heavily on the letter-sound relationships, even if they do so in different ways.

---

[18] NFL – National Football League; NHL – National Hockey League; NBA – National Basketball Association.

The Three Components of Orthographic Mapping

In essence, orthographic mapping has three components (see Figure 4.4). To be good orthographic mappers, children need to develop three skills: 1) Automatic letter-sound associations, 2) highly proficient phoneme awareness, and 3) word study. Word study represents an unconscious or conscious process of connecting the phonemes in spoken words to the written form of the word, which does not happen efficiently if the first two components (letter-sound proficiency and phoneme proficiency) are not in place. Basically, *word study is the process of matching the oral phonemes to the letters to establish secure memory for future retrieval.* When beginning to read, while the first two components are still developing, the word study process may be somewhat conscious. But as letter-sound and phoneme skills become automatic, the word-study aspect of the orthographic mapping process generally occurs without conscious effort, as we encounter unfamiliar words. Thus, word study (conscious or unconscious) is the connection making process used to remember words. The word-study aspect of mapping is the superglue that anchors words in permanent memory. But for this to happen, students must have letter-sound proficiency and phonemic proficiency.

FIGURE 4.4
THREE CRITICAL SKILLS NEEDED FOR ORTHOGRAPHIC MAPPING

Traditional approaches like *whole language* (now called *balanced instruction*) and the *whole word* approach do not adequately address the three components of permanent word storage. Most children develop these three skills naturally, without being directly taught. Through exposure to letters and words, children destined to be good readers naturally make connections between sounds and letters. But students with phonological awareness difficulties do not make those connections, so reading is a major struggle for them. We then blame the student and give him or her names like "dyslexic," "learning disabled," or "reading disabled." The inadequate

Chapter 4

attention that our current teaching approaches give to letter-sound skills and phoneme awareness helps explain why we have 27-34% of fourth graders in the U.S. reading substantially below grade level. Instead of "learning disabled," Dr. Philip McInnis preferred "curriculum disabled." Others use the term "curriculum casualty." Our curricula only seem to help the top two thirds of students who are bound to learn to read regardless of the approach we use. Phonics fares better than whole language/balanced literacy because it explicitly teaches the letter-sound component. But phonics programs typically do an insufficient job with the other two components. All three components of orthographic learning should be explicitly taught and reinforced, starting in kindergarten, and yet no currently popular approach does that. The classic methods (phonics, whole word, whole language/balanced instruction) were developed before the discovery of orthographic mapping. Thus, they cannot be faulted for not anticipating that discovery. However, given the research findings, we can now make the development of these components a central part of reading instruction and remediation. Studies show this will result in substantial reductions in the percentage of struggling readers.

A study conducted at the State University of New York at Albany showed that the researchers were able to reduce the number of students with reading problems to a tiny fraction of the usual number of poor readers. How? They addressed the issue of permanent word storage by teaching skills consistent with the mapping process. Students were trained in phoneme awareness, letter-sound skills, and word-study skills. This allowed them to map words efficiently to permanent memory. As a result, they became good readers and no longer required extra reading help. Others studies have shown similar results.

In addition, similar results have been found for many years among schools using McInnis' ARL program. ARL was using these techniques long before researchers began to understand the mapping process. Rather, McInnis used these techniques *because they worked*. Only in recent years have we figured out *why* they worked. But the kind of training used in the Albany study and in ARL have not been commonly used in our schools. This is likely because of the prominent role the whole language/balanced instruction philosophy has played in our educational systems. The whole language/balanced instruction approach stresses meaning, context, and good literature, but puts insufficient emphasis on phonological awareness and word study, virtually guaranteeing poor reading among about one-third of our students.

Getting Orthographic Mapping into the Knowledge Base of Teachers

Since 2001, I have presented this information about mapping to hundreds of teachers, school psychologists, school administrators, parents, and undergraduate college students. I realize that it is usually not well understood the first time through. Do not get discouraged if it is difficult to understand the orthographic mapping concept. It took a while for me to grasp it as well. Rereading this chapter may help.[19]

---

[19] Also it is covered in depth in *Essentials of Assessing, Preventing, and Overcoming Reading Difficulties* and it is presented in a YouTube video (https://www.youtube.com/watch?v=VBx3zBzrL5I).

What you really need to know is the bottom line: we use our oral filing system as the basis for sight word storage and retrieval. The point of entry into our permanent filing system for written words is at the level of letters and phonemes, not "whole words," despite how badly our intuitions have mislead us. If students notice that the phonemes in spoken words are represented by letters in printed words, they can make those written sequences familiar. If students do not easily notice the phoneme structure of spoken words (i.e., they lack sufficient phoneme awareness), then for them, there is nothing special or meaningful about the letter order in printed words. As a result, it is very difficult to remember those letter sequences and make them familiar. This means that words are added to a student's sight vocabulary very slowly. A limited sight vocabulary is the primary basis for poor reading fluency. If a student is poor at word recognition and fluency, reading comprehension typically suffers. When reading comprehension suffers, all of a student's school experience is negatively affected. This entire chain of events is preventable in most cases if we make sure that all students have adequate phoneme awareness and letter-sound skills, right from the start. This book contains a comprehensive and carefully sequenced curricula of phonological awareness skills starting in kindergarten that you can use to help prevent most reading difficulties. It is designed to supplement the many phonic programs already available.

My goal in giving a detailed account of orthographic mapping in this chapter is for the reader to understand that:

- We do not store and retrieve words based on visual memory. Any strictly visually-based teaching techniques represent an inefficient use of instructional time.
- Our phonological filing system is the basis for word memory/word recognition.
- Phoneme awareness and letter-sound skills are not optional—they are central to the process of permanent word storage and sight vocabulary development. Either we are going to leave children on their own to figure it out themselves, or we will directly train them. They cannot read efficiently without these skills.

The next step is to look at how we should approach teaching reading now that we have a good understanding of how words are learned. What should schools do to make sure children become efficient orthographic mappers? The following two chapters address this question.

CHAPTER 5

TEACHING READING IN LIGHT OF ORTHOGRAPHIC MAPPING

The previous chapter described how we permanently store (i.e., learn) words. Now that scientists have a basic understanding of how that process works, we are in a position to take a fresh look at how we teach reading. This may involve significant changes. We cannot continue with our current approaches because doing so virtually guarantees that we will continue to have about 30% of our students reading substantially below grade level.

What needs to change? The following list of recommendations is based on our understanding of orthographic mapping. We will look at each one in turn:

- Train the prerequisite skills for orthographic mapping: letter-sound skills, phoneme awareness to the level of phonemic proficiency, and word study.
- Teach reading in a developmental sequence that 1) is consistent with the sequence of phonological awareness development, and 2) is consistent with what we know about the development of how children efficiently build a sight word vocabulary.
- Avoid or postpone teaching word-reading strategies that do not promote orthographic mapping.
- Teach and use specific word-study strategies that directly promote or reinforce orthographic mapping (i.e., word memory).

Train the Prerequisite Skills for Mapping

The skills necessary for mapping are letter-sound proficiency, phonemic proficiency, and word study. *Letter-sound proficiency* refers to automatic and effortless recognition of consonants, vowels, blends, and digraphs. *Phoneme awareness* training is described in detail in Chapters 7-11. *Word study* is the unconscious or conscious mental habit of connecting what is heard in the mind (phoneme awareness) with what is seen on the page (letter-sound skills). Unless children have phonemic proficiency and letter-sound proficiency, word study will be inefficient.

Phoneme awareness should *not* be trained as an isolated skill. Unless students are able to *apply* their phoneme awareness skills to the process of mapping sounds to letters, you will not see the benefits of phoneme awareness training. This is especially true of students who develop phoneme awareness skills later as a result of remedial instruction. These students need to "re-learn" how to approach words in a way that will make those words memorable. Words will become more memorable by applying their newly developed phoneme awareness skills to those words. In the next chapter, a wide variety of strategies that promote word study are presented. Many of these strategies can be used as a routine part of reading instruction in first through third grade. They can also be used to remediate older students who developed phoneme awareness skills late. Without such strategies, older students may not reap the benefits of newly developed phoneme awareness skills. *Note:* Some of the word-study techniques in Chapter 6 presume that the student has developed basic phoneme-level skills (e.g., Levels H, I, & J), and are making good progress on the advanced phoneme levels.

Teach Reading Using a Developmentally Appropriate Sequence of Reading Approaches

Too often, educators believe they must choose from among the traditional reading approaches; 1) phonics, 2) whole word, and 3) whole language. Yet all of these approaches have been used in schools since the 1800s, long before the explosion of scientific research on reading over the last 40 years. None of these approaches is based upon an accurate understanding of how words are remembered. We cannot rely on them to boost the sight vocabularies and fluency of weak readers. However, they can be salvaged and reworked somewhat to accommodate recent scientific findings, but in ways that may not be so obvious.

To establish a developmentally appropriate reading program, we need to look at two issues. First, because phoneme awareness is necessary for reading efficiency, *we must make sure our approach to teaching reading is consistent with what we know about the development of phoneme awareness*. Second, we must be sure our approach to teaching reading takes account of the development of sight-word acquisition (i.e., orthographic mapping). Researchers have identified the sequence of phases students go through as they develop their sight vocabularies. Researcher Linnea Ehri has described the four phases of sight word development. These phases are based on a broad range of research and are depicted in Table 5.1.

The first phase is rather brief and is called the *pre-alphabetic phase*. When children are introduced to reading at the preschool or early kindergarten levels, they typically do not have enough letter-sound knowledge to map words to permanent memory. Instead, they use visual cues to remember words. For example, they may remember that the word *look* has two "eyes" in the middle or that the word *camel* has two humps in the middle. In the pre-alphabetic phase, the cues children use have nothing to do with the sound properties of the words.

During the pre-alphabetic phase, children learn what have been called *concepts about print*. These include things like reading from left to right, starting at the top of the page, etc. After doing over 1,000 evaluations of students with reading difficulties, I have never seen a student whose reading difficulties were influenced by poor concepts about print. Also, there is no research to indicate that weak readers struggle because of poor concepts about print. So while concepts about print are foundational, they are not the source of reading difficulties.

The second phase is the *partial alphabetic phase*. Here the student uses *some* alphabetic knowledge to store words. They usually can match the first sound with the first letter or maybe one or two other sound/letter combinations as well. For example, a child may see the word *stand* and map the first and last letters/sounds (the /s/ ⇢ s and /d/ ⇢ d), so when he sees *stand* again he may remember it. However, when he sees *sand* or *strand*, he is likely to say *stand*, because only part of the word is mapped. Students at this phase do not have the phoneme awareness or letter-sound skills necessary to efficiently map all the letter-sound combinations in the words they see. It is at the partial alphabetic phase that many weak readers get stuck.

Ehri's Phases of Sight Word Development	Sample Word
1. Pre-Alphabetic Phase	LOOK
2. Partial Alphabetic Phase	s p e n t / /s/ /e/ /t/
3. Full Alphabetic Phase	b l a n k / /b/ /l/ /a/ /n/ /k/
4. Consolidated Alphabetic Phase	car pen ter / /car/ /pen/ /ter/

TABLE 5.1

EHRI'S PHASES OF SIGHT WORD DEVELOPMENT

When students are at the *full alphabetic phase,* they can map every sound-letter combination in the words they see. To return to the word *stand,* a child would have the word fully mapped and would therefore not confuse it with *sand* or *strand.* A student needs good phoneme-level awareness and letter-sound skills to reach this phase of sight word learning.

The *consolidated alphabetic phase* is when many word parts have been mapped, so students can efficiently handle multi-syllabic words. At this phase, students attend to bigger chunks and patterns in words, which speeds mapping and fluency. Studies show that first graders and weaker second grade readers pronounce nonsense words like *nalk* to rhyme with *talc,* based on phonetic decoding. Stronger second graders and older students pronounce *nalk* to rhyme with *talk, chalk,* and *walk.* Why? Because they are at the consolidated alphabetic phase and have stored memories for word parts such as *–alk, –ing,* or *–tion.* This stage of mature word recognition requires well-developed phoneme awareness.

Using the levels of phonological awareness development (syllable, onset-rime, phoneme; see Chapter 3) and the four phases of sight word development (pre-, partial, full, and consolidated alphabetic phases), we are in a position to suggest a developmentally appropriate sequence of reading instruction. Table 5.2 organizes the developmental progression of these reading-related skills to provide us with the raw materials we can use to piece together a developmentally appropriate reading curriculum. Such a curriculum, along with the other considerations in this chapter (e.g., train the prerequisite skills for mapping) should dramatically decrease the likelihood of reading difficulties.

Based on what we know about phonological awareness development and the phases of sight word development, we must carefully consider the reading materials we use early on to

Chapter 5

minimize reading difficulties and maximize reading success. It must be noted that this careful sequencing is primarily intended for students at-risk for reading difficulties. There is a much greater flexibility for the students who will become good readers no matter what approach is used. But we often do not know which students are destined to struggle, so it is essential to keep a close watch on students' development of letter-sound skills and phonological awareness so we do not require them to read developmentally inappropriate material.

Approximate Grade Level	Phonological Awareness Development	Mapping Development (Ehri's Phases of Sight Word Development)	Developmentally Appropriate Reading Approach for this Level
Pre-K Early Kindergarten	Syllable Level	Pre-Alphabetic	Read to students and teach letters
Mid-Kindergarten	Onset-Rime Level	Partial Alphabetic	Linguistic Approach
Late Kindergarten Early First Grade	Basic Phoneme Level	Full Alphabetic	Phonics Approach
Late First Grade to Late Second Grade	Advanced Phoneme Level	Consolidated Alphabetic	Reinforce code knowledge, morphology, and expand reading experience

TABLE 5.2
THE SEQUENCE OF TYPICAL DEVELOPMENT OF PHONOLOGICAL AWARENESS AND ORTHOGRAPHIC MAPPING/SIGHT WORD DEVELOPMENT IN RELATION TO THE TRADITIONAL READING APPROACHES

For beginning reading instruction, we need to make use of reading materials that are appropriate to *the level at which the student can phonologically and orthographically deal with words*. If we present students with words that are too difficult for them to phonetically decode and remember, we may accidentally push them toward using inefficient compensating strategies. If they are at-risk readers, this could negatively affect reading acquisition and start them down a path toward a habit of compensation and inefficient reading skills. Weak readers use compensating strategies (see Chapter 13) while good readers develop good orthographic mapping skills early on and apply their phoneme awareness skills to remembering words.

In kindergarten, children usually work on mastering letter names and sounds. This should be done alongside phonological awareness development and extensive reading to children. In kindergarten, train the students in phonological awareness at the levels of the syllable (Levels D & E) and eventually the onset-rime (F & G). And, of course, read to them daily.

Many schools in the U.S. teach reading in kindergarten due to state mandates. This may work for many students, but not for students at risk for reading difficulties. Those responsible for such state mandates would have difficulty finding any scientific research to support the push to teach all or most children to read in kindergarten. Teaching reading before students are ready inadvertently promotes bad compensating habits for those with weak readiness skills. If schools are required to teach 50 or 100 words in kindergarten, then for at-risk readers you may want to consider using word families (e.g., *at, bat, cat, fat, hat, mat, pat, rat, sat*). A few common word families can go a long way toward reaching a target number of words.[1] You may also want to teach a limited number of high frequency words (e.g., *a, the, is, was*) that are not in word families to allow teachers to generate sensible sentences and stories based upon the word families. It is advisable to limit the high frequency words that are phonetically irregular because exposure to words with inconsistent letter patterns makes it difficult for some children to develop letter-sound skills. But some irregular words, like those mentioned (*a, the, is, was*), are unavoidable.

For the formal teaching of reading, research has shown that phonics instruction has superior outcomes compared to the whole language/balanced literacy or classic whole word approaches. However, phonics is *not* the developmentally most appropriate introduction to reading. This is because, in order to be successful, *students must do phoneme-level processing right from the start*. Phonic programs typically begin with words with a single, short vowel, like short *a*. Then, children are expected to sound out and remember words such as *hat, bag, cab, nap, cat, sad*, etc. But to do this, beginning readers must attend to the beginning, middle, and ending sounds in order to "map" these words to permanent memory (e.g., *h-a-t, b-a-g*). However, the majority of beginning readers cannot do the phoneme-level processing that phonetic decoding requires. Phonics works best when students are at the *full alphabetic phase* of reading development. Yet most students are at the *partial alphabetic phase* when first given reading instruction. Most children *survive* this early speed bump in literacy instruction. However, far too many do not. The whole language/balanced literacy and whole word approaches are even more developmentally inappropriate because they do not explicitly and systematically teach the code of written English and expect beginning readers to figure much of it out on their own.

What is the alternative? There are two approaches to the initial teaching of reading that are easier than phonics. Each one matches up with the first two phases of sight-word acquisition. The first "reading" method, which aligns with the pre-alphabetic phase, is an old method that is only appropriate for a child's first exposure to the *concept* of reading. It is called Rebus reading, which uses small pictures in place of words. This is not real reading. However, it is a supplemental technique in some older phonic and linguistic programs.[2] I am not necessarily recommending the use of the Rebus approach nor am I discouraging it. I am simply pointing out one of the two reading approaches that are developmentally easier than phonics.

The second method that is developmentally easier than phonics is called the *linguistic approach*.[3] The linguistic approach aligns itself quite well with the *partial-alphabetic phase* of sight word acquisition and the onset-rime level of phonological awareness, which is where most students are functioning when they begin formal reading instruction.

---

[1] A useful word family to teach because it contains very commonly used words is *be, he, me, she, we*. This presumes they have learned the consonant digraph *sh* (see Chapter 12) and have learned how the word *the* breaks that pattern.
[2] Rebus was used in order to include words in a story that had a spelling pattern not yet introduced in the beginning reading series. Thus, if the pattern *–ouse* had not yet been taught, the story could incorporate words like *mouse* and *house* using a little picture of those items. As spelling patterns were learned, the pictures were phased out.
[3] In order for the linguistic approach to work, students *must* have basic letter-sound knowledge.

Chapter 5

Often confused with phonics, the linguistic approach focuses on the *rime unit* (e.g. m<u>at</u>, c<u>at</u>, s<u>at</u>, b<u>at</u>, h<u>at</u>,). Recall that a *rime unit* is the part of the syllable that contains the vowel and any consonants following the vowel in that syllable. This is often called the *word family approach*. This approach is less demanding than phonics in terms of prerequisite phonological awareness skills, making it more developmentally appropriate than phonics for an introductory approach to reading. Students working at the onset-rime level of phonological awareness can be taught successfully using a linguistic approach. In fact, most students by late kindergarten to early first grade are precisely at these onset-rime and partial alphabetic levels of development, right when formal reading instruction begins. Phonics requires phoneme-level abilities, which few children have at the start of first grade. By contrast, the linguistic approach requires onset-rime abilities, which most children have at the beginning of first grade. The linguistic approach is therefore developmentally more appropriate for beginning readers than the phonics approach. Linguistic materials allow children to begin reading sentences and short stories while their basic phoneme-level skills are developing.

Rime units play different roles at different points in reading development. During the *partial alphabetic phase*, they assist with word *identification*, but not with word *recognition*. This is because students are not yet able to map the individual phonemes within rime units to permanent memory. Studies show that children can *identify* words that share a rime unit (*lip, dip, sip*, etc.) more quickly than words with different rime units. However, children do not necessarily *remember* these words for the long haul. Efficient permanent storage of rime units comes when a student can map each element in a rime (e.g. i - p = ip). This happens during the *full alphabetic phase*, when students have the phoneme awareness needed to map words and word parts (such as rime units) to permanent memory. In the *consolidated alphabetic phase*, students use mapped rimes to quickly learn new words and access the words they already know. This helps foster the huge sight word explosion that occurs during and after third grade.

The linguistic reading approach is like "training wheels" for learning to read. This approach often allows at-risk readers to start reading in early first grade without requiring them to struggle or compensate. They can thus practice basic reading while their phonological awareness abilities are developing to the phoneme level, at which point they are ready for phonic materials. It is my opinion that the linguistic approach is a developmentally more appropriate starting point than phonics. If you use this "linguistics first, phonics second" approach, while systematically training phonological awareness, you will reduce the number of struggling readers to a fraction of what any traditional method (including phonics alone) would produce.[4]

Once children start developing phoneme-level skills, they can move to phonic materials. For most students, this will be early first grade, but often later for at-risk students. Phonic materials use words with regular spelling patterns. Studies show that children learn words with regular spelling patterns more quickly than irregular words. Research shows it takes about half of first

---

[4]Linguistic materials are harder to find these days. Some phonics programs include some word families. Available linguistic readers include 1) *Let's Read* by Bloomfield and Barnhardt; 2) *Let's Read* student readers published by Educators Publishing Service; and 3) Merrill Linguistics. Note that there are other programs that are also called *Let's Read*, so be sure to find the books by Bloomfield and Barnhardt.

grade for children to master reading in languages with consistent writing systems (Italian, Spanish, Turkish, etc.). By contrast, it takes until late second to early third grade to master English phonetic decoding because of all the irregular words, plus the many consonant digraphs (e.g., *ch, ph, sh*), vowel digraphs (*au, ea, ee, oo, ou*), beginning and ending blends (e.g., *bl, str, tr; –nt, –rd*) and diphthongs (e.g., *oi, oy*).[5]

For beginning readers, words with regular spelling patterns reinforce the mapping concept, due to the consistent connection between letters and sounds. Thus, phonic materials are suitable for typically developing students, but not necessarily for at-risk students with limited phonological awareness skills. Such students will likely struggle with phonics instruction and may benefit from continuing with linguistic materials until the basic phoneme-level skills emerge. Otherwise, we force students to come up with ways of remembering words that are not consistent with efficient sight word development.

Once children have 1) phoneme-level skills, and 2) basic mapping skills, and 3) sufficient experience reading phonic materials with consistent sound-letter patterns, they are ready for any reading approach, including the whole word and whole language approaches. This might be late first grade to early second grade, depending on the student's progress. Whole word readers and children's literature (whole language) contain many phonetically irregular words. Yet when children have good mapping skills, they can handle irregular words. However, continued refinement of letter-sound skills, orthographic patterns, and morphological knowledge should continue throughout elementary school.

Table 5.2 shows the relationship between the development of phonological awareness skills, mapping skills, and the appropriate sequence for introducing various reading approaches. The point here is that *each of the conventional approaches is developmentally appropriate for different points along the sequence of reading development*. Historically, educators have felt the need to choose between phonics and whole word approaches, or some mixture or "balance" between the two. It turns out that each approach is developmentally appropriate at one stage of reading development, and inappropriate at others. I believe that failure to recognize this has contributed to the high rate of reading difficulties.

Research suggests that for 60%-70% of students, any reading approach will work. However, if we take all children through the developmental sequence of the linguistic approach first, followed by the phonic approach, we will find that very few children will struggle. This assumes their phonological awareness skills are developing appropriately.

---

[5]Contrary to popular belief, consistent writing systems have about the same percentage of students with reading problems as found in English readers, but these difficulties present themselves differently. Students with reading difficulties in consistent languages develop phonetic decoding skills more easily because of the regularity of those languages. However, this development takes about twice as long as their typically developing peers. In writing systems that are consistent, poor readers struggle in orthographic mapping and thus have limited sight vocabularies. As a result, the most common symptom of a reading problem in those languages (beyond second grade) is poor fluency. This poor fluency is a direct result of having too few words in their sight vocabularies so they must sound out many of the words they read. While the letter-sound aspect of mapping is far more easily mastered in those languages, the phoneme proficiency aspect of mapping continues to be a problem, just like in English. This implies that simplifying the English spelling system would not, by itself, result in fewer individuals with reading problems because reading problems are found in those languages with very simple and consistent writing systems.

Chapter 5

Avoid or Postpone Teaching Strategies that Do Not Promote Orthographic Mapping

The practice of teaching students to guess words based on context or picture cues has been controversial. Some teachers are in favor of this practice while others are not. Who is right? From what we have learned about mapping, the question should be: *Who* should be taught guessing techniques and *when?* If children are good orthographic mappers, then it is appropriate to teach them to supplement their phonics skills with contextual guessing. Using a combination of good phonics skills and guessing, good orthographic mappers can figure out many new words on their own. Once a good mapper figures out a new word, he or she naturally maps the new word to long-term memory, so guessing is no longer needed for that particular word.

However, teaching guessing strategies to children who are *not* good orthographic mappers hinders word reading development. If a student guesses a word, he does not have to pay attention to the internal structure of that word. *Yet attending to the internal structure of words is the very process needed to store words for future retrieval!* For students weak in phoneme awareness, guessing becomes a compensating strategy that inhibits the growth of sight vocabulary. For poor mappers, guessing does nothing to help remember the word for the next time. Guessing will not help an unfamiliar word become a familiar, automatic sight word. We must not teach weak mappers to compensate via guessing. *Guessing will not help a weak reader become a strong reader!* It is a dead end for weak readers.

Children should *not* be encouraged to guess at words during the earliest stages of reading instruction, plain and simple. Such guessing accidentally promotes compensation in weaker readers.[6] I am keenly aware that this advice goes against the prevailing practice in which many teachers were trained. However the "guessing" advice was developed before we understood mapping. Those promoting guessing as a reading strategy for beginning readers will be very hard pressed to find *any* scientific research to support that practice with weak or at-risk readers.

Summary

Now that we understand how words are stored, we cannot continue to do "business as usual," using the same approaches that have consistently yielded 30% reading failure. We need to work backward from what scientists have discovered about how reading works. We need to 1) teach the skills needed to map words to permanent memory, 2) teach reading in a developmentally appropriate manner, and 3) avoid teaching reading techniques, such as guessing strategies, that circumvent the mapping process needed to efficiently remember words. Following these principles will minimize reading difficulties. In addition to these, we should use specific teaching techniques that directly promote orthographic mapping and thus promote a large sight vocabulary and reading fluency. Such teaching techniques are presented in the next chapter.

---

[6]Children can *identify* more words in context than in isolation (called *contextual facilitation*). Yet this involves word *identification* not word *recognition*. Good readers do not require context for instant word *recognition*.

CHAPTER 6

WORD-STUDY ACTIVITIES THAT PROMOTE ORTHOGRAPHIC MAPPING

In the previous chapter, some of the broader educational recommendations based on our understanding of orthographic mapping were discussed. These include: 1) training phonological awareness and letter-sound skills, 2) teaching reading in a developmentally appropriate way, and 3) postponing reading approaches that do not promote mapping. This chapter provides a toolkit full of strategies to train, support, and highlight the word-study aspect of orthographic mapping. This is the chapter that provides the proverbial "bag of tricks."

The strategies in this chapter are consistent with orthographic mapping (see Chapter 4). If you do not understand orthographic mapping, some of these strategies will not make much sense to you. But if you understand mapping, the point of all these interventions will be clear.

These strategies also assume that students will have some basic phoneme-level skills. To profit best from this chapter students should have 1) at least mastered Levels H, I, J, in the program, 2) can segment phonemes,[1] 3) are making progress on Levels K, L, M, and 4) have developed good letter-sound skills (see Chapter 12). *If any of these are not the case, then many of the strategies in this chapter may not work very well.*

Activities That Promote Mapping

When children are involved in various literacy activities, teachers and parents should point out the relationship between what students hear in spoken words (i.e., the phonemes), and how the order of the letters matches up with the order of those oral phonemes. Many of the following methods should be used routinely for beginning reading instruction. Right from the start, we want students to become efficient orthographic mappers, which is the key to building a large sight vocabulary. However, techniques described in this chapter should also be used for remedial efforts. Older students who have developed inefficient or compensating strategies must "undo" bad habits and "relearn" how to approach words. These techniques are divided into 1) strategies to use for beginning reading and remedial reading and 2) strategies for remedial reading only. This second group includes some unusual or "extreme" strategies that are unnecessary for beginning reading and should be reserved for helping older students (past second grade) break their compensating habits. Appendix D lists and summarizes each technique to provide a quick reference to assist in lesson planning.

---

[1] See the next chapter on the distinction between segmentation and phonological manipulation. After reading the next chapter, this assumption should be quite clear.

Chapter 6

Strategies for Beginning Reading Instruction and Remedial Reading Interventions

1) Teach Students the Vocabulary of Mapping

We all learn best when we have labels attached to the concepts we are learning. Therefore, it is useful to provide students with the vocabulary they need to understand the mapping process. A proper vocabulary helps sharpen their thinking, enhances communication between teacher and student, and allows them to look at words more analytically. Such critical analysis naturally fosters word study, which in turn fosters permanent word storage.

If you teach these words, model them, and *routinely* use them. Also, have the children use them and they will learn them. These words are developmentally appropriate because they represent concrete concepts. Providing labels for these concepts will help the learning process (see the Glossary for help with any of the words in Figure 6.1).

Vowel	Consonant	Phoneme	Automaticity
Onset	Consonant digraph	Vowel diagraph	Letter Strings
Rime	Rime Unit	(Oral) Blending	Map (verb)
Rhyming	Syllable	Phonics	Irregular Word
Grapheme	Multisyllabic	Schwa	Diphthong
Sight Word	Sight Vocabulary	Nonsense Word	Orthographic Mapping
Phonological Awareness	Alliteration	Onset-Rime Level	
	Blend	Voiced & Unvoiced Consonants[2]	Stressed/Unstressed Syllables[3]

FIGURE 6.1
EXAMPLES OF MAPPING-RELATED TERMS
STUDENTS SHOULD KNOW AND USE

2) Phoneme-to-Grapheme Mapping Technique

Phonetic decoding goes letter-to-sound but in order to be skilled at orthographic mapping, it is important that students master the reverse: sound-to-grapheme. Recall that a grapheme is one or more letters that represent a single phoneme, so *b, t, ph, sh, ee, oa,* and *-igh* are all graphemes because they each represent a single phoneme.

The phoneme-to-grapheme technique involves a teacher saying a sound and students pointing to the grapheme on a card that represents that sound. For example, the students may have a card in front of them with the letters *t, s,* and *k*. The teacher says "Which of these says /t/?" and the students point to the *t*. "Which says /s/?" and they point to the *s*. The teacher may say "Which says /m/?" The students should respond that none of the letters make that sound.

---

[2] See Chapter 12.

[3] This refers to the situation when vowels in non-stressed syllables in multisyllabic words are reduced to either a schwa sound such as the *i* in *holiday* or *marigold*, or to the short *i* sound as the *e* in *market* or *magnet*. In such non-stressed syllables, the vowel uses neither its "short" nor "long" sound.

For kindergarteners or older students with cognitive impairments, it is best to begin with cards that have only two letters on them. This keeps it simple and improves the chances of success. Then the cards get more letters, such as three, then four, and finally five. More than five in an array turns this into a visual tracking/search task in addition to a sound matching task. Figure 6.2 shows what some of the cards may look like.

The goal is to progress from simple sound-to-letter relationships to more complex graphemes that have two letters, like consonant digraphs (*ch, sh, th*) and vowel digraphs (*ai, oo*). Eventually, you would move beyond individual graphemes to diphthongs, blends, rime units, and common suffixes. This can even be used with common words, particularly words that look alike (see the example in Figure 6.2). The goal is for students to make quick responses. This would require a large number of cards, or it could be done whole group with PowerPoint slides. Rather than pointing, students are asked to call out the letters that go with the sounds presented. So, when presented with *wh, kn, ck,* and *mb*, the teacher may say, "Which one says /n/ at the beginning of the word?" and the students would say "*kn.*" "How about /m/ at the end of the word" They respond "*mb.*"

r t	t s k	a o e
b g n w	p n j z l	th ch sh ph
bl st rm kl cr	oo oy ea ai	ip ap ut et
wh– kn– –mb –ck	–ing –tion –ent –ence	one on once or of

FIGURE 6.2

EXAMPLES OF SOUND-TO-GRAPHEME CARDS

3) Teach Students to Map Rime Units

Studies show we map rime units, not just words. Children can instantly recognize rime units like *ip, ut, um, ot, een, ame, ake,* etc. Rime units facilitate mapping and help with sounding out multi-syllabic words. Rime units can play a key role in early reading but also support more advanced fluent word recognition as evidenced by their role in the consolidated alphabetic phase (see Chapter 5). Appendix F lists rime units to use when teaching.

As students learn rime units, they can be put on a "word wall." You can organize a word wall in different ways. The most practical and space-efficient way is by using rime units, not actual words. Any rime unit can represent many different words, which makes good use of limited wall space. The first five sections of the word wall organize the rime units based on the vowels. A sixth section could include common but irregular words (e.g., *the, of, one*). This word wall would list the rime units in alphabetical order within each vowel for easier reference (see Figure 6.3). This was used successfully in the ARL program.

Chapter 6

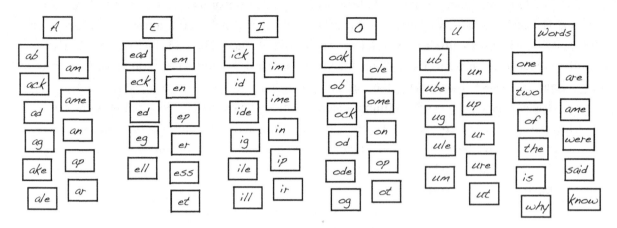

FIGURE 6.3
SAMPLE WORD WALL BASED ON RIME UNITS

With this word wall, there is a quick reinforcement activity that can be used at various times during the day. With a pointer, the teacher can randomly point to the rime units on the word wall and have the children call them out. Also, the teacher should have a set of flash cards with the rime units that have been learned to that point. These flash cards could be used in large and small group situations (see Chapter 12 for the effective use of flash cards).

Use phoneme awareness activities on rime units. In order to get students to map rime units to permanent memory, teachers should do phoneme awareness activities on the rime units. This will help students secure the rime units in memory. The following are examples of phoneme awareness activities with rime units. These activities follow the pattern of the One Minute Activities (covered in the next chapter). The examples below demonstrate both phoneme deletion and phoneme substitution. Notice how the teacher has the student manipulate both parts of the rime unit, vowel and consonant:

Phoneme Deletion with Rime Units
Teacher: "Say *im*." (Student says *im*) "Now say *im* again but don't say /i/." (Student: /m/)
Teacher: "Say *ot*." (Student says *ot*) "Now say *ot* but don't say /t/." (Student: /o/)

Phoneme Substitution with Rime Units
Teacher: "Say *ad*." (Student says *ad*) "Now say *ad* but instead of /d/ say /b/." (Student: *ab*)
Teacher: "Say *ib*." (Student says *ib*) "Now say *ib* but instead of /i/ say /u/." (Student: *ub*)

Having students map rime units will pay great dividends in building a sight vocabulary, in sounding out new words, and even in spelling. Appendix F lists many common rime units to assist teachers with this activity. You can take words from Appendix F to create One Minute Activity-type exercises to map rime units to permanent memory.

4) Introduce Words Orally First

Rather than introduce a word in print first, present it orally. Then, you direct attention to the various sound properties of the oral word (e.g., how many syllables, beginning, middle and ending sounds, etc.). When introducing a new word, whether in a story, a spelling list, or as a vocabulary item, have children concentrate on the oral properties of the word *before* showing it to them in print. Then, when they see the printed form of the word, they are in a much better position to map the written letters used to represent the word onto the oral phonemes in the spoken word. For example, consider a first grade teacher introducing a new word:

> One of the new words in our story is *street*. How many syllables are in *street*? That's right, one. Okay, how many phonemes? Wow, five, you guys are great at this. What is the first sound you hear in *street*? That's right. What's the last sound you hear in street? Good. What is the second sound you hear? Yes, and how about the third? Great!
>
> Now that you know the sounds, let's look at the letters that are used to spell the word . . . (The teacher then shows them the word and points out the connections between the printed word and the oral sounds in the word, or has the students point them out.)

It is not necessary to ask about every element in the word. Just sample some phoneme elements to prepare them to remember the word. Beginning readers and weak readers tend to notice beginning and ending sounds, and not medial sounds. So, be sure to focus on the sounds in the middle or end of the word. A great time to use this technique is when a student gets stuck on a word while reading. Cover the word and ask questions about its oral features. Then, uncover the word and show how the oral features "map" onto the printed word.

5) Use Look-Alike Words

The Look-Alike Words strategy may be one of the most powerful tools in your "bag of tricks" to assist word storage. When you do exercises, such as flash cards, word searches, or other activities, use words that look alike (e.g., *black, block, brick, brink, break, brake, braid, blink, brand, bland, blend, blind*). This forces students to attend to *every* letter in the words they are learning. This has been shown by multiple research studies to reinforce mapping.

Three of the most common compensating strategies used by weak readers are 1) using the first letter as a cue, 2) visual memory, including the length and overall "look" of the word, and 3) guessing based on context. None of these strategies work with the look-alike words task. All the words used in this activity begin with the same letter, have about the same number of letters, have no context, and "look" alike. This forces students to map and not compensate. Appendix G contains sample groups of look-alike words for this activity. You do not need to train every look-alike word in English. Rather, *you are training the mental habit* of attending to every letter-sound correspondence within words. This promotes mapping. As this habit develops, children should begin to naturally apply it to other words instead of compensating. This strategy can be used along with the *direct mapping technique* described below. Also, this look-alike concept can assist in some of the other strategies in this chapter.

When using a group of look-alike words in a packet of flash cards, eventually students may not attend to the first letter because they already know what it is. To counteract this, combine three groups of look-alikes together after they are proficient at the individual card packs. Grouping a pack of words beginning with the letter *b* with a pack of *d* words would be a good idea to force attention to the b/d distinction.

Chapter 6

6) Mapping So-Called "Irregular" Words

Given our understanding of mapping, we may want to avoid the term "irregular word." Instead, we should talk about irregular letter-sound connections. Most "irregular" words have only *one* irregular letter/sound connection. Consider the irregular word *said*. The letters *s* and *d* perform their jobs just fine. The *ai* represents only one phoneme. There is an irregular relationship between the *ai* and the sound it makes. In the word "island," five of the six letter-sound relationships are normal. Only one letter is irregular (*s* is rarely silent). In the past, students were encouraged to "just learn" irregular words, through some type of visual memorization. Research has shown that attending to the letter-sound correspondences in irregular words promotes memory for those words compared to trying to remember such words as unanalyzed wholes. This is because research has shown that we store irregular words in long-term memory in a similar manner to how we store regular words. We use the normally performing letter-sound combinations to "anchor" those irregular words in memory. Researchers call this a "phonological framework," which means noticing and anchoring the stable or regular letters and phonemes within the word. Then, the reader makes a mental note of the irregular element of the word. Only a tiny fraction of "irregular" words are off by more than one phoneme (e.g., *said* is off by two letters, but only one phoneme). Only a few of these rare exception words happen to be words children need to learn early in their careers (*one, none, once,* and *of*). These words are inconsistent by more than one phoneme.[4]

The instructional implication of this is that we should point out the regular elements within all words (which many teachers already do). This will help anchor words in memory. Appendix I has dozens of irregular words for the purposes of word study.

7) Direct Mapping

Years ago, Gerald Glass developed *Glass Analysis*. It involved a method of asking students questions about the letters and sounds in words. Glass Analysis took two forms. One was a phonetic decoding/analysis task. The teacher shows a word on a card and asks what sounds the individual letters in that word make. This reinforces letter-sound skills.

This second form of Glass Analysis directly taught children to map! This *direct mapping* technique (not a term Glass used) started with the oral word and had the student connect the oral parts of the word to the printed letters of the word. For example, the student is presented with the word *best*. The teacher asks "In *best*, what[5] makes the /st/ sounds?" then "What makes the /b/ sound?" then "What makes the /ĕ/ sound?" and "what makes the /s/ sound?"[6] The teacher says the sounds and the student indicates the letters onto which those sounds map. This was also done with word parts (rime units, blends, digraphs, etc.). For example, with the word *sharp*, the

---

[4]Rarely do words have multiple "violations." Examples are *aisle, isle, iron, tomb, sugar, ocean, tongue, rhythm, stomach, bouquet, suede, chauffeur, ukulele,* and *colonel*. However, most of these are not first or second grade words. Also, there are larger patterns that have multiple violations but because they are pronounced consistently in English, they are considered "regular" from a phonic standpoint, such as *–alk* (talk, walk), *–ight* (right, sight) and the suffix *–tion* (action, nation).

[5]Notice the wording, "What makes . . ." or "What says . . ." as opposed to "What letter says . . ." or "What two letters say . . ." This way the student must determine which letter or letters are used to represent the sounds.

[6]Recall that the letters between slash marks represent the *sound* those letters make, not the letters themselves.

teacher may say "What letter or letters say /arp/?" (the teacher says the sound made by *arp,* not the letters) or "What says /sh/."

Phoneme awareness can be incorporated into this activity. Before presenting a word, have the student orally segment the word.

Teacher: Say all of the sounds you hear in *brush.*

Student: /b/ /r/ /u/ /sh/

Teacher: (Holds up a card with the word or writes it on the board) Good, now in the word *brush,* what makes the /ŭ/ sound?
(Do the same with some or all of the other sounds or word parts of sounds, e.g., "What says /br/?")

The teacher should present the sound/letter connections to be mapped onto letters *out of order.* This forces the student to do phoneme isolation (see next chapter). This means the student must be able to *determine the position* of the sound in the word (i.e., isolate its location). If you do the analysis *in* order, you remove some of the phoneme analysis that will assist in the mapping process. Also, be sure to present blends, rime units, etc., together *and* separately (e.g., "What says /br/?" [later] "What says /r/?").

With this direct mapping technique, the child learns to focus on the oral phonemes because you start by segmenting the word. Then, the teacher draws attention to the connection between the phonemes the student just segmented and the letters that are used to represent those sounds. Thus, this is a very "direct" method for teaching mapping/word study. Like other techniques in this chapter, this whole process assumes the student has letter-sound skills and phoneme awareness skills (at least phoneme segmentation, see the next chapter).

A major criticism of the old *Glass Analysis* method was that there are too many questions and that the lessons were long and boring, for both student and teacher. I'm suggesting some important modifications to this technique to avoid these criticisms. First, the phonics portion of the program is eliminated. That is the part described above in the first paragraph of this section. Phonics can be taught via other methods. Only the "mapping" portion of the program is retained. This cuts the time of the old Glass method in half. Second, I'd suggest paring down the time even more by using this technique about 2-4 minutes per lesson. This may involve only 4-10 words per lesson, depending on student proficiency. Third, teachers should not feel the need to highlight every possible combination of letters and sounds in every word (which the Glass method did, making the lessons tedious). Finally, the pacing of the lesson should be as quick as the student can handle, which increases the number of reinforcements in the time allotted, and keeps the activity fresh and interesting.

You cannot train every word this way. There are thousands of words kids need to learn to become proficient readers. Rather, *you are training a mental habit.* You are teaching students a way to approach words so they more naturally map new words to permanent memory.

This direct mapping technique can be especially helpful in mapping words with irregular letter-sound combinations (see *Mapping "irregular" words,* above). Direct mapping allows students to see what combinations of letters are used to represent oral words, regardless of whether they are regular or irregular.

Chapter 6

Direct mapping helps students apply both their phoneme awareness skills and their letter-sound skills to actual words. Again, the goal is to map those words to permanent memory. In addition to a formal demonstration and practice with a few words a day, teachers can use this technique informally at other times. A great time to use this informally is when a student becomes "stuck" on a particular word when orally reading a passage. A combination of the analysis of the word structure along with the time spent on this process, even though brief, should increase the likelihood that the word will be remembered in the future. This technique can be combined with other techniques, like oral spelling (see below), which could logically follow this method using the word or words just analyzed.

The *direct mapping* technique is rather easy for students because they have the letters in front of them. They can "cheat" in a sense, by relying on their phonics skills. However, as mentioned, you are developing a mental habit. You want children to be able to listen for the individual sounds in words that you present, and "map" them onto the letters on the page.

8) Backward Decoding

Another technique to promote orthographic mapping is to have children sound out words from back to front. Backward decoding activates the reader's onset-rime skills and assists in word study. For example, let's say a student sees the word *sent*. Cover up the *s* and the student says *ent*. Then uncover the *s* and the student says *sent*. Teachers have done this for years with single syllable words. I'm suggesting we use it with many multi-syllabic words, too.

Why this works. In my workshops, I do the following demonstration. Teachers get 20 seconds to write as many words as they can that rhyme with *at*. After 20 seconds, they feel they could have come up with more words if given more time. Next, I have them write as many words as they can that begin with *m*. Again, at 20 seconds, they are on a roll. Twenty seconds is not enough time. Next, I ask teachers to write down as many words as they can that have a short *e* in the middle (e.g., *get*). They are instructed that they must not turn it into a rhyming task (e.g., *get, yet, met, set*) because we already did the rhyming demonstration. After 10 seconds they start groaning. By 20 seconds they feel a sense of relief that the task is over. It is extremely difficult to rapidly recall words based upon a middle vowel sound. Finally, I give them 20 seconds to write words that end with *t* (again they are told not to turn it into a rhyming task). This is also very difficult. What they learn from this demonstration is that our mental recall system for oral words is organized according to first sounds and rhyming patterns. Our memory system is *not* organized by isolated middle sounds or isolated ending sounds. So with a word like *sent*, you cover up all but the *s*, the student says *ent*. Now all the words that rhyme with *ent* are "primed," meaning they are in a higher state of readiness in the memory system. Adding the *s* at the beginning activates the word *sent* with relative ease.

The traditional left-to-right phonetic decoding is inconsistent with how our memory system is organized. This left-to-right approach seems perfectly logical, because we read from left to right. However, despite the intuitive logic, it may not be the most efficient way. Consider when a first grader sees the word *tap* for the first time. Left-to-right phonetic decoding would suggest starting at the beginning with the /t/ sound. So far, so good. We learned from the demonstration described above that the first sound is a critical cue in our memory system for oral words. In the phonics approach, the next step is to sound out and blend the first and second letters: *ta–*. Do you notice what is happening here? The left-to-right decoding splits the rhyming portion of the word. This nullifies the other important cue for verbal memory activation. By splitting the rime unit *ap,* the student loses the benefit of a powerful verbal organizational principle already built into our memory system. As logical as left-to-right decoding may seem, it is not as efficient as preserving the rhyming part of the word (i.e., the oral rime). By contrast, when we use the backward decoding technique, we capitalize on *both* forms of verbal organization in our memory system: first sound *and* rhyming pattern. Unfortunately, phonetic decoding uses the first powerful cue and throws away the second.

As mentioned, backward decoding can be used with many multi-syllable words. Let's say a student sees the word *carpenter,* but doesn't recognize it. Have the student cover up all of the letters except the final rime unit, in this case *er*. The student says *er*. Then, expose the onset, and the student says *ter,* then reveal the next rime unit, *enter,* then the next onset, *penter*. Then the next rime unit, *arpenter;* then finally the next onset, *carpenter*. For many multi-syllabic words, children will do better with this technique than the traditional left to right decoding. Backward decoding involves less guessing, especially guessing based upon the first letter and the length of the word, which are typical compensating strategies. It also draws attention to the internal structure of the word in a different way than the traditional left-to-right decoding. This technique does *not* work well with many multi-syllable words. You must use your judgment and decide which words are appropriate for backward decoding and which are not.

When my son Brendan was in first grade, I taught him the backward decoding technique. I was surprised to see him reading his science textbook in fourth grade, covering up some difficult, long scientific words with his thumb and decoding them back to front!

Backward decoding works well combined with the "Give students the vocabulary of mapping" technique above. If they have the vocabulary, you can say, "When you approach a new word, cover the whole word except the last rime unit. Then uncover the onset . . ." etc.

9) Highlight Rime Units and Syllables in Words

This technique draws a student's attention to the structure of the word, and will minimize guessing. When children guess, they use the overall "look" of the word as a cue. They don't take account of every letter or syllable. But when you highlight the internal structure of words, you increase the likelihood that they will pay attention to the letter sequence. The simplest way to do this is to underline the rime units in words you present to children.

s<u>at</u>   h<u>im</u>   st<u>ack</u>   D e•cem•b<u>er</u>   c<u>am</u>•c<u>or</u>•d<u>er</u>

Another technique built into the examples above is that all the multi-syllabic words have the syllables separated by a dot. This breaks the word down for students. Weak readers often sound out the first syllable of multi-syllabic words and gloss over the rest.

This strategy assumes you have explained the highlighting and the students make use of it. Another suggestion is to use a yellow highlighter on rime units. If you are introducing words on a chalkboard or whiteboard, use a different color for the rime unit than the rest of the word. If

Chapter 6

you are more acclimated to the computer, there are many possibilities for highlighting rime units. You can use the "format type" command in your word processor and make the onsets gray instead of black, so rime units stand out:[7]

    carpenter   yesterday   student   afternoon

Another idea is to put rime units in uppercase. This way, students have no choice but to notice the internal structure of the words because of the way the words are printed:

    sAND   nICE   wEST   cAT-ER-pILL-ER   AF-tER-nOON

Notice how unusual words look when printed this way. This kind of technique is quite contradictory to the classic "whole word" approach used for over a century. But that approach incorrectly assumed that words are stored based on visual memory (see Chapter 4). While children will never read text printed this way, this exercise forces them to attend to the letter sequence, which is necessary for mapping.

10) Use Oral Spelling to Reinforce Mapping

Oral spelling bees in school have gone the way of the 8-track tape player because poor spellers were always eliminated early. I am not advocating going back to traditional classroom spelling bees. However, oral spelling can be a useful tool in a teacher's repertoire. It involves a faster response than written spelling. Used as an informal technique, teachers can have students orally spell either new words or words that are difficult for them to remember. This can be done with the whole class (together, not singling out anyone), a small reading group, or even with individual students. Oral spelling can 1) reinforce a student's phoneme awareness of a given word, 2) reinforce the letter-sound relationships, and 3) help him or her make the word a familiar letter string, which helps spelling and reading. One idea is to have students work in groups of two as "study buddies," quizzing one another orally with spelling words. Even weak spellers can do this because they will be looking at the printed words when they are quizzing the other student. Be sure to have them review past words, not just that week's spelling list.

11) Oral Decoding — Identifying Orally Spelled Words

Spell a word aloud and have the student identify the word based on your oral spelling. This reinforces orthography and therefore orthographic memory. This teaching technique is different from oral blending (see Chapter 7) and oral spelling (above). Oral blending is when a student identifies words after hearing the *sounds* of the word. With oral decoding, students hear you say the *letter names*, not the letter sounds, and they have to determine the word you spelled. You can use words from the weekly spelling lists, words that students find difficult, new vocabulary words, or use this in any other way that will reinforce orthography and thus, orthographic mapping. One quick activity would be "oral flash cards," in which the teacher quickly spells 3-4 words and expects the student(s) to identify the word.

---

[7] An efficient way to prepare words this way in Microsoft Word is to get one letter or word in a shade of gray then double click the "format painter." This will make any words parts you highlight match that shade of gray. When done, click again on the format painter to return the cursor to normal.

– 62 –

12) Invented Spelling

Invented spelling involves students spelling new words using letter-sound and phoneme awareness skills. For students in kindergarten or early first grade, *cat* may be spelled *kat,* or *knit* spelled *nit,* because that is how those words sound. Having them try to spell words independently sharpens both letter-sound skills and phoneme awareness. Invented spelling has been criticized because some teachers did not hold students accountable for the correct spellings of words. But an inappropriate use of this technique should not negate its appropriate use. In kindergarten and early first grade, invented spelling is a great tool for both phoneme awareness and letter-sound-skills. After students attempt a new word, teachers can praise the child's efforts. This is a "teachable moment" to show 1) how the oral phonemes relate to what the student wrote and 2) how those phonemes related to the actual spelling of the word. Even beyond early first grade, when a student comes to a new word he wants to write, he should be encouraged to try to spell it out on his own, sound by sound. This gets the student to focus on the internal structure of the spoken word. After making a best guess, the student gets feedback from the teacher, highlighting the relationship between the sounds and the actual spelling. This can work well with the *introduce words orally first* technique described above.

13) Reading Nonsense Words

Have children read 5-10 nonsense words per lesson. This is a quick activity that reinforces letter-sound skills and blending. Some educators object to using nonsense words in instruction or assessment. They overlook two realities. First, every new word a student encounters is functionally a nonsense word until he or she has successfully figured it out. Second, many syllables in multisyllabic real words are functionally nonsense words (e.g., con-tro-ver-sy; mag-ne-tic). Thus, being proficient in nonsense word reading has "authentic" applications. Appendix H includes over 3,000 nonsense words that can be worked into lessons.

Research suggests there are different levels of nonsense word reading proficiency. The first involves one of two types. One type would be when a student sounds out each letter, but cannot sound out the word. This is a problem with oral blending (see next chapter). Another type would be the student who cannot get the letter-sounds correct. This is a problem with basic letter-sound skills. However, once oral blending and letter sound skills develop, the second and third level of proficiency emerges. The second level is when a student sounds out each letter then correctly pronounces the nonsense word. For example, when shown *blap*, the student says, "/b/ /l/ /a/ /p/, *blap!*" The third level involves a student seeing the word and instantly pronouncing the entire nonsense word holistically *"blap!"* without any obvious or lengthy sounding out process. Researchers found that each of these three levels of nonsense word reading proficiency predicted later reading outcomes. Students at the first level had the lowest reading outcomes and the students at the third level had the highest.

What can be taken from this is that nonsense word reading proficiency is related to real word reading proficiency. The instructional purpose of nonsense word reading is to develop the ability to quickly and accurately decode single syllable words.

Chapter 6

14) Spelling Nonsense Words

Have children spell nonsense words (e.g., *ap, blim, frabe, coaf*). To correctly spell nonsense words, a student must 1) listen carefully and be *aware* of the phonemes he or she is hearing (i.e., phoneme awareness), and 2) use the correct letters to represent those sounds (i.e., letter-sound skills). Thus, this task reinforces both phoneme awareness and letter-sound skills, two skills essential for orthographic mapping. The advantage of spelling nonsense words over spelling real words is that the student is forced to use both phoneme awareness and letter-sound skills. When spelling real words, students may be able to bypass this if they have had past experience with any given word. One suggestion is to have students spell four to five nonsense words per lesson (large or small group lesson). This way, you sharpen their skills without investing too much time in this activity. Appendix H lists over 3000 nonsense words to support this activity (see Appendix H for more explanation).

If you use this technique, be aware that there may be two or more correct answers for some nonsense words. For example, *frabe* could also be spelled *fraib* (but not *frab*) and *coaf* could also be spelled *cofe* (but not *cof*). Give students credit for alternative spellings if they are phonetically accurate.

15) Spelling Irregular Words

Irregular words do not conform to the basic grapho-phoneme regularities of printed English. However, they include many very common words. Getting students to spell irregular words reinforces orthography, that is, the correct letter string used to represent that specific word. Like other instructional techniques in this chapter, it is essential that students have been progressing very well in their phoneme awareness skills. The goal of spelling irregular words is to have them learn the precise spelling of those particular words. This will assist in turning those irregular words into familiar letter strings. Once familiar, they are instantly recognized.

Appendix I contains over 300 of the most common irregular words to use for this activity. Words with an asterisk are Dolch words.[8] It will be important that students can spell these Dolch words accurately before moving on to tackle the other words in Appendix I.

Researchers have shown that it is helpful is to give students a mnemonic pronunciation to guide their spelling. An example would include teaching them to say/spell *Wednesday* as wed-ness-day (we pronounce it like *Wenzday*). Obviously this alternative pronunciation is designed to match the spelling pattern. Other examples include *iz-land* for *island*, *an-chore* for *anchor*, and *co-lo-nel* for *colonel*. While this technique does not work for the spelling of all irregular words, it works for many. We want words to become familiar letter strings, and knowing the correct spelling of any given word helps to make it a familiar letter string. This technique can be used in conjunction with other techniques in this chapter, such as *mapping irregular words, oral spelling, oral decoding,* and *spelling nonsense words.*

---

[8] Dolch words represent the 220-320 most common words in printed English. Only those Dolch words that are irregular are included in Appendix I.

16) Word Structure Analysis

Have students identify the onsets and rime units in words.[9] This should be done both verbally and in print. For example, ask a student how many syllables are in a word. Or, you can ask him or her to identify any onset(s) or rime(s) in a word. In print, have students underline the rime units, and circle the onsets. Do not have them do it in the same order each time or else they will guess the last feature of the word by process of elimination. You can give them a list of words, or you can have them structurally analyze an entire sentence.

I am reluctant to include syllabification as part of this activity. Syllabification can be very tricky. Even dictionaries do not always agree on syllabification. Consider the words *hopping* and *hoping*. *Hopping* does not have two separate *p* sounds. The second *p* exists to indicate that the *o* is short, not long. The double *p* in *hopping* sounds the same as the single *p* in *hoping*.[10] Thus, *hopping* should be broken up *ho/pping* (as awkward as that looks), just as *hoping* is divided as *ho/ping*. Some may argue it should be *hop/ing*. Say it both ways: *ho/ping* vs. *hop/ing* and I suspect you will prefer the first. Even if you do not, we must be aware that often a consonant functions as both the last sound in one syllable *and* the first sound in the next syllable. That double-duty is one reason why the syllable divisions in printed words are tricky. If you want to use syllabification of written words as part of this activity, you can have students draw lines between syllables. But you must teach them about the "trickiness" described here. Sometimes, they may put the line through a consonant, indicating that it functions as the end of one syllable and the beginning of the next. Here are examples:

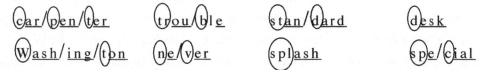

Analyzing the structure of words helps students to focus on the sound sequence that is present in oral words and the corresponding letter sequences in the printed form. This fosters the word-study aspect of mapping.

17) Making/Breaking Words

There are whole books devoted to this technique. This is actually a phonics technique but it can reinforce the word-study component of mapping (and indirectly, phoneme segmentation). Students start with letters which form a big word (e.g., *independent*). The students do not know what the big word is. They try to see how many words they can make from the set of letters they are given, including trying to figure out the big word. They write down each smaller word they make. Because of the ongoing interaction with the internal structure of words, this directly reinforces letter-sound skills and indirectly reinforces phoneme segmentation and the word-study portion of orthographic mapping. A simple way to do this is to type out words in large type and put a space between each letter, like this:

---

[9] Do not confuse this technique with the "Highlight phonograms and syllables in words" technique described above. In the previous technique, the *teacher* highlights the structure of the word. Here, the *student* takes the active role.

[10] Say *hopping* carefully and you will see we don't say *hop/ping* (i.e., we don't make the *p* sound twice).

Chapter 6

<pre>
YESTERDAY   INVESTIGATOR
TELEVISION   HOUSEBOAT
</pre>

You should use type larger than this. Cut up the letters (they don't need to be perfect cuts) and give them to the students. A practical way to organize the words is to use one small Ziploc-type bag to hold the letters for each word. The bags could be numbered with a list the teacher keeps to know what is the "big word" associated with each bag. Also, there are computer programs that can be used for this activity.[11]

18) Words Their Way

Words Their Way is a spelling/phonics program. *Words Their Way* does not deal extensively with phoneme awareness, but it focuses on orthography. Orthography refers to the correct spelling of words but also is the study of patterns in written words. This program teaches the developmental stages of spelling. These stages roughly parallel the development of sight word learning (i.e., mapping) described in Chapter 5. *Words Their Way* helps mapping skills indirectly by focusing attention on the orthographic structure of words.

The following techniques are unusual but are designed to help students break compensating habits. They should be reserved for students who have mastered the phonological awareness program in this manual to the point where all responses to each level are automatic. If, despite this mastery, a student continues to display compensating habits (guessing words based on first sound, length of word, and context), the following techniques may be useful. These techniques promote (or force) students to attend to the internal structure of words.

19) The Reversed Sentence Reading Technique

This must not be confused with the *backward decoding* mentioned above. That technique is a method for sounding out words. This technique is designed to prevent guessing based on context. The "backward decoding" technique can be taught to all students while the "reverse sentence" technique is for those who need to break the habit of guessing based on context.

The reversed sentence technique is very simple and direct. Before having a student read a sentence the normal way, have him or her read it in reverse order, starting with the last word and working toward the first. A similar approach would be to point to words in a sentence randomly and out of order and have the student identify the words prior to reading it normally. These techniques limit the use of context for identifying words. After correctly identifying each word in the sentence, the student then reads the sentence in its proper order.

---

[11]One is *Word Maker* (from Don Johnston, Inc.) for younger students and *Text Twist* computer program and the *Jumbline* app for older students. Be advised that *Text Twist* includes some inappropriate words in their database of possible words, although it does not include profanity.

20) Use All Capitals and Other Forms of Presenting Words

Writing or typing words in all capitals decreases the likelihood that students will guess based on the "look" of the word. They will more likely attend to the letter sequence, which is central to mapping. During a lesson, present 5-10 words for students to read in all capitals. Doing so helps them train the habit of attending to the letter order in words. For example:

HELP   CARPET   ELEPHANT   RED   WINDOW   CAME

Another (rather unusual) suggestion is to write words in a vertical orientation (Figure 6.4). This also forces students to attend to the letter sequence and not the "look" of the word. This strategy springs from our understanding of mapping and the concept of developing familiar *sequences* of letters. At first, presenting letters in all capitals or vertically may be challenging. You will be surprised, however, how quickly most weak readers adjust to this. Students who do not adjust well are likely to be students who lack letter-sound skills or phoneme awareness. Creating words this way on the computer is difficult so you can do it more easily by hand.

```
w    s    c    t    p    c    a    t    f
i    t    a    r    l    r    b    h    r
s    o    m    e    a    e    l    i    i
h    r    e    e    c    w    e    n    e
     e    r    s    e         k    n
               a                        d
```

FIGURE 6.4
SAMPLE WORDS PRINTED VERTICALLY

21) Reading Sideways and Upside Down

Take paragraphs, sentences, word lists or flash cards and present them to a student rotated 90 degrees counterclockwise. Have the student try to read the words this way without letting him turn the paper or tilt his head. This will prompt the student to carefully consider the letter sequence in order to respond correctly. Sometimes rotate the text 90 degrees clockwise, just so students don't get too good at the other orientation and start compensating again. Finally, you can turn the text upside down and have the student read that way, with similar effect. As unusual as this strategy sounds from the perspective of the classic reading methods, it must be borne in mind that this technique gets the student to focus on the *sequence of letters,* which is the key to the word-study aspect of mapping. This strategy is designed to keep the student from guessing based on the first letter and the "look" of the word, though some students may still try to do this when the words are presented this way.

22) Multiple Font and Mixed Case Reading

With computers, we have the ability to alter type for instructional purposes. Print words in isolation or sentences, with different fonts per word (if a word is repeated, make sure it is in a different font). The more ornate or unusual the font, the better this will work, as long as the letters are clearly identifiable. Words can also be printed in mixed case which also disrupts any strategy of remembering the "look" of the word (see Chapter 4). Like other extreme strategies in this section, the goal is to get students to attend to the letter sequence, not the visual aspects of the word. The multiple font approach may be too easy for some older students, but may be helpful for younger students. Samples include:

Words in isolation:

stand   **meet**   WASH   *calculator*   BRIDGE   **stairway**

mUsT   fIsHiNg   hAnD   nEvEr   wHeThEr   sToRaGe

Words in sentences:

THE *quick* **brown** *fox jumped* **over** the *lazy* DOG'S **back**.

THe qUiCk BrOwN fOx JuMpEd oVEr thE lAzY dOg'S bACk.

23) The Spaced Out Letters Approach

Researchers have found that for typical readers, words are easier to read or more difficult to read depending on how close the letters are. So, the word *stand* is easier to read than either *stand* or s t a n d. Careful attention to the letter sequence is needed to identify a word that has a large amount of space between its letters. Words can be expanded this way using the "format font" feature in Microsoft Word. A whole group of words can be expanded this way all at once, making it an easy technique to use. Examples would be:

s t o p   h e l p e r   f r i e n d

Viewing distance is important. If the word is farther away, it will be easier to read.

24) The Linked Words Technique

In ancient times, words were written without spaces in between, as any ancient Greek or Roman inscription will show. Spaces between words came into use in the Middle Ages. We can use that older writing format to get students to pay closer attention to the spelling patterns in words. For example, like ancient times, sentences could be written without spaces like this:

Somekidslikecatsandotherkidslikedogs.Mostkidslikebothcatsanddogs.Butthere arealsomanykidswhodonotlikecatsordogs.

A more challenging way to do this is to link words together that do not form sentences, so there is no help from context, like this:

helpchairmousefreeanswernowapplebikenevercampdustflyingsandpapercart

---

Providing Feedback During Oral Reading

The National Reading Panel's review of research indicated that while oral reading practice *with feedback* leads to reading gains, silent reading did not. If students read orally and get feedback from a teacher, they develop a mental habit of approaching reading more accurately.

During silent reading, students might make all kinds of mistakes and not know it. They may even "practice" their mistakes by repeating the wrong pronunciation silently.

Other research has shown that oral reading with feedback resulted in better reading skills than oral reading without feedback. That is no surprise. What may be surprising is that oral feedback that corrects *every* mistake was more effective than oral feedback that only corrects mistakes that affect the meaning. Limiting oral feedback to reading errors that only affect meaning is a practice that does not improve reading any more than providing no feedback at all! How could this be? One guess is that oral feedback for every reading error helps hold students accountable for what they are reading. By contrast, when feedback is only given when mis-readings affect the meaning, the student is not held accountable for accuracy and can gloss over many words, so long as his or her mis-readings don't affect the meaning. These two approaches to feedback develop two different mental habits. One promotes accuracy and attention to detail while the other promotes "just getting by."

When I tell teachers about this research, they say, "If I had to correct every oral reading error, I would be correcting the student constantly." There are two responses to this. First, if the student is making that many mistakes, he is reading material above his reading level. The teacher should use easier reading material to reinforce his reading skills.[12] Second, it *may* be true that initially there would be many corrections. However, you are developing a new mental habit. The amount of feedback will diminish as the student's accuracy increases.

When a Student Gets "Stuck" on a Word or Mis-Reads a Word

This section illustrates how some of the techniques described above can help when a student gets stuck or incorrectly reads a word. Traditionally, there are four things a teacher can do when a student is reading aloud and gets stuck on a word: 1) have the student sound out the word, 2) have the student guess based on context, 3) have them think of a similar word (read *prince* by analogy to *since*), or 4) simply tell the student the word. Teachers can expand their toolboxes with some of the techniques from this chapter:

- *Introduce the word orally first*. Have the student cover up the difficult word. Then do oral analysis of the word before exposing the printed form again.
- *Backward decoding*. Have the student sound out the word in reverse order, chunked by onsets and rimes. But first you must make a quick judgment as to whether it is one of the words that works well with this technique.
- *Direct mapping*. Say the oral parts of the word and have the student identify which letters represent those phonemes, rime units or other word parts (blends, digraphs, & diphthongs).
- *Map irregular words*. Point out the regularities in "irregular" words. Then draw attention to the irregular element. Indicate that this must be remembered for future reference.

---

[12]There is an old strategy that is helpful for students with reading difficulties. Tell the student ahead of time that he will be reading paragraph number two during class. Go over it with him and let him practice it. Then, when the class is reading, select a student for the first paragraph and select the student with the reading disability for the second and he will be as proud as can be that he accurately read aloud in class like everyone else.

These techniques all promote permanent word storage. They go beyond just telling the student the word or having the student guess. They also go a step beyond sounding out the word. When a student sounds out a word phonetically, there is no guarantee that he will remember the word the next time he sees it.

None of these techniques should be used every time a student needs help with a word. It is sometimes best to supply the word and move on, particularly when it is an uncommon word, including names, places, or foreign words they are not likely to encounter later. Just supply the word and move on. An exception is when the unusual word illustrates a letter pattern the children have been taught. Such a word can be used to reinforce previously learned patterns.

In a given reading group, you may want to consciously attempt to use each technique mentioned in this section at least once, or even twice. If you use them more than this, it is easy to bog down the group. One idea behind using these techniques regularly is that you are training a mental skill, namely the word-study aspect of orthographic mapping. With time, children learn this skill, so you may rely less and less on these techniques. The exception is with beginning readers, who will benefit from these techniques all year. If a word is a new word, let students try to sound it out. If a student misses a word more than once, then the *oral word first* or *direct mapping* approaches would be appropriate. With careful use of these techniques, they will become a natural part of reading with students.

Effective Use of Independent Work Time

Some of the techniques in this chapter can boost student learning during independent work time. If the students are familiar with the techniques listed below, they can be used during such times. Some can be done alone, and some require a "study buddy."

Independent Tasks that Can be Used Alone

- *The "backward decoding" technique.* Encourage students to use this when they are stuck on a word while reading independently.
- *Use invented spelling to reinforce mapping.* When students are doing independent written work, and when they want to spell previously untaught words, encourage invented spelling in first and second grade. However, simultaneously you will want to transition them to using a dictionary for these situations.
- *Analyze the structure of words.* Provide students with sentences for them to analyze the words in these sentences or analyze a short list of words (5-10 words – keep it brief).
- *Making/Breaking Words.* This is a great independent activity. Also, the software mentioned above can be used independently.
- *Words Their Way.* This program includes some independent activities.
- *Linked words technique.* With proper planning, you can have students read some stories printed this way. Including comprehension questions would make this more productive.

Independent Tasks With a Study-Buddy

- *Do phoneme awareness activities.* Have one team of two students at a time use this book during the independent study time. Students get to administer a One Minute Activity to their study-buddy. Once students learn this from their teacher, they love to do it with each other. The one quizzing the other has the correct answer in front of him so he need not be proficient at the particular level he is quizzing.
- *Directly map words using word-study questions.* If students have done this technique with you enough, they "get the routine" and can do it with peers. They each get a supply of words and they take turns being the teacher.
- *Use oral spelling to reinforce mapping.* Have students quiz each other orally.
- *Oral decoding (identifying orally spelled words).* Have students take turns spelling a word aloud while the other identifies the spelled word.
- *Spelling nonsense words.* Give students lists of nonsense words and have them take turns being the teacher.

Providing study-buddy pairs with a list of items that sample from a few of these techniques can make this independent work time very productive.

Sample Lesson Plan Outlines

I once watched a practice session of a very successful high school basketball team. During the first 15 minutes, not a word was spoken. The players knew the routine and went from one drill to another. No drill lasted more than 2-3 minutes. Like clockwork, each player had extensive practice in dribbling, passing, shooting, and defense. They had more reinforcement of these skills in 15 minutes than most teams get in an hour. I thought this could be adapted to small group instruction. Imagine the first 6-8 minutes of a small group time, moving through various fast-paced activities that allow multiple opportunities of skill reinforcement, many drawn from this chapter. Each activity would last between 30 seconds and 3 minutes. With a little planning, teachers can use the techniques in this chapter to build a rapid-fire routine that will dramatically increase the number of exposures and reinforcements to various words and skills compared to what students ordinarily receive.

Below are some very basic lesson planning outlines, one for large group, one for small group, and one for remedial purposes. These represent more conventional plans, but you can create your own rapid-fire routine and rework these plans. Use Appendix D to assist in lesson planning. Also keep this manual handy because you will be using the One Minute Activities.

Whole Class or Small Group (First Grade)

- Start with a One Minute Activity at the appropriate level (1 min.)
- Briefly teach/review the next level in their phonological awareness skills (2 to 5 min.)
- Review mapping vocabulary, introduce new term(s) if needed (30 sec. to 2 min.)
- Review rime units on word wall (1 min.); Introduce new rime unit(s) (3 min.)

Chapter 6

- Introduce new words in story (2 to 4 min.)
    Use "Introduce words orally first" on 1 or 2 of them
    Select 1-3 other word-study techniques from earlier in this chapter
- Do another One Minute Activity at the appropriate level (1 min.)
- Have students read a story; Stop to discuss story/monitor comprehension (10 to 15 min.)
    (During reading, use 2 to 3 of the techniques above to address mis-readings)
- End with a One Minute Activity at the appropriate level (1 min.)

Small Group – Remedial

- Start with a One Minute Activity at the appropriate level (1 min.)
- Briefly teach/review the next level in their phonological awareness skills (2 to 5 min.)
- Review mapping vocabulary, introduce new term(s) if needed (1 to 2 min.)
- Review rime units on word wall. Introduce new rime unit(s) with related words (3 min.)
- Do another One Minute Activity (1 min.)
- Word Study: Select 1 to 3 word-study techniques from this chapter (see Appendix D)
- Introduce new words in story (2 to 4 min.)
    Use "Introduce words orally first" or "direct mapping" on 1 to 3 of them
- Have students read story, stopping to discuss story/monitor comprehension (10 to 15 min.)
    (During reading, use 2 to 3 of the techniques above to address mis-readings)
- End with a third One Minute Activity (1 min.)

These lesson plans are samples only. Given what we know about permanent word storage, a good reading lesson will always include:

1) Phonological/phoneme awareness. This should never be considered an extra. It must be part of the hard landscape of early and remedial reading instruction.

2) Letter-sound skills. This should not be optional. It is essential for sounding out new words and storing words for instant recognition. Letter-sound skills must be proficient.

3) Word Study. Whether you want to teach beginning readers good mental habits for approaching words or break bad habits in older, weak readers, these techniques are designed to promote mapping words to permanent memory.

Summary

Orthographic mapping is a mental process, not a teaching method. However, there are a variety of instructional techniques that promote orthographic mapping. These can apply to early reading instruction or with older, struggling readers. Some techniques can be used to assist students when they get "stuck" on a word. Some can be used during independent work time in addition to formal teaching situations. The goal of these techniques is to train a mental habit that allows students to approach words using their letter-sound proficiency and phoneme proficiency to map words to permanent memory. This, in turn, is intended to promote fluent word reading which is important for reading comprehension.

CHAPTER 7

ONE MINUTE ACTIVITIES AND OTHER PHONOLOGICAL AWARENESS TASKS

The preceding chapters show that phonemic proficiency is central to developing a large sight vocabulary. The following chapters teach how to train phoneme awareness. There are several different types of phonological awareness *tasks* available that have been used for assessment and instruction. Which is the best? Or, should we use all of them? This chapter introduces the most common phonological awareness tasks that have been used for assessment and instruction. It explains why the *Equipped for Reading Success* program uses *phonological manipulation* for the assessment, instruction, and remediation of phonological awareness.

Types of Phonological Awareness Tasks

Researchers have used several types of tasks to assess the concept of phonological awareness, including *rhyming, alliteration, segmentation, blending, categorization, isolation,* and *manipulation*. Studies have shown that all of these tasks are tapping into a single, underlying phonological awareness skill. In other words, these tasks do not assess separate phonological awareness skills. This is exciting news because it means that we do not have to train many separate phonological awareness skills, as some programs do. With that said, let's look at the ways in which phonological awareness has been tested.

Oral Blending/Phonological Blending

Phonological blending is essential for sounding out words. When a student sees a new word, she will give a sound for each letter and *blend* those sounds to read the word. Blending puts sounds together while phonological analysis tasks (segmentation, manipulation, etc.) pull words apart. Blending is required for phonetic decoding while analysis is required for orthographic mapping and spelling. Most weak readers eventually develop blending skills without developing phoneme analysis skills. I have tested many poor readers with normal blending skills but poor phoneme analysis skills. A blending task should never be the only assessment of phonological awareness. When a student does well on blending and poorly on an analysis task, he has poor phonological awareness. Difficulties with analysis *and* blending suggest more serious phonological difficulties.

Chapter 7

Rhyming, Alliteration, and First-Sound Awareness

Rhyming, alliteration, and first-sound awareness are some of the easiest phonological tasks. They typically develop during preschool and kindergarten. At-risk readers often develop rhyming skills later than their peers. Alliteration and first-sound awareness involve the same underlying skill, but the tasks are different.

Categorization/Identification

The most common categorization/identification task is the "oddity task." The student is asked, "which of these words ends with a different sound than the others, *truck, bike, brush?*" This requires more working memory than other phonological tasks. It is a slow-moving activity and is therefore not very efficient compared to other phonological awareness tasks.

Segmentation

This involves segmenting words into parts, whether *syllables*, *onset-rimes*, or *phonemes*:

1) Teacher: Say *flashlight* one syllable at a time.	Student:	/flash/ /light/
2) Teacher: What are the onset and rime in *sight?*	Student:	/s/ /ight/
3) Teacher: Tell me all of the sounds you hear in *fix*.	Student:	/f/ /i/ /k/ /s/

Isolation

Isolation requires the student to focus on one part within the word and isolating it from the rest of the word:

Teacher: What is the second syllable in *under?*	Student:	*der*
Teacher: Where is the *ate* in *plate?*	Student:	*the rime* (or *last*, or *second*)
Teacher: What is the last sound you hear in *ran?*	Student:	/n/
Teacher: Where is the /l/ sound in *clap?*	Student:	*second* (or *after the c*)

Manipulation

Manipulation requires a student to make a change to a word, the two most common tasks involve *deleting* or *substituting* sounds.[1] Below are examples of these tasks. They are given emphasis here because they comprise the phonological training program in this manual.

Deletion involves deleting a syllable, onset-rime unit, or phoneme.

Say *enter*. Now say *enter* but don't say *ter*	Student:	*en*
Say *pin*. Now say *pin* again without saying /p/	Student:	*in*
Say *smile*. Now say *smile* without saying /s/	Student:	*mile*
Say *seen*. Now say *seen* without saying /n/	Student:	*see*
Say *club*. Now say *club* without saying /l/	Student:	*cub*

---

[1] Other manipulation tasks like *transposition, reversal, Pig Latin,* and *Spoonerisms* are not as practical as deletion and substitution for instruction and assessment. Phonological *addition* is often called a manipulation task but does not involve phoneme analysis but is actually a blending task (e.g., "Say *nap* with a /s/ at the beginning" – *snap*).

Substitution involves exchanging an onset, a rime, or a phoneme.[2]

Say *path*. Say it again but instead of /p/ say /m/	Student: *math*
Say *blue*. Now say it again but instead of /b/ say /g/	Student: *glue*
Say *hit*. Say *hit* again but instead of /i/ say /a/	Student: *hat*
Say *sat*. Say it again but instead of /t/ say /d/	Student: *sad*

Which Tasks Should be Trained?

Phonological awareness is such a powerful reading-related skill that *every* task mentioned above correlates with word reading. So which task should we use for training and assessment? Segmentation is the most commonly used phonological awareness assessment task in schools. However segmentation has a weaker correlation with reading than phonological manipulation, blending, isolation, and categorization. Many poor readers can segment phonemes well, but cannot manipulate phonemes, which skilled readers can do. Thus, if we rely on segmentation to assess phonological awareness, we overlook poor readers who can segment but do not have the more developed phoneme awareness skills. When this happens, students may not get the intensive phoneme awareness training they need because we mistakenly assume the student does not have a phonological awareness problem. Unfortunately, most of the available phonological awareness tests rely on segmentation (e.g., DIBELS, Aimsweb, easyCBM).

A related concern is the reliance on segmentation training to correct phonological awareness. Studies of reading intervention in students with poor word-level reading display very different results. An interesting pattern is that studies that train no phoneme awareness show minimal reading gains. Studies that train segmentation and blending show modest gains. However, studies that train phoneme manipulation show very large positive results, results that are maintained at one to three year follow ups. So not only does phonological manipulation appear to be a superior way to assess word-level reading skills, it appears to be superior for training phonological awareness.

Manipulation tasks are superior to the other tasks for assessing and training phonological awareness because they actually have the other phonological tasks built in. Consider the manipulation activity of changing *sling* to *sing* by deleting the /l/. To do this successfully, the student must first pull the sounds of *sling* apart (*segmentation*). Second, she needs to locate where in the word she hears the /l/ sound (*isolation*). Third, she needs to pull that sound out (*manipulation*). Finally, she needs to combine the remaining sounds to form the word *sing* (*blending*).[3] In addition, with onset-rime manipulation, you are also training rhyming (e.g., "Say *cat*;" "Now say *cat* but instead of saying /k/ say /s/" "*sat*").

We can conclude from this that phonological manipulation represents the best way to address phonological awareness assessment and intervention. It has a stronger correlation with reading

---

[2]This program does not have syllable-level substitution. The pilot version of this manual (2002) field-tested syllable substitution. It was very problematic and did not contribute to the training so it was deleted from the program.

[3]While all manipulation items require segmentation and isolation, not all deletion items require blending, like the illustration above did. For example, deleting /c/ from *cat* to get *at* requires no blending. However, all substitution activities require blending in addition to segmentation and isolation.

than any of the other tasks, it has the other tasks built into it, and it produces the best results in reading intervention studies.

Phonological Manipulation Using One Minute Activities

Equipped for Reading Success is based on manipulation tasks. The training portion of the program makes heavy use of what Dr. Philip McInnis called *One Minute Activities*. These activities involve 10 rapid-fire manipulation items at a given level. This typically takes less than a minute. While *Equipped for Reading Success* uses phonological manipulation for both assessment and training, I felt it was important to present the other types of phonological awareness tasks so you have a better understanding of what else has been used to test or train phonological awareness. It should be clear from this presentation that One Minute Activities (i.e., manipulation tasks) represent what is arguably the most efficient way to develop phonological awareness skills. They incorporate segmentation, isolation, and blending and are better at building the phonemic proficiency needed for efficient orthographic mapping. Segmentation training is not as likely to do that.

Summary and Conclusion

Researchers have used various phonological awareness tasks for assessment and instruction. These tasks include *rhyming, alliteration, categorization, blending, segmentation, isolation*, and *manipulation*. Phonological manipulation stands out as the most efficient way to train phonological awareness because it incorporates segmentation, isolation, and blending. Manipulation training typically includes deleting and substituting sounds in words. When students respond instantly to a phonemic manipulation task, you are assured that their phoneme analysis skills (the ability to pull the word apart into phonemes) are automatic and unconscious. This is because segmentation is the first of four phonemic awareness processes that occur in one second when phoneme manipulation responses are responded to instantly. Segmentation tasks explicitly involve *conscious* segmentation (i.e., that is what students are asked to do!). By contrast, when students respond instantly to a phoneme manipulation task, they are not even aware that the first step they performed involved efficient, unconscious segmentation of the target word. As a result, teachers can be assured that segmentation is automatic and unconscious. This represents phonemic proficiency and is the foundation of efficient orthographic mapping. It is for this reason that the *Equipped for Reading Success* program is based upon phonological manipulation activities. This training provides the assurance of the development of phonemic proficiency.

CHAPTER 8

BECOMING PROFICIENT IN PHONEMIC AWARENESS

The techniques in this chapter are intended to promote *proficient* phonemic awareness. The goal is for students to develop their skills to the point where they consistently respond accurately, automatically, and effortlessly to all levels in the program. Below are three different stages or phases students go through to become proficient at any given level in the program.[1]

Multisensory Stage: The student can only do the task with external prompts or helps. The student often makes mistakes.

Knowledge Stage: The student can do the task mentally, with no external prompts, but not quickly. He or she may still make mistakes.

Automatic Stage: The student can do a task quickly and with no apparent effort. The student rarely makes mistakes.

This manual is designed to get all students to the automatic stage for every phonological awareness level in the program. *You are not likely to see the desired reading gains until children have mastered all of the levels in this manual to the point of automaticity.*

Multisensory Stage

Students at the multisensory stage for any level in the program cannot complete tasks at that level *mentally*, but can do so with external visual or verbal prompts. For example, Nicholas cannot change the /i/ in *hit* to an /o/ (i.e., *hot*). But using tokens and demonstrations by his teacher, he can do it. He is thus at the multisensory stage for that particular level in the program.

In the research on successful phonological awareness training, a variety of effective multisensory teaching strategies have been used. *Equipped for Reading Success* arranges these effective techniques into a continuum of activities progressing roughly from the easiest to the most difficult. Because each of these techniques has been shown to be effective in research studies, having all of them available on a continuum of difficulty helps assure smooth progress through the levels. There is simply no point on the continuum of difficulty for a student to get stuck. While listed in order of difficulty, these techniques are not steps students must go through instructionally. Rather, they can be used as needed to assist skill development.

As students move through the program levels, the techniques listed in Table 8.1 can provide assistance in developing skills at each new level in the program. Use them in any order needed to assure that students understand what you are asking them to do phonologically. You can start

---

[1] These three levels are adapted from the *McInnis Learning Construct*, a component of ARL.

Chapter 8

the teaching of any new program level with an oral activity, but if there is a struggle or uncertainty, these techniques can help students understand what you are expecting them to do.

Type of Activity	Type of Assistance Provided	Skills Developed or Reinforced
Use *letters* to illustrate phonemic awareness concepts	Visual-spatial & auditory, plus letter prompts	• Letter-sound skills • Segmentation • Oral blending
Use *visual-spatial* cues (e.g., tokens) to illustrate phonological manipulations	Visual-spatial & auditory only (no letters)	• Segmentation • Isolation • Oral blending
Use *visual-sequential* cues (e.g., clapping) to reinforce segmentation skills	Visual-sequential & auditory only (no lasting visual-spatial prompts)	• Segmentation • Isolation
Use oral cues (e.g., stretching or repeating sounds) to emphasize sounds and assist in phonological isolation	Oral prompts only (no visual cues)	• Isolation • Oral blending
One Minute Activities	None (except task-related isolation cues)[2]	• Segmentation • Isolation • Oral blending

TABLE 8.1
CONTINUUM OF DIFFICULTY FOR
PHONOLOGICAL AWARENESS TEACHING TECHNIQUES

The techniques in Table 8.1 follow a pattern from top to bottom, ranging from providing the most help to providing the least help. When you introduce a new level in the program, you can start with *any* of the above and see how they respond. If they are not successful with a technique you have chosen, back up to an easier technique (i.e., one that provides more help). There is usually no need to use all of these at a given level, just use what is needed to move forward.

Appendix A gives a "bird's eye" view of the entire phonological awareness training program. It helps to track individual student progress. The Multisensory Stage in Appendix A is divided into four sections, representing the first four types of strategies in Table 8.1: (1) L/S (letter-sound); (2) VSp (visual-spatial); (3) VSeq (Visual-sequential); and (4) Oral (oral only).

You can use the multisensory strategies in a small group, large group, or individual tutoring. Feel free to move up and down the continuum in Table 8.1 depending on the needs of the group. If they seem to be getting the idea with a particular strategy, move to a more difficult one. If

---

[2] Most One Minute Activities manipulate sounds in a specific position. After the first item, students know the position of the sound they need to manipulate within the word. This means the One Minute Activity helps them with the phonological isolation. This is why mixed activities are so valuable because they remove this phonological isolation help because the target position changes from item to item.

they are having difficulty with a technique, move back to an easier one. The teaching techniques in Table 8.1 are described in detail in the following pages:

- Use *letters/spelling* to illustrate phonemic awareness concepts
- Use *visual-spatial* cues
    – *Three dimensional tokens*   – *Two dimensional tokens*   – *Invisible token technique*
- Use *visual-sequential* cues to reinforce segmentation skills
    – *Clapping* or *table tapping*   – *Hand puppet*
- Use oral cues to emphasize sounds
    – *Whisper technique*   – *Stretching and repeating sounds*
- Use *One Minute Activities* to train phonological awareness to automaticity

Multisensory Activities for Training Phonological Awareness

Use Letters/Spelling to Illustrate Phonemic Awareness Concepts

This technique is typically not appropriate in kindergarten or beginning of first grade with at-risk readers. But for readers with basic letter-sound knowledge, this may help them understand the phonemic awareness task you are trying to teach.

An example would be when teaching Level J, you could write *bat* on a chalkboard then erase the letter *a* and replace it with the letter *e* to create *bet*. This helps the student understand *exactly* what you are trying to accomplish in the oral/phonological realm at Level J. Then repeat this with other words. *It must be kept in mind that this activity is not phoneme awareness.* Rather, it is phonics (see page 15). Do not assume if students can do this successfully that they are demonstrating phoneme awareness. This technique is simply a *written* example to illustrate an *oral* activity. Once a child understands the task using letters, move to the next technique in which the letters are not used but are replaced with non-lettered tokens.

Use Visual-Spatial Cues

Going from an activity that uses letters to illustrate phoneme awareness to this next approach removes the help students receive from the letters. The visual-spatial cue technique still provides visual-spatial reference points to refer back to, so the transition is not a big jump.

Three-dimensional tokens. Use blocks or other objects as tokens to represent syllables, onsets, rimes, and/or phonemes. For syllable-level activities, each token represents a syllable. For onset-rime activities, one token represents the onset and another represents the rime. Because onset-rime work focuses attention on first sounds, the whole rime unit is represented by a single token. For example, you would use two tokens for *fast,* one for /f/ and one for /ast/. Exchange the token representing /f/ and say the new one represents /l/ to make *last*. At the phoneme level, each token represents a phoneme. You can do deletion and substitution activities with tokens. You can say, "When I take away this sound (move a token away), what word is left?" (deletion), or "let me take away this /k/ sound (remove a token) and put in a /t/ (move a different token to that spot), now what word do I have?" (substitution).

Chapter 8

Two-dimensional tokens. This works much like 3D tokens. Students draw boxes, circles, or dashes on paper, which represent "tokens" on the 2D paper. They write one 2D token for each sound in a word. For deletion activities, ask them to cross out the token representing a given sound and say what remains. For substitution activities, they cross out a token and put a different one above it and say what remains.

You do not need to go from 3D tokens to 2D tokens, but can go from the 3D tokens to the visual-sequential or oral techniques described below. The 2D token approach can provide additional reinforcement after using 3D tokens. However, it can be used in place of 3D tokens given it is a more convenient way to instruct than 3D tokens in large or small group settings.

Invisible tokens technique. This is a natural extension of the above technique. Rather than place tokens in front of the student, you tap the table, from the student's left to right,[3] with one tap representing each sound you are focusing on. Each tap should a good distance apart, as if you are touching invisible tokens.[4] For example, at level E, you tap the syllables from the student's left to right. For level F & G, you tap the onset then the rime. From H onward, you tap out each phoneme, in sequence, from left to right. If you need to delete a sound (e.g., D, E, F, H1, etc.), you make a wiping motion over the spot where you want the sound removed. If you substitute a sound (e.g., G, H2, J, etc.), you pull one hand away like you are sliding away an invisible token, then push the other hand toward that spot as if you are replacing one invisible token with another. In essence, this technique is the same as the 3D token approach except you are doing it with invisible tokens. This approach maintains a visual reference point like with 3D tokens, but is more abstract and presumably more difficult. It is thus a good transition from the visual-spatial to the visual-sequential techniques. It requires no prior preparation by the teacher (locating tokens). With older students, you may want to try this first and you may find you do not need actual tokens.

Use Visual-Sequential Skills to Reinforce Segmentation Skills

Segmentation tasks do not adequately assess the phonemic proficiency needed for good word-reading skills (see Chapter 7). Some poor readers can segment words yet lack phonological proficiency. However, segmentation is foundational for phonological manipulation tasks, so it is important to determine if a student can segment sounds.

The second and third techniques in Table 8.1 involve a visual prompt. However, this third technique is a little harder than the second one because it removes any spatial reference points. It focuses on segmentation, but without anything visual to refer back to for each segment.

Clapping. One of the most popular segmentation activities involves having students clap out each sound you are working on. If you are working at the syllable level, students clap once for each syllable in the word (e.g., *yes-ter-day*). If you are at the onset-rime level, the student claps

---

[3] It is essential that this is from the student's left to right. If you are directly across from the student, you would tap from your own right to left, so the student sees it left to right, to reinforce the left to right movement in reading.

[4] To avoid confusion in terms of the position of the taps, these taps should be *much* farther apart than if you were using real tokens.

– 80 –

once for the onset, and once for the rime unit (e.g., *cl-ap*). At the phoneme level, students clap once for each phoneme (e.g., *s-t-a-n-d*).

Tapping. One of the earliest phoneme awareness tasks from the early 1970s was table tapping. A student taps the table with the tip of his or her finger or the eraser side of the pencil. One tap is made for each sound segment. This approach is quieter and less distracting than clapping and is more appropriate in the context of small group instruction. Clapping would be better suited in a whole class activity.

Hand puppet. Hand puppets can be a great way to teach the segmental nature of spoken language. Because a syllable basically represents one opening and closing of our mouths, puppets easily teach syllable segmentation. Researchers have found they can also be used to teach onset-rime and phoneme segmenting. One research team introduced a frog puppet and told the children he "talks funny." The puppet opened his mouth once for each onset in the word and once for each rime. The same could be done with phonemes. After demonstrating this, the teacher has the students do this. They could take turns with the puppet or the whole kindergarten or first grade class could make puppets out of paper lunch bags and then use them in small groups.

Use Oral Cues to Emphasize Sounds

These oral cues are easy to use and require no prep time. They can be used in systematic instruction or at teachable moments. The second of these (stretching and repeating sounds) has had strong research support.

Whisper technique. This works best when doing phonological awareness activities at the syllable levels (D and E). Say a word by whispering the syllable that you want a child to delete. For example,

Teacher:	"Say *sail* boat" (the small print represents a whispered syllable)
Student:	"Sailboat"
Teacher:	"I didn't say *sailboat*, I said *sailboat*."
Student:	"*Sail* boat"
Teacher:	"Now say *sailboat* but don't say *sail*."

Students quickly acquire syllable skills with this technique. It is especially helpful with the more difficult syllable levels, E3, E4, and E5.

Stretching and repeating sounds. An important aspect of phonological awareness is *phoneme isolation,* which is the ability to determine where a sound is located within a word (see Chapter 7). We do not want to *tell* children where the sound is located in the word. We want them to figure it out. For example, don't say "change the /l/ sound at the beginning of *light* to a /s/," or "delete the /d/ and the end of *bead*." It is important that you let the child figure out where in the sound is within the word. If he or she cannot locate the sound, you accentuate the target sound by stretching or repeating it. While the whisper technique works best at the syllable level, the stretching/repeating technique works best at the phoneme level. For example,

Teacher: "Nicholas, say *hiiiiiit*."

Chapter 8

>   Student: *"Hit."*
>   Teacher: "No, I didn't say *hit*, I said *hiiiiiit*."
>   Student: *"Hiiiiit."*
>   Teacher: "Now say *hiiiiiit* but instead of *iiiii*, say *aaahhhh*" (the short /o/ sound).

Nicholas correctly responds with the word *hot*, with the middle vowel stretched out. You can easily stretch out all of the vowels, but not all of the consonants can be easily stretched. To deal with sounds that cannot be easily stretched, researchers use the technique of repeating sounds. An example would be to go from *hat-t-t* to *had-d-d*. Because the /t/ and /d/ sounds cannot be stretched, they are repeated to draw attention to the position of the sound. Stretching or repeating sounds lets the student know exactly which part of the word you want him or her to manipulate. Stretching and repeating can be mixed in the same item, e.g. "Say *map-p-p*. Now say it again but instead of *p-p-p* say *nnnnnn*" → *man* (the /n/ can stretch, the /p/ cannot).

The following are the consonant sounds that can be easily stretched and those that cannot:

>   Sounds to stretch:[5] /f/, /l/, /m/, /n/, /r/, /s/, /sh/, /th/, /v/, /w/, /z/
>   Sounds to repeat:[6]   /b/, /ch/, /d/, /g/ (hard g), /j/, /k/, /p/, /t/

Level 4 is harder than Level 3 for most students because it removes any visual prompts (e.g., clapping or a puppet). Level 4 is strictly oral, but you are still providing help by isolating the sound's position through whispering, stretching, or repeating. At Level 4, you can gradually shorten the length of the sound you are emphasizing. As students need less and less help of this sort, they are ready for the One Minute Activity*s* at that particular level.

The first four techniques from Table 8.1 can function as precursors to competence in phonological development at any given level (again these need not be done in order). Unfortunately, some phonological awareness tests assume that a student has adequate phonological awareness skills when they can demonstrate phoneme-level processing with manipulatives. It is then assumed that further phoneme training is not necessary. This is unfortunate. *There are many children who are poor readers who can do phoneme processing with manipulatives but who do not have automatic phoneme awareness*. Teachers then assume that these weak readers do not have phoneme awareness difficulties, so the source of their reading problem does not get addressed. The techniques in Table 8.1 help us move toward the goal of automatic phoneme awareness that is strictly oral. Success with multisensory activities is not the end goal, but only a step toward the goal of phoneme proficiency.

Selecting Words for Phonological Awareness Instruction

When teaching any given level in the program (e.g., E4, H, K), there is no need to try to figure out appropriate words to use in the lesson. Teachers can get words for their lessons simply by pulling them from the section of the One Minute Activities appropriate for that level. For

---

[5] It should be noted that the breakdown of letters here differs somewhat from Chapter 12 and Appendix E. That's because the material here is serving a more specific function of making this technique easy to use.

[6] Actually, you can stretch out the /ch/, hard /g/, /j/, and /k/ by following the suggestions in Chapter 12. Otherwise, you can repeat these sounds.

example, if you want to teach Level K (e.g., go from *fry* to *fly*), turn to the section for Level K of the One Minute Activities and select words to use instructionally.

Knowledge Stage

This is the stage at which students are able to do a task *mentally,* yet they still cannot do it quickly or automatically. Also, they may still make mistakes at that phonological level.

Let's return to Nicholas. We already saw that he is at the *multisensory stage* with the Level J task. However, he is at a *Knowledge Stage* with tasks at Level H, which involves splitting an initial blend. So when you ask Nicholas to go from *blue* to *glue,* he can do it. However, it often takes him a few seconds to figure it out. He needs no external visual or oral prompts. He can do it totally in his head. Nicholas still makes some mistakes with Level H activities, but much of the time he is correct. This degree of competence is called the *knowledge stage* because the child *knows* how to do it. He just cannot do it automatically.

I have evaluated many students in 4th to 12th grade with reading difficulties who can correctly respond to untimed phoneme-level tasks. These students were at the Knowledge Stage. However, they could not do these tasks automatically, while younger students who are good readers can. For efficient orthographic mapping (i.e., sight vocabulary development), students need *automatic* phoneme awareness. Thus, the knowledge stage must be viewed as a step toward the goal of phoneme proficiency, but not the goal itself. Unfortunately, most training programs stop when students can do these tasks, regardless of speed. You will know a student is at this level if he can do phonological awareness tasks mentally, but his or her response often takes more than 2 seconds or he or she continues to make mistakes. Students at the knowledge stage should receive multiple One Minute Activities each day at that particular level. The One Minute Activities are designed to develop automatic, effortless phoneme proficiency, which is a prerequisite for skilled orthographic mapping.

Automatic Stage

This is the stage at which students are able to do a given phonological awareness task quickly, accurately, and effortlessly. Students respond correctly within about one second, or at most, two seconds. I have had the opportunity to screen large groups of average and above average readers at the first through sixth grade levels. It amazes me how instantly they respond to phoneme awareness tasks, and these students had never been exposed to these tasks before. By contrast, students with reading difficulties of all ages struggle with these same tasks.

Automaticity appears to be a key ingredient in phoneme awareness. *Struggling readers are not likely to show substantial improvements in reading until they can do phoneme-level processing automatically.* A student will be prepared to expand his sight vocabulary when he can automatically process sounds in every position within words—quickly and automatically.

To return to Nicholas, he is at the Automatic Stage for the onset-rime levels. Remember that he could not swap middle phonemes (Level J) unless provided with external prompts. Thus, he is at the Multisensory Stage for Level J. He can split an initial blend mentally (Level H), but it

Chapter 8

takes him a few seconds to do it. This means he is at the Knowledge Stage for Level H. However, he can do Levels F and G automatically. These involve onset-rime skills. He nearly always responds in about one second and rarely makes mistakes. Nicholas is also automatic for most of the earlier level activities as well (Levels D1 through E3).

Nicholas' profile is typical of children with reading difficulties past the second grade. This same profile may apply to a 3rd, 5th or 11th grader. For weak readers, phonological awareness skills get "stuck" at this late 1st grade/early 2nd grade level and do not progress unless directly trained. As mentioned, if students cannot do phoneme-level processing automatically, they are not likely to make substantial reading gains. Because automatic phoneme awareness is necessary for efficiently building a large sight vocabulary (i.e., orthographic mapping), poor or non-automatic phonemic awareness will limit a student's progress.

Look at the *Phonological Awareness Development Chart* (Appendix A). This chart can be reproduced so that there is one for each student to keep track of their progress, starting in kindergarten.[7] Keep track of progress until the student has demonstrated proficiency (i.e., automaticity) at all levels. You know they are at proficiency at any given level when their accuracy rate is about 98%-100% and they consistently respond instantly.

Remember that phonological awareness is 1) a critical mental skill needed to acquire a large sight vocabulary; 2) the most common source of word reading difficulties; and 3) not meaningfully related to intelligence, so we cannot assume who will struggle in this skill. Thus, phonological awareness should be trained and monitored with *all* students. Regardless of grade level (1st to 12th) *continue using the progress chart in Appendix A until a student has mastered all the skills to the point of automaticity.*

The chart is easy to understand. Check off each box as the student progresses through each level. If you are instructing a student on a task, that student is at the multisensory stage for that phonological awareness level. Note how in Appendix A, the multisensory stage is divided into four sections to represent the first four techniques from Table 8.1. If a student can successfully perform at a given level, but not immediately and (nearly) flawlessly, he is at the knowledge stage. When he can do it consistently and accurately in less than 1 to 2 seconds, he has automaticity. You can use check marks or can write dates in the boxes to log student progress. Check a box if a student has been successful at a given level for a few days to a week or so (assuming you are doing One Minute Activities a few times a day).

The teaching techniques from this chapter should be integrated into lesson plans, like the examples at the end of Chapter 6. These techniques will be your primary methods for teaching a given level in the program until the student reaches the knowledge stage with that level. At that point, the One Minute Activities will be used to train students so they can reach the automatic stage at that level.

---

[7] To get a free pdf copy of Appendix A to print one for each student, go to www.equippedforreadingsuccess.com

CHAPTER 9

HOW TO TRAIN PHONOLOGICAL AWARENESS

Training phonological awareness does not involve long, boring lessons or drills. In fact, it involves very little time. As a bonus, kids really enjoy these activities. The suggestions below will help keep these activities fresh and engaging, while maximizing learning opportunities.

There are at least three ways you can train phonological awareness. Doing all three of these guarantees that students will have sufficient opportunities for skill development.

Type of Learning Opportunity	Amount of Time Per Activity	Number of Times Per Day
1) Direct Teaching	2 to 10 minutes	0, 1, or 2
2) *One Minute Activities*	45 seconds to 1 minute	4 to 8
3) Incidental Teaching	3 to 10 seconds	Many "teachable" moments

Direct Teaching of Phonological Awareness

Direct teaching means explicitly instructing students in phonological awareness skills. This involves 1) explanation, 2) demonstration, 3) practice, and 4) feedback. Direct teaching should focus on the *levels* of phonological skill within the program (i.e., Level D1 through Level M2). Direct teaching occurs when students are at the multisensory stage of skill development (see Chapter 8). At the multisensory stage, a student does not have a good grasp of the skill or concept and requires demonstrations, external prompts, manipulatives, and much practice.

You should *not* do a 20-30 minute lesson on phonological awareness. Direct teaching should only take between 2 and 10 minutes. How much time you spend will depend on whether this is the first time you have exposed the students to a new level. Typically, this teaching is incorporated into a broader literacy lesson. Techniques for direct teaching are described in Chapter 8 and can include:

TEACHING TECHNIQUES
•Use phonics to illustrate phonemic awareness
•Use 3-D tokens, 2-D tokens, and/or the invisible token technique
•Reinforce segmenting skills via clapping, tapping, and/or a hand puppet
•Stretching and/or repeating sounds or use the whisper technique

TRAINING/REINFORCING
•One Minute Activities

Chapter 9

One Minute Activities

Once a student understands a given phonological awareness level (Level E, G, etc.), he or she is ready for One Minute Activities. One Minute Activities are your main tool for developing skill and automaticity at each phonological awareness level. One Minute Activities were developed by Dr. Philip McInnis[1] and were used successfully in his Assured Readiness for Learning (ARL) program for decades. The vast majority of children enjoy the One Minute Activities. To them, it is a game. In over 30 years of using this activity, McInnis said that he always got great feedback from teachers about how much the kids enjoy One Minute Activities. I hear the same feedback from teachers, parents, and students. I hear stories about students lining up to leave the room and making up One Minute Activities to quiz one another!

Children must be at the knowledge stage of development to do One Minute Activities. If the child struggles with a One Minute Activity at a given level, he or she may not be ready for that level, and will require more instruction (see the techniques in Chapter 8). For children at the knowledge or automatic stages of development at a given level, the One Minute Activities will be the primary way to train phonological awareness. Appendix A provides an overview of the levels and stages. A few points must be clearly understood:

Students Should Be Working on Two Levels of the Program at the Same Time

On one level, students will be developing automaticity through One Minute Activities. On a second, more difficult level, students will be learning with help from the activities found in Chapter 8. For example, Erin is a first grader who can do Levels F and G fairly well. Her teacher is giving Erin's reading group One Minute Activities at Level G. Yet Erin and others in her group are being instructed at Level H. The teacher uses various multisensory techniques to demonstrate how to do Level H manipulations. In her small reading group, the teacher spends a few minutes every day instructing the students at Level H. But she begins the group with a Level G One Minute Activity. At some time in the middle of the reading group, the teacher does a second One Minute Activity. She concludes the group with a third One Minute Activity at F or G. Thus, in one reading group, the students have had three One Minute Activities to reinforce their skills. Additionally, they have been instructed so they can move up to the next level of phonological awareness development (in this case, Level H). This means that these students will receive 15 One Minute Activities a week in that small group setting alone.

One Minute Activities Should Take a Minute or Less

One Minute Activities are intended to reinforce the skill at a given level and develop automaticity. If students have to be prompted through a One Minute Activity, they are not yet ready for a One Minute Activity at that level. Go back and do One Minute Activities with an easier level. More direct teaching is needed at the level at which the students are struggling.

---

[1] Phonological manipulation activities pre-date McInnis' ARL by a few years, but he developed the idea of organizing them into groups of 10 for instructional purposes. I believe he coined the term *One Minute Activity*.

One Minute Activities Can Be Used to "Punctuate" the School Day

In addition to the three One Minute Activities per reading group (see above), teachers should also do whole class One Minute Activities during transition times. Just before lunch, bus dismissal, the daily special (art, music, P.E., etc.), do a whole class One Minute Activity. When teachers transition to another subject, they can do a One Minute Activity. When one combines the One Minute Activities children receive in their reading groups with these whole class One Minute Activities that "punctuate" the day, children could easily get 6 to 10 One Minute Activities each day.[2] This will have a significant impact on their development of phonological awareness.

One Minute Activities in Small Groups and Large Groups

When you do One Minute Activities in a group setting, you can either have all students respond in unison, or you can have them respond choral-solo-choral-solo. For the first item, the group responds. Then, every other item could be directed to an individual student. When you have a single student respond in a group setting, make sure it is an item the student can do. You don't want to embarrass a student or turn anyone off to One Minute Activities.

For groups, keep your finger in two places in the manual (three, if you have good fine motor skills). You may give the group an item at one level but may give a weaker individual an item an easier level. Or, the reverse may be true. You could give the group a Level F activity, but give students with good skills more difficult items when it is their turn.

Why One Minute Activities Are So Effective

One Minute Activities have several important advantages. First, as mentioned in Chapter 7, One Minute Activities use phonological manipulation. Thus, they incorporate the other phonological tasks: segmentation, isolation, and blending. For this reason, they are the most efficient way to train phonological awareness. Second, the administration of One Minute Activities requires almost no planning by the teacher. Simply grab this manual and do the next One Minute Activity at the appropriate level. You don't need to come up with examples—it is all laid out in this manual. Third, you can provide many reinforcements in a short amount of time compared to other types of phonological awareness training, which are often slower moving activities. Fourth, ongoing assessment is built into the One Minute Activities. By using these activities, you know a student's degree of proficiency and at what level he or she is proficient. Fifth, it is easy to track student progress using the Phonological Awareness Development Chart (Appendix A). Finally, students enjoy One Minute Activities.

Incidental Teaching

Phonological awareness can be taught and reinforced in many ways each school day. There are "teachable moments" available for teachers who are in the habit of looking for them:

---

[2] Depending on the grade level and skill level of the class or group, you can also punctuate your day by reviewing rime units, letter sounds/names, blends, digraphs, diphthongs, or Dolch words. The goal is to provide ongoing review and reinforcement to make these basic skills automatic.

Chapter 9

- In the early weeks of kindergarten or first grade, teachers can have students clap out their names in syllables. They can also do this with days of the week, months, etc. In mid to late first grade, teachers can have the class clap out the *phonemes* of each student's name or days of the week, months, etc.
- Each week's spelling words can be phonologically analyzed according to the level of the students' current phonological awareness development.
- When new vocabulary words are introduced, or unfamiliar words are encountered in a story, a brief 5 to 10 second analysis of the new words can be done. For example, first graders encounter the printed form of the word *house* for the first time while reading a story. The teacher asks an "analyzing question" that taps into Level I (appropriate for mid first grade with most students) "What is the *sound* you hear at the end of *house?*" A bright student says "/E/" because he's already familiar with the spelling of *house*. The teacher says, "I'm not talking about *letters*, I want you to tell me the last *sound* you hear when I say *house?*" Once identified, the teacher moves on. You don't have to ask a bunch of questions for each word. Rather, sprinkle in questions that direct the students' attention to the sound properties of words. Those questions must be consistent with the students' phonological awareness development. This works in large or small group contexts.

Phonological *segmentation* and *isolation* are the most practical types of phonological tasks to use informally, because they do not require any pre-planning. The previous paragraph already mentioned informal segmentation (i.e., clapping out syllables or phonemes). Informal isolation would involve simple questioning of students about where in the word they hear certain sounds (e.g., "where do you hear the /n/ in Spain?"). This could also involve the reverse, asking what sound they hear in a given position (e.g., "What's the last sound you hear in Greece?"). See Chapter 7 for a description of segmentation and isolation. It is possible to use other phonological tasks informally (e.g., blending and manipulation) but segmentation and isolation are the easiest for unplanned reinforcement via incidental teaching.

The Power of Punctuating Your Day

Studies show that when you keep coming back to things throughout the day, memory for the content gets better solidified in a student's long-term memory system and learning is more successful. So, whether it is One Minute Activities, or a review of letter-sound skills, rime units, or taught sight words, the use of multiple exposures throughout the day is a powerful way to promote success.

Summary and a Challenge

Phoneme awareness training is easy to do, takes very little time, and is fun for students. Yet over the years I have heard teachers say, "But I don't have time . . ." Those teachers cannot possibly understand how important phoneme awareness is to reading. Otherwise, they would know how inefficient their reading instruction is when they try to teach reading to students with inadequate phoneme awareness. Children with weak phoneme awareness will not develop adequate reading abilities if that weakness is not corrected. *Make time for phoneme awareness training!*

CHAPTER 10

HOW TO USE THE ONE MINUTE ACTIVITIES

Let's review what has been said about the One Minute Activities:

- One Minute Activities involve phonological manipulation. Phonological manipulation represents a very efficient approach to phonological awareness training because it simultaneously provides practice in segmentation, isolation, manipulation, and blending.
- There are two types of manipulation tasks found in the One Minute Activities, deletion and substitution.[1]
- One Minute Activities should take a minute or less.
- One Minute Activities are a fast-paced activity that children usually enjoy.
- Children should do about 4 to 8 One Minute Activities spread throughout their school day.

Below are additional explanations of the various levels and special features of the One Minute Activities section of the manual.

General Considerations

Where to Start?

Kindergarten. Start beginning kindergarteners with D1. If you do at least four One Minute Activities a day (you can do more), you will complete D1 in the second week of school, as long as all students in the class or small group can do D1 activities quickly and accurately for a few days in a row. Use instructional strategies as needed (Chapter 8). Follow this same procedure with D2, then move on to E2. You can skip E1 (see comments on pages 92 and 135).

While doing E2 One Minute Activities, use instructional approaches from Chapter 8 to teach E3, preparing them for the E3 One Minute Activities when they finish the E2 activities. The jump from E2 to E3 can be difficult without that instructional support ahead of time. Follow this "one ahead" approach throughout the program as described on page 86. The goal is to get to phoneme-level activities as soon as is reasonably possible because it is phoneme-level skills, not syllable-level skills, that affect reading development. The syllable-level activities are a very easy introduction for young children to learn how to recognize that words are made up of smaller parts. Also, it helps acclimate them to the One Minute Activities.

---

[1] *Reversal* is a third type of manipulation task used in the One Minute Activities, but only in the optional Level N.

Chapter 10

Either after E3, or concurrent with it, start work on Level F. You have now reached the first phoneme-level activities. While Levels F and G are called "onset-rime," they are actually the easiest phoneme activities because they work on initial phonemes. Continue through the various levels at as fast a pace as at-risk students can handle. There is no stopping point. If the children can master Levels H and I in kindergarten, that's great. But it is important that you primarily support the progress of the at-risk readers. Providing at-risk students with extra individual or small group help on these skills may be necessary for them to keep pace.

First grade and beyond, including older, remedial students. As just mentioned, phoneme activities are what support reading, so you do not want to spend time on anything but phoneme-level activities from first grade and beyond (i.e., Levels F and higher). While PAST test results might suggest a starting point, it is recommended that you start all students with One Minute Activities at D1, but only a single One Minute Activity at that level. The very next One Minute Activity would be a D2 activity, but only one at that level as well. Continue doing only one at each level until students begin to struggle. That will tell you where you need to work on teaching.

The reason for taking all students back to D1, D2, etc., even if for only a single One Minute Activity, is to be sure that students have mastered the skills needed for those earlier level activities. For example, E4 and E5 help children notice a single phoneme in the middle of a multisyllabic word. F and G have very important multisyllabic/applied levels (see below) that should not be skipped—but would likely get skipped—if students started the program above those levels. Thus it is encouraged that all students begin with at least one D1 activity. A classroom teacher doing four or more One Minute Activities distributed throughout the day could get through these early levels and get to the instructional level in one or two days. The key is to not miss Levels E4, E5, and the multisyllabic/applied activities for F and G.

Also, *teachers have a tendency to spend too much time at one level!* If students can respond accurately and automatically to the One Minute Activities at a given level for three or four days in a row, they are ready to move on. Review activities are built into the program at the bottom of each page starting with Level F. Teachers can always go back to earlier levels if needed.

Note the Samples at the Top of Each Page

At the top of each page of the One Minute Activities are examples of what to say. There are three ways to do it. The first is when you say the word and repeat the word, like this:

Say: ***classroom*** Now say ***classroom*** again, but this time don't say ***class.***

When you repeat the word a second time, students are less likely to forget the word. Because these activities are fast moving, it would be easy for a student to lose track of the target word. Repeating the word every time is monotonous, so an alternative is:

Say: ***classroom*** Now say it again, but don't say ***class.***

When students are nearly automatic at a given level, the phrase can be shortened further:

Say: ***classroom*** without saying ***class.***

When students move up to the next level, use the fuller instructions at the new level.

Avoid Doing Levels Out of Sequence—With Two Exceptions

This program is sequenced based upon research on phonological awareness development plus decades of field-testing. Going out of sequence can make it difficult for students with weak phonological skills. There are two exceptions to this. The first has to do with Level E, explained on page 135. Levels E3, E4, and E5 are more difficult than Levels F and G for most students. *After students has mastered E2, move on to Level F.* Do Level E3 alongside Levels F and G and do Levels E4 and E5 alongside Levels H and I. The second exception is that the Levels F and G multisyllabic/applied activities don't have to be mastered before moving on to Level H (see below). Aside from these exceptions, it is recommended to follow the suggested sequence.

Re-using Levels

If you use up all of the One Minute Activities at a given level, and the students have not mastered that level yet, you can go back and re-use the items. Most levels have 280-290 manipulations arranged into 28-29 One Minute Activities. This should be enough under most circumstances. If you need to cycle back around, rest assured, the students will not have memorized the correct responses to nearly 300 items! When re-using a substitution exercise, you can do the items in the opposite direction. For example, if the activity says to go from *sat* to *hat*, the second time around you can go in the reverse order, from *hat* to *sat*.

Using Words for Other Tasks

When doing multisensory teaching tasks (see Chapter 8), you can draw words from the One Minute Activities at the respective level. For example, when teaching students about Level K, draw the words you need for your lessons from the Level K section of the One Minute Activities. There is no need to struggle to come up with words to fit a given instructional level.

Extra Levels and Special Activities

Mixed Activities and Supplemental Activities

Starting with Level F1, there are mixed activities on most pages that combine the newest level with previously learned levels. With standard One Minute Activities, students can get "into a groove," because all items manipulate a sound in the same position. Mixed activities sharpen their skills because students must use their isolation skills to determine *where* the target sound is within the word. Also, I have added 8 or 9 "supplementary" One Minute Activities at most levels in the event that the original 20 are not enough.

Multisyllabic/Applied Activities

Skilled orthographic mapping presumes students can process phonemes within multisyllabic words. Levels F1, G1, I2, J, and L have *Multisyllabic/Applied* activities,[2] which apply skills

---

[2] Finding appropriate word pairs for these multisyllabic/applied activities was very difficult. Other levels (H, K, M) do not have multisyllabic/applied activities because not enough word pairs could be found.

learned at those levels to internal phonemes within multisyllabic words. At F1, for example, in the word *hamper,* you first set aside *ham*, delete the onset of *per* and blend that with *ham* to get *hammer*. Thus, F1 first-sound deletion is applied to the middle of a multisyllabic word.

Multisyllabic/applied activities are harder than other items at those levels, so you may need to use instructional strategies from Chapter 8. Also, students do not need to master these before moving on to the next level. However, it is very important to come back to these later because skilled reading requires efficient mapping of multisyllabic words. E4 and E5, while syllable-level activities, actually get students to notice single phonemes in the middle of multisyllabic words. Thus, these also help students to notice sounds in all positions of words, whether single syllable words or multisyllabic words.

Challenge Words—Three Phoneme Blends

So that students can apply their phoneme skills to any type of written word they encounter, words with three phoneme blends are included. There are "challenge words" at the end of Levels H1, K1, and K2. These activities use words beginning with three phonemes (e.g., *spring, split*) and can be done separately, or mixed in with other words at their corresponding levels.

The Number of Activities Per Level

Some levels have fewer than 28 activities. This was because I "ran out" of appropriate words at those levels. The vast majority of levels have the full 28-29 activities. The exception is that I did not run out of words at E1. Only 16 are included in E1 because if students can do D1, they can do E1. It is not necessary to provide extra items for a level that could be skipped altogether (it is fine to go from D2 to E2). Treat E1 as an introduction to three syllable words. If they can do the first few E1 activities, move on to E2.

Optional Level N

Level N uses phoneme reversal. This is not necessary for the successful completion of the program. However, this optional phoneme reversal task is included for students who have mastered the other levels, and still want to participate in One Minute Activities (see introductory page for Level N) while their fellow students are catching up. A good differentiated instructional technique was described in a previous chapter in which different students in the group got different item levels, depending on their progress in the program.

Chapter 11

Assessment of Phonological Awareness:
The Phonological Awareness Screening Test (PAST)

The *Equipped for Reading Success* program provides three ways to evaluate phonological awareness skills, two informal and one formal.

1) The simplest way to evaluate phonological awareness is to note the level at which a student is working in the program. Is he or she able to do Level E3? Level H? Level K? This informal assessment tells you how far along in the program a student has progressed. It is important to notice a student's *speed* when doing One Minute Activities to see if he or she is at the knowledge stage or the automatic stage.

2) If you want a quick assessment of a student's skill, you can simply give half of a One Minute Activity (i.e., five items) from any given level. How well the student does lets you know how well he or she is progressing. Also pay close attention to speed of response.

3) Use the formalized *Phonological Awareness Screening Test* (PAST)[1] in Appendix C. This chapter provides detailed instructions for administering the PAST. The PAST is best used with students as part of a whole class screening in K-2 or a formal reading assessment. A comprehensive reading assessment should include tests of working memory, rapid automatized naming, as well as phonological awareness and oral blending.[2] All of these lower-level linguistic skills are assessed on the *Comprehensive Test of Phonological Processing-Second Edition* (CTOPP-2),[3] which I strongly recommend. The CTOPP-2 should be used alongside the PAST. I have found the PAST and the *Elision* subtest, which is the CTOPP-2's phonological awareness test, tend to yield similar results. However, in the cases where they differ, the PAST is usually (but not always) more consistent with a student's reading skill (i.e., weak PAST, weak reading, strong PAST, better reading).

---

[1] An Internet search will turn up another test that uses the acronym PAST called the *Phonological Awareness Skills Test*. This test samples from the various classical tasks like rhyming, segmentation, etc. Like most other phonological awareness tests, it does not provide a timing element.

[2] These tests would be, of course, in addition to tests of context-free word identification, nonsense word reading, and perhaps reading comprehension and language/listening comprehension.

[3] As mentioned in an earlier chapter, blending may be average in weak readers with poor phonemic analysis skills. Thus, the CTOPP-2's *Blending Words* subtest must be interpreted with caution. If it is average, it does not rule out phonological awareness difficulties. The *Blending Words, Elision* (manipulation/deletion) and *Phoneme Isolation* subtests all are combined on the CTOPP-2 for an overall Phonological Awareness Composite. Be wary of that composite score if Blending Words is average and the Elision and/or Phoneme Isolation are weak.

Chapter 11

Instructions for the
Phonological Awareness Screening Test (PAST)

The *Phonological Awareness Screening Test* (PAST) can be found in Appendix C. There are four forms; A, B, C, and D. This allows teachers to do a formal assessment a few times a year to track a student's progress.

There is a "history" behind the title "PAST." First, PAST stands for Phonological Awareness Screening Test. Second, the acronym acknowledges the work of others in the *past*. The PAST originated as the *Auditory Analysis Test* (AAT) of Rosner & Simon (*Journal of Learning Disabilities*, 1971). Dr. Philip J. McInnis revised the AAT by adding substitution items (the AAT only used deletion items) and adding levels to make it more developmentally appropriate. His version was first called the *Language Processing Assessment* (LPA) and then the *Phonological Processing Test* (PPT). Since 2003, I have used a modified, updated version of this time-tested assessment.[4] Thus, while the PAST is my "version" of the test, it is based upon the work of my predecessors (hence, the "PAST").

General Principles of Administration

Do not administer the PAST unless you have 1) carefully read the directions in this chapter; 2) read the section in Chapter 12 that covers pronouncing phonemes in isolation; and 3) practiced on someone, preferably with feedback before testing a student, preferably feedback from a school psychologist or speech pathologist. Those professions receive formal training in individualized testing.

No Practice Items

There are no practice items. Feedback is given for every incorrect item (see below), so incorrect items function like practice items. Follow the sample line at the beginning of each level. All items at a given level are administered the same way. *Delete or substitute the sound represented by the letter or letters in the parentheses.* With *cow(boy)*, "boy" gets deleted.

Proper Pronunciation of Sounds

When giving directions for Levels F through M, use letter *sounds*, not letter names. When you say "change /a/ to /i/," you say the *sound* made by the letter, not the name of the letter. The exception is with the "long" vowel sounds in Level J. Long vowel sounds are represented by uppercase letters in brackets (i.e., /A/). These long vowel sounds match the letter name (e.g., the *a* in words like *cake, tame,* or *made*).

Do not add an "uh" sound when pronouncing consonants (e.g., /m/ is pronounced *mmm*, not *muh*). *Proper pronunciation of sounds in isolation is essential for children to understand which*

---

[4]My version 1) adds a timing element to assess automaticity; 2) adds or modifies levels to make smoother transitions (see Appendix B for program comparisons); 3) provides corrective feedback for *every* incorrect item, and 4) for Forms A, B, C, and D in Appendix C, most items are "orthographically inconsistent" to decrease the possibility of correctly responding to test items via a mental spelling strategy rather than by phonological awareness. For example, going from *gave* to *game* by exchanging an /m/ for a /v/ can occur via mental spelling while going from *both* to *boat* by exchanging a /t/ for a /th/ does not as easily yield to a mental spelling strategy.

phoneme you are asking them to manipulate. For help with pronunciation when administering the PAST, see Chapter 12 and Appendix E.

The Assessment of Automaticity

All items are timed. When administering an item, immediately upon finishing speaking, count in your head "one thousand *one*, one thousand *two*." To be sure your counting is really two seconds, use a stop watch for practice (most smart phones have a stopwatch app). If the student responds correctly before you get to the word *two* in the phrase "one thousand two," he or she receives credit for an automatic response. Put an "X" in the blank next to the word to indicate an automatic response. If the student answers correctly, but after the two second count, mark a "1" next to that item. Incorrect items are marked with a zero (0). See Figure 11.1 below.

When doing the mental count, continue counting until the student responds. If you reach "one thousand five" and the student has not responded, repeat the same item and resume the mental counting, starting with "one thousand one." If the student responds correctly within five seconds of this second chance, score the item as correct (i.e., a "1"). However, *an automatic score can only occur within the first two seconds of the first try*. A second chance is given because students sometimes forget what you asked. Also, if a student asks you to repeat the item, do so, but repeated items cannot be scored as automatic, only as correct or incorrect. If the student does not respond after the second five-second count, score the item as incorrect and demonstrate the correct response for that item (see below on providing feedback).

If you mis-speak a word, excuse yourself, skip the item, and go on to the next one, so long as it was not the last item at that level. Go back to the item you spoiled before going on to the next level and score normally (i.e., they can receive an automatic score if they respond in less than two seconds). If this occurs on the last item of a level, repeat that item immediately and use your best judgment about scoring.

Occasionally, a student will respond to the previous item. For example, you have the student go from *sit* to *sat* (Level J). On the next item, you ask the student to go from *hid* to *had*, but instead of *had*, the student says *sad*, accidentally carrying over sounds from the previous item. This may not be the result of a phonological awareness problem, but may result from an attentional lapse. If you judge that a student has carried something over from the previous example, re-administer the item. However, the student cannot receive an automatic score on a re-administered item, only correct (1) or incorrect (0).

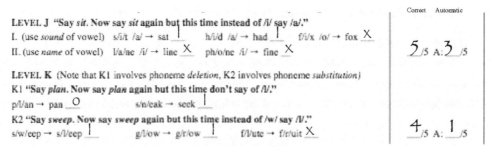

FIGURE 11.1
SAMPLE SCORING

Automatic responding typically takes about a second or less, so a two second count is generous. Therefore, only give automatic credit if students have begun a correct response by the time you have mentally said *two* in the silently phrase "one thousand *two*."

Repeating an Item

If a student seems confused, or seems to have a lapse in attention, it is okay to repeat an item. However, when you repeat an item, that item cannot be scored as automatic. Students can only receive a score of correct (1) or incorrect (0).

Pacing

One important reason to be thoroughly familiar with the administration procedures and to be well practiced with the test beforehand is *pacing*. It is important to administer the PAST at a good pace to keep things moving. A moderately quick pacing prevents lapses of attention, boredom, or prevents you from unnecessarily burdening a student's working memory.

Providing Feedback

A unique feature of the PAST is that students receive corrective feedback for every incorrect item. Students are not going to develop phonological awareness skills in the 4 to 8 minutes it takes to administer this test. Yet they may get items incorrect because they are confused about the task expectations given that phonological awareness tests are unusual for most students. Thus, give feedback for *every* incorrect response. That lets them know precisely what you want.

The standard correction is provided on the test form for each level. No further demonstration or explanation is permitted (especially, no visual cues). Correct every incorrect item, even if it is the last item at a given level. Positive feedback is permitted ("that's right!"), especially if a child responds tentatively. *However,*

1) Do *not* teach any item or level. This is a test, not a teaching session. Although spoken feedback is provided, no teaching, manipulatives, or explanations are allowed.

2) *Never* say anything about the *position* of the sound within the word because this is a big part of what you are testing. For example, never say anything like "see how I switched the /b/ to a /t/ at the beginning of the word?" An important part of phonological awareness is being able to determine where a sound is located within a word. Saying anything about the position of the sound is like giving the student the correct answer.

Routing Procedure to Speed Administration

Students are not administered all 52 PAST items. For younger students, many of the later items are too difficult and there is a discontinue rule (described below). For more skilled students, it would be unnecessarily tedious to administer all of the easy items. To keep the test a reasonable length, there is a routing procedure, which works differently at each of the *syllable, onset-rime,* and *phoneme* levels.

Syllable Levels (D1 to E3)

- *Everyone* who is administered the PAST, including older students and adults, start at Level D1. Explain to students that this "word game" starts out very easy. The easy ones help students understand the nature of the task without ever having to explain the nature of the task. There are no explanations or practice items when administering the PAST.

- For kindergarteners and potentially at-risk beginning first graders, give every item at levels D and E and follow the discontinue rule, below.

- For most first graders and all students beyond first grade, if the first item of D1 is responded to automatically (i.e., 2 seconds or less), skip down to the first item of D2. If that is automatic, skip to first item of E2, then E3. When you score later, if the first D1 through E3 items are automatic, score any un-administered items at those levels as automatic (thus a 3/3 at that level).

- However, if any item is either 1) incorrect, or 2) correct but not automatic (i.e., correct response after 2 seconds), administer *all* items at that level and score normally. For example, if the first D2 item is correct but not automatic, administer the other D2 items. However, the routing procedure resumes with E2. If the first item in E2 is automatic, do not administer the other E2 items and score those un-administered items as automatic.[5]

Onset-Rime Levels (F & G)

For kindergarten to second grade:

- If the first three F or G items are automatic, skip the final two items at that level and score them as automatic.
- If any of the first three F or G items are incorrect, or correct but not automatic, administer all five items at that specific level (i.e., F or G) and score normally.

For third grade through adults:

- Use the same general procedure as with the kindergarten through second graders except only the first *two* items need to be automatic before skipping on to the next level.

Phoneme Levels (H to M)

- For Levels H through M, give *all* items at each level. Continue administering until the discontinue rule is reached or you come to the end of the test.

Discontinue Rule

If the combined "correct" score on two levels in a row is 0, 1 or 2 out of 10, discontinue the test. Consider all items in the levels beyond the discontinue level as incorrect. For example, if a student gets only two items at Level I and none at level J (thus 2/10 across the two levels), discontinue the test. Do not administer K, L, or M. All un-administered levels are scored 0.

---

[5] The reasoning is that if students can do a higher syllable level (E2 or E3), they likely can do the easier ones, but were incorrect or not automatic due to the novelty of the task or lapse in attention rather than a lack of phonological awareness. It is not unusual for a student to get one of these earlier items incorrect or correct but not automatically and then go on and display automatic responding at higher levels. In such cases, administering all subsequent syllable-level items after an early error or slow response is unnecessarily tedious. If they have an automatic response to the first item at any given syllable level, do not administer any more at that level and score unadministered items as automatic, even if they had an incorrect or slow response on an easier syllable level.

Chapter 11

Scoring the PAST

Passing a Level

Levels D and E are considered passed if all items are correct. Levels F through M are considered passed if at least 4 out of 5 are correct. Similarly, D and E are considered automatic if all 3 items are responded to automatically. For Levels F to M, at least 4 of 5 items must be responded to automatically. Levels with 3 out of 5 or fewer automatic responses represent a level that should receive instructional attention. Each level yields two scores, a correct score and an automatic score. Students commonly pass levels with correct scores but not with automatic scores. These differences are reflected in the total scoring (see Figure 11.2 below). Only levels passed at the automatic level do not require instructional attention.

Item Scoring

It should be clear by now that items are scored in one of three ways:

1) Incorrect (Score = 0)
2) Correct but not automatic (Score = 1). The student responds in more than two seconds.
3) Automatic (Score = X) The student responds in two seconds or less.

At each level, count every score of 1 and X and put the total in the "correct" column on the right. In the "automatic" column, only include the items with Xs for that level (see Figure 11.1 above for an illustration).

The Total Scores

As mentioned, students receive two scores at each level, a correct score and an automatic score. Transfer the totals from the right hand columns to the top of the first page of the test. There are two sides to this. First, the student receives a score indicating how many were correct and how many were automatic at the *syllable, onset-rime,* and *phoneme* levels. Second, the other side gives the highest level passed. Remember that a level is passed as *correct* if at least 4 out of 5 at that level are correct. The exceptions to this are the syllable levels which require at least 3 out of 3 to be considered passing. A level is considered *automatic* if at least 4 out of 5 items were automatic (or 3 out of 3 for the syllable levels). For most children, the highest correct level will be higher than his or her highest automatic level (see Figure 11.2 for an illustration). It is also important to note any levels not passed that were below the highest level passed.

RESULTS:	Correct	Automatic		
Basic Syllable	12/12	10/12	Highest Correct Level:	J
Onset-Rime	10/10	10/10	(Levels not passed below the highest correct level)	—
Basic Phoneme	8/10	4/10		
Advanced Phoneme	6/20	2/20	Highest Automatic Level:	I
Test Total	36/52	26/52	(Non-automatic levels below highest automatic level)	E, H

FIGURE 11.2

SAMPLE OF SCORING RESULTS

Interpreting the *PAST*

The PAST correlates powerfully with reading but is not a normed test. However, the following is a guide to interpreting the results of the PAST based on 1) several studies that did not use the PAST that show when children developmentally can do specific phonological manipulations; 2) Dr. Philip McInnis' 35 years using very similar levels on his LPA/PPT; 3) my 14 years working with the PAST; and 4) several studies I have directly done on the PAST.

Note: The data used to piece together Table 11.1, based on the sources mentioned above, were gathered from schools that had *not* been doing phonological/phonemic awareness instruction. If you use the *Equipped for Reading Success* program, the expectations should be somewhat higher than found in Table 11.1. Also, the information sources behind Table 11.1 were from the 1980s to early 2000s, when formal reading instruction began in first grade. Now that reading instruction starts in kindergarten in U.S. schools, it will be important to get through the early levels more quickly and get to levels H and I by late kindergarten.

Grade Level	Typically Achieving Readers	Low Achieving Readers
Mid Kindergarten	D1-E2, F, sometimes higher	D1-D2 or none correct at all
Late Kindergarten	D1-E2, F, G, sometimes higher	D1-D2; E2 or lower
Mid First Grade	E3, E4, F, G, I or higher	E2, F, G or lower
Late First Grade	F, G, H, I, J	F, G, I, or lower
Mid Second Grade	H, I, J, K or higher	F, G, H, I, or lower
Late Second/Early Third Grade	H to M mostly automatic	H, I, maybe J or lower
Mid Third Grade	All levels, mostly automatic	Many levels correct, I to M mostly not automatic
Fourth Grade to Adulthood	All levels automatic	Most levels correct, but J to M not all automatic

TABLE 11.1

APPROXIMATE DEVELOPMENTAL LEVELS FOR AUTOMATIC RESPONSES

If a student's performance matches the shaded *Low Achieving Readers* column, it suggests that phonological awareness may be a concern. If a student's level is lower than is listed in that column, then a phonological awareness problem is very likely. In either case, those students will require training beyond what they may be receiving in whole-class instruction.

Notice in Table 11.1 how small the differences can be, especially early on (i.e., K-1). Except for obvious cases of very low performance, the differences may be very slight. This is why all students should get whole class or small group phonological awareness training in kindergarten and first grade. Next, note that over time, typically developing readers start to pull away from those with reading difficulties. Automaticity becomes a bigger factor with time, especially after second grade. After third grade, lack of automaticity at any level may indicate that a phonological awareness difficulty may be present.

Do not be surprised by inconsistent performance across some levels. An individual student may struggle with a lower level and yet pass a higher level. This is because different levels involve different types of manipulations. For example, H and K involve splitting initial blends.

If a student struggles with sounds in blends, he may not pass H, but may pass J, which does not involve blends. Students who struggle with awareness of ending sounds may do poorly with Level I and L but do well with H, J, and K. While based upon group data I have gathered, the leveling system is quite accurately laid out, for any given student there may be some inconsistencies.

Below is a table showing the average score out of five attained on each level of the PAST from among three first grade classes and two second grade classes from a lower middle class elementary school. The first graders were tested in December to January and the second graders from February to March. You can see there is an increasing degree of difficulty based upon a smaller average number of correct items as the test progresses. Also, with time, the gap between automatic and non-automatic responses widens. Based upon the note on the previous page, you should expect better results than this if you instruct/train your students with *Equipped for Reading Success* because the school where this data gathering occurred was not doing any instruction in phonemic awareness.

Grade Level:		Grade 1		Grade 2	
Scoring Approach:		Correct	Automatic	Correct	Automatic
Highest possible score:		5/5	5/5	5/5	5/5
Syllable	D	4.3	3.9	4.9	4.7
Levels	E	3.6	3.2	4.6	4.1
Onset-Rime	F	4.9	4.8	5.0	4.8
Levels	G	4.5	4.2	4.9	4.4
Phoneme	H	2.6	2.0	3.7	2.8
Levels	I	2.9	1.5	4.2	2.4
	J	1.6	1.0	3.8	2.1
	K	1.7	0.7	2.7	1.0
	L	2.0	0.9	2.9	1.0
	M	1.3	0.4	2.4	0.6

Note: All raw scores reported above are out of a possible 5 points. The current version of the PAST uses different scoring at the syllable levels than when these data were collected.

Table 11.2

AVERAGE RAW SCORES ON EACH LEVEL OF THE PAST

NOTE: PDFs of all four forms of the PAST, to print out and use with students, are available at www.thepasttest.com.

CHAPTER 12

Letter–Sound Learning

Letter-sound proficiency refers to the automatic, unconscious activation of letter-sound knowledge. This level of proficiency is foundational for both efficient phonetic decoding and for permanent word storage via orthographic mapping. Equipped for Reading Success is designed to supplement existing phonics programs. Without explicit and systematic phonics instruction, the benefits of the Equipped for Reading Success program will be substantially diminished.

Letter-sound knowledge, phonetic decoding, and *phonics* are not the same thing. Phonics is an instructional approach designed to develop letter-sound skills and phonetic decoding. Letter-sound knowledge refers to the skill of instantly recognizing the sounds that go with letters, digraphs and blends. Phonetic decoding is a word-reading strategy. It combines letter-sound skills with oral/phonological blending to sound out unfamiliar words:

FIGURE 12.1

THE SKILLS NEEDED FOR PHONETIC DECODING

Explicit and systematic phonics instruction can occur at three general levels of specificity:

Level 1 *Basic phonetic decoding instruction* teaches 1) letter-sound knowledge and 2) oral blending to sound out unfamiliar words. There are no rules at this level, per se, just instruction in the sounds of letters, digraphs, and blends, along with blending. This parallels the definition of phonics instruction used by the National Reading Panel.

Level 2 *Simple-rules phonics instruction* teaches a limited set useful phonic rules (e.g., the "silent *e* rule"), often rules centered around the six syllable types of printed English.[1]

Level 3 *Detailed syllable analysis instruction.* Students learn all the exceptions to the six syllable types of printed English and then the exceptions to the exceptions.

Phonic rules are not technically necessary for orthographic mapping, only letter-sound knowledge and phoneme awareness/proficiency. However, knowing basic phonic rules can be helpful to make sense when creating a "map" between oral phonemes and written letter sequences (written words). For example, the word *cake* has three sounds (/k/ /A/ /k/) but four letters. Knowing the silent e rule would presumably help with the connection forming process

---

[1] The six syllable types are 1) closed (*had, much*); 2) open (*be, why*); 3) silent *e* (*make, ride*); 4) vowel digraphs (*boat, feed*); 5) r controlled (*car, her*); and 6) *le* syllables (*table, idle*).

process of going from pronunciation to written form (phonetic decoding goes in the other direction, from written form to pronunciation).

The word-study aspect of orthographic mapping (see Chapter 4) most commonly occurs in the context of what researchers call the *self-teaching hypothesis*. The self-teaching hypothesis says that when students successfully sound out new words while reading, that sounding-out process allows them to interact with the word's sounds and letters and promotes memory for that letter sequence. In other words, it provides them opportunities to map words to permanent memory. There is a strong correlation between children who have good phonetic decoding skills early in their reading careers and those who are successful readers later on. But not all students with good phonetic decoding skills become good readers. If they lack sufficient phoneme proficiency, they will struggle. I have evaluated many "graduates" of popular phonics programs who remained weak readers.

Some Orton-Gillingham-based programs (e.g., Wilson) take phonics instruction to "Level 3." This is the level of detailed syllable analysis. These intensive programs are popular interventions for students with reading disabilities because they get better results than non-phonics programs. Nonetheless, with a large portion of weak readers, progress is slow and gradual and even plateaus below grade level. Such students often display dramatic improvements in nonsense word reading (a good test of phonetic decoding skills), yet only show modest improvements in their ability to remember real words for later, instant recognition.

The philosophy behind the intensive Orton-Gillingham inspired programs was developed before the discovery of orthographic mapping and is thus based on older beliefs about word-reading. We now know that if students have letter-sound proficiency and phoneme awareness proficiency, they can learn to read. If a student displays Level 1 and 2 phonics skills yet is not efficiently storing words and building fluency, then more intensive phonics is not the answer. For such struggling readers, the missing element is almost always phoneme proficiency. Orton-Gillingham-based programs include some phoneme awareness, but they rely on segmentation training, which is insufficient to facilitate efficient sight-word storage in a large proportion of struggling readers.

With that said, Orton-Gillingham-based programs have many attractive features. They provide help in developing letter-sound skills (via their Level 1 phonics instruction). They have many great materials to assist with the phonetic aspects of the reading process (i.e., help students sound-out words). In fact, those programs can be used alongside Equipped for Reading Success, as long as their strengths and weaknesses are recognized. The strength is in the development and reinforcement of the letter-sound relationships. Their weaknesses include their inadequacy in training phoneme awareness, their lack of direct help in fostering permanent word storage, and their use of the largely unnecessary "Level 3" instruction in phonics (i.e., systematic coverage of the multiple exceptions to each of the six syllable types and the exceptions to those exceptions). In addition, if you use these approaches, you may want to use a linguistic approach for word reading before the phonetic word reading, because the linguistic approach is a developmentally more appropriate introduction to reading for students at the onset-rime or basic phoneme level of phonological awareness and the partial alphabetic phase of sight word development (see Chapter 5). As students reach the phoneme level of phonological awareness and the full alphabetic phase of sight-word learning, the phonetic word reading in these programs would be more appropriate and helpful.

If you are working with a poor reader who has good letter-sound skills, chances are, he has weak phoneme awareness. Do not be misled by the fact that he can segment phonemes. Chances are, he cannot do advanced phoneme manipulations (Levels J through M) to the automatic level. Attention should be directed toward the mastery of phoneme awareness skills. It is the combination of strong phoneme awareness and solid letter-sound skills that will enable the student to do the kind of word study needed to efficiently acquire sight words.

Phonetic approximation

Because of the inconsistency of the spelling of many English words, phonetic decoding is not as reliable as it is in other languages (e.g., Spanish or Italian). However, the majority of English words are phonetically regular or consistent.[2] That's the good news. The bad news is that many irregularities occur with the most common words, referred to as the Dolch Words. These are the 220-320 most frequently used words in English. They account for about 50% of all the words in print (common words like *it, the, a, with,* etc.). Only half of the Dolch words are regular or consistent. Yet children need to learn these words early in their reading careers because they are so common. Consider the phonetic irregularities of these Dolch words:[3]

> of   one   the   been   said   was   two

It is unreasonable to expect students with poor phoneme awareness to learn words with phonetic irregularities at the earliest stages of learning to read. Irregularities typically mean that the one-to-one correspondence between the oral/phoneme structure of the word and the written/phonetic structure of the word is broken in some way. This makes it more difficult for students to truly grasp the *alphabetic principle*. The alphabetic principle is the insight children gain that the written letters are supposed to represent the oral sounds within spoken words.

In real-life reading, a child can combine phonetic decoding skills with context to figure out many irregular words, if sounding out and blending the letters provides a close enough *approximation* to the oral word. For example, a child reads a sentence aloud "The weather has *bean* great this week" (*bean* is the phonetically regular pronunciation of *been*). Many children self-correct and say "The weather has *been* great . . ." The mispronunciation was close enough that the context helped the child determine the word.[4]

---

[2] A *regular* spelling pattern in a written word follows basic phonic rules. A *consistent* spelling pattern is not technically regular, but it is consistent so it is easy to learn. For example, *–alk* has a consistent pronunciation in English (e.g., *chalk, talk,* and *walk*). Phonetic regularity would suggest *–alk* should be pronounced like *–alc* in *talc*. Regular and consistent words tend to be grouped together and distinguished from irregular words.

[3] If the irregularities are not obvious: *of* – neither letter makes its usual sound; *one* – no letter represents the /w/ sound in the oral word, the *o* makes a short /u/ sound and the *e* does nothing; *the* – an *e* at the end of the word does not normally make the short /u/ sound; *been* – the *ee* is almost always long *e* as in *seen*; *said* – *ai* doesn't usually make the short /e/ sound; *was* – the *a* represents the short *u* sound and the *s* makes a /z/ sound; *two* – *wo* is an atypical way to represent the /oo/ sound.

[4] Teachers get frustrated when students do not self-correct when their mis-readings do not make sense. However, this does not automatically mean the student has a comprehension problem. Typically this is an index of the mental effort required to decode the sentence. Due to limitations in our working memory, too much attention to decoding

Chapter 12

How to Develop Letter-Sound Skills

It should be clear from Chapter 4 that word recognition is *not* based on visual memory. However letter-sound skills are partially based on what is called *visual-phonological paired-associate learning*. To know that the letter *w* has a name ("double-you") and that it makes a /w/ sound, involves matching a visual memory of that figure *W* to a name and a sound, both of which involve phonology. So, oddly, memory for letters involves visual memory, while memory for words does not. Letter-sound learning is based on matching visual memory with phonological memory. The squiggly lines we call letters represent sounds in our oral language. There is nothing about the letter *m* that makes one think of the /m/ sound unless it has been learned. Children need hundreds of exposures to those letters before they can recognize them effortlessly and flawlessly. Students need to learn them based on visual-phonological memory via paired-associate learning. However, recent research out of Oxford University in the UK has indicated that when there are problems with this visual-phonological paired associate learning process, it is the phonological aspect that is typically the culprit. Poor letter name and letter sound learning is not based on poor visual memory, but rather on a difficulty with the phonological retrieval of those letter sounds and names.

Several well-established methods for learning letters include 1) providing many exposures, 2) using multisensory methods, 3) teaching a small set of letters at a time, 4) pointing out visual features of letters, 5) teaching letter sounds in a developmentally appropriate manner, and 6) teaching letters using embedded mnemonic letters.

Provide multiple exposures. This cannot be emphasized enough. Children require hundreds of exposures to the letters to make those letter names and sounds effortless and automatic. Until the letters are automatic, reading will not be efficient.

To reinforce letters, teachers can "punctuate" their day with brief reviews. For example, during a transition time, kindergarten teachers can either begin or end a lesson by taking a pointer and pointing randomly at the letters learned so far and have the students give the sounds. For first grade, include digraphs, blends, and vowel digraphs. Teachers can also do a very quick flash card review. The more reinforcements, the stronger the letter-sound skills.

Use multi-sensory methods of learning. It is often not enough to look at letters and say them. Young children need to experience the letters in three dimensions. They need to make letters with modeling clay, trace letters two feet tall with sidewalk chalk, draw letters in whipped cream, paint letters with finger paints, etc. They should see letters and recognize them in uppercase, lowercase, cursive, and print. Programs like the *Assured Readiness for Learning* provide many suggestions for multi-sensory activities that develop letter skills.

---

can crowd out the meaning. That is why good comprehenders have effortless word recognition (see Chapter 4). They do not put effort into determining the words. Therefore, they are able to focus their attention and working memory on comprehension. When they can do this, they are more likely to self-correct a misreading.

Teach a small set of letters at a time. It would be unreasonable to expect children to learn all of the letters at the same time. It is important to start with a few letters and build on those. One might think that this goes without mentioning because this is typically done in kindergarten. However, there is something that teachers often overlook. When students do not acquire complete letter knowledge by the end of kindergarten, teachers must not assume a "window of opportunity" has been missed. These children should not be expected to learn to read words in first grade. Rather, they will need to have individualized work on the letters until they are mastered. Expecting them to read words, even simple ones, forces them to "compensate" because they do not have the letter-sound or phoneme skills necessary to anchor words in permanent memory. When students have not mastered the alphabet and sounds, teaching efforts should be geared toward selecting a restricted set of new letters to learn using multisensory approaches and multiple exposures. Then add new letters to this set of letters while reinforcing the previous letters until all letter sounds are automatic.

Teach letter sounds in a developmentally appropriate manner. Some letter sounds are easier to learn than others, and this should affect our approach to teaching them. Research has shown that students more easily learn the sounds of the letters whose sounds appear first in the letter's name. The letter sounds *b, c, d, g, p, t, v,* and *z* are easy to learn because the sound they make matches the first sound in their letter's name (*b* (*bee*), *c* (*cee*), *d* (*dee*), *g* (*gee*), *j* (*jay*), *k* (*kay*), *p* (*pee*), *t* (*tee*), *v* (*vee*), *z* (*zee*). It is harder for them to learn the sounds of letters whose sounds appear second in their name. These letters, such as *f, l, m, n, r, s,* and *x*, have sounds that come second in the letter's name, after a vowel sound (*ef, el, em, en, ar, es, ex*). Most difficult are letter names in which the letter's sound is not present in the letter's name (e.g., *h, w, y*). It has been shown that letter sounds are easier to learn if we teach the easier ones before the more difficult ones. Teaching sounds in alphabetical order is not as efficient.[5]

Point out visual features of letters. Some may think that teaching letters like *t* and *c* at the same time may be a good idea because they look so different they will not be confused.[6] Actually, it would be better to teach the letters *t, f,* and *l* together, and the letters *c, o,* and *e* together because these groups of letters share similar features and must be distinguished from one another. Teaching similar looking letters at the same time forces students to pay attention to detail. Teachers can directly draw attention to the similarities between the visual features of letters and even have the students point out the differences. Also, attention should be drawn to the differences between a letter's uppercase vs. lowercase version. The point is to make sure students have a thorough command of the letters and do not confuse similar looking letters.

Teach letter sounds using embedded mnemonic letters. Often, children are taught the letters with a key word and an accompanying picture, such as "*a* is for *apple.*" Studies have shown that such pictures that accompany a key word provide no advantage over teaching with a key word without such a picture. However, several studies have shown that when the picture

---

[5]They should still learn the alphabet in alphabetical order and recite it, etc. The point here is when teachers begin the process of systematically teaching letter *sounds*, doing it in alphabetical order is not as effective as doing it in the more developmentally appropriate way just described.

[6]Teaching visually distinct letters at the same time is a valid approach for preschoolers and students with low cognitive skills. However, after mastering a few letters this way, it will be useful to transition to the approach described in this paragraph.

accompanying the keyword is drawn in the shape of the letter it is representing, students learn the letter sounds more quickly. The clearest example is "*s* is for *snake*" with the drawing of a snake that looks like the letter *s*. Some partial or complete sets of these embedded picture mnemonic alphabets can be found via an Internet search.

Teaching the Letter Sounds

Most readers of this manual have taken a foreign language in high school or college. Using your background with a foreign language, identify these words by sounding them out:

cuhahtuh, tuhuhguh, guhehtuh.

Can you recognize those words? Did you take Spanish? French? German? Well, none of those languages will help here. They're English. The words are *cat*, *tug*, and *get*, respectively. Did you have a hard time identifying them? Yet this is how we often present letter sounds to students: /c/ /a/ /t/ as *cuh – ah – tuh*. However, *c* does not say *cuh* and the letter *t* does not say *tuh*. We must not tell students that these are the sounds of those letters. When presenting consonant sounds, we must not add a vowel sound (usually a short /u/ sound). Adding vowels sounds to consonants disrupts the process of phonological blending when students sound out words. Just like *cat, tug,* and *get* were difficult to recognize because of those extra sounds, children also struggle when they sound out words if they think *t* says *tuh* and *b* says *buh*.

How to Pronounce Phonemes in Isolation

When teaching children the letter sounds, we must learn to *correctly* pronounce the sounds in isolation. For most letters, this is easy. However, there are a few that are very difficult. Below is a guide to assist in this process. In addition to the teacher using the correct pronunciations, students should learn these as well. Not only is accurate pronunciation of sounds in isolation needed for sounding out words, but students and teachers need precise pronunciations during phoneme awareness activities and assessments.

Vowels

The vowels are the easiest to say in isolation. Vowels include both the short and long forms of *a, e, i, o,* and *u*.[7] They also include the various vowel combinations (*ou, oo, ee, ea, ey,* etc.), and the letters *y* and *w* when they are not the first sound in a syllable. Vowels represent the flow of air through the activated vocal cords and out the mouth.

Easy consonants and digraphs.[8]

The easiest consonants to pronounce in isolation are the ones that you can "stretch out" as long as you'd like. For example, there is no excuse for saying that *m* says *muh* because it is very

---

[7] The terms "long" and "short" for vowels are used here based upon their relative familiarity as an old convention in reading instruction, despite lacking a precise linguistic basis. Short vowels are those in *pat, pet, pit, pot,* and *putt.*

[8] I am including the consonant digraphs (*ch, ph, sh, th*) in this breakdown because they should be taught right along with the letters of the alphabet. Like the letters, they produce a single sound. In contrast to digraphs, blends retain the sounds of both letters (e.g., *st, pl, br*). See Appendix E for more on blends.

easy to make the /m/ sound in isolation and drag it out: *mmmmmm*. Several letters are easy to stretch out like this and therefore are easy to produce in isolation. These include the following: soft *c, f, l, m, n, ph, s, sh, th* (voiced), *th* (unvoiced), *v, z*. There is absolutely no reason /m/ should be presented as *muh*, because /m/ and the other consonants presented here are easy to say and stretch out (e.g., *mmmmm* . . .) without an *–uh* at the end.

"Soft *c*" refers to when the letter *c* makes the /s/ sound (e.g., *cent, space*). Notice there are two different pronunciations of *th*. One is the *th* as in *the, they, this,* and *though*. The other is the *th* as in *think, thin, thank*. Do you notice why these are different? Speech pathologists and linguists refer to the difference as *voiced* vs. *unvoiced*. Put your fingers on your throat and say *think*. Then say *these*. Notice how your vocal cords vibrate when you said the *th* in *these* but not the *th* in *think*. However, your mouth, lips, and tongue were in virtually the same position for both versions of *th*. The only difference was the use of the vocal cords. When the vocal cords are used (e.g., *this, the*), it is called a "voiced" *th*. When the vocal cords are not used (*think, thank*), it is called an "unvoiced" *th*. Either version of *th* can be easily pronounced in isolation. Children should be taught both of the sounds for *th*. Have them do the demonstration with the vocal cords. That will make the two sounds more memorable for them.[9]

Even though the consonants in this section are the easy ones, practice pronouncing them in isolation until they are automatic. Appendix E has more help with letter sounds.

Moderately difficult consonants

There are consonants that require more thought and practice to properly pronounce in isolation: *h, j, k, q, r, w, x, y* plus hard *c*, soft *g* and hard *g*. It is tempting to put an *–uh* after many of these the consonant sounds. Below are suggestions on how to avoid this.

Hard *c* and *k* make the same sound (/k/). With effort and concentration, you can get your mouth in position to make this sound, but send air through your mouth restricting the flow somewhat. If you hold that sound, it should sound like the static you hear when your car radio is tuned between stations. After holding the sound, learn to shorten it up to less than a second and you are pronouncing the *k* in isolation. There is no reason to say *kuh*.

The soft *g* and the letter *j* both make the /j/ sound. While this is pronounceable in isolation, it takes some concentration. Say the word *just*. Now start to say it but hold the /j/ sound before you get to the /u/. With practice you will be able to pronounce the /j/ without any vowel sound. The /j/ sound is voiced, meaning you should hear your vocal cords vibrate. If you take away the voicing, you will find yourself making something closer to the /ch/ sound.

Hard *g*, as in *go* or *get*, is difficult, but pronounceable. If done correctly, you'll be making a scraping noise or it may sound a bit like the radio static, like the /k/ mentioned above, except you are adding voicing (i.e., using your vocal cords). Say *go* very slowly but stop short of shifting from the /g/ to the /O/ sound. The hard /g/ should sound halfway between radio static

---

[9] The distinction between "voiced" and "unvoiced" is a concrete concept that kindergarteners and first graders can understand. Do the demonstration with the fingers on the throat and point out that they use their voice with one and not the other. There are other examples of voiced and unvoiced letters (*v/f; j/ch, b/p, d/t*). Having children think about these letters and sounds in this way adds one additional layer to the multisensory presentation of letters and phonemes. The more ways information is "plugged in," the greater likelihood it will be remembered.

and an electric vibrating/humming sound. Simply make the radio static sound (which is unvoiced) and vibrate the vocal cords to provide voicing to get the hard /g/.

The *h* is rather easy but I included it here because it requires comment. The /h/ is actually a breathing sound that can be held. If you were to breathe on your glasses to fog them up to clean them, you'd be making the /h/ in isolation.

In English words, *q* does not appear without the letter *u* immediately following.[10] We should not teach *q* in isolation. It should be taught as *qu*. We pronounce *qu* as /kw/ and sounds very close to *coo* like in *coo-coo clock*.[11] *Qu* does not say *kwuh*, i.e., with an /uh/ sound.

The *r* is tricky. However, if you can produce the sound of a fire engine, you can produce the /r/ in isolation. Start to say *ruh*, but hold the /r/ sound and don't say the *uh* in *ruh*. Hold that /r/ and you will sound like a child playing with a toy fire engine. Make that sound very briefly and you've pronounced the /r/ in isolation.

The *x* is fairly easy but takes practice. It is really two phonemes combined: /k/ and /s/.[12] Think of a word like *socks*, and focus on the last two sounds /k/ and /s/. That's how you produce the /x/ sound in isolation.[13]

The /w/ is made by forming a small, tight circle with your lips and making an *oo* sound as in *food*, except that your lips are almost closed while in that circular position.[14] Normally when making the *oo* sound you leave a slightly larger circular opening in your lips than when you are trying to make the /w/ sound.

The *y* requires a bit of thought. Start to say *yes* but hold that initial sound before getting to the vowel sound. With a little practice, you can do it in isolation, with no vowel sound.

Difficult consonants

There are four consonants that *cannot* be pronounced in isolation, so all we can do is make as close of an approximation as possible. These approximations are designed to minimize the likelihood of extra sounds being added, which can interfere with phonemic blending. The difficult consonants are *b, d, p,* and *t*. These consonants stop the flow of air entirely, so you must put a vowel sound or whisper before or after them to pronounce them. The problem can be seen if you listen carefully as you say one of these consonants at the beginning of a word and then the end of a word. For example, slowly say *bat*. The /b/ represents a full restriction of airflow out of your mouth until the airflow begins as you start producing the /a/ sound while your mouth is already in the /b/ position. You can't really pull the /b/ as a separate sound apart from the /a/ that follows. Now try the /b/ at the end of the word *cab*. This time, the /b/ represents the way

---

[10] The exceptions to this are proper names: *Iraq* and *Shaq*, the latter being short for Shaquille (O'Neal).

[11] If this does not sound right to you, listen to what you are saying as you begin to say *quick, queen,* and *quiet*. So, for example, *quick* is like saying coo followed by wick. The /w/ sound in *quick* results as air continues from your mouth while you shift between the /oo/ and the /i/.

[12] That is why the baseball teams, the Boston Red Sox and the Chicago White Sox can get away with their unusual spellings. *Sox* and *socks* are pronounced identically.

[13] The actual letter *x* only makes the /ks/ sound at the end of a syllable or word (e.g., *mix, tax*). In the very rare cases in which the letter *x* begins a syllable, it makes the /z/ sound (xylophone, Xavier). In x-ray, the x is actually the ending of the first syllable which begins with an unwritten short *e* sound (i.e., ex-ray).

[14] Here's a little trick to see what I mean. Start to say the word *food*. As you say the /foo/, before getting to the /d/, change mid-stream and say *wish*. Notice how the /oo/ in *food* glides right into the /w/ in *wish*. All you are doing here is ever so slightly closing the circle your mouth a little tighter before producing the /w/.

you completely stop the airflow after making the /a/. So to get the proper sound of the /b/ you seem forced to put a vowel either before it or after it. This is also the case with *d, p,* and *t*. How, then, do we produce these in isolation? Simple. We cheat! Rather than follow these sounds with a full-fledged vowel sound (/uh/), with practice, we train ourselves to let a whisper or hiss of air come out of our mouth after trying to produce the sound in isolation.

To pull off this difficult feat, we must first notice that all vowels, whether long or short, are *voiced*. You can verify this by putting your fingers on your throat and try each vowel sound. However, whispers and hisses are *unvoiced*. They don't use our vocal cords.[15] In order to produce a stop consonant (*b, d, p, t*) in isolation, we replace an unwanted voiced vowel sound (i.e., /uh/) with an unvoiced whisper or hiss. This will avoid confusion when it comes time to blend sounds into words. It will also assist in producing sounds in isolation for phoneme awareness tasks, where precise pronunciation of sounds in isolation is important.

With a little concentration and practice, getting this whisper effect from the /t/ and /p/ is not too hard. Start to say a *t* and let out a short hiss of air, like the sound when you let air out of a car tire.[16] With *p,* you're letting out an unvoiced puff of air, as if you were at the beach and got some sand on your lips. The *p* and *t* are unvoiced, so this is fairly easy. The *b* and *d* are more difficult because they require at least some voicing to produce. The /b/ almost requires a slight amount of a short u sound (the schwa). With practice, you can make the schwa extremely short and almost unnoticeable, so it is less likely to interfere with blending. The /d/ almost requires a very shortened version of the short *i* sound (/i/), but keep it very short. Practice these. Concentrate on eliminating as much as possible any trace of a vowel sound, and you can rid yourself of *buh, duh, puh* and *tuh*!

It is important to teach children how to produce sounds in isolation. This will assist them with phonological blending as they sound out words and also helps with phoneme awareness activities. Additionally, such instruction is itself a form of phoneme awareness training. Learning and practicing the correct pronunciations of phonemes in isolation helps focus on the sound structure of spoken language, which is the very nature of phoneme awareness.

Using Flash Cards to Reinforce Letter-Sound Skills

When students have had many multisensory opportunities to learn the letters, the time will come to use flash cards. Below are a few tips to maximize the use of flash cards.

Use a restricted group of cards. Only use 5-10 cards, depending on the students' proficiency. Don't use a whole stack of 26 cards (at least not at first). With some struggling learners, you may need to use only 2-3 cards at a time.

Use multiple forms. Present the letter cards in uppercase and lowercase. These may be done separately, but eventually mix them. Also, make sure students see words printed in cursive too.

---

[15] That is why when people are sick and "lose their voice," they can still whisper.

[16] It is more like a release of air pressure starting with an explosive /t/. For those familiar with drums, it's a bit like imitating with your mouth the sound of hitting a *closed* high-hat on a drum set.

Chapter 12

Select type of response. Sometimes, the child responds with the letter *name*. At other times, the letter *sound* should be expected. Sometimes you may expect students to give both name and sound. The goal is automatic, effortless knowledge of letter *sounds*.

Require multiple responses. Students must learn that many letters have more than one common sound. So when you show the *s* flash card, the student should say "/s/ or /z/" because /z/ is a very common sound for the letter *s* when it ends a word (e.g., *is, his, was, has, hers* and many plurals like *birds, meals, hands*). For vowels, have students give the long *and* short sounds, instantly and back-to-back.[17] If a student only gives one sound, prompt him or her for the other(s). Don't consider any letter mastered unless a student can give both sounds instantly and consistently for a few weeks.[18] The goal is automaticity.

It is not necessary for students to give multiple sounds for every possible variation of every letter. For example, *s* should be learned as /s/ and /z/. The letter *c* should be learned as /k/ and /s/. However, there is no need to teach (at this point) that *s* can say /sh/ (*sugar, sure*) or /zh/ (*collision*) or that c can say /ch/ (*cello*) because these instances are so rare and are bound to produce confusion. Just stick with the common variations. Other examples include: *g* should be responded to with /g/ (hard g in *get*) and /j/ (soft as in *gem*); *ch* is /ch/ (*chair*) and /k/ (*character*). Beyond these, other variations can be taught as they come up.

Treat digraphs like letters. Train the digraphs – *ch, ph, th, sh* – right along with the letters. Have them give both responses for *th* (see Appendix E).

Add blends, rime units, and other word parts. Flash cards are a great way to help students learn the blends, rime units, and other common words parts (prefixes, suffixes), as well as Dolch words, and punctuation (see Appendices E and F).

Work for speed. Part of the goal is immediate, effortless recognition. Emphasize speed. Using a restricted set of letters (see above) can help with this.

When a student makes an error. When a student cannot identify a letter sound (or letter name), correct the error immediately. However, *do not* put that card at the back of the stack. Put it 1 or 2 cards back in the pile so the student will see it again soon. Do the same when the student responds slowly but correctly. If the student gets it correct the second time, still refrain from putting it in the back. Rather, put the card back 4-5 cards behind the front card. This gives the student further opportunity for reinforcement. *Only correct items responded to instantly the first time go to the back of the deck.*

Expand the pack of cards as the student masters them. As the student develops mastery of the letters and digraphs, expand the pack size for review and to increase speed.

Additional Helps for Letter-Sound Learning

There are helps for letter-sound learning in Appendices E and F. I encourage the reader to consult those appendices to supplement this chapter. They will also be helpful as a quick reference for lesson preparation.

---

[17]This is essentially the same as giving the letter name and sound (see previous paragraph) because a vowel's long sound corresponds to the sound of its name. The exception is *u*, which has two "long" sounds, e.g., 1) *cute*, and 2) *flute*. The first sounds like the entire word *you*, and the second sounds like the *oo* in *boot*. Remember the phrase *cute flute*, and you'll remember the two versions of the long *u* sound.

[18]Do not use the same stack of cards for a few weeks unless it is necessary. The "few weeks" mentioned above includes later review.

CHAPTER 13

Addressing Compensating Students

There are some students with weak phonological awareness skills that go unnoticed. This can result in significant difficulties later on. These students perform average to low average in reading, especially in the early years, but with much effort. They are called "compensators."

Compensating students have strong language abilities but have a weakness in one of the key skills needed for reading, usually phonemic proficiency. This prevents them from attaining reading comprehension skills consistent with their language comprehension skills. Compensators' reading comprehension is typically within the average range, but well below their language skills. This means compensators rarely get "flagged" for extra help. They use their intellectual strengths to cover up their weaknesses—thus the term *compensator*.

The average-level reading comprehension performance of the compensating student comes at a great cost. For him, reading is a chore. Compensators usually do not like to read because of the effort involved. Many compensators get frustrated and discouraged about school. Compensators sometimes show behavior problems, which are likely based on work avoidance or frustration. Interestingly, based on many years of experience in evaluating students for behavioral and academic problems, I have found that "compensators" are often brought to my attention because of behavioral or writing concerns, not reading concerns. When I evaluate, there is often a reading difficulty that lies behind the behavior problems and the writing problems. With these students, language skills are high, while reading is mediocre, at best. The initial impression is that the behavior problems are causing the underachievement. While this may be true in some cases, many of these students showed no behavioral difficulties in the earliest years of school. But with time, the work becomes harder. Compensators see other students out-performing them, even students who are not as bright as they are. Teachers see the behavioral difficulties and look for the reasons for the student's misbehavior. They often overlook how underachievement contributes to behavior because the compensator's achievement is within the average range.

As mentioned, written expression is also a problem for compensators. Phoneme awareness affects spelling,[1] and poor spelling drags down written expression. It is often harder for compensators to hide writing problems than it is to hide reading difficulties.

---

[1] Some compensators may be decent spellers. This is often a testimonial to effort some parents put into preparing their son or daughter for spelling tests.

Chapter 13

The sad irony is that many compensators are among our most intellectually endowed students. They do not perform anywhere near their potential, typically due to poor phoneme awareness. This is most unfortunate. Children who could be among our "best and brightest" are turned off to school, all due to a correctable problem. If we only knew earlier that the student was compensating, we could have prevented the problem.

Common Signs of Compensating

To assist in identifying a compensator, it will be helpful to be aware of some of the common signs of compensating. Once a compensating student is identified, teachers can provide the proper help needed to allow him to become a better reader. Such extra help may prevent a great deal of frustration, which may affect behavior and attitude toward school. Below are some common signs of compensating (see Table 13.1). Many of these "signs" are seen among weak readers in general. However, with weak readers, we know they are weak because of poor word recognition and poor reading comprehension. But with the bright compensator, we may overlook the problem because reading comprehension is fairly normal. The point of these "signs" is that they are present despite acceptable reading comprehension. A student does not need to show all these signs to be a compensator. Sometimes, they may only display a single sign (such as forgetting previously learned words or requiring many exposures to words before learning them). The basic signs are:

Strong general intellectual skills yet average reading skills. Compensators could not be compensators without the practical intelligence needed to figure out compensating strategies.

Weak or non-automatic phoneme awareness. Not only is this another sure sign of a compensator, it is probably the reason the student has to compensate in the first place. We usually test phoneme awareness on weak students, but fail to screen "average" readers. But because of weak phoneme awareness, maintaining average reading comprehension requires much effort. We are not doing students any favors by allowing them to operate this way.[2]

Heavy reliance on context to determine words. This is a sure sign of compensation. When students frequently guess based on context, it tells you they don't have a large enough sight vocabulary. If they did, there would be no need for such a heavy reliance on context.

Forgets words previously learned. Once good readers learn words, they're permanently stored. If students return from school vacations or long weekends and have forgotten words they knew before, it is because they compensated with little tricks and clues to remember the words the last time. However, they often forget their little mnemonic clues. The point is that they have not efficiently mapped these words to permanent memory.

Requires many exposures to words before they are permanently remembered. This is another sure sign of compensation. Students who are good at mapping words need only about 1-5 exposures to words to store them permanently. If a student requires 10-20 or more exposures, that tells you he is not a good mapper.

---

[2]Traditional segmentation or blending tasks may not catch the phonological awareness difficulties in these students. Only a test like the PAST will look at the automaticity on a phonological manipulation task, the best way to assess phonemic proficiency.

Weak spelling skills. Compensators are often (but not always) poor spellers.

Weak written expression skills. Compensators tend to be weak in written expression. They may communicate well orally but cannot do so in writing.

Irregular words are harder to identify than regular words. Once words are in a person's sight vocabulary, irregular and regular words are recognized equally quickly. But compensators have smaller sight vocabularies than typical readers, so they often have to use phonetic decoding skills to identify words. Such skills are not as reliable with irregular words.

- Has strong general intellectual skills without strong word recognition
- Weak phoneme awareness
- Heavy reliance on context to identify words
- Forgets words previously learned
- Requires many exposures to words to learn them
- Weak spelling skills
- Weak written expression skills
- Irregular words harder to recognize than regular words
- Discrepancies among reading related skills

TABLE 13.1

COMMON SIGNS OF COMPENSATION

Discrepancies among reading related skills. Finally, compensators show a common pattern of difficulties in reading-related skills. Usually, they display below average phoneme awareness and/or phonics. Because many teachers and schools do not assess phoneme awareness in all students,[3] many compensators go unnoticed. Also, compensating students typically have average to low average reading comprehension, which is high enough to keep them from getting extra reading help. Their word recognition ability falls somewhere between their phoneme awareness and their reading comprehension (see Table 13.2 below).

Given this pattern, compensators experience a mental "tug of war." On one end of the rope is their strength in the area of language, which is pulling them toward high comprehension. However, on the other end of the rope, their phoneme awareness (and possibly phonics) is pulling them toward low word recognition. These weaknesses mean that word identification is a struggle, which limits reading comprehension. If, however, these students had good phoneme awareness and phonics, they would be good orthographic mappers and therefore have good word recognition skills. If they had good word recognition, they would have much better reading comprehension. But due to these lower-level weaknesses, they struggle through school, often with a dislike of reading, despite their potential for being top students.

---

[3]Or, more recently, schools *are* assessing phoneme awareness, but with the less sensitive segmentation-type tests. As discussed in Chapter 7, segmentation is the most popular method for evaluating phoneme awareness, but is much less reliable than phoneme manipulation. Thus, some students with weak phoneme awareness will be mistakenly judged to have good phoneme awareness because they pass a segmentation test.

Chapter 13

The best way to assess compensating is to get scores from tests/subtests for each of the following skills. Granted, some scores, like an IQ score, may not be available. Teachers can determine that a student has strong language skills simply by interacting with him or her:

1) Language/listening comprehension[4] and/or verbal intelligence (VIQ)[5]
2) Reading comprehension (RC)
3) Context-free word identification (Word ID) (i.e., from a graded word list)
4) Word identification in sentences and paragraphs (Word ID in context) (i.e., words in context)
5) Phonetic decoding skills (Phon Dec) (assessed by reading nonsense words)[6]
6) Phoneme awareness/proficiency (PA/PP) (such as the PAST; see Chapter 11 and Appendix C)

Generally the compensator will follow one of the following four patterns (see Table 13.2; recall that the < symbol means "less than," and ≤ means "less than or equal to").

1) PA/PP ≤	Phon Dec	<	Word ID	<	RC		<	LC/VIQ
2) Phon Dec ≤	PA/PP	<	Word ID	<	RC		<	LC/VIQ
3) PA/PP	<	Word ID	<	Phon Dec	<	RC	<	LC/VIQ
4) PA/PP < RC	≤	Word ID	<	Phon Dec	≤	Word ID in context	<	LC/VIQ
WEAK AREA		LOW AVERAGE		AVERAGE				STRONG AREA

TABLE 13.2

SKILL PATTERNS OF COMPENSATORS

In the first two patterns, phonetic decoding and phoneme skills are lower than word identification. With the third pattern, the student can sound out new words, but can't remember them for the long term. So, the student must sound words out again and again. This happens because the student's phoneme awareness/proficiency—the super-glue of written word memory—is too weak to allow for efficient orthographic mapping.

The fourth pattern is rather interesting and complex. In this case, the word recognition in context may seem fine. However, reading comprehension is weak. If the listening comprehension was also weak, this would make more sense. But listening comprehension is strong. The reason for this pattern is that the compensator is making good use of context and some decent phonetic decoding skills to identify the words. He's getting good at it so that he can move along and *sound* fluent. But he is relying on context and phonetic decoding and not on a large sight vocabulary to identify words, so reading is fluent on the surface, but mentally it is very effortful. Because reading is effortful, he has precious little working memory and attention available to comprehend what he is reading.

---

[4]The speech pathologist can provide this data, if it is available. Otherwise, a teacher or parent can informally assess this by simply asking him or herself, "does this student understand stories that are read *to* him or her?" If the answer is yes, then the student likely has good listening comprehension.

[5]The school psychologist can provide this if IQ testing was done. Some schools give group "IQ" tests, which can give a fairly decent estimate of verbal intelligence, as long as reading is not required to complete the test.

[6]Several individualized achievement tests include a subtest that involves nonsense word reading. This is a good assessment of phonetic decoding skills.

Addressing Compensating Students

The "compensator" phenomenon provides a good argument for why *all* children should be formally instructed in phonological awareness starting in kindergarten. Unfortunately, schools tend to only provide phoneme awareness training for students who have already demonstrated reading failure. This practice needs to change. Prevention is far more efficient than after-the-fact remediation.

Addressing the Compensator

When you discover a compensating student, the solution is simple. First, work directly on her phonological awareness skills. If she has poor phonetic decoding, work on her letter-sound skills. Until she has mastered these skills to automaticity, you will not likely see reading gains.

Second, you need to help "undo" inefficient word recognition habits. The compensator has accomplished what she has accomplished through compensating, not through skills in orthographic mapping. You will need to "re-train" how she approaches words. Explain to her that she will need to look at words differently in order to remember them. Then, select an assortment of strategies from Chapter 6 that train the mental habit of orthographic mapping. *It is critical to understand that by itself, improved phoneme awareness and letter-sound skills may not be enough.* Those newly developed skills must be directly and explicitly tied back into word recognition. The activities in Chapter 6 are designed to do just that.

Prevention of Compensation

There is only one way to prevent compensation. That is to make sure students arrive at first grade with the prerequisite skills to learn to read. Emerging research is showing that children start to map earlier than we once thought. This begins as soon as students learn letter names, and before they even know letter sounds to sound out words! For example, researchers created artificially printed forms of real words for kindergarten non-readers to learn. One type involved representing the word "bead" as BD and "team" as TM, while a second type involved representing "bag" as BG and "toad" as TD. They trained students with flash cards on several words like these and found that students learned the first type of word much more quickly than the second type. What's the difference? Well, the first type has the *name* of the first letter in it. *Bead* and *team* have the sound of the name of the letters B and T in them (bee and tee). However, *bag* and *toad* don't begin with the sounds of the *names* of their first letters (*baa* and *toe* vs. *bee* and *tee*). Keep in mind, the students in this study did not know the *sounds* of letters yet, only the letter names. Thus, they could not sound out words, and couldn't associate the isolated /b/ sound with *bag* or the isolated /t/ sound with *toad*. But they *did* use what little knowledge of letters they had to associate the name of the first letter to remember the words *bead, team,* and others like them. The point is that at the earliest stage of exposure to reading, students try their best to find some way to remember words. They naturally connect sounds they can hear in words to the letters on the page (mapping) consistent with their skill level. Children with poor phonological awareness and/or poor phonetic decoding skills cannot do this very well. These students are behind, right out of the starting gates. They are left to come up with weak, compensating strategies to remember words, because they cannot access the efficient

– 115 –

orthographic mapping process used by good readers. If they only arrived at first grade with good letter-sound and phonological awareness skills, they would learn to map and "take off" in reading, just like their classmates.

This emerging research, which shows that students start to map words before they can even sound out words is exciting, but challenging. We must train students in letter-sound skills and phonological awareness in kindergarten to be sure they have the skills needed to start the mapping process when they are expected to learn to read. We can also incorporate direct help with the mapping process to facilitate this early reading development (see Chapters 5 & 6). When children begin to read in early first grade, and they do not possess the prerequisite phonological and letter-sound skills, we may be accidentally creating compensators. Add to this the fact that many states around the country are pushing schools to formally teach reading in kindergarten. Fewer students have the prerequisite skills in kindergarten, so by starting reading early, we accidentally encourage a greater number of students to compensate and we institutionalize the production of compensating students via state mandates. Granted, there is no research that I know of which suggests that students who were bound to be good readers will not become good readers as a result of inappropriate instructional decisions. However, inappropriate early reading instruction may accidentally promote weak reading among students who are at-risk for reading difficulties.[7]

The exciting news is that we can prevent most reading difficulties. Strangely, that is old news among researchers. This prevention phenomenon has been demonstrated in numerous studies over the years, reports of which almost never cross the divide between reading researchers to our K-12 classrooms. However, if we are aware of how the reading process develops, we *can* prevent reading difficulties in the first place. The challenge is in the willingness to apply these findings, in spite of trends in education that may be accidentally promoting the very difficulties we are trying to prevent.

---

[7]Risk factors for kindergarteners and early first graders include: weakness in vocabulary, letter name knowledge, letter sound knowledge, phonological awareness, as well as a family history of reading difficulties.

CHAPTER 14

Remediation, Learning Disabilities, Dyslexia, and Response to Intervention (RTI)

In this final chapter, I would like to tie up some loose ends and suggest some new, more accurate perspectives on reading difficulties and reading disabilities. I want to answer the question: How do the ideas, strategies, and materials in Equipped for Reading Success relate to students with learning disabilities? How about students with dyslexia? And what about the concepts of RTI (Response to Intervention) and MTSS (Multi-Tier System of Supports)?

Understanding the Nature of Dyslexia

To begin with, it is important to know that reading skills fall along a continuum, with highly skilled readers on one end, poor readers on the other, and most everyone else at various points in between. Unfortunately, we have given the term "dyslexia" a mystique it does not deserve. I'm referring to the popular notion that somehow dyslexia involves reversing letters and seeing things backwards. This notion misunderstands both the nature of dyslexia and the phenomenon of letter reversals and letter transpositions.

Until recently, dyslexia has not been an educational term, but rather a medical, psychological, and neuropsychological term. Dyslexia comes from the Greek *dys* ("bad") and *lexia* ("speech"; but in this usage it refers to the written form of speech, namely reading). In education, what scientists call "dyslexia," the federal special educational law calls "learning disabled in basic reading and/or reading fluency." However, as of October 2015, the U.S. Department of Education says it is now okay to use the term dyslexia in an educational context. Since then, many states have passed dyslexia legislation.

There are at least two broad definitions of dyslexia. The first is used by *Webster's II New College Dictionary* and by many reading researchers. This definition says that dyslexia is simply an "impairment of the ability to read." That's it. By this definition, anyone who is a poor word-level reader would be considered to have dyslexia. Often, researchers add the idea that dyslexia applies to individuals who generally have normal verbal language skills. Nonetheless, there is no agreement on how severe the word reading difficulty has to be.

This definition contrasts with the second definition of dyslexia, which is the "popular" definition. The popular definition of dyslexia refers to an unusual type of reading disorder in which the reader reverses and transposes letters. It is presumed that those with dyslexia "see things backwards" or have some other type of visual-perceptual problems. However, contrary to this common belief, dyslexia is not a "special type" of reading disability. Most individuals with dyslexia have normal visual-spatial skills[1] and they do *not* see things backwards. Other than some letters (usually b, d, and less commonly p, and q), and occasionally some numbers, these individuals do *not* mix things up in their visual world. A child with dyslexia may be able to easily track a flying baseball hit from home plate to center field while running full speed as that ball reaches the point where he or she will intercept it at its precise trajectory to catch it. Other children with dyslexia may be outstanding at building with Lego or other hand-eye coordination activities. This is not what you'd expect from someone whose visual-spatial world is all mixed up! What, then, is the source of the reversals?

Understanding and Dealing with Reversals and Transpositions

Some students reverse or transpose letters. *Reversal* means that a letter is written backwards or misread as the backward version of that letter. For example, a student may read bib as did or write a b for a d. *Transposition* refers to reading or spelling words with the letter order transposed, such as reading the word *on* as *no, saw* as *was,* or spelling *said* as *siad.*

For years, the reversals and transpositions seen in some with dyslexia (i.e., poor word readers) puzzled scientists. Various theories floated around, but few had any merit. Finally, in the late 1970s, researchers figured it out. They began with an observation about beginning reading that can be confirmed by any first grade teacher: Reading and spelling errors involving reversing and/or transposing letters are very common among typical first graders who are learning to read. The researchers discovered that approximately 25% of reading and spelling errors made by average first graders involved reversing or transposing letters. These researchers then looked at third and fourth graders with dyslexia who were reading at a first grade level. The researchers found that approximately 25% of the reading and spelling errors of these third and fourth graders were also reversals or transpositions. What does this mean? It means that there is no mysterious basis for reversals and transpositions among those with dyslexia. Rather, these weak readers are making the kinds of mistakes anyone would make who are *at that early reading level.* In other words, if you are reading at a first grade level, it doesn't matter what your actual grade level is (second, third, fourth), you are likely to make the kinds of reading and spelling mistakes that readers at the first grade level make. No more puzzle. No more mystique. Thus, reversals and transpositions are a *side effect* of continuing to be at the earliest stages of reading development. In other words, *they are not poor readers because they are reversing or transposing letters. Rather, they are reversing and transposing letters because they are poor readers!* Their reading problems are not due to faulty visual input. Interestingly, this was discovered in the late 1970s and still has not made its way to the popular culture, where the "seeing things backwards" mystique continues.[2]

What, then, should be done about reversals and transpositions? What if a kindergartener, first grader, or older student continues to confuse the letters b and d? First, make sure the student is

---

[1] Recall from Chapter 4 that there is extensive evidence against the notion that reading difficulties are caused by visual-spatial problems.

[2] Some students also have visual-spatial difficulties in addition to the phonological difficulties, but only the latter causes dyslexia. Visual-spatial skills have been shown to affect math and reading comprehension, but not word reading.

progressing all around in reading. As mentioned, these types of errors are a side effect of weak reading and not a cause. Second, make sure the student knows his right from left. Reversals tend to be as much a language/labeling difficulty as a visual-spatial difficulty. Those who know their left from right can more easily be instructed, and more easily remember that the "circle" is on the right of the line in a b, and the circle is on the left of the line in a d. They can learn the phrase "be right" (i.e., b has the circle to the right). If the circle is not on the right, it must be a d ("Dee left").

So how do you get students to learn their left from their right? Well, the best way for that to happen is for that skill to be part of pre-K and kindergarten curriculum, and reinforced in first grade. The Assured Readiness for Learning (ARL) program addressed this beautifully. One quick trick is to teach right-handed kids that when they get confused which is their left or right, squeeze the hand they write with.[3] Left-handers, of course, learn the opposite.

Another way to address reversals is to use spelling and reading (via flashcards) of words that force students to distinguish confusable letters. For example, b/d are the most commonly confused letters, so have students with b/d issues learn to read the words listed below quickly and accurately, with flash cards. Also, have them spell these words. Reading and spelling are both needed to help make sure students will overcome the b/d reversals. Other letter confusions can be treated the same way. Included with the words in the flash cards (or when you ask them to spell) should be the letters b and d in isolation. They need to practice instant recognition (or in the case of spelling, production) of those letters.

Below is a group of words that will assist in this process. Put these words on flash cards. With the third group of words, the "word contrasts," make two cards for each contrasting set. For example, one card would be bid/did while the other would be did/bid. They should learn to see these and identify them immediately. Also, have them spell these words:

Three, four, and five letter words with two bs and/or ds in them:

bad	bib	bob	dab	dib	dub
bed	bid	bud	dad	did	dud
babe	bead	blab	dead	dude	buddy
baby			deed	dumb	daddy

Three, four, and five letter "nonsense words" to "keep them honest":

bab	bod	deb	dob	bede	boad
beb	bub	ded	dod	boad	dabe
debe	deeb	doab	dube	bubby	dabby

Word contrasts, to also "keep them honest":

bad/dad	bib/dib	bid/did	bad/dab	blab/blade	bland/blab
bid/dib	bib/did	bud/dud	bead/deed	dumb/bum	
dead/bead	dread/bread	blade/bland	buddy/daddy	daddy/baby	

---

[3] Or, have them shake the hand they write with side to side, as if writing something in the air.

Chapter 14

A New Perspective on Word-Reading Disabilities

Like dyslexia, the concept of "learning disabilities" has been shrouded in mystery both inside and outside of education. There is much about learning disabilities that we still would like to know. However, researchers know a great deal about reading disabilities, and more than enough knowledge exists to prevent and correct most of these disabilities.

So, rather than look at reading disabilities and dyslexia with awe and mystery, there is a better way of viewing them. In Chapter 1, we learned about mental and academic skills that contribute to word recognition and word identification. If we selected any one of these skills, we would find that some students are very good at that skill, some are very poor, and most are in between. Each skill has its own continuum of skill levels, as illustrated in Figure 14.1.

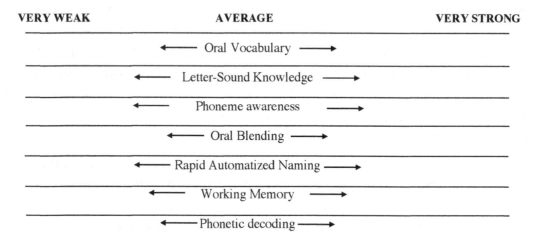

FIGURE 14.1

THE SKILLS THAT DETERMINE WORD RECOGNITION AND
WORD IDENTIFICATION EACH VIEWED ALONG ITS RESPECTIVE CONTINUUM

The fact that specific skills contribute directly to word recognition and these skills lie along a continuum suggests to us a different and more useful way of looking at weak readers, regardless of the severity of their reading problem. Rather than labeling students *reading disabled, learning disabled,* or *dyslexic,* it makes more sense to look at what determines skilled reading and find out which skill area or areas are holding these students back. If a student is competent in all the key skills that underlie word-level reading, that student will be a good word reader. However, if one or more of these skills is significantly compromised, the student is likely to struggle in reading. Would it not make more sense to evaluate these key skill areas and address any weaknesses directly, rather than considering him or her "disabled?" A term like "disabled" implies that the student is destined to struggle in reading.

From this perspective, reading disabilities, dyslexia, or even mild reading difficulties can be better understood when we identify the *source* of the difficulty. The important question is: In

Remediation, Learning Disabilities, Dyslexia, and RTI

which of these skills, or combination of skills, does a student struggle? If all of these skills were evaluated and the student's skill levels were plotted, you would get a profile that usually can tell you why a student is struggling in word-level reading. Consider Figure 14.2, which reflects a very common skill profile of a poor word reader.

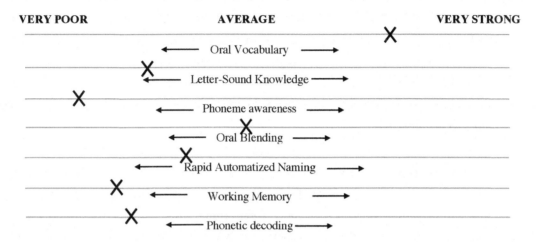

FIGURE 14.2

A COMMON SKILL PROFILE OF A STUDENT
WITH WORD RECOGNITION DIFFICULTIES

After establishing the profile of the student in Figure 14.2, we see he is strong in his higher-level language skills (vocabulary), but poor in phoneme awareness. His rapid naming, oral blending, and letter-sound skills may all be average. He has some mild weaknesses in working memory (about half of kids with reading difficulties do).

Unfortunately, there is no research to guide us on how to address rapid automatized naming problems. It is therefore a relief that this student does not have a difficulty in this area.[4] His letter-sound skills are okay, but not great, so this is an area that could use some improving. Working memory, like rapid naming, is not so easily "fixed." However, as a student builds up a large sight vocabulary, working memory plays less of a role in word reading. This is because if a student instantly and effortlessly identifies a word, he does not need to make use of his working memory. That is, he doesn't need to direct working memory capacity to the process of figuring out the word—he already knows it. Thus, we can "work around" the weakness in working memory by focusing on expanding the student's sight vocabulary.

It is clear from the profile above that phoneme awareness is the biggest difficulty for this student. He will need training, regardless of his grade level. His word recognition skills will not substantially improve until the phoneme awareness problem has been addressed.

---

[4] It is interesting that several studies have shown that when the phoneme awareness and letter-sound skills were corrected and students displayed large improvements in word-level reading, their rapid automatized naming also improved. Researchers have not yet determined why this is the case. Also, students with *only* rapid automatized naming difficulties can show a pattern of slow, accurate reading with good comprehension. Studies show it does not have as significant of an impact on reading as phoneme awareness does.

Chapter 14

This sample student profile illustrates how you can evaluate and address a student's reading concerns without relying on diagnosing the student as *dyslexic* or *learning disabled*. Keep in mind, the concepts of dyslexia and learning disabilities originated in two different eras, neither of which had the benefit of the last 40 years of research into the reading process. Now, we no longer need to treat reading difficulties, mild, moderate, or severe, as mysterious conditions that defy logic (such as the classic case of the fifth grader with a 120 IQ who is reading at a first grade level, despite his best efforts). So we can now redefine *learning disability* and *dyslexia* to refer to a situation in which a student struggles in one or more of the key areas that determine reading skill. Poor phoneme awareness is almost always the main culprit, though weaknesses in other skills (working memory, rapid automatized naming, letter-sound skills) are also common contributors to the problem.

Researchers have discovered that dyslexia and reading disabilities do not differ *qualitatively* from the simple concept of poor word reading. Rather, they are terms that describe students at the bottom end of the continuum of reading skills. Thus, we need to address all word reading difficulties with a similar approach, namely determining what parts of the process are not working and then address those concerns. Better yet, we need to design our curriculum starting in kindergarten to take account of these skills in order to prevent reading difficulties in the first place. Programs such as Equipped for Reading Success provide the information needed to do that. Equipped for Reading Success is well suited for 1) the prevention of reading difficulties, 2) remediating mild reading problems, and 3) addressing and correcting serious reading disabilities. The research findings and the techniques found in Equipped for Reading Success should be used in both general and special education. This approach also provides content for the process referred to as RTI.

Equipped for Reading Success for
Response to Intervention and Multi-Tier Systems of Supports

In 2004, the U.S. Congress re-appropriated the Individuals with Disabilities Education Act, commonly known as IDEA. They added an additional way of designating a student with a specific learning disability (SLD)[5] based on what is called *Response to Intervention* (or RTI). Under the RTI approach, a student is designated as having a learning disability if he or she does not respond adequately to high quality, research-based instruction and intervention. Much has already been written about RTI. It is often conceptualized as having three phases or "tiers." Tier 1 covers all students and expects high quality research-based reading instruction in the general education classroom. Students who do not make adequate progress in the general education context would receive more targeted, small group remediation, using research-based remediation methods. This is Tier 2. Only students who are substantially behind after Tier 2

---

[5]The federal IDEA legislation uses the term *specific learning disability* for what nearly everyone else calls *learning disability*. Researchers, advocacy groups (e.g., Learning Disabilities Association), college textbooks, and even some states (e.g., New York) use the simpler term *learning disability*. There is no difference in meaning between *learning disability* and *specific learning disability*.

intervention can be considered to have a learning disability. Those students move to Tier 3 and continue with research-based remedial techniques as "disabled" students.[6]

The material in the Equipped for Reading Success program is very well suited for addressing all tiers of RTI and MTSS approaches. Below is a listing of some of the ways the Equipped for Reading Success program can support RTI and MTSS.

Tier 1: High quality, research-based instruction for all students in general education classrooms

- Train phonological awareness from kindergarten to early third grade
- Train letter-sound skills from kindergarten to late second grade
- Use the developmental reading approach, which starts reading instruction using a linguistic reading approach then moves to a phonics approach (see Chapter 5)
- Use various teaching techniques that promote mapping (see Chapter 6)

Tier 2: Research-based intervention in a small group, general education remedial setting

- Train phonological awareness from kindergarten until mastered
- Train letter-sound skills from kindergarten until mastered
- Continue with the developmental reading approach, making sure a student's reading materials match his or her level of phonological awareness, letter-sound skills, and sight word development (see Chapter 5)
- Use various teaching techniques that promote mapping (see Chapter 6), which may include some of the more "extreme" techniques designed for remediation
- The biggest difference between Tier 2 and Tier 1 is not the content of instruction, but the intensity (i.e., more instructional time for reading acquisition, more multisensory opportunities, pacing, etc.)

Tier 3: Research-based instruction for students with reading disabilities

- Train phonological awareness from kindergarten until mastered
- Train letter-sound skills from kindergarten until mastered
- Continue with the developmental reading approach, making sure a student's reading materials match his or her level of phonological awareness and sight word development
- Use various teaching techniques that promote mapping (see Chapter 6), which would include some of the more "extreme" techniques designed for remediation
- Note that Tier 3 does not necessarily differ from Tier 2 in content; however Tier 3 students represent the most severe reading difficulties and may involve smaller group size and more instructional time per week.

You will note much overlap between the levels. All involve the key components of orthographic mapping. By its very nature, RTI is just a process and a framework. Equipped for Reading Success provides the much needed instructional content for that framework.

---

[6] This is only one version of RTI. In some versions, Tier 3 is still a general educational service, but with more intensive services (smaller group size, and more time per week).

Chapter 14

Summary Comments

I wrote *Equipped for Reading Success* out of a desire to close the gap between what scientists *know* about the reading process and what educators actually *do* to teach children to read. Since the 1997-1998 school year, I have been closely following the scientific research on reading acquisition and reading difficulties. Also, though my association with the late Dr. Philip McInnis, I have seen firsthand how incredibly powerful this research can be. I saw this as I traveled to schools using his ARL program. Roughly speaking, ARL was simply a "brand name" for reading research's "greatest hits." In addition, I saw a 75% reduction in the number of students designated with reading difficulties in a public elementary school building in which I previously worked. This happened after our reading teachers began using these research-based approaches that were included in an earlier version (2002) of this manual. Our amazing results were no more amazing that the same results found in the research reports from which we drew our approaches. We basically did "monkey see, monkey do" and mimicked the instruction/intervention in those successful studies and got similar results to what they got.

I often present this material to educational professionals at conferences and professional development training workshops. I am sometimes asked if I have a child with a reading difficulty, because they detect a great deal of passion in my presentation. This is a reasonable question to ask. The woman who is arguably the world's most well-versed expert on dyslexia, Margaret Snowing of Oxford University (England), had a younger brother with dyslexia, and she says this contributed to her choice of a career as a researcher. However, none of my many family members ever struggled in reading. Rather, my "passion" derives from my 28 years of experience as a school psychologist. I have done over 1,000 evaluations of students with reading difficulties, sat through countless Committee on Special Education meetings, and consulted with hundreds of parents of students who struggle in reading. I have seen youngsters begin school with an excitement and eagerness to learn but eventually hate school because it was such a struggle due to their reading problems. So, after immersing myself in the scientific research on reading acquisition and reading difficulties, it became clear to me that most reading problems are preventable, and those that are not preventable can still be substantially improved. When I combined this research knowledge with my firsthand experience, it was difficult *not* to become enthusiastic about this information. I have thus developed a passion to get the word out to teachers and administrators that we can make an incredible difference in the lives of students who are at a grave educational disadvantage. Word-level reading difficulties take their toll psychologically, educationally, behaviorally, and often in terms of future career opportunities. So, no—I have no family members with reading difficulties. But yes—I do have a passion for this cause, and I'm not embarrassed that it shows.

One Minute Activities

Syllable–Level Activities

Levels D and E

Preschool, Kindergarten, Early First Grade, and Older, Struggling Readers

Basic Syllable Processing
Levels D1, D2
Levels E1, E2

Advanced Syllable Processing
Levels E3, E4, and E5

LEVEL D

Syllable–Level Processing with Two Syllable Words

D1   Delete one syllable from a two-syllable compound word

Examples: sail(boat) → sail
(toy)box → box

D2   Delete one syllable from a two-syllable word (not a compound word)

Examples: (ham)per → per
sil(ver) → sil

Special Administration Considerations for Level D

- Many of the syllable breaks are arbitrary. They are made to facilitate this activity. For example, it may be awkward at first to see a syllable break like ni-bble (one would expect nib-ble). However, we don't say two /b/ sounds, only one. Consider the words *hoping* and *hopping*. The /p/ sound is identical in both words, even though one has the letter *p* twice while the other has it once. Only the vowel is different. Thus in *ni-bble,* you are separating the syllable before the first consonant sound and including that consonant sound in the second syllable.

- In the One Minute Activities, pronounce the syllables that are printed in isolation exactly the way they are pronounced *in the context of the word*. Do not pronounce them the way they are printed. For example, in *(Mon)day,* "mon" is pronounced "mun," rhyming with *fun* and not "mon," rhyming with *on*. It is important to preserve the *sounds* of the syllables. *The spellings just tell you which syllable is being manipulated, and where the syllable break is for that item*. This is an oral activity and the children will not be seeing the words during One Minute Activities.

- Some of the D1 words are technically not compound words (e.g., *forecast, endless*). However, they appear to be phonologically closer to compounds than to the D2 non-compound words.

One Minute Activities Level D1

Say: (birth)day — Now say (birth)day, but don't say (birth) → day
Or say: (birth)day — Now say it again, but don't say (birth) → day

1. Say:
(birth)day → day
(day)time → time
(air)port → port
(eye)sight → sight
(foot)ball → ball

(disk)drive → drive
(bed)time → time
(ice)berg → berg
(flash)light → light
(door)bell → bell

2. Say:
(key)board → board
(hay)stack → stack
(grey)hound → hound
(clock)wise → wise
(half)way → way

(grand)son → son
(book)case → case
(post)mark → mark
(race)track → track
(sand)box → box

3. Say:
(gold)fish → fish
(black)board → board
(head)light → light
(gum)drop → drop
(base)ball → ball

(down)town → town
mail(box) → mail
(cart)wheel → wheel
hair(cut) → hair
(foot)print → print

4. Say:
(sun)set → set
life(guard) → life
(door)step → step
rail(road) → rail
(free)way → way

sea(shell) → sea
(row)boat → boat
draw(bridge) → draw
(him)self → self
in(come) → in

5. Say:
(tad)pole → pole
moon(light) → moon
(side)walk → walk
grass(land) → grass
(text)book → book

some(thing) → some
(leap)frog → frog
there(fore) → there
(saw)horse → horse
grand(stand) → grand

6. Say:
(jig)saw → saw
sand(wich) → sand
(tight)rope → rope
door(way) → door
(soft)ball → ball

fore(head) → fore
(pass)port → port
home(land) → home
(in)doors → doors
hill(top) → hill

7. Say:
(grape)fruit → fruit
out(side) → out
(mid)night → night
bill(board) → bill
(out)look → look

(air)craft → craft
hill(side) → hill
(ice)box → box
side(ways) → side
(in)field → field

8. Say:
(space)craft → craft
back(ground) → back
(play)pen → pen
out(grow) → out
(pay)roll → roll

hand(ball) → hand
(neck)tie → tie
bull(dog) → bull
(sky)line → line
land(slide) → land

One Minute Activities Level D1

	Say:	(card)board	Now say (card)board, but don't say (card)	→	board
	Or say:	(card)board	Now say it again, but don't say (card)	→	board

9. Say:	(card)board	→	board	10. Say:	(rain)coat	→	coat
	out(line)	→	out		snow(flake)	→	snow
	(ping)pong	→	pong		(doll)house	→	house
	grape(vine)	→	grape		tip(toe)	→	tip
	(blind)fold	→	fold		(side)show	→	show
	(oat)meal	→	meal		house(boat)	→	house
	news(cast)	→	news		(drive)way	→	way
	(scare)crow	→	crow		scrap(book)	→	scrap
	air(plane)	→	air		(thumb)tack	→	tack
	(see)saw	→	saw		up(stairs)	→	up

11. Say:	(red)wood	→	wood	12. Say:	(bare)foot	→	foot
	stop(watch)	→	stop		class(mate)	→	class
	(box)car	→	car		(fly)wheel	→	wheel
	wind(mill)	→	wind		hand(bag)	→	hand
	(air)field	→	field		(out)field	→	field
	some(how)	→	some		wood(chuck)	→	wood
	(nick)name	→	name		(some)one	→	one
	work(book)	→	work		black(bird)	→	black
	(ear)drum	→	drum		(hedge)hog	→	hog
	sea(board)	→	sea		fore(arm)	→	fore

13. Say:	(some)day	→	day	14. Say:	(tool)box	→	box
	night(fall)	→	night		home(made)	→	home
	(base)ball	→	ball		(work)bench	→	bench
	tooth(paste)	→	tooth		sky(lark)	→	sky
	(proof)read	→	read		(blue)print	→	print
	off(shore)	→	off		wrist(watch)	→	wrist
	(hand)book	→	book		(kick)off	→	off
	sun(rise)	→	sun		search(light)	→	search
	(coast)line	→	line		(high)way	→	way
	ply(wood)	→	ply		ground(hog)	→	ground

15. Say:	(class)room	→	room	16. Say:	(touch)down	→	down
	snow(man)	→	snow		sea(shore)	→	sea
	(tooth)brush	→	brush		(ware)house	→	house
	green(house)	→	green		net(work)	→	net
	(stair)case	→	case		(some)what	→	what
	out(doors)	→	out		trade(mark)	→	trade
	(earth)quake	→	quake		(house)fly	→	fly
	rain(drop)	→	rain		smoke(stack)	→	smoke
	(saw)dust	→	dust		(week)day	→	day
	fox(hound)	→	fox		pitch(fork)	→	pitch

One Minute Activities Level D1

	Say:	(snow)plow	Now say (snow)plow, but don't say (snow)	→	**plow**
	Or say:	(snow)plow	Now say it again, but don't say (snow)	→	**plow**

17. Say:	(snow)plow	→	plow	18. Say:	(wind)shield	→	shield
	wild(cat)	→	wild		snap(shot)	→	snap
	(care)less	→	less		(bag)pipe	→	pipe
	steam(boat)	→	steam		cat(fish)	→	cat
	(pin)wheel	→	wheel		(day)break	→	break
	sea(shell)	→	sea		new(born)	→	new
	(week)end	→	end		(sun)shine	→	shine
	air(line)	→	air		wild(life)	→	wild
	(sun)down	→	down		(arch)way	→	way
	house(work)	→	house		skate(board)	→	skate

19. Say:	(rain)fall	→	fall	20. Say:	(back)board	→	board
	pin(point)	→	pin		sun(burn)	→	sun
	(in)side	→	side		(eye)lash	→	lash
	life(boat)	→	life		work(shop)	→	work
	(tooth)pick	→	pick		(arm)chair	→	chair
	watch(dog)	→	watch		wish(bone)	→	wish
	(air)mail	→	mail		(suit)case	→	case
	off(spring)	→	off		note(book)	→	note
	(sound)proof	→	proof		(south)west	→	west
	whirl(pool)	→	whirl		sea(plane)	→	sea

Supplemental Activities for Level D1

S1		S2		S3		S4	
(stage)coach		(air)borne		(with)out		(no)where	
back(bone)		cup(cake)		chess(board)		quick(sand)	
(hard)wood		(horse)shoe		(nine)teen		(egg)plant	
spring(board)		land(mark)		steam(ship)		foot(note)	
(horse)back		(hall)way		(teen)age		(dash)board	
cloud(burst)		on(to)		lock(smith)		out(fit)	
(head)line		(pass)word		(your)self		(north)east	
day(dream)		shell(fish)		zig(zag)		there(by)	
(foot)step		(take)off		(song)bird		(stock)yard	
count(down)		fog(horn)		rose(bud)		wood(work)	

S5		S6		S7		S8	
(jack)pot		(short)stop		(sun)light		(gate)way	
draw(back)		out(run)		world(wide)		surf(board)	
(some)time		(life)time		(cross)road		(night)mare	
light(house)		full(back)		sea(weed)		(blue)bird	
(out)let		(some)where		(house)hold		saw(mill)	
head(phone)		rain(bow)		white(wash)		(pad)lock	
(drift)wood		(lime)stone		(road)side		(use)ful	
court(yard)		out(board)		soy(bean)		(ship)yard	
(ship)wreck		(sub)way		(vine)yard		safe(guard)	
fore(ground)		drum(stick)		stove(pipe)		(sea)food	

One Minute Activities Level D2

	Say:	(can)dy	Now say (can)dy, but don't say (can)	→	dy
	Or say:	(can)dy	Now say it again, but don't say (can)	→	dy

1. Say:	(can)dy	→	dy	2. Say:	(sil)ver	→	ver
	(en)ter	→	ter		(Nep)tune	→	tune
	(mem)ber	→	ber		(mon)key	→	key
	(hum)ble	→	ble		hur(dle)	→	hur
	(dan)cer	→	cer		su(per)	→	su
	(but)ler	→	ler		(bar)gain	→	gain
	(fab)ric	→	ric		dis(pense)	→	dis
	(laugh)ter	→	ter		(men)tal	→	tal
	(mar)ket	→	ket		man(sion)	→	man
	(hard)ly	→	ly		(cor)ner	→	ner

3. Say:	(fen)der	→	der	4. Say:	(nor)mal	→	mal
	(jer)sey	→	sey		Mon(day)	→	Mon
	(ca)ble	→	ble		(jour)ney	→	ney
	(mag)net	→	net		mon(ster)	→	mon
	(ig)nite	→	nite		(an)swer	→	swer
	hus(band)	→	hus		lan(tern)	→	lan
	gen(tle)	→	gen		(mus)tache	→	tache
	laun(dry)	→	laun		num(ber)	→	num
	ad(vice)	→	ad		(fac)tor	→	tor
	jour(nal)	→	jour		ca(boose)	→	ca

5. Say:	(hu)man	→	man	6. Say:	(har)bor	→	bor
	on(ly)	→	on		nim(ble)	→	nim
	(be)gin	→	gin		(ac)tor	→	tor
	ou(ter)	→	ou		parch(ment)	→	parch
	(gol)den	→	den		(kind)ly	→	ly
	in(sect)	→	in		fal(ter)	→	fal
	(la)zy	→	zy		(par)ka	→	ka
	mum(ble)	→	mum		mol(ding)	→	mol
	(gob)let	→	let		(cam)per	→	per
	nei(ther)	→	nei		mar(shal)	→	mar

7. Say:	(cen)ter	→	ter	8. Say:	(em)blem	→	blem
	(sim)ple	→	ple		mer(cy)	→	mer
	(kin)dle	→	dle		(or)der	→	der
	em(ber)	→	em		hy(brid)	→	hy
	like(ly)	→	like		(ig)nore	→	nore
	(ba)lloon	→	loon		pan(da)	→	pan
	lum(ber)	→	lum		(can)dle	→	dle
	(las)ting	→	ting		par(don)	→	par
	hun(dred)	→	hun		(shoul)der	→	der
	(gin)ger	→	ger		(high)ly	→	ly

One Minute Activities Level D2

	Say:	(**near**)ly		Now say (**near**)ly, but don't say (**near**)	→	ly
	Or say:	(**near**)ly		Now say it again, but don't say (**near**)	→	ly

9. Say:	(near)ly	→	ly	10. Say:	(month)ly	→	ly
	mar(ble)	→	mar		in(vade)	→	in
	(el)der	→	der		(be)ing	→	ing
	in(dex)	→	in		cir(cus)	→	cir
	(neigh)bor	→	bor		(mus)tang	→	tang
	cen(tral)	→	cen		frac(tion)	→	frac
	(ob)ject	→	ject		(ma)ttress	→	tress
	hus(ky)	→	hus		o(ver)	→	o
	(fal)con	→	con		(par)cel	→	cel
	shel(ter)	→	shel		don(key)	→	don
11. Say:	(men)u	→	u	12. Say:	(im)pact	→	pact
	pas(try)	→	pas		mis(chief)	→	mis
	(ran)dom	→	dom		(fa)ble	→	ble
	fron(tier)	→	fron		or(chard)	→	or
	(jum)bo	→	bo		(la)ther	→	ther
	mer(chant)	→	mer		ker(nel)	→	ker
	(per)suade	→	suade		(bor)der	→	der
	ba(ker)	→	ba		far(ther)	→	far
	(pic)ture	→	ture		(per)son	→	son
	in(stant)	→	in		can(yon)	→	can
13. Say:	(me)ow	→	ow	14. Say:	(sig)nal	→	nal
	ox(ford)	→	ox		(nas)ty	→	ty
	(plas)ter	→	ter		(boul)der	→	der
	nap(kin)	→	nap		mon(arch)	→	mon
	(ac)tion	→	tion		(por)poise	→	poise
	ser(mon)	→	ser		lan(ding)	→	lan
	(ol)der	→	der		(or)dain	→	dain
	mo(tel)	→	mo		im(pair)	→	im
	(pes)ter	→	ter		(cap)tain	→	tain
	o(cean)	→	o		os(trich)	→	os
15. Say:	(fum)ble	→	ble	16. Say:	(neu)tral	→	tral
	dri(ver)	→	dri		in(vent)	→	in
	(dan)ger	→	ger		(mor)ning	→	ning
	pen(cil)	→	pen		ner(vous)	→	ner
	(men)tion	→	tion		(par)tial	→	tial
	pan(ther)	→	pan		ad(vance)	→	ad
	(oy)ster	→	ster		(per)fect	→	fect
	ear(ly)	→	ear		la(dy)	→	la
	(par)lor	→	lor		(ow)ner	→	ner
	cac(tus)	→	cac		han(dle)	→	han

One Minute Activities Level D2

Say: (**fum**)ble   Now say (**fum**)ble, but don't say (**fum**) → ble
Or say: (**fum**)ble   Now say it again, but don't say (**fum**) → ble

17. Say:	(pen)guin	→	guin	18. Say:	(pic)nic	→	nic
	fil(ter)	→	fil		san(dal)	→	san
	(pa)tience	→	tience		(ham)ster	→	ster
	car(pet)	→	car		poin(ter)	→	poin
	(per)tain	→	tain		(an)tique	→	tique
	sel(dom)	→	sel		mor(sel)	→	mor
	(em)ploy	→	ploy		(jum)ble	→	ble
	or(nate)	→	or		or(gan)	→	or
	(plen)ty	→	ty		(res)cue	→	cue
	for(mal)	→	for		per(sist)	→	per

19. Say:	(mer)it	→	it	20. Say:	(pam)per	→	per
	in(vert)	→	in		sen(tence)	→	sen
	(ban)jo	→	jo		(lof)ty	→	ty
	or(chid)	→	or		plas(tic)	→	plas
	(ser)vice	→	vice		(ser)geant	→	geant
	o(mit)	→	o		pil(grim)	→	pil
	(per)ceive	→	ceive		(fan)cy	→	cy
	mas(ter)	→	mas		her(mit)	→	her
	(pas)tel	→	tel		(en)gine	→	gine
	oc(tave)	→	oc		par(sley)	→	par

Supplemental Activities for Level D2

S1		S2		S3		S4	
	(squad)ron		(trum)pet		(chow)der		(sam)ple
	en(ding)		in(struct)		un(cle)		in(cline)
	(per)haps		(pon)der		(char)ming		(sis)ter
	in(vite)		chap(ter)		var(nish)		gar(den)
	(thim)ble		(mis)ty		(sar)dine		(no)ble
	sub(ject)		sur(vey)		fic(tion)		scram(ble)
	(in)sist		(mas)cot		(ven)dor		(pen)sion
	stur(dy)		hin(der)		jum(per)		be(gun)
	(al)bum		(tur)nip		(ur)ban		(ob)tuse
	pop(per)		me(tric)		bill(ion)		ham(per)

S5		S6		S7		S8	
	(mic)robe		(trans)fer		(slen)der		(snor)kel
	for(tress)		pam(phlet)		dol(phin)		bum(per)
	(pos)ter		(shar)pen		(ton)sil		(pow)der
	sim(ply)		ex(plore)		splen(dor)		splin(ter)
	(Kan)sas		(ster)ling		(free)zer		(pos)tage
	spon(sor)		lec(ture)		stum(ble)		in(stead)
	(ob)tain		(ob)serve		(in)clude		(or)phan
	per(plex)		scam(per)		com(fort)		nick(el)
	(cen)sus		(an)them		(slum)ber		(en)dorse
	por(trait)		mar(vel)		mor(tal)		cir(cle)

LEVEL E

Syllable–Level Processing with
Three Syllable Words

IMPORTANT! *Do not* expect students to master all of Level E before moving on to Levels F and G. When a student has mastered Level E2, go on to Level F1. Levels E3 through E5 can be done alongside Levels F, G, H, and I.

Basic Syllable-Level Deletion

E1 NOTE: *E1 is optional. Students can go from D2 to E2.* E1 is normally as easy as D1, but functions as an introduction to three-syllable words. This level involves deleting the first or last syllable from a three-syllable compound word. The number of E1 exercises was deliberately limited to keep teachers from spending too much time at this level.
    Samples: (pine)apple ⇢ apple   after(noon) ⇢ after

E2 This involves deleting the first syllable from a three-syllable word. E2 words have their stress (or "accent") on the second syllable, which makes it easier than E3, E4, and E5.
    Samples: (im)provement ⇢ provement   (sub)scription ⇢ scription

Advanced Syllable-Level Deletion

E3 This involves deleting the first syllable from a three-syllable word. E3 words have their stress (or "accent") on the first syllable. The removal of the stressed syllable makes E3 more difficult than E2.
    Samples: (ar)chitect ⇢ chitect   (won)derful ⇢ derful

E4 Like E3, the student deletes the first syllable from a three-syllable word, but E4 words are more difficult because not only is the first (stressed) syllable removed, the remaining middle syllable is made up of only a vowel sound with no consonant sounds.
    Samples: (el)ephant ⇢ ephant   (man)ager ⇢ ager

E5 This involves deleting the last syllable from a three-syllable word. Level E5 uses E4 words but deletes the last syllable rather than the first. For many, this is easier than E4.
    Samples: clari(net) ⇢ clari   daffo(dil) ⇢ daffo

Special Administration Instructions for Level E

- The syllable breaks are often arbitrary. They are designed to facilitate this activity and are *not* a guide to pronunciation.

- In the *One Minute Activities,* you are to pronounce the syllables that are printed in isolation exactly the way they are pronounced in the context of the spoken word, not the way the printed form would suggest (see instructions to Level D for further explanation of this).

- **REMEMBER: After completing E2, proceed to F1 activities and do E3, E4, and E5 alongside Levels F and G.**

One Minute Activities Level E1

	Say:	(pine)apple	Now say (pine)apple but don't say (pine)	→	apple
	Or say:	(pine)apple	Now say it again, but don't say (pine)	→	apple

1. Say:	(pine)apple	→	apple	2. Say:	(straw)berry	→	berry
	basket(ball)	→	basket		any(how)	→	any
	after(noon)	→	after		(what)ever	→	ever
	lady(bug)	→	lady		water(front)	→	water
	motor(boat)	→	motor		butter(milk)	→	butter
	ginger(bread)	→	ginger		fire(wood)	→	fire
	(news)paper	→	paper		over(lap)	→	over
	finger(nail)	→	finger		honey(comb)	→	honey
	neighbor(hood)	→	neighbor		country(side)	→	country
	butter(fly)	→	butter		under(line)	→	under

3. Say:	(sand)paper	→	paper	4. Say:	(sun)glasses	→	glasses
	every(one)	→	every		over(hear)	→	over
	(out)standing	→	standing		(air)liner	→	liner
	(post)master	→	master		rattle(snake)	→	rattle
	pocket(book)	→	pocket		(black)berry	→	berry
	thunder(storm)	→	thunder		(wood)worker	→	worker
	(sky)scraper	→	scraper		water(proof)	→	water
	fisher(man)	→	fisher		(loud)speaker	→	speaker
	volley(ball)	→	volley		over(do)	→	over
	fire(place)	→	fire		dragon(fly)	→	dragon

5. Say:	(near)sighted	→	sighted	6. Say:	(sun)flower	→	flower
	every(thing)	→	every		(sub)marine	→	marine
	over(coat)	→	over		(grand)daughter	→	daughter
	meadow(lark)	→	meadow		passage(way)	→	passage
	honey(bee)	→	honey		(salt)water	→	water
	over(look)	→	over		arrow(head)	→	arrow
	finger(print)	→	finger		butter(scotch)	→	butter
	(grand)mother	→	mother		(grass)hopper	→	hopper
	police(man)	→	police		(scout)master	→	master
	(out)spoken	→	spoken		express(way)	→	express

7. Say:	(which)ever	→	ever	8. Say:	(pace)maker	→	maker
	fire(proof)	→	fire		under(stood)	→	under
	jelly(fish)	→	jelly		over(hand)	→	over
	(wheel)barrow	→	barrow		minute(man)	→	minute
	master(piece)	→	master		auto(graph)	→	auto
	under(stand)	→	under		(when)ever	→	ever
	service(man)	→	service		figure(head)	→	figure
	body(guard)	→	body		(out)number	→	number
	pepper(mint)	→	pepper		(hand)writing	→	writing
	silver(ware)	→	silver		(horse)power	→	power

One Minute Activities Level E1

	Say:	(water)fall	Now say (water)fall but don't say (water)	→	**fall**
	Or say:	(water)fall	Now say it again, but don't say (water)	→	**fall**

9. Say:	water(fall)	→	water	10. Say:	every(day)	→	every
	(grand)parent	→	parent		window(pane)	→	window
	scholar(ship)	→	scholar		partner(ship)	→	partner
	pocket(knife)	→	pocket		fire(fly)	→	fire
	candle(stick)	→	candle		(book)keeper	→	keeper
	over(came)	→	over		silver(smith)	→	silver
	(top)soil	→	soil		other(wise)	→	other
	any(thing)	→	any		table(spoon)	→	table
	fire(works)	→	fire		golden(rod)	→	golden
	(pen)manship	→	manship		taxi(cab)	→	taxi

11. Say:	(left)over	→	over	12. Say:	(type)writer	→	writer
	(bad)minton	→	minton		(steam)roller	→	roller
	(fore)finger	→	finger		after(ward)	→	after
	butter(cup)*	→	butter		honey(moon)	→	honey
	(fly)catcher	→	catcher		butter(nut)	→	butter
	second(hand)	→	second		(drum)major	→	major
	fire(house)	→	fire		bumble(bee)	→	bumble
	(straight)forward	→	forward		over(come)	→	over
	under(ground)	→	under		English(man)	→	English
	(out)going	→	going		(run)away	→	away

13. Say:	(wood)working	→	working	14. Say:	under(brush)	→	under
	cobble(stone)	→	cobble		checker(board)	→	checker
	(sky)diving	→	diving		(bull)dozer	→	dozer
	under(growth)	→	under		(fore)runner	→	runner
	fiber(glass)	→	fiber		(wood)cutter	→	cutter
	tattle(tale)	→	tattle		over(cast)	→	over
	over(time)	→	over		any(way)	→	any
	water(way)	→	water		under(took)	→	under
	any(one)	→	any		piggy(back)	→	piggy
	under(sea)	→	under		super(man)	→	super

15. Say:	(grand)father	→	father	16. Say:	any(where)	→	any
	water(works)	→	water		brother(hood)	→	brother
	every(where)	→	every		(sledge)hammer	→	hammer
	paper(back)	→	paper		humming(bird)	→	humming
	(sky)rocket	→	rocket		(Thanks)giving	→	giving
	(blue)berry	→	berry		(wall)paper	→	paper
	under(went)	→	under		(fresh)water	→	water
	kettle(drum)	→	kettle		wild(life)	→	wild
	over(board)	→	over		(sports)manship	→	manship
	(turn)table	→	table		lumber(jack)	→	lumber

One Minute Activities Level E2

	Say:	**(De)cember**	Now say **(De)cember** but don't say **(De)**	→	**cember**
	Or say:	**(De)cember**	Now say it again, but don't say **(De)**	→	**cember**

1. Say:	(De)cember	→	cember	2. Say:	(ma)gician	→	gician
	(to)morrow	→	morrow		(tax)ation	→	ation
	(fla)mingo	→	mingo		(i)llusion	→	lusion
	(pre)vention	→	vention		(cre)ative	→	ative
	(im)provement	→	provement		(sub)scription	→	scription
	(o)fficial	→	ficial		(do)nation	→	nation
	(com)puter	→	puter		(a)ttendance	→	tendance
	(dal)mation	→	mation		(vol)cano	→	cano
	(terr)ific	→	ific or rific		(no)tation	→	tation
	(lo)cation	→	cation		(som)brero	→	brero

3. Say:	(pro)fession	→	fession	4. Say:	(re)ception	→	ception
	(re)public	→	public		(ad)mission	→	mission
	(dis)traction	→	traction		(for)getful	→	getful
	(for)gotten	→	gotten		(de)duction	→	duction
	(tra)dition	→	dition		(trans)mission	→	mission
	(mu)sician	→	sician		(com)panion	→	panion
	(trans)lation	→	lation		(de)cided	→	cided
	(in)vention	→	vention		(re)bellion	→	bellion
	(pro)peller	→	peller		(con)tagious	→	tagious
	(um)brella	→	brella		(de)fensive	→	fensive

5. Say:	(re)corder	→	corder	6. Say:	(re)cover	→	cover
	(de)tergent	→	tergent		(pe)tition	→	tition
	(va)nilla	→	nilla		(be)ginning	→	ginning
	(con)tinue	→	tinue		(de)molish	→	molish
	(de)lightful	→	lightful		(chi)huahua	→	huahua
	(i)guana	→	guana		(per)sistent	→	sistent
	(chin)chilla	→	chilla		(e)leven	→	leven
	(pa)jamas	→	jamas		(de)partment	→	partment
	(va)cation	→	cation		(pro)cedure	→	cedure
	(par)tition	→	tition		(re)moval	→	moval

7. Say:	(re)action	→	action	8. Say:	(di)vision	→	vision
	(quo)tation	→	tation		(O)lympic	→	lympic
	(de)cision	→	cision		(his)toric	→	toric
	(car)nation	→	nation		(gym)nastics	→	nastics
	(sur)vival	→	vival		(en)durance	→	durance
	(foun)dation	→	dation		(lieu)tenant	→	tenant
	(spa)ghetti	→	ghetti		(e)lastic	→	lastic
	(in)formal	→	formal		(ma)ternal	→	ternal
	(a)ttention	→	tention		(com)pletely	→	pletely
	(mu)seum	→	seum		(per)spective	→	spective

One Minute Activities Level E2

	Say:	(No)vember	→	Now say (No)vember but don't say (No)	→	vember
	Or say:	(No)vember		Now say it again, but don't say (No)	→	vember

9. Say:	(No)vember	→	vember	10. Say:	(Sep)tember	→	tember
	(mag)netic	→	netic		(il)legal	→	legal
	(de)licious	→	licious		(de)liver	→	liver
	(com)pletion	→	pletion		(co)mmander	→	mander
	(Vir)ginia	→	ginia		(de)tective	→	tective
	(em)ployer	→	ployer		(im)portant	→	portant
	(con)clusion	→	clusion		(tri)umphant	→	umphant
	(sug)gestive	→	gestive		(ig)nition	→	nition
	(in)terpret	→	terpret		(stra)tegic	→	tegic
	(so)lution	→	lution		(de)termine	→	termine
11. Say:	(e)dition	→	dition	12. Say:	(Wy)oming	→	oming
	(de)cipher	→	cipher		(de)cisive	→	cisive
	(in)stallment	→	stallment		(suc)cessful	→	cessful
	(re)cording	→	cording		(ath)letic	→	letic
	(pap)rika	→	rika		(fi)nancial	→	nancial
	(con)sistent	→	sistent		(e)quator	→	quator
	(i)magine	→	magine		(per)mission	→	mission
	(de)scendant	→	scendant		(de)velop	→	velop
	(pro)fessor	→	fessor		(e)normous	→	normous
	(be)ginner	→	ginner		(stu)pendous	→	pendous
13. Say:	(re)member	→	member	14. Say:	(per)fection	→	fection
	(Wis)consin	→	consin		(or)ganic	→	ganic
	(en)rollment	→	rollment		(sus)penders	→	penders
	(do)mestic	→	mestic		(in)vestment	→	vestment
	(sur)render	→	render		(di)gestion	→	gestion
	(de)voted	→	voted		(in)centive	→	centive
	(gi)gantic	→	gantic		(co)mmercial	→	mercial
	(con)tainer	→	tainer		(pho)netic	→	netic
	(E)gyptian	→	gyptian		(qua)drupled	→	drupled
	(com)partment	→	partment		(de)parture	→	parture
15. Say:	(e)lectric	→	lectric	16. Say:	(ma)jestic	→	jestic
	(syn)thetic	→	thetic		(im)pression	→	pression
	(im)patient	→	patient		(pro)gressive	→	gressive
	(ob)jection	→	jection		(tran)sistor	→	sistor
	(dy)namic	→	namic		(con)struction	→	struction
	(Mon)tana	→	tana		(sub)traction	→	traction
	(be)havior	→	havior		(e)lection	→	lection
	(con)vention	→	vention		(u)tensil	→	tensil
	(pro)portion	→	portion		(in)ventor	→	ventor
	(re)hearsal	→	hearsal		(re)lation	→	lation

One Minute Activities Level E2

Say: **(tor)nado** Now say **(tor)nado** but don't say **(tor)** → **nado**
Or say: **(tor)nado** Now say it again, but don't say **(tor)** → **nado**

17. Say:
(tor)nado	→	nado
(co)mmittee	→	mittee
(me)chanic	→	chanic
(pro)vided	→	vided
(en)joyment	→	joyment
(re)ceiver	→	ceiver
(pro)tection	→	tection
(tre)mendous	→	mendous
(i)dea	→	dea
(con)sumer	→	sumer

18. Say:
(re)mainder	→	mainder
(de)posit	→	posit
(re)cital	→	cital
(con)sider	→	sider
(per)formance	→	formance
(se)lection	→	lection
(e)quation	→	quation
(de)pendent	→	pendent
(in)surance	→	surance
(po)etic	→	etic

19. Say:
(re)union	→	union
(em)bargo	→	bargo
(i)talic	→	talic
(di)stinctive	→	stinctive
(ca)thedral	→	thedral
(tor)pedo	→	pedo
(fan)tastic	→	tastic
(Mi)ssouri	→	souri
(em)ployment	→	ployment
(Sep)tember	→	tember

20. Say:
(pneu)monia	→	monia
(en)deavor	→	deavor
(re)triever	→	triever
(trans)lucent	→	lucent
(con)dition	→	dition
(per)former	→	former
(mo)mentum	→	mentum
(im)pressive	→	pressive
(me)tallic	→	tallic
(re)garded	→	garded

One Minute Activities Level E3
NOTE: After completing E2, move on to F1 and do E3 simultaneously with Level F

Say: **(tri)angle** Now say **(tri)angle** but don't say **(tri)** → **angle**
Or say: **(tri)angle** Now say it again, but don't say **(tri)** → **angle**

1. Say:	(tri)angle	→	angle	2. Say:	(wil)derness	→	derness
	(spec)tator	→	tator		(xy)lophone	→	lophone
	(com)pensate	→	pensate		(sim)plify	→	plify
	(fur)niture	→	niture		(ro)deo	→	deo
	(bal)cony	→	cony		(mic)rophone	→	rophone
	(tam)bourine	→	bourine		(wol)verine	→	verine
	(por)cupine	→	cupine		(ad)vertise	→	vertise
	(fes)tival	→	tival		(en)velope	→	velope
	(vic)tory	→	tory		(tan)gerine	→	gerine
	(or)chestra	→	chestra		(ul)timate	→	timate
3. Say:	(com)pliment	→	pliment	4. Say:	(sym)phony	→	phony
	(tur)moil	→	moil		(um)pire	→	pire
	(ac)robat	→	robat		(ten)dency	→	dency
	(won)derful	→	derful		(clean)liness	→	liness
	(per)manent	→	manent		(dan)gerous	→	gerous
	(car)nival	→	nival		(hi)bernate	→	bernate
	(mar)garine	→	garine		(quar)terly	→	terly
	(sub)stitute	→	stitute		(vi)deo	→	deo
	(stu)dio	→	dio		(work)manship	→	manship
	(bar)becue	→	becue		(a)gency	→	gency
5. Say:	(fur)thermore	→	thermore	6. Say:	(com)pany	→	pany
	(ar)gument	→	gument		(in)terval	→	terval
	(tri)cycle	→	cycle		(for)merly	→	merly
	(an)cestor	→	cestor		(per)fectly	→	fectly
	(des)tiny	→	tiny		(live)lihood	→	lihood
	(en)terprise	→	terprise		(or)nament	→	nament
	(tech)nical	→	nical		(Ger)many	→	many
	(mas)querade	→	querade		(in)dustry	→	dustry
	(dip)lomat	→	lomat		(mer)chandise	→	chandise
	(trans)mitter	→	mitter		(car)penter	→	penter
7. Say:	(supp)lement	→	lement	8. Say:	(pho)tograph	→	tograph
	(yes)terday	→	terday		(con)fidence	→	fidence
	(al)phabet	→	phabet		(like)lihood	→	lihood
	(per)sonal	→	sonal		(sci)entist	→	entist
	(Wash)ington	→	ington		(bra)very	→	very
	(com)promise	→	promise		(Af)rica	→	rica
	(turn)stile	→	stile		(al)ternate	→	ternate
	(har)mony	→	mony		(en)tertain	→	tertain
	(por)table	→	table		(Sat)urday	→	urday
	(cal)culate	→	culate		(com)plicate	→	plicate

One Minute Activities Level E3

Say: **(sym)pathy** Now say **(sym)pathy** but don't say **(sym)** → **pathy**
Or say: **(sym)pathy** Now say it again, but don't say **(sym)** → **pathy**

9. Say:	(sym)pathy	→	pathy	10. Say:	(es)timate	→	timate
	(ca)pital	→	pital		(fac)tory	→	tory
	(den)sity	→	sity		(mock)ingbird	→	ingbird
	(al)titude	→	titude		(in)cident	→	cident
	(in)terview	→	terview		(con)ference	→	ference
	(em)peror	→	peror		(in)stantly	→	stantly
	(can)taloupe	→	taloupe		(ad)vocate	→	vocate
	(al)manac	→	manac		(In)dian	→	dian
	(mag)nify	→	nify		(mul)tiply	→	tiply
	(car)dinal	→	dinal		(in)fluence	→	fluence

11. Say:	(mar)malade	→	malade	12. Say:	(pre)vious	→	vious
	(op)tional	→	tional		(sym)bolize	→	bolize
	(in)terview	→	terview		(pro)perly	→	perly
	(pen)tagon	→	tagon		(in)strument	→	strument
	(cus)tomer	→	tomer		(aw)fully	→	fully
	(mic)roscope	→	roscope		(nine)tieth	→	tieth
	(pri)mary	→	mary		(tour)nament	→	nament
	(sur)gery	→	gery		(con)template	→	template
	(per)secute	→	secute		(mar)velous	→	velous
	(in)finite	→	finate		(pub)lisher	→	lisher

13. Say:	(ver)tebrate	→	tebrate	14. Say:	(bi)nary	→	nary
	(ab)solute	→	solute		(har)monize	→	monize
	(em)phasis	→	phasis		(cor)duroy	→	duroy
	(in)tercept	→	tercept		(dy)nasty	→	nasty
	(con)centrate	→	centrate		(con)stable	→	stable
	(dra)pery	→	pery		(ac)tivate	→	tivate
	(Cel)sius	→	sius		(In)dia	→	dia
	(spec)tacle	→	tacle		(Ar)kansas	→	kansas
	(con)fident	→	fident		(cal)endar	→	endar
	(do)berman	→	berman		(em)bassy	→	bassy

15. Say:	(ar)chitect	→	chitect	16. Say:	(mul)titude	→	titude
	(mer)cury	→	cury		(ad)miral	→	miral
	(mis)pronounce	→	pronounce		(mus)cular	→	cular
	(coll)ection	→	ection		(sta)dium	→	dium
	(mul)tiple	→	tiple		(plen)tiful	→	tiful
	(at)mosphere	→	mosphere		(ra)diant	→	diant
	(mys)tery	→	tery		(al)gebra	→	gebra
	(sen)sible	→	sible		(prin)cipal	→	cipal
	(ab)domen	→	domen		(ter)minal	→	minal
	(con)sequence	→	sequence		(in)fantry	→	fantry

One Minute Activities Level E3

Say: (su)pervise Now say (su)pervise but don't say (su) → pervise
Or say: (su)pervise Now say it again, but don't say (su) → pervise

17. Say:
(su)pervise	→	pervise
(ther)mostat	→	mostat
(con)tinent	→	tinent
(to)tally	→	tally
(al)batross	→	batross
(in)digo	→	digo
(tex)tile	→	tile
(mem)orize	→	orize
(cen)tury	→	tury
(am)bulance	→	bulance

18. Say:
(dig)nity	→	nity
(con)gregate	→	gregate
(tes)tify	→	tify
(char)acter	→	acter
(mess)enger	→	enger
(cu)cumber	→	cumber
(app)rehend	→	rehend
(ob)stacle	→	stacle
(pan)tomime	→	tomime
(in)dicate	→	dicate

19. Say:
(coun)selor	→	selor
(por)tico	→	tico
(com)petent	→	petent
(ap)ricot	→	ricot
(in)tercom	→	tercom
(sen)timent	→	timent
(prac)tical	→	tical
(cer)tainty	→	tainty
(in)terfere	→	terfere
(ver)tical	→	tical

20. Say:
(tem)perate	→	perate
(pro)perty	→	perty
(or)ganize	→	ganize
(agg)ravate	→	ravate
(boom)erang	→	erang
(mill)ionaire	→	ionaire
(ar)tery	→	tery
(sac)rifice	→	rifice
(mu)tiny	→	tiny
(in)tricate	→	tricate

Supplemental Activities for Level E3

S1
(el)derly
(coun)terfeit
(du)plicate
(cul)tivate
(bi)cycle

(all)ergy
(cor)nea
(an)tonym
(col)orful
(harp)sicord

S2
(gra)vity
(fre)quency
(gro)cery
(li)brary
(dec)orate

(han)dicraft
(di)gital
(im)provise
(hu)morous
(in)tellect

S3
(nour)ishment
(i)rony
(diff)erent
(nu)meral
(in)terest

(fed)eral
(ma)jesty
(o)pening
(des)ignate
(jus)tify

S4
(pen)dulum
(hy)drogen
(cyl)inder
(cour)tesy
(dem)onstrate

(cul)tural
(con)queror
(fif)tieth
(pro)bably
(hyp)notize

S5
(in)ternal
(ap)titude
(con)stitute
(att)ribute
(can)didate

(ig)norance
(cour)teous
(mas)culine
(fla)voring
(cor)poral

S6
(for)tunate
(in)stitute
(mag)nitude
(in)quiry
(dy)namo

(gar)goyle
(con)trary
(in)sulate
(nu)merous
(ig)norant

S7
(or)thodox
(pa)triot
(light)ening
(in)jury
(per)forate

(dig)nified
(pro)bable
(fa)vorite
(pun)ishment
(lu)bricate

S8
(guar)dian
(fu)gitive
(gen)erous
(i)vory
(am)plify

(o)pener
(pro)bably
(im)plement
(em)phasize
(in)tegrate

One Minute Activities Level E4

Say: **(an)imal**   Now say **(an)imal** but don't say **(an)** → **imal**
Or say: **(an)imal**   Now say it again, but don't say **(an)** → **imal**

	1. Say:				2. Say:		
	(an)imal	→	imal		(circ)ular	→	ular
	(fab)ulous	→	ulous		(happ)ily	→	ily
	(el)ephant	→	ephant		(man)ager	→	ager
	(cat)alog	→	alog		(bull)etin	→	etin
	(diff)icult	→	icult		(med)icine	→	icine
	(fin)ally	→	ally		(pyr)amid	→	amid
	(hurr)icane	→	icane		(tel)escope	→	escope
	(ben)efit	→	efit		(ed)itor	→	itor
	(luck)ily	→	ily		(vi)olet	→	olet
	(par)agraph	→	agraph		(qual)ity	→	ity

	3. Say:				4. Say:		
	(clar)ify	→	ify		(class)ical	→	ical
	(din)osaur	→	osaur		(heav)ily	→	ily
	(hol)iday	→	iday		(lin)ear	→	ear
	(buff)alo	→	alo		(mus)ical	→	ical
	(mag)azine	→	azine		(hes)itant	→	itant
	(ed)ucate	→	ucate		(sen)ator	→	ator
	(pres)ident	→	ident		(doc)ument	→	ument
	(reg)ular	→	ular		(ser)ious	→	ious
	(par)akeet	→	akeet		(char)ity	→	ity
	(par)achute	→	achute		(sal)ary	→	ary

	5. Say:				6. Say:		
	(class)ify	→	ify		(flamm)able	→	able
	(loll)ipop	→	ipop		(en)emy	→	emy
	(her)itage	→	itage		(disc)ipline	→	ipline
	(aud)io	→	io		(acc)urate	→	urate
	(ox)ygen	→	ygen		(di)alogue	→	alogue
	(clar)ity	→	ity		(cent)igrade	→	igrade
	(dram)atize	→	atize		(dram)atist	→	atist
	(cav)ity	→	ity		(terr)ible	→	ible
	(rel)ative	→	ative		(nom)inate	→	inate
	(ic)icle	→	icle		(vin)egar	→	egar

	7. Say:				8. Say:		
	(clar)inet	→	inet		(mag)ical	→	ical
	(poss)ible	→	ible		(sim)ilar	→	ilar
	(qual)ify	→	ify		(im)itate	→	itate
	(aer)ospace	→	ospace		(lull)aby	→	aby
	(par)adise	→	adise		(def)inite	→	inite
	(Id)aho	→	aho		(av)enue	→	enue
	(Mich)igan	→	igan		(del)icate	→	icate
	(cas)ual	→	ual		(rid)icule	→	icule
	(par)allel	→	allel		(ev)idence	→	idence
	(opp)osite	→	osite		(carr)ier	→	ier

One Minute Activities Level E4

Say: **(clar)**inet Now say **(clar)**inet but don't say **(clar)** → **inet**
Or say: **(clar)**inet Now say it again, but don't say **(clar)** → **inet**

9 Say:	(char)iot	→	iot	10. Say:	(daff)odil	→	odil
	(man)ual	→	ual		(Mar)yland	→	yland
	(Hall)oween	→	oween		(jan)itor	→	itor
	(Del)aware	→	aware		(car)avan	→	avan
	(sat)ellite	→	ellite		(res)ident	→	ident
	(ann)ual	→	ual		(pel)ican	→	ican
	(tel)ephone	→	ephone		(mir)acle	→	acle
	(ster)eo	→	eo		(is)olate	→	olate
	(vis)ible	→	ible		(eas)ily	→	ily
	(gull)ible	→	iot		(glor)ify	→	ify
11. Say:	(flex)ible	→	ible	12. Say:	(Flor)ida	→	ida
	(del)egate	→	egate		(com)ical	→	ical
	(ex)ecute	→	ecute		(tel)egraph	→	egraph
	(bod)ily	→	ily		(cel)ebrate	→	ebrate
	(pol)itics	→	itics		(av)alanche	→	alanche
	(min)imum	→	imum		(chlor)ophyll	→	ophyll
	(com)edy	→	edy		(mol)ecule	→	ecule
	(ded)icate	→	icate		(dom)inant	→	inant
	(phon)ograph	→	ograph		(irr)itate	→	itate
	(terr)ify	→	ify		(di)agram	→	agram
13. Say:	(pharm)acy	→	acy	14. Say:	(nov)elist	→	elist
	(chem)ical	→	ical		(friv)olous	→	olous
	(pred)icate	→	icate		(pat)io	→	io
	(ant)elope	→	elope		(rel)evant	→	evant
	(plat)inum	→	inum		(cell)ophane	→	ophane
	(ad)equate	→	equate		(vi)olate	→	olate
	(ep)isode	→	isode		(man)icure	→	icure
	(dev)iate	→	iate		(lig)ament	→	ament
	(meg)aphone	→	aphone		(et)iquette	→	iquette
	(pur)ity	→	ity		(aer)ial	→	ial
15. Say:	(man)uscript	→	uscript	16. Say:	(cat)apult	→	apult
	(col)ony	→	ony		(mon)itor	→	itor
	(occ)upant	→	upant		(jav)elin	→	elin
	(Or)egon	→	egon		(cit)izen	→	izen
	(cer)amics	→	amics		(chem)istry	→	istry
	(ar)ea	→	ea		(pit)iful	→	iful
	(po)etry	→	etry		(corr)idor	→	idor
	(vis)ual	→	ual		(neg)ative	→	ative
	(el)ement	→	ement		(par)aphrase	→	aphrase
	(dil)igent	→	igent		(el)egant	→	egant

One Minute Activities Level E4

Say: **(form)**ula Now say **(form)**ula but don't say **(form)** → ula
Or say: **(form)**ula Now say it again, but don't say **(form)** → ula

17. Say:	(form)ula	→	ula	18. Say:	(kil)ogram	→	ogram
	(barr)icade	→	icade		(hel)ium	→	ium
	(long)itude	→	itude		(i)odine	→	odine
	(acc)ident	→	ident		(cam)ouflage	→	ouflage
	(can)opy	→	opy		(imm)igrant	→	igrant
	(dep)uty	→	uty		(dom)ino	→	ino
	(an)alyze	→	alyze		(tel)egram	→	egram
	(fort)ify	→	ify		(ap)athy	→	athy
	(chanc)ellor	→	ellor		(sax)ophone	→	ophone
	(rev)enue	→	enue		(dec)imal	→	imal
19. Say:	(tel)evise	→	evise	20. Say:	(cer)eal	→	eal
	(cap)ital	→	ital		(garr)ison	→	ison
	(am)ateur	→	ateur		(pur)ify	→	ify
	(grat)ify	→	ify		(an)imate	→	imate
	(el)oquent	→	oquent		(var)ious	→	ious
	(cel)ery	→	ery		(cab)inet	→	inet
	(par)asol	→	asol		(suit)able	→	able
	(ev)ident	→	ident		(occ)upy	→	upy
	(bar)itone	→	itone		(grad)ual	→	ual
	(arr)ogant	→	ogant		(leg)ible	→	ible

Supplemental One Minute Activities for Level E4

S1	(mod)ify	S2	(sol)uble	S3	(ab)acus	S4	(Can)ada
	(pharm)acist		(ed)ible		(li)able		(app)etite
	(al)ibi		(par)ody		(hom)onym		(Mex)ico
	(rev)eille		(lar)iat		(ag)ony		(dur)able
	(car)ibou		(skel)eton		(glor)ious		(barr)ier
	(gel)atin		(par)affin		(pal)isades		(for)eigner
	(pro)minent		(mocc)asin		(naus)ea		(gal)axy
	(em)inent		(al)ien		(ol)eo		(aer)osol
	(jov)ial		(gen)uine		(pen)etrate		(or)igin
	(terr)ier		(em)igrate		(om)inous		(glor)ify
S5	(scen)ery	S6	(vis)itor	S7	(ker)osene	S8	(ad)enoids
	(sed)iment		(id)iom		(or)iole		(Mex)ican
	(cur)ious		(nav)igate		(irr)igate		(lyr)ical
	(met)aphor		(ag)itate		(sec)ular		(al)ias
	(des)olate		(med)ia		(jeal)ousy		(fur)ious
	(pen)alize		(cell)uloid		(imm)igrate		(gloss)ary
	(el)evate		(stren)uous		(pess)imist		(kil)owatt
	(fil)ament		(hes)itate		(aff)able		(ad)amant
	(cop)yright		(fem)inine		(dem)ocrat		(hal)ogen
	(bot)any		(the)ater		(boul)evard		(cal)ico

One Minute Activities Level E5

Say: **ani(mal)** Now say **ani(mal)** but don't say **(mal)** → **ani**
Or say: **ani(mal)** Now say it again, but don't say **(mal)** → **ani**

1. Say:	ani(mal)	→	ani	2. Say:	circu(lar)	→	circu
	fabu(lous)	→	fabu		happi(ly)	→	happi
	ele(phant)	→	ele		mana(ger)	→	mana
	cata(log)	→	cata		bulle(tin)	→	bulle
	diffi(cult)	→	diffi		medi(cine)	→	medi
	fina(lly)	→	fina		pyra(mid)	→	pyra
	hurri(cane)	→	hurri		tele(scope)	→	tele
	bene(fit)	→	bene		edi(tor)	→	edi
	lucki(ly)	→	lucki		vio(let)	→	vio
	para(graph)	→	para		quali(ty)	→	quali
3. Say:	clari(fy)	→	clari	4. Say:	classi(cal)	→	classi
	dino(saur)	→	dino		heavi(ly)	→	heavi
	happi(ness)	→	happi		line(ar)	→	line
	buffa(lo)	→	buffa		musi(cal)	→	musi
	maga(zine)	→	maga		hesi(tant)	→	hesi
	edu(cate)	→	edu		sena(tor)	→	sena
	presi(dent)	→	presi		docu(ment)	→	docu
	regu(lar)	→	regu		seri(ous)	→	seri
	oxy(gen)	→	oxy		chari(ty)	→	chari
	para(chute)	→	para		sala(ry)	→	sala
5. Say:	classi(fy)	→	classi	6. Say:	flamma(ble)	→	flamma
	lolli(pop)	→	lolli		ene(my)	→	ene
	heri(tage)	→	heri		disci(pline)	→	disci
	audi(o)	→	audi		accu(rate)	→	accu
	para(keet)	→	para		dia(logue)	→	dia
	clari(ty)	→	clari		centi(grade)	→	centi
	drama(tize)	→	drama		drama(tist)	→	drama
	cavi(ty)	→	cavi		terri(ble)	→	terri
	rela(tive)	→	rela		nomi(nate)	→	nomi
	ici(cle)	→	ici		vine(gar)	→	vine
7. Say:	clari(net)	→	clari	8. Say:	magi(cal)	→	magi
	possi(ble)	→	possi		simi(lar)	→	simi
	quali(fy)	→	quali		imi(tate)	→	imi
	aero(space)	→	aero		lulla(by)	→	lulla
	para(dise)	→	para		defi(nite)	→	defi
	Ida(ho)	→	Ida		ave(nue)	→	ave
	Michi(gan)	→	Michi		deli(cate)	→	deli
	casu(al)	→	casu		ridi(cule)	→	ridi
	para(llel)	→	para		evi(dence)	→	evi
	oppo(site)	→	oppo		carri(er)	→	carri

One Minute Activities Level E5

	Say:	clari(net)	Now say clari(net) but don't say (net) → clari
	Or say:	clari(net)	Now say it again, but don't say (net) → clari

9. Say:	coco(nut)	→	coco	10. Say:	daffo(dil)	→	daffo
	manu(al)	→	manu		Mary(land)	→	Mary
	holi(day)	→	holi		jani(tor)	→	jani
	Dela(ware)	→	Dela		cara(van)	→	cara
	satell(ite)	→	satell		resi(dent)	→	resi
	annu(al)	→	annu		peli(can)	→	peli
	tele(phone)	→	tele		mira(cle)	→	mira
	stere(o)	→	stere		iso(late)	→	iso
	visi(ble)	→	visi		easi(ly)	→	easi
	chari(ot)	→	chari		platy(pus)	→	platy

11. Say:	flexi(ble)	→	flexi	12. Say:	Flori(da)	→	Flori
	dele(gate)	→	dele		comi(cal)	→	comi
	exe(cute)	→	exe		tele(graph)	→	tele
	bodi(ly)	→	bodi		cele(brate)	→	cele
	poli(tics)	→	poli		ava(lanche)	→	ava
	mini(mum)	→	mini		chloro(phyll)	→	chloro
	come(dy)	→	come		mole(cule)	→	mole
	dedi(cate)	→	dedi		domi(nant)	→	domi
	phono(graph)	→	phono		irri(tate)	→	irri
	terri(fy)	→	terri		dia(gram)	→	dia

13. Say:	formu(la)	→	formu	14. Say:	kilo(gram)	→	kilo
	barri(cade)	→	barri		heli(um)	→	heli
	longi(tude)	→	longi		io(dine)	→	io
	acci(dent)	→	acci		camou(flage)	→	camou
	cano(py)	→	cano		immi(grant)	→	immi
	depu(ty)	→	depu		domi(no)	→	domi
	ana(lyze)	→	ana		tele(gram)	→	tele
	forti(fy)	→	forti		apa(thy)	→	apa
	chance(llor)	→	chance		saxo(phone)	→	saxo
	reve(nue)	→	reve		deci(mal)	→	deci

15. Say:	manu(script)	→	manu	16. Say:	cata(pult)	→	cata
	colo(ny)	→	colo		moni(tor)	→	moni
	occu(pant)	→	occu		jave(lin)	→	jave
	Ore(gon)	→	Ore		citi(zen)	→	citi
	cera(mics)	→	cera		chemi(stry)	→	chemi
	are(a)	→	are		piti(ful)	→	piti
	poe(try)	→	poe		corri(dor)	→	corri
	visu(al)	→	visu		nega(tive)	→	nega
	ele(ment)	→	ele		ani(mate)	→	ani
	dili(gent)	→	dili		ele(gant)	→	ele

ONSET-RIME LEVEL ACTIVITIES

KINDERGARTEN, FIRST GRADE, AND
SOME OLDER STRUGGLING READERS

LEVELS F1, F2
LEVELS G1, G2

ONSET-RIME LEVELS

The earliest phonological awareness programs date from the late 1960s and early 1970s. These programs mixed together the activities that involved the first, middle, and ending phonemes in syllables. By the 1980s researchers demonstrated that initial phonemes were much easier to manipulate than middle and ending phonemes. Even though the initial phoneme in a syllable is a true phoneme, it is much simpler to manipulate than phonemes located in the middle or end of a word. Thus, to be truly developmental in our teaching of phonological awareness, we must acknowledge that the onset-rime level comes before the phoneme level. There is now ample research to support this.

You may find that this is the level where some students with reading difficulties get "stuck." Children with reading difficulties can do onset-rime level activities but struggle with the true phoneme levels. They usually become automatic with onset-rime activities. Yet some students with the most severe reading problems may even struggle with this level. However, most children without reading difficulties can do onset-rime level activities, if taught, by late kindergarten. For an extensive description of the onset-rime level, see Chapter 3 *Levels of Phonological Awareness*.

Level F1 represents deleting the initial sound in a word. Level G1 involves substituting a new sound in the onset position. For example:

| *deletion* | Level F1 | (s)it → it | (ch)air → air |
| *substitution* | Level G1 | (t)ied → (r)ide | (t)ask → (m)ask |

Levels F2 and G2 approach the onset-rime juncture from the other direction. These levels involve deleting or substituting the rime rather than the onset. For example:

| *deletion* | Level F2 | s(ing) → /s/ | m(at) → /m/ |
| *substitution* | Level G2 | t(ime) → t(ack) | s(un) → s(ip) |

In these cases, the entire rime unit is deleted or exchanged. Like F1 and F2, the split is at the onset-rime juncture. Many children will find F2 and G2 more difficult than F1 and G1 activities. However, they will find the rime deletion and substitution easier than deleting or substituting a middle or ending phoneme.

Note on multisyllabic/applied activities: These activities are important (see p. 91) but are usually much harder than the regular activities at their levels (e.g., F1, G1). They do not need to be done before moving on to higher levels. However, once students are working H, I, and higher levels, it will be important to cycle back around and work on these multisyllabic activities.

Remember: THE FOCUS IS ON THE SOUNDS, NOT SPELLING PATTERNS.

LEVEL F

ONSET-RIME LEVEL PROCESSING
DELETION TASK

    F1   Level F1 involves deleting a single consonant (the onset) from a single syllable word.
            Samples: (t)ap → ap   (r)un → un

    F2   Level F2 involves deleting the rime unit from a single syllable word.
            Samples: m(an) → /m/   s(ay) → /s/

Multisyllabic/Applied Activities

The *Multisyllabic/Applied* activities are designed to help children apply the phoneme awareness skills that they have learned to multi-syllabic words. If students struggle with these, it is okay to move on, but it is important to come back to these (see p. 91).

    F1   This activity deletes the first sound of the second syllable in a two syllable word.
            Samples: dri(v)er → dryer   buil(d)ing → billing

Special Administration Instructions for Level F

- An effort was made to match the sounds rather than the letters to make the activities easier for the teacher. For example, when deleting the onset of the word *here*, the result is not printed as *ere* (a word fragment) but as *ear*, which the teacher can quickly recognize during the activities. Other illustrations include: *love* → *of; lone* → *own*; and *pour* → *or*. Because One Minute Activities are *oral* so students never *see* the words. These adjustments should make administration easier. The reading teachers that have used this for years preferred this way. Note that this differs from the way syllables are represented in Levels D and E (see the introduction to those sections).

- In Level F2, consonants must be isolated. To make this simpler, only consonants that can be easily pronounced in isolation were used (*f, l, m, n, r, s, sh, z*). Please note that /m/ is not pronounced "muh." You can say all of these consonants sounds without the "uh" sound at the end. Adding this vowel sound (the "uh") at the end of the consonant sound only makes phoneme awareness and blending more difficult and confusing for children. For help in producing sounds in isolation, see Chapter 12 and Appendix E.

- Starting with F1, *mixed levels* are introduced. For explanation of mixed levels, see Chapter 10. Mixed levels are located in the bottom right corner of each page and combine the current level with levels previously learned. They are designed to sharpen a student's skills and add additional practice in phoneme isolation (for a description of phoneme isolation, see Chapter 7). They also function as a review of previous material.

Remember: THE FOCUS IS ON THE SOUNDS, NOT SPELLING PATTERNS.

One Minute Activities Level F1

            Say: **fall**   Now say **fall** again, but don't say /f/ ⇢ **all**
    Or: Say: **fall**   Now say it again, but don't say /f/ ⇢ **all**

1. Say:	fall	don't say /f/	all	2. Say:	peer	don't say /p/	ear
	bad	don't say /b/	add		chair	don't say /ch/	air
	here	don't say /h/	ear		rise	don't say /r/	eyes
	rat	don't say /r/	at		wake	don't say /w/	ache
	pair	don't say /p/	air		game	don't say /g/	aim
	ties	don't say /t/	eyes		chase	don't say /ch/	ace
	birth	don't say /b/	earth		ham	don't say /h/	am
	leaves	don't say /l/	eves		shown	don't say /sh/	own
	call	don't say /k/	all		than	don't say /th/	an
	peg	don't say /p/	egg		con	don't say /k/	on
3. Say:	meek	don't say /m/	eek	4. Say:	leave	don't say /l/	eve
	hide	don't say /h/	I'd		bit	don't say /b/	it
	love	don't say /l/	of		wheel	don't say /wh/	eel
	lone	don't say /l/	own		coil	don't say /k/	oil
	gate	don't say /g/	ate		seat	don't say /s/	eat
	pour	don't say /p/	or		till	don't say /t/	ill
	shawl	don't say /sh/	all		came	don't say /k/	aim
	paid	don't say /p/	aid		pose	don't say /p/	owes
	she's	don't say /sh/	ease		pouch	don't say /p/	ouch
	nice	don't say /n/	ice		fame	don't say /f/	aim
5. Say:	wise	don't say /w/	eyes	6. Say:	side	don't say /s/	I'd
	dial	don't say /d/	aisle		whiz	don't say /w/	is
	seal	don't say /s/	eel		pan	don't say /p/	an
	kit	don't say /k/	it		chin	don't say /ch/	in
	hall	don't say /h/	all		lore	don't say /l/	ore
	mice	don't say /m/	ice		Nile	don't say /n/	I'll
	shove	don't say /sh/	of		cheer	don't say /ch/	ear
	neat	don't say /n/	eat		hive	don't say /h/	I've
	sought	don't say /s/	ought		fizz	don't say /f/	is
	rate	don't say /r/	ate		hit	don't say /h/	it

Mixed Levels

7. Say:	tear	don't say /t/	ear	(F1)	here	don't say /h/	ear
	fit	don't say /f/	it	(D2)	(can)dy	don't say (can)	dy
	sour	don't say /s/	our	(F1)	gate	don't say /g/	ate
	wheat	don't say /w/	eat	(E2)	(o)fficial	don't say (o)	ficial
	road	don't say /r/	owed	(F1)	fit	don't say /f/	it
	five	don't say /f/	I've	(D2)	(sil)ver	don't say (sil)	ver
	dice	don't say /d/	ice	(F1)	wheat	don't say /w/	eat
	wall	don't say /w/	all	(E2)	(lo)cation	don't say (lo)	cation
	bait	don't say /b/	ate	(F1)	wall	don't say /w/	all
	joke	don't say /j/	oak	(E2)	(vol)cano	don't say (vol)	cano

One Minute Activities Level F1

	Say:	**has**	Now say **has** again, but don't say **/h/** → **as**
Or:	Say:	**has**	Now say it again, but don't say **/h/** → **as**

8. Say:				9. Say:			
	has	don't say /h/	as		mad	don't say /m/	add
	led	don't say /l/	Ed		time	don't say /t/	I'm
	dill	don't say /d/	ill		war	don't say /w/	or
	sown	don't say /s/	own		lad	don't say /l/	add
	seize	don't say /s/	ease		mile	don't say /m/	aisle
	bake	don't say /b/	ache		cone	don't say /k/	own
	beg	don't say /b/	egg		kneel	don't say /n/	eel
	quill	don't say /qu/	ill		rage	don't say /r/	age
	couch	don't say /k/	ouch		can	don't say /k/	an
	hose	don't say /h/	owes		wit	don't say /w/	it

10. Say:				11. Say:			
	wore	don't say /w/	or		cod	don't say /k/	odd
	yam	don't say /y/	am		jam	don't say /j/	am
	shout	don't say /sh/	out		year	don't say /y/	ear
	your	don't say /y/	or		race	don't say /r/	ace
	zeal	don't say /z/	eel		shore	don't say /sh/	or
	cheese	don't say /ch/	ease		tall	don't say /t/	all
	shape	don't say /sh/	ape		shake	don't say /sh/	ache
	chime	don't say /ch/	I'm		fan	don't say /f/	an
	rake	don't say /r/	ache		chill	don't say /ch/	ill
	chore	don't say /ch/	ore		teach	don't say /t/	each

12. Say:				13. Say:			
	his	don't say /h/	is		tore	don't say /t/	or
	shale	don't say /sh/	ale		view	don't say /v/	you
	ball	don't say /b/	all		bar	don't say /b/	are
	shade	don't say /sh/	ade		tin	don't say /t/	in
	jar	don't say /j/	are		shame	don't say /sh/	aim
	bat	don't say /b/	at		deer	don't say /d/	ear
	beach	don't say /b/	each		coat	don't say /k/	oat
	ran	don't say /r/	an		tax	don't say /t/	ax
	tar	don't say /t/	are		quit	don't say /qu/	it
	core	don't say /k/	oar		bill	don't say /b/	ill

Mixed Levels

14. Say:							
	that	don't say /th/	at	(F1)	wise	don't say /w/	eyes
	wheeze	don't say /wh/	ease	(D2)	(en)ter	don't say (en)	ter
	boat	don't say /b/	oat	(F1)	has	don't say /h/	as
	base	don't say /b/	ace	(E2)	(com)puter	don't say (com)	puter
	shear	don't say /sh/	ear	(F1)	reach	don't say /r/	each
	reach	don't say /r/	each	(D2)	(dan)cer	don't say (dan)	cer
	tan	don't say /t/	an	(F1)	chin	don't say /ch/	in
	has	don't say /h/	as	(E2)	(terr)ific	don't say (ter)	ific or rific
	phone	don't say /f/	own	(F1)	can	don't say /k/	an
	hill	don't say /h/	ill	(D2)	mon(key)	don't say (key)	mon

One Minute Activities Level F1

| | | Say: | **toad** | Now say **toad**, but don't say /t/ → **owed** |
| | | Or: Say: | **toad** | Now say it again, but don't say /t/ → **owed** |

15. Say:	toad	don't say /t/	owed	16. Say:	whiz	don't say /wh/	is
	size	don't say /s/	eyes		bought	don't say /b/	ought
	van	don't say /v/	an		fade	don't say /f/	aid
	doze	don't say /d/	owes		bone	don't say /b/	own
	wage	don't say /w/	age		these	don't say /th/	ease
	Ron	don't say /r/	on		dive	don't say /d/	I've
	box	don't say /b/	ox		cage	don't say /k/	age
	case	don't say /k/	ace		far	don't say /f/	are
	pad	don't say /p/	add		loan	don't say /l/	own
	will	don't say /w/	ill		fed	don't say /f/	Ed

17. Say:	real	don't say /r/	eel	18. Say:	thought	don't say /th/	ought
	bus	don't say /b/	us		fill	don't say /f/	ill
	like	don't say /l/	Ike		said	don't say /s/	Ed
	fake	don't say /f/	ache		boil	don't say /b/	oil
	sheet	don't say /sh/	eat		can't	don't say /k/	ant
	red	don't say /r/	Ed		sat	don't say /s/	at
	wax	don't say /w/	ax		car	don't say /k/	are
	page	don't say /p/	age		poke	don't say /p/	oak
	weave	don't say /w/	eve		sail	don't say /s/	ail
	ride	don't say /r/	I'd		wait	don't say /w/	ate

Mixed Levels

19. Say:	shall	don't say /sh/	Al	(F1)	shout	don't say /sh/	out
	cough	don't say /k/	off	(D2)	in(dex)	don't say (dex)	in
	cup	don't say /k/	up	(F1)	beach	don't say /b/	each
	share	don't say /sh/	air	(E2)	(um)brella	don't say (um)	brella
	deal	don't say /d/	eel	(F1)	quiz	don't say /qu/	is
	tame	don't say /t/	aim	(D2)	(nor)mal	don't say (nor)	mal
	rash	don't say /r/	ash	(F1)	chill	don't say /ch/	ill
	tape	don't say /t/	ape	(E3)	(fur)niture	don't say (fur)	niture
	quiz	don't say /qu/	is	(F1)	deer	don't say /d/	ear
	care	don't say /k/	air	(E3)	(por)cupine	don't say (por)	cupine

Mixed Levels

20. Say:	wedge	don't say /w/	edge	(F1)	wage	don't say /w/	age
	load	don't say /l/	owed	(D2)	(an)swer	don't say (an)	swer
	sill	don't say /s/	ill	(F1)	box	don't say /b/	ox
	pin	don't say /p/	in	(E2)	(spa)ghetti	don't say (spa)	ghetti
	sit	don't say /s/	it	(F1)	bus	don't say /b/	us
	soak	don't say /s/	oak	(E2)	(O)lympic	don't say (O)	lympic
	fuss	don't say /f/	us	(F1)	soak	don't say /s/	oak
	pit	don't say /p/	it	(E3)	(tri)angle	don't say (tri)	angle
	sod	don't say /s/	odd	(F1)	bought	don't say /b/	ought
	lime	don't say /l/	I'm	(E3)	(tan)gerine	don't say (tan)	gerine

Supplemental One Minute Activities for Level F1

      Say: **ledge**   Now say **ledge**, but don't say /l/ → **edge**
Or: Say: **ledge**   Now say it again, but don't say /l/ → **edge**

S1.	(l)edge	→	edge	S2.	(s)ame	→	aim	S3.	(m)ill	→	ill
	(l)eg	→	egg		(s)hed	→	Ed		(p)each	→	each
	(g)ill	→	ill		(r)od	→	odd		(m)oan	→	own
	(f)ear	→	ear		(w)ear	→	air		(m)oat	→	oat
	(th)us	→	us		(sh)one	→	own		(f)or	→	or
	(n)od	→	odd		(p)od	→	odd		(n)ame	→	aim
	(f)use	→	use		(s)oar	→	oar		(n)ear	→	ear
	(n)or	→	or		(c)ape	→	ape		(l)ace	→	ace
	(f)ox	→	ox		(p)ies	→	eyes		(f)ought	→	ought
	(f)in	→	in		(wh)ile	→	aisle		(p)arch	→	arch

S4.	(p)ill	→	ill	S5.	(sh)ears	→	ears	S6.	(g)uide	→	I'd
	(c)ash	→	ash		(n)ose	→	owes		(h)ad	→	add
	(f)oil	→	oil		(p)ace	→	ace		(p)ear	→	air
	(w)here	→	air		(th)ere	→	air		(h)ead	→	Ed
	(g)ear	→	ear		(s)ad	→	add		(p)eel	→	eel
	(p)ile	→	aisle		(th)in	→	in		(kn)it	→	it
	(w)hose	→	ooze		(r)ich	→	itch		(kn)own	→	own
	(r)ide	→	I'd		(r)ose	→	owes		(m)ore	→	or
	(r)ice	→	ice		(t)ide	→	I'd		(l)ad	→	add
	(w)in	→	in		(c)are	→	air		(l)ake	→	ache

S7.	(l)ate	→	ate	S8.	(g)oat	→	oat	S9.	(f)our	→	or
	(l)it	→	it		(sh)in	→	in		(p)eat	→	eat
	(f)eel	→	eel		(h)eal	→	eel		(h)air	→	air
	(h)eave	→	eve		(w)eight	→	ate		(g)oes	→	owes
	(w)ed	→	Ed		(f)ace	→	ace		(m)itt	→	it
	(d)ime	→	I'm		(h)edge	→	edge		(h)at	→	at
	(f)eet	→	eat		(f)air	→	air		(p)ants	→	ants
	(d)oor	→	or		(l)ash	→	ash		(h)ear	→	ear
	(h)eat	→	eat		(w)ide	→	I'd		(p)at	→	at
	(wh)ale	→	ale		(c)at	→	at		(rh)yme	→	I'm

Multisyllabic/Applied
One Minute Activities Level F1

See note about multisyllabic/applied activites on pages 91 and 151

		Say:	**driver**	Now say **driver**, but don't say **/v/** →	**dryer**
Or:		Say:	**driver**	Now say it again, but don't say **/v/** →	**dryer**

1. Say:	driver	don't say /v/	dryer	2. Say:	driving	don't say /v/	drying
	hamper	don't say /p/	hammer		hiker	don't say /k/	hire
	beaming	don't say /m/	being		freezing	don't say /z/	freeing
	seating	don't say /t/	seeing		stating	don't say /t/	staying
	floating	don't say /t/	flowing		fiber	don't say /b/	fire
	winter	don't say /t/	winner		moaning	don't say /n/	mowing
	laser	don't say /z/	layer		loafer	don't say /f/	lower
	fighter	don't say /t/	fire		spraining	don't say /n/	spraying
	silence	don't say /l/	science		soaker	don't say /k/	sower
	storming	don't say /m/	storing		molar	don't say /l/	mower

3. Say:	powder	don't say /d/	power	4. Say:	planter	don't say /t/	planner
	roaming	don't say /m/	rowing		monkey	don't say /k/	money
	grocer	don't say /s/	grower		spider	don't say /d/	spire
	stormy	don't say /m/	story		pager	don't say /j/	payer
	waiting	don't say /t/	weighing		siding	don't say /d/	sighing
	worthy	don't say /th/	worry		later	don't say /t/	layer
	soaking	don't say /k/	sewing		gracing	don't say /s/	graying
	building	don't say /d/	billing		primer	don't say /m/	prior
	freezer	don't say /z/	freer		seedling	don't say /l/	seeding
	beating	don't say /t/	being		loiter	don't say /t/	lawyer

5. Say:	roller	don't say /l/	rower
	seeking	don't say /k/	seeing
	groaning	don't say /n/	growing
	butler	don't say /l/	butter
	maker	don't say /k/	mayor
	staging	don't say /j/	staying
	trooper	don't say /p/	truer
	sized	don't say /z/	sighed
	tiger	don't say /g/	tire
	seeding	don't say /d/	seeing

Multisyllabic/Applied
One Minute Activities Level F1

See note about multisyllabic/applied activites on pages 91 and 150

	Say:	**saving**	Now say **saving**, but don't say **/v/** → **saying**
Or:	Say:	**saving**	Now say it again, but don't say **/v/** → **saying**

6. Say:	saving	don't say /v/	saying	7. Say:	bloomer	don't say /m/	bluer
	praising	don't say /z/	praying		keeping	don't say /p/	keying
	motor	don't say /t/	mower		Laker	don't say /k/	layer
	shelving	don't say /v/	shelling		fielder	don't say /d/	feeler
	pacing	don't say /s/	paying		paging	don't say /j/	paying
	straining	don't say /n/	straying		gloating	don't say /t/	glowing
	loaner	don't say /n/	lower		stooping	don't say /p/	stewing
	banter	don't say /t/	banner		filter	don't say /t/	filler
	fleeting	don't say /t/	fleeing		sterling	don't say /l/	stirring
	settler	don't say /l/	setter		fleecing	don't say /s/	fleeing

8. Say:	roping	don't say /p/	rowing	9. Say:	liner	don't say /n/	liar
	wormy	don't say /m/	worry		pleading	don't say /d/	pleaing
	transmission	don't say /m/	transition		tiling	don't say /l/	tying
	bumper	don't say /p/	bummer		hoping	don't say /p/	hoeing
	waking	don't say /k/	weighing		starling	don't say /l/	starring
	planeing	don't say /n/	playing		piercing	don't say /s/	peering
	moping	don't say /p/	mowing		needing	don't say /d/	kneeing
	banking	don't say /k/	banging		muster	don't say /s/	mutter
	waning	don't say /n/	weighing		grading	don't say /d/	graying
	noting	don't say /t/	knowing		invert	don't say /v/	inert

10. Say:	soaping	don't say /p/	sewing
	admission	don't say /m/	addition
	priming	don't say /m/	prying
	soothing	don't say /th/	suing
	recorder	don't say /k/	reorder
	signing	don't say /n/	sighing
	toning	don't say /n/	towing
	tender	don't say /d/	tenor
	lining	don't say /n/	lying
	paving	don't say /v/	paying

One Minute Activities Level F2

		Say:	**more**	Now say **more**, but don't say /ore/ → /**m**/
	Or:	Say:	**more**	Now say it again, but don't say /ore/ → /**m**/

1. Say	more	don't say /ore/	/m/	2. Say	mice	don't say /ice/	/m/
	lake	don't say /ake/	/l/		feet	don't say /eet/	/f/
	news	don't say /ooze/	/n/		ride	don't say /ide/	/r/
	like	don't say /ike/	/l/		lean	don't say /ean/	/l/
	rose	don't say /ose/	/r/		mine	don't say /ine/	/m/
	sill	don't say /ill/	/s/		fill	don't say /ill/	/f/
	ledge	don't say /edge/	/l/		leaves	don't say /eaves/	/l/
	mill	don't say /ill/	/m/		fit	don't say /it/	/f/
	fall	don't say /all/	/f/		last	don't say /ast/	/l/
	fan	don't say /an/	/f/		nice	don't say /ice/	/n/

3. Say	name	don't say /ame/	/n/	4. Say	foil	don't say /oil/	/f/
	real	don't say /eal/	/r/		zoo	don't say /oo/	/z/
	shed	don't say /ed/	/sh/		thaw	don't say /aw/	/th/
	seat	don't say /eat/	/s/		fan	don't say /an/	/f/
	view	don't say /iew/	/v/		rice	don't say /ice/	/r/
	feat	don't say /eat/	/f/		fox	don't say /ox/	/f/
	fed	don't say /ed/	/f/		rake	don't say /ake/	/r/
	shout	don't say /out/	/sh/		late	don't say /ate/	/l/
	think	don't say /ink/	/th/		van	don't say /an/	/v/
	race	don't say /ace/	/r/		reach	don't say /each/	/r/

5. Say:	mall	don't say /all/	/m/	6. Say:	fun	don't say /un/	/f/
	leave	don't say /eave/	/l/		rum	don't say /um/	/r/
	same	don't say /ame/	/s/		five	don't say /ive/	/f/
	led	don't say /ed/	/l/		lamb	don't say /am/	/l/
	made	don't say /ade/	/m/		nail	don't say /ail/	/n/
	leg	don't say /eg/	/l/		said	don't say /aid/	/s/
	she	don't say /E/	/sh/		mode	don't say /ode/	/m/
	move	don't say /oove/	/m/		sail	don't say /ail/	/s/
	red	don't say /ed/	/r/		near	don't say /ear/	/n/
	lash	don't say /ash/	/l/		neat	don't say /eat/	/n/

Mixed Levels

7. Say	zeal	don't say /eal/	/z/	(F2)	more	don't say /ore/	/m/
	like	don't say /ike/	/l/	(D2)	in(dex)	don't say (dex)	in
	vine	don't say /ine/	/v/	(F2)	name	don't say /ame/	/n/
	file	don't say /ile/	/f/	(F1)	shown	don't say /sh/	own
	size	don't say /ize/	/s/	(F2)	vine	don't say /ine/	/v/
	thin	don't say /in/	/th/	(E3)	(stu)dio	don't say (stu)	dio
	shade	don't say /ade/	/sh/	(F2)	feet	don't say /eet/	/f/
	soup	don't say /oup/	/s/	(F1)	than	don't say /th/	an
	fear	don't say /ear/	/f/	(F2)	thaw	don't say /aw/	th
	veil	don't say /eil/	/v/	(F1)	gate	don't say /g/	ate

One Minute Activities Level F2

	Say:	**sit**	Now say **sit**, but don't say **/it/** → **/s/**
Or:	Say:	**sit**	Now say it again, but don't say **/it/** → **/s/**

8. Say	sit	don't say /it/	/s/	9. Say	mile	don't say /ile/	/m/
	zone	don't say /own/	/z/		side	don't say /ide/	/s/
	fuss	don't say /uss/	/f		rail	don't say /ail/	/r/
	meal	don't say /eal/	/m/		think	don't say /ink/	/th/
	lad	don't say /ad/	/l/		line	don't say /ine/	/l/
	feel	don't say /eel/	/f/		seal	don't say /eal/	/s/
	ran	don't say /an/	/r/		light	don't say /ight/	/l/
	vase	don't say /ase/	/v/		moat	don't say /oat/	/m/
	lame	don't say /ame/	/l/		fin	don't say /in/	/f/
	far	don't say /ar/	/f/		man	don't say /an/	/m/

10. Say	loan	don't say /oan/	/l/	11. Say	thin	don't say /in/	/th/
	mask	don't say /ask/	/m/		rise	don't say /ise/	/r/
	zap	don't say /ap/	/z/		miss	don't say /iss/	/m/
	face	don't say /ace/	/f/		list	don't say /ist/	/l/
	roar	don't say /oar/	/r/		fiz	don't say /iz/	/f/
	sat	don't say /at/	/s/		lap	don't say /ap/	/l/
	four	don't say /our/	/f/		zinc	don't say /ink/	/z/
	live	don't say /ive/	/l/		near	don't say /ear/	/n/
	fuel	don't say /uel/	/f/		rhyme	don't say /ime/	/r/
	nap	don't say /ap/	/n/		ship	don't say /ip/	/sh/

Mixed Levels

12. Say	thick	don't say /ick/	/th/	(F2)	sit	don't say /it/	/s/
	share	don't say /air/	/sh/	(D2)	lum(ber)	don't say (ber)	lum
	for	don't say /or/	/f/	(F2)	leave	don't say /eave/	/l/
	rat	don't say /at/	/r/	(F1)	ties	don't say /t/	eyes
	laid	don't say /aid/	/l/	(F2)	fame	don't say /ame/	/f/
	soap	don't say /oap/	/s/	(E3)	(car)nival	don't say (car)	nival
	vest	don't say /est/	/v/	(F2)	line	don't say /ine/	/l/
	road	don't say /oad/	/r/	(F1)	birth	don't say /b/	earth
	fame	don't say /ame/	/f/	(F2)	moat	don't say /oat/	/m/
	lost	don't say /ost/	/l/	(F1)	peg	don't say /p/	egg

Mixed Levels

13. Say	sore	don't say /ore/	/s/	(F2)	mask	don't say /ask/	/m/
	ripe	don't say /ipe/	/r/	(D2)	(cen)ter	don't say (cen)	ter
	fad	don't say /ad/	/f/	(F2)	list	don't say /ist/	/l/
	rich	don't say /ich/	/r/	(F1)	fall	don't say /f/	all
	night	don't say /ight/	/n/	(F2)	real	don't say /eal/	/r/
	sought	don't say /ought/	/s/	(E3)	(ac)robat	don't say (ac)	robat
	fade	don't say /ade/	/f/	(F2)	flip	don't say /ip/	/fl/
	moose	don't say /oos/	/m/	(F1)	chair	don't say /ch/	air
	real	don't say /eal/	/r/	(F2)	neat	don't say /eat/	/n/
	she	don't say /E/	/sh/	(F1)	game	don't say /g/	aim

LEVEL G

Onset-Rime Level Processing Substitution Task

Onset-Rime Level Substitution

G1 Level G1 involves exchanging single-phoneme onsets at the beginning of words.

   Samples: (wh)ite ⇢ (r)ight   (c)ub ⇢ (t)ub

G2 Level G2 involves exchanging rime units in words.

   Samples: f(it) ⇢ f(or)   t(ell) ⇢ t(ag)

Multisyllabic/Applied Activities

The *Multisyllabic/Applied* activities are designed to help children apply the phoneme awareness skills that they have learned at Level G to multi-syllabic words.

G1 This involves substituting the first sound of the second syllable of a multi-syllabic word.

   Samples: so(d)a ⇢ so(f)a   cen(t)er ⇢ sen(d)er

Special Administration Instructions for Level G

•An effort was made to match the sounds rather than the letters to make the One Minute Activities easier to administer. For example, in the above illustration *(wh)ite* ⇢ *(r)ight,* the /w/ sound is represented by a *wh,* with the *h* being silent. Also in that same example, *ite* and *ight* represent the same sound, even though the spelling is different. Remember, One Minute Activities are oral activities, so the students never see the words. These adjustments should make it easier for the teacher.

Remember: THE FOCUS IS ON THE SOUNDS, NOT SPELLING PATTERNS.

One Minute Activities Level G1

Say: **wood** Now say **wood**, but instead of **/w/** say **/g/** → **good**
Or say: **wood** Now say it again, but instead of **/w/** say **/g/** → **good**

1. Say:	wood	instead of /w/ say /g/	good	2. Say:	bad	instead of /b/ say /h/	had
	fed	instead of /f/ say /r/	red		men	instead of /m/ say /t/	ten
	sun	instead of /s/ say /f/	fun		sheep	instead of /sh/ say /k/	keep
	tab	instead of /t/ say /k/	cab		cow	instead of /k/ say /h/	how
	load	instead of /l/ say /r/	road		bake	instead of /b/ say /l/	lake
	lime	instead of /l/ say /d/	dime		joke	instead of /j/ say /w/	woke
	rain	instead of /r/ say /ch/	chain		keep	instead of /k/ say /l/	leap
	came	instead of /k/ say /g/	game		meet	instead of /m/ say /w/	wheat
	box	instead of /b/ say /f/	fox		cut	instead of /k/ say /w/	what
	mix	instead of /m/ say /s/	six		niece	instead of /n/ say /p/	piece
3. Say:	moan	instead of /m/ say /k/	cone	4. Say:	night	instead of /n/ say /b/	bite
	cane	instead of /k/ say /r/	rain		house	instead of /h/ say /m/	mouse
	bad	instead of /b/ say /m/	mad		hub	instead of /h/ say /k/	cub
	look	instead of /l/ say /b/	book		hot	instead of /h/ say /l/	lot
	care	instead of /k/ say /f/	fair		hose	instead of /h/ say /n/	nose
	kneel	instead of /n/ say /w/	wheel		six	instead of /s/ say /f/	fix
	south	instead of /s/ say /m/	mouth		hum	instead of /h/ say /s/	some
	sad	instead of /s/ say /h/	had		dime	instead of /d/ say /r/	rhyme
	fell	instead of /f/ say /b/	bell		made	instead of /m/ say /sh/	shade
	dig	instead of /d/ say /w/	wig		call	instead of /k/ say /b/	ball
5. Say:	pool	instead of /p/ say /t/	tool	6. Say:	real	instead of /r/ say /s/	seal
	hug	instead of /h/ say /t/	tug		bowl	instead of /b/ say /g/	goal
	ride	instead of /r/ say /g/	guide		pick	instead of /p/ say /k/	kick
	sing	instead of /s/ say /th/	thing		feel	instead of /f/ say /r/	real
	chill	instead of /ch/ say /f/	fill		mail	instead of /m/ say /n/	nail
	wedge	instead of /w/ say /h/	hedge		mood	instead of /m/ say /f/	food
	soup	instead of /s/ say /h/	hoop		mouse	instead of /m/ say /h/	house
	bell	instead of /b/ say /f/	fell		hush	instead of /h/ say /r/	rush
	base	instead of /b/ say /f/	face		bid	instead of /b/ say /h/	hid
	peel	instead of /p/ say /m/	meal		beach	instead of /b/ say /p/	peach

Mixed Levels

7. Say:	knife	instead of /n/ say /w/	wife	(G1)	wood	instead of /w/ say /g/	good
	hid	instead of /h/ say /k/	kid	(E3)	(bar)becue	don't say (bar)	becue
	cool	instead of /k/ say /p/	pool	(G1)	came	instead of /k/ say /g/	game
	fan	instead of /f/ say /r/	ran	(F1)	wore	don't say /w/	or
	net	instead of /n/ say /s/	set	(G1)	kneel	instead of /n/ say /w/	wheel
	guess	instead of /g/ say /y/	yes	(E3)	(mag)nify	don't say (mag)	nify
	ball	instead of /b/ say /t/	tall	(G1)	cool	instead of /k/ say /p/	pool
	rid	instead of /r/ say /d/	did	(F1)	yam	don't say /y/	am
	tax	instead of /t/ say /w/	wax	(G1)	tax	instead of /t/ say /w/	wax
	bought	instead of /b/ say /k/	caught	(F2)	shoe	don't say /oo/	/sh/

One Minute Activities Level G1

Say: **cub** Now say **cub**, but instead of **/k/** say **/t/** → **tub**
Or say: **cub** Now say it again, but instead of **/k/** say **/t/** → **tub**

8. Say:	cub	instead of /k/ say /t/	tub	9. Say:	cheese	instead of /ch/ say /n/	knees
	gum	instead of /g/ say /th/	thumb		lock	instead of /l/ say /s/	sock
	hair	instead of /h/ say /sh/	share		right	instead of /r/ say /w/	white
	wreath	instead of /r/ say /t/	teeth		cube	instead of /k/ say /t/	tube
	yawn	instead of /y/ say /g/	gone		like	instead of /l/ say /h/	hike
	wool	instead of /w/ say /f/	full		cave	instead of /k/ say /g/	gave
	loss	instead of /l/ say /s/	sauce		moose	instead of /m/ say /g/	goose
	look	instead of /l/ say /k/	cook		lot	instead of /l/ say /h/	hot
	rhyme	instead of /r/ say /t/	time		mad	instead of /m/ say /h/	had
	pin	instead of /p/ say /t/	tin		beef	instead of /b/ say /l/	leaf
10. Say:	neat	instead of /n/ say /f/	feet	11. Say:	tune	instead of /t/ say /n/	noon
	cap	instead of /k/ say /m/	map		tongue	instead of /t/ say /h/	hung
	foil	instead of /f/ say /b/	boil		wake	instead of /w/ say /l/	lake
	good	instead of /g/ say /w/	wood		nap	instead of /n/ say /k/	cap
	these	instead of /th/ say /ch/	cheese		white	instead of /w/ say /m/	might
	don't	instead of /d/ say /w/	won't		tide	instead of /t/ say /h/	hide
	give	instead of /g/ say /l/	live		beat	instead of /b/ say /f/	feet
	five	instead of /f/ say /d/	dive		weave	instead of /w/ say /l/	leave
	mat	instead of /m/ say /s/	sat		thought	instead of /th/ say /s/	sought
	kit	instead of /k/ say /n/	knit		bean	instead of /b/ say /s/	seen
12. Say:	door	instead of /d/ say /m/	more	13. Say:	woke	instead of /w/ say /j/	joke
	hut	instead of /h/ say /k/	cut		deep	instead of /d/ say /sh/	sheep
	jam	instead of /j/ say /l/	lamb		chore	instead of /ch/ say /m/	more
	vote	instead of /v/ say /k/	coat		was	instead of /w/ say /d/	does
	wait	instead of /w/ say /d/	date		done	instead of /d/ say /w/	won
	put	instead of /p/ say /f/	foot		hope	instead of /h/ say /r/	rope
	ring	instead of /r/ say /k/	king		lawn	instead of /l/ say /g/	gone
	rock	instead of /r/ say /n/	knock		than	instead of /th/ say /k/	can
	deal	instead of /d/ say /m/	meal		mile	instead of /m/ say /w/	while
	peace	instead of /p/ say /g/	geese		pat	instead of /p/ say /k/	cat

Mixed Levels

14. Say:	down	instead of /d/ say /t/	town	(G1)	hair	instead of /h/ say /sh/	share
	fall	instead of /f/ say /w/	wall	(E3)	(tri)cycle	don't say (tri)	cycle
	her	instead of /h/ say /f/	fur	(G1)	sing	instead of /s/ say /th/	thing
	goes	instead of /g/ say /r/	rose	(F1)	year	don't say /y/	ear
	beak	instead of /b/ say /w/	week	(G1)	down	instead of /d/ say /t/	town
	hoof	instead of /h/ say /r/	roof	(F2)	lap	don't say /ap/	/l/
	shore	instead of /sh/ say /d/	door	(G1)	goes	instead of /g/ say /r/	rose
	king	instead of /k/ say /r/	ring	(F1)	cheese	don't say /ch/	ease
	boat	instead of /b/ say /n/	note	(G1)	like	instead of /l/ say /h/	hike
	loss	instead of /l/ say /t/	toss	(E4)	(el)ephant	don't say (el)	ephant

One Minute Activities Level G1

Say: **fur** Now say fur, but instead of /f/ say /h/ → **her**
Or say: **fur** Now say it again, but instead of /f/ say /h/ → **her**

15. Say:	fur	instead of /f/ say /w/	were	16. Say:	knock	instead of /n/ say /l/	lock
	gain	instead of /g/ say /r/	rain		lack	instead of /l/ say /t/	tack
	dial	instead of /d/ say /m/	mile		nut	instead of /n/ say /w/	what
	took	instead of /t/ say /sh/	shook		pack	instead of /p/ say /t/	tack
	need	instead of /n/ say /f/	feed		hid	instead of /h/ say /d/	did
	cuff	instead of /k/ say /r/	rough		tough	instead of /t/ say /k/	cuff
	met	instead of /m/ say /p/	pet		voice	instead of /v/ say /ch/	choice
	night	instead of /n/ say /w/	white		bush	instead of /b/ say /p/	push
	does	instead of /d/ say /w/	was		chair	instead of /ch/ say /h/	hair
	near	instead of /n/ say /y/	year		sun	instead of /s/ say /n/	none
17. Say:	peach	instead of /p/ say /r/	reach	18. Say:	path	instead of /p/ say /m/	math
	wait	instead of /w/ say /g/	gate		booth	instead of /b/ say /t/	tooth
	save	instead of /s/ say /w/	wave		deck	instead of /d/ say /ch/	check
	set	instead of /s/ say /m/	met		rack	instead of /r/ say /b/	back
	read	instead of /r/ say /n/	need		bet	instead of /b/ say /g/	get
	much	instead of /m/ say /s/	such		toss	instead of /t/ say /l/	loss
	boot	instead of /b/ say /r/	root		math	instead of /m/ say /p/	path
	tooth	instead of /t/ say /b/	booth		meal	instead of /m/ say /w/	wheel
	map	instead of /m/ say /t/	tap		dock	instead of /d/ say /r/	rock
	tick	instead of /t/ say /k/	kick		chip	instead of /ch/ say /l/	lip

Mixed Levels

19. Say:	kid	instead of /k/ say /l/	lid	(G1)	door	instead of /d/ say /m/	more
	heat	instead of /h/ say /s/	seat	(E3)	(pho)tograph	don't say (pho)	tograph
	raise	instead of /r/ say /d/	days	(G1)	wait	instead of /w/ say /g/	gate
	gate	instead of /g/ say /l/	late	(F1)	rake	don't say /r/	ache
	cup	instead of /k/ say /p/	pup	(G1)	raise	instead of /r/ say /d/	days
	book	instead of /b/ say /t/	took	(F2)	zinc	don't say /ink/	/z/
	fun	instead of /f/ say /n/	none	(G1)	seal	instead of /s/ say /w/	wheel
	seal	instead of /s/ say /w/	wheel	(F1)	his	don't say /h/	is
	cone	instead of /k/ say /ph/	phone	(G1)	mile	instead of /m/ say /w/	while
	feed	instead of /f/ say /r/	read	(E4)	(hurr)icane	don't say (hurr)	icane

Mixed Levels

20. Say:	kite	instead of /k/ say /m/	might	(G1)	does	instead of /d/ say /w/	was
	goat	instead of /g/ say /r/	wrote	(E3)	(in)fluence	don't say (in)	fluence
	pan	instead of /p/ say /r/	ran	(G1)	five	instead of /f/ say /d/	dive
	choose	instead of /ch/ say /sh/	shoes	(F1)	tall	don't say /t/	all
	note	instead of /n/ say /b/	boat	(G1)	gone	instead of /g/ say /l/	lawn
	head	instead of /h/ say /sh/	shed	(F2)	food	don't say /ood/	/f/
	seek	instead of /s/ say /w/	week	(G1)	wake	instead of /w/ say /l/	lake
	gone	instead of /g/ say /l/	lawn	(F1)	race	don't say /r/	ace
	get	instead of /g/ say /s/	set	(G1)	white	instead of /w/ say /m/	might
	feet	instead of /f/ say /h/	heat	(E4)	(tel)escope	don't say (tel)	escope

Supplemental One Minute Activities for Level G1

Say: **lit**   Now say **lit** but instead of /l/ say /b/ → **bit**
Or say: **lit**   Now say it again, but instead of /l/ say /b/ → **bit**

S1				S2				S3			
	lit	/l/ to /b/	bit		reach	/r/ to /t/	teach		hive	/h/ to /f/	five
	man	/m/ to /p/	pan		file	/f/ to /w/	while		ripe	/r/ to /t/	type
	chin	/ch/ to /w/	win		coat	/k/ to /b/	boat		line	/l/ to /f/	fine
	this	/th/ to /m/	miss		less	/l/ to /g/	guess		hop	/h/ to /t/	top
	bike	/b/ to /l/	like		name	/n/ to /k/	came		lid	/l/ to /h/	hid
	guide	/g/ to /w/	wide		rim	/r/ to /h/	him		jar	/j/ to /f/	far
	news	/n/ to /h/	whose		wide	/w/ to /s/	side		more	/m/ to /r/	roar
	chime	/ch/ to /t/	time		run	/r/ to /d/	done		late	/l/ to /w/	wait
	nose	/n/ to /t/	toes		same	/s/ to /g/	game		rope	/r/ to /h/	hope
	pouch	/p/ to /k/	couch		rice	/r/ to /m/	mice		join	/j/ to /k/	coin

S4				S5				S6			
	pull	/p/ to /w/	wool		rich	/r/ to /w/	which		mine	/m/ to /s/	sign
	wing	/w/ to /r/	ring		chick	/ch/ to /k/	kick		nail	/n/ to /p/	pail
	bug	/b/ to /r/	rug		loop	/l/ to /s/	soup		chain	/ch/ to /m/	main
	cage	/k/ to /p/	page		note	/n/ to /g/	goat		cop	/k/ to /m/	mop
	height	/h/ to /s/	sight		mine	/m/ to /n/	nine		for	/f/ to /sh/	shore
	chief	/ch/ to /l/	leaf		choice	/ch/ to /v/	voice		cheap	/ch/ to /k/	keep
	bed	/b/ to /s/	said		mop	/m/ to /sh/	shop		root	/r/ to /b/	boot
	full	/f/ to /w/	wool		more	/m/ to /f/	four		lease	/l/ to /n/	neice
	game	/g/ to /s/	same		dish	/d/ to /f/	fish		jet	/j/ to /g/	get
	make	/m/ to /t/	take		nudge	/n/ to /b/	budge		bat	/b/ to /h/	hat

S7				S8				S9			
	mall	/m/ to /k/	call		pup	/p/ to /k/	cup		hill	/h/ to /w/	will
	hide	/h/ to /r/	ride		rig	/r/ to /b/	big		lane	/l/ to /g/	gain
	got	/g/ to /n/	not		mice	/m/ to /n/	nice		light	/l/ to /k/	kite
	check	/ch/ to /n/	neck		coil	/k/ to /b/	boil		fur	/f/ to /h/	her
	noise	/n/ to /t/	toys		job	/j/ to /n/	knob		hat	/h/ to /s/	sat
	moon	/m/ to /s/	soon		chew	/ch/ to /d/	do		nice	/n/ to /r/	rice
	code	/k/ to /t/	toad		laugh	/l/ to /k/	calf		case	/k/ to /r/	race
	hall	/h/ to /t/	tall		beam	/b/ to /t/	team		jeep	/j/ to /k/	keep
	page	/p/ to /k/	cage		heal	/h/ to /m/	meal		rip	/r/ to /l/	lip
	cheer	/ch/ to /h/	hear		led	/l/ to /s/	said		road	/r/ to /k/	code

Multisyllabic/Applied
One Minute Activities Level G1

See note about multisyllabic/applied activites on page 91 and 160

Say: **center** Now say **center**, but instead of /t/ say /d/ → **sender**
Or say: **center** Now say it again, but instead of /t/ say /d/ → **sender**

1. Say:	center	instead of /t/ say /d/	sender	2. Say:	reading	instead of /d/ say /ch/	reaching
	laser	instead of /z/ say /t/	later		linen	instead of /n/ say /s/	listen
	flicker	instead of /k/ say /p/	flipper		either	instead of /th/ say /t/	eater
	sofa	instead of /f/ say /d/	soda		tiger	instead of /g/ say /m/	timer
	stunning	instead of /n/ say /f/	stuffing		clipping	instead of /p/ say /k/	clicking
	clover	instead of /v/ say /s/	closer		raisin	instead of /z/ say /v/	raven
	washer	instead of /sh/ say /t/	water		dinner	instead of /n/ say /p/	dipper
	speeder	instead of /d/ say /k/	speaker		supper	instead of /p/ say /f/	suffer
	quicker	instead of /k/ say /t/	quitter		heading	instead of /d/ say /m/	hemming
	meeting	instead of /t/ say /n/	meaning		seven	instead of /v/ say /sh/	session

3. Say:	odor	instead of /d/ say /v/	over	4. Say:	coaxing	instead of /ks/ say /t/	coating
	dimmer	instead of /m/ say /n/	dinner		rhymer	instead of /m/ say /d/	rider
	trading	instead of /d/ say /n/	training		pudding	instead of /d/ say /l/	pulling
	stable	instead of /b/ say /p/	staple		differ	instead of /f/ say /m/	dimmer
	covering	instead of /v/ say /l/	coloring		patient	instead of /sh/ say /m/	payment
	slimmer	instead of /m/ say /v/	sliver		sliver	instead of /v/ say /p/	slipper
	ocean	instead of /sh/ say /p/	open		cyber	instead of /b/ say /d/	cider
	scatter	instead of /t/ say /n/	scanner		quiver	instead of /v/ say /k/	quicker
	reaping	instead of /p/ say /ch/	reaching		liken	instead of /k/ say /t/	lighten
	lather	instead of /th/ say /d/	ladder		plucking	instead of /k/ say /m/	plumbing

5. Say:	lesser	instead of /s/ say /t/	letter
	stocking	instead of /k/ say /p/	stopping
	crossing	instead of /s/ say /l/	crawling
	shimmer	instead of /m/ say /v/	shiver
	coming	instead of /m/ say /t/	cutting
	richer	instead of /ch/ say /v/	river
	glimmer	instead of /m/ say /t/	glitter
	pushing	instead of /sh/ say /l/	pulling
	lever	instead of /v/ say /t/	letter
	rougher	instead of /f/ say /n/	runner

Multisyllabic/Applied
One Minute Activities Level G1

See note about multisyllabic/applied activites on page 91 and 160

Say: **wager**   Now say **wager**, but instead of /j/ say /t/ → **waiter**
Or say: **wager**   Now say it again, but instead of /j/ say /t/ → **waiter**

6. Say:
wager	instead of /j/ say /t/	waiter
numbing	instead of /m/ say /th/	nothing
roughing	instead of /f/ say /sh/	rushing
winning	instead of /n/ say /sh/	wishing
ruler	instead of /l/ say /m/	rumor
meager	instead of /g/ say /t/	meter
steamer	instead of /m/ say /p/	steeper
property	instead of /t/ say /l/	properly
tripping	instead of /p/ say /m/	trimming
supper	instead of /p/ say /m/	summer

7. Say:
shocking	instead of /k/ say /p/	shopping
resolution	instead of /z/ say /v/	revolution
rover	instead of /v/ say /l/	roller
shaping	instead of /p/ say /v/	shaving
zither	instead of /th/ say /p/	zipper
wither	instead of /th/ say /n/	winner
rebel	instead of /b/ say /v/	revel
warping	instead of /p/ say /m/	warming
trimming	instead of /m/ say /k/	tricking
cloaking	instead of /k/ say /th/	clothing

8. Say:
grating	instead of /t/ say /z/	grazing
webbing	instead of /b/ say /d/	wedding
receiving	instead of /s/ say /l/	relieving
seeding	instead of /d/ say /p/	seeping
wafer	instead of /f/ say /j/	wager
liver	instead of /v/ say /t/	litter
pretention	instead of /t/ say /v/	prevention
upper	instead of /p/ say /sh/	usher
teaser	instead of /z/ say /ch/	teacher
clatter	instead of /t/ say /p/	clapper

9. Say:
robber	instead of /b/ say /k/	rocker
tenor	instead of /n/ say /l/	teller
sever	instead of /v/ say /t/	setter
roper	instead of /p/ say /l/	roller
profession	instead of /f/ say /s/	procession
rehiring	instead of /h/ say /t/	retiring
deter	instead of /t/ say /f/	defer
rudder	instead of /d/ say /n/	runner
other	instead of /th/ say /d/	udder
walking	instead of /k/ say /sh/	washing

10. Say:
owner	instead of /n/ say /v/	over
rubbing	instead of /b/ say /n/	running
prevent	instead of /v/ say /z/	present
missing	instead of /s/ say /ks/	mixing
shipper	instead of /p/ say /v/	shiver
warping	instead of /p/ say /n/	warning
rather	instead of /th/ say /p/	wrapper
waver	instead of /v/ say /t/	waiter
reliever	instead of /l/ say /s/	receiver
professional	instead of /f/ say /s/	processional

One Minute Activities Level G2

Say: **his** Now say **his**, but instead of **/is/** say **/ad/** → **had**
Or say: **his** Now say it again, but instead of **/is/** say **/ad/** → **had**

1. Say:				2. Say:			
	his	instead of /iz/ say /ad/	had		back	instead of /ack/ say /ug/	bug
	far	instead of /ar/ say /un/	fun		man	instead of /an/ say /iss/	miss
	big	instead of /ig/ say /at/	bat		fan	instead of /an/ say /or/	for
	mad	instead of /ad/ say /en/	men		gag	instead of /ag/ say /um/	gum
	pet	instead of /et/ say /ack/	pack		fax	instead of /ax/ say /ib/	fib
	rug	instead of /ug/ say /eck/	wreck		buck	instead of /uck/ say /us/	bus
	what	instead of /ut/ say /ell/	well		win	instead of /in/ say /eb/	web
	did	instead of /id/ say /un/	done		sun	instead of /un/ say /ed/	said
	tall	instead of /all/ say /op/	top		nick	instead of /ick/ say /od/	nod
	sob	instead of /ob/ say /ad/	sad		calm	instead of /om/ say /ut/	cut

3. Say:				4. Say:			
	run	instead of /un/ say /ed/	red		fit	instead of /it/ say /ed/	fed
	cab	instead of /ab/ say /op/	cop		jab	instead of /ab/ say /og/	jog
	leg	instead of /eg/ say /ip/	lip		map	instead of /ap/ say /itt/	mitt
	tap	instead of /ap/ say /uck/	tuck		lick	instead of /ick/ say /eg/	leg
	mall	instead of /all/ say /et/	met		big	instead of /ig/ say /us/	bus
	six	instead of /ix/ say /ack/	sack		tan	instead of /an/ say /ub/	tub
	guess	instead of /ess/ say /ut/	gut		fed	instead of /ed/ say /ill/	fill
	well	instead of /ell/ say /un/	won		tick	instead of /ick/ say /ab/	tab
	cat	instead of /at/ say /um/	come		sack	instead of /ack/ say /ill/	sill
	fin	instead of /in/ say /ox/	fox		cup	instead of /up/ say /an/	can

5. Say:				6. Say:			
	ball	instead of /all/ say /ox/	box		map	instead of /ap/ say /itt/	mitt
	cab	instead of /ab/ say /up/	cup		safe	instead of /afe/ say /ink/	sink
	hat	instead of /at/ say /im/	him		wreck	instead of /eck/ say /un/	run
	run	instead of /un/ say /ed/	red		sun	instead of /un/ say /ed/	said
	dad	instead of /ad/ say /ig/	dig		web	instead of /eb/ say /all/	wall
	cup	instead of /up/ say /an/	can		mix	instead of /ix/ say /utt/	mutt
	west	instead of /est/ say /ink/	wink		ring	instead of /ing/ say /est/	rest
	rack	instead of /ack/ say /ib/	rib		weed	instead of /eed/ say /in/	win
	where	instead of /air/ say /in/	win		rock	instead of /ock/ say /ag/	rag
	net	instead of /et/ say /ock/	knock		pup	instead of /up/ say /in/	pin

Mixed Levels

7. Say:							
	rough	instead of /uff/ say /at/	rat	(G2)	far	instead of /ar/ say /un/	fun
	top	instead of /op/ say /in/	tin	(F1)	chill	don't say /ch/	ill
	maam	instead of /am/ say /ill/	mill	(G2)	tall	instead of /all/ say /op/	top
	cub	instead of /ub/ say /at/	cat	(F2)	sixth	don't say /ixth/	/s/
	let	instead of /et/ say /am/	lamb	(G2)	cub	instead of /ub/ say /at/	cat
	fun	instead of /un/ say /all/	fall	(G1)	knife	instead of /n/ say /w/	wife
	net	instead of /et/ say /ock/	knock	(G2)	fan	instead of /an/ say /or/	for
	pick	instead of /ick/ say /ad/	pad	(G1)	net	instead of /n/ say /s/	set
	rid	instead of /id/ say /ug/	rug	(G2)	sun	instead of /un/ say /ed/	said
	cup	instead of /up/ say /ar/	car	(F2)	ring	don't say /ing/	/r/

One Minute Activities Level G2

Say: **ball** Now say **ball**, but instead of /all/ say /ox/ → **box**
Or say: **ball** Now say it again, but instead of /all/ say /ox/ → **box**

8. Say:	well	instead of /ell/ say /un/	won	9. Say:	has	instead of /az/ say /it/	hit
	box	instead of /ox/ say /ike/	bike		knock	instead of /ock/ say /et/	net
	read	instead of /eed/ say /uff/	rough		time	instead of /ime/ say /ap/	tap
	tip	instead of /ip/ say /ag/	tag		pat	instead of /at/ say /in/	pin
	head	instead of /ed/ say /ill/	hill		lack	instead of /ack/ say /id/	lid
	lack	instead of /ack/ say /it/	lit		tan	instead of /an/ say /ub/	tub
	mail	instead of /ail/ say /ite/	might		map	instead of /ap/ say /ice/	mice
	tab	instead of /ab/ say /ick/	tick		tell	instead of /ell/ say /ug/	tug
	fed	instead of /ed/ say /ill/	fill		six	instead of /ix/ say /ack/	sack
	miss	instead of /iss/ say /ud/	mud		fax	instead of /ax/ say /ib/	fib
10. Say:	zap	instead of /ap/ say /oom/	zoom	11. Say:	nose	instead of /ose/ say /oon/	noon
	lamb	instead of /am/ say /aust/	lost		tug	instead of /ug/ say /ell/	tell
	pick	instead of /ick/ say /ad/	pad		hall	instead of /all/ say /en/	hen
	goat	instead of /oat/ say /ide/	guide		what	instead of /ut/ say /en/	when
	lid	instead of /id/ say /ap/	lap		seal	instead of /eal/ say /it/	sit
	neck	instead of /eck/ say /ob/	knob		man	instead of /an/ say /iss/	miss
	tough	instead of /uff/ say /ax/	tax		nest	instead of /est/ say /ot/	not
	tub	instead of /ub/ say /an/	tan		sad	instead of /ad/ say /ick/	sick
	man	instead of /an/ say /et/	met		tape	instead of /ape/ say /in/	tin
	rut	instead of /ut/ say /ib/	rib		fill	instead of /ill/ say /ar/	far

Mixed Levels

12 Say:	peg	instead of /eg/ say /in/	pin	(G2)	ball	instead of /all/ say /ox/	box
	leg	instead of /eg/ say /id/	lid	(F1)	tin	don't say /t/	in
	red	instead of /ed/ say /im/	rim	(G2)	mail	instead of /ail/ say /ix/	mix
	wall	instead of /all/ say /ut/	what	(F2)	rich	don't say /ich/	/r/
	let	instead of /et/ say /am/	lamb	(G2)	red	instead of /ed/ say /im/	rim
	den	instead of /en/ say /im/	dim	(G1)	fan	instead of /f/ say /r/	ran
	pop	instead of /op/ say /en/	pen	(G2)	rid	instead of /id/ say /at/	rat
	wax	instead of /ax/ say /in/	win	(G1)	net	instead of /n/ say /s/	set
	pen	instead of /en/ say /up/	pup	(G2)	knock	instead of /ock/ say /et/	net
	what	instead of /ut/ say /ell/	well	(F2)	night	don't say /ight/	//n/

Mixed Levels

13. Say:	well	instead of /ell/ say /ish/	wish	(G2)	lamb	instead of /am/ say /ap/	lap
	car	instead of /ar/ say /ut/	cut	(G1)	cool	instead of /k/ say /p/	pool
	boat	instead of /oat/ say /us/	bus	(G2)	mill	instead of /ill/ say /op/	mop
	knit	instead of /it/ say /un/	none	(F1)	chime	don't say /ch/	I'm
	tax	instead of /ax/ say /uff/	tough	(G2)	guess	instead of /ess/ say /ift/	gift
	mat	instead of /at/ say /ix/	mix	(F2)	she	don't say /ee/	sh
	nap	instead of /ap/ say /ice/	nice	(G2)	fell	instead of /ell/ say /ox/	fox
	top	instead of /op/ say /all/	tall	(F1)	tore	don't say /t/	or
	won	instead of /un/ say /ig/	wig	(G2)	mat	instead of /at/ say /ix/	mix
	pat	instead of /at/ say /op/	pop	(G1)	net	instead of /n/ say /s/	set

PHONEME-LEVEL ACTIVITIES

LEVELS H THROUGH N

First Grade, Second Grade, and Older Struggling Readers (including adults)

Basic Phoneme Processing
Levels H1, H2
Levels I1, I2

Advanced Phoneme Processing
Level J
Levels K1, K2
Levels L1, L2
Levels M1, M2
Levels N1, N2 (optional)

BASIC PHONEME LEVELS

The position of a sound within the syllable and the type of phoneme manipulation (deletion or substitution) are the factors which separate the basic phoneme levels from the advanced ones. Level H is easier than Levels J through M because it involves manipulating the *first sound* within a word. However, to do this, the student must split an initial blend. Levels F and G also manipulate the first sound within a word, but they are easier than H because they break the word at the onset-rime juncture. Level H qualifies as a true phoneme manipulation because it involves splitting a blend, and does not break at the onset-rime juncture. The following examples illustrate how Level H differs from Levels F and G:

		BASIC PHONEME TASK The split is between two consonants within a blend		ONSET-RIME TASK The split is before the vowel, at the onset-rime juncture
deletion	Level H1	(b)lock ⇝ lock	Level F1	(s)at ⇝ at
substitution	Level H2	(t)ried ⇝ (f)ried	Level G1	(t)in ⇝ (w)in

Thus, while F, G, and H all manipulate the first sound within the syllable, H is more difficult because it involves splitting two phonemes within a blend. Though more difficult than F and G, Level H is one of the easiest phoneme-level manipulations because it involves the first sound.

Deletion and substitution are of a similar level of difficulty when splitting initial blends, so these tasks are both part of Level H (i.e., H1 and H2). However, manipulating ending sounds is different. It is much easier for a student developing phoneme awareness to delete an ending sound than to substitute an ending sound. Most students can delete an ending sound in first grade but cannot substitute ending sounds until second grade. For this reason, deleting and substituting sounds are separate levels in the program. Level I involves deleting ending sounds, which is a basic phoneme task. Level L substitutes ending sounds, and it is an advanced phoneme level. Level I1 and I2 appear to be of similar difficulty, even though the final sound in I1 words represents the second sound in a blend (e.g., go from *card* to *car*). For many students, I1 will be easier than I2.

There is some research to suggest that I is a little easier than H. My own experience evaluating hundreds of children is that these levels are very similar in difficulty. I recently analyzed data on 130 referred students, and the group totals for H and I were identical. However, what is important is that H and I are more difficult than F and G, and most definitely easier than Levels J through N. Because of this, the distinction is made between basic and advanced phoneme processing.

In addition to splitting two phoneme blends (H1, H2, I2) students need to be able to develop phoneme awareness with three phoneme blends. To allow children to sharpen their phonological awareness for blends, Level H1 *Challenge Words* are included after the supplementary H1 *One Minute Activities*. These *Challenge Words* all include three phoneme blends. All initial three phoneme blends begin with the letter *s* (e.g., *spring, split, street*). Thus, there can be no substitution of the initial phoneme, which is why there are no *Challenge Word*s for H2.

Remember: THE FOCUS IS ON THE SOUNDS, NOT SPELLING PATTERNS.

LEVEL H

Basic Phoneme-level Processing
Manipulating the First Sound in Initial Blends

H1 Level H1 involves deleting the first sound in a word, but the student must split an initial blend in order to delete this first sound.
   Samples: (t)rim → rim   (s)nail → nail

H2 Level H2 involves substituting the first sound in a word, but the student must split an initial blend in order to make the substitution.
   Samples: (b)lue → (g)lue   (d)ry → (f)ry

H1 Challenge Words (Three Phoneme Blends)

H1 has an extra, Challenge Words section that involves deleting one or two phonemes from words with three phoneme blends (see p. 91) These can be done after students have mastered H1 activities or done alongside the regular H1 activities. For most children, this will present no difficulty. For others, you may need to provide additional instruction about these three phoneme blends.

   Samples: (s)tray → tray or dray   (sc)rub → rub

Note that in some instances, the first of the three sounds in the blend is removed while in others, the first two sounds are deleted. Both are instances of H1 type manipulations.

Multiple correct answers for some items

Some words have more than one correct answer listed because many blends that begin with the letter *s* (*sp, st, sc,* etc.) change the sound of the second consonant. For example, the sound made by the letter *t* in the word *stray* is actually a /d/ sound. The /d/ and /t/ use the same mouth position, but the /d/ is *voiced* (uses vocal cords) while the /t/ is *non-voiced* (does not use vocal cords). To illustrate this issue, say: *spot*. Now say *spot* without the /s/. Most people respond "*pot.*" But if you say *spot* slowly, you will notice the second sound is the voiced /b/ and not the unvoiced /p/. You are not saying *s-pot,* but more like *sbot*. So, in a case like this, the student would get credit for either *pot* or *bot*. This is why more than one answer is listed for some of the *s* blends, especially in the *Challenge Words* (e.g., *strain* → *train* or *drain; sprint* → *print* or *brint*).

Problems with the manipulation of phonemes within blends

A small subset of students with phoneme awareness difficulties struggle more with blends than with other aspects of phoneme awareness. This means that Levels H, K, and M are particularly difficult and may require additional instructional help. The techniques described in Chapter 8 can be used to assure that students will master the manipulation of blends.

Remember: THE FOCUS IS ON THE SOUNDS, NOT SPELLING PATTERNS.

One Minute Activities Level H1

	Say:	brush	Now say **brush**, but don't say /b/	rush
	Or say:	brush	Now say it again, but don't say /b/	rush

1. Say:	brush	don't say /b/	rush	2. Say:	plane	don't say /p/	lane
	great	don't say /g/	rate		snip	don't say /s/	nip
	ski	don't say /s/	key *or* ghee		claim	don't say /k/	lame
	trim	don't say /t/	rim		shrug	don't say /sh/	rug
	scare	don't say /s/	care *or* gare		trail	don't say /t/	rail
	clap	don't say /k/	lap		scan	don't say /s/	can *or* gan
	snap	don't say /s/	nap		fried	don't say /f/	ride
	climb	don't say /k/	lime		fled	don't say /f/	led
	snail	don't say /s/	nail		sneeze	don't say /s/	knees
	drawer	don't say /d/	roar		throw	don't say /th/	row

3. Say:	Fred	don't say /f/	red	4. Say:	scoop	don't say /s/	coop *or* goop
	shrub	don't say /sh/	rub		dry	don't say /d/	rye
	trend	don't say /t/	rend		slip	don't say /s/	lip
	broom	don't say /b/	room		truth	don't say /t/	Ruth
	skate	don't say /s/	gate *or* Kate		skit	don't say /s/	kit *or* git
	clean	don't say /k/	lean		crash	don't say /k/	rash
	flyer	don't say /f/	liar		swish	don't say /s/	wish
	scant	don't say /s/	can't *or* gant		glide	don't say /g/	lied
	twin	don't say /t/	win		speech	don't say /s/	peach *or* beach
	span	don't say /s/	pan *or* ban		glump	don't say /g/	lump

5. Say:	fright	don't say /f/	right	6. Say:	grave	don't say /g/	rave
	glad	don't say /g/	lad		skid	don't say /s/	kid *or* gid
	sleep	don't say /s/	leap		troll	don't say /t/	roll
	bland	don't say /b/	land		clock	don't say /k/	lock
	slack	don't say /s/	lack		flute	don't say /f/	loot
	grow	don't say /g/	row		slap	don't say /s/	lap
	phrase	don't say /f/	raise		ply	don't say /p/	lie
	snow	don't say /s/	no		grail	don't say /g/	rail
	frail	don't say /f/	rail		trap	don't say /t/	rap
	glee	don't say /g/	Lee		crave	don't say /k/	rave

Mixed Levels

7. Say:	brake	don't say /b/	rake	(G1)	look	instead of /l/ say /k/	cook
	slam	don't say /s/	lamb	(F1)	same	don't say /s/	aim
	flake	don't say /f/	lake	(F2)	mat	don't say /at/	/m/
	smile	don't say /s/	mile	(H1)	drain	don't say /d/	rain
	bread	don't say /b/	red	(G1)	cold	instead of /k/ say /s/	sold
	slow	don't say /s/	low	(H1)	sleep	don't say /s/	leap
	proof	don't say /p/	roof	(H1)	flap	don't say /f/	lap
	school	don't say /s/	cool *or* ghoul	(G1)	time	instead of /t/ say /d/	dime
	tweak	don't say /t/	weak	(G2)	cat	instead of /at/ say /up/	cup
	scab	don't say /s/	cab *or* gab	(G1)	team	instead of /t/ say /s/	seem

One Minute Activities Level H1

	Say:	**fright**	Now say **fright**, but don't say **/f/** → **right**
	Or say:	**fright**	Now say it again, but don't say **/f/** → **right**

8. Say:	slight	don't say /s/	light	9. Say:	space	don't say /s/	pace or base
	breach	don't say /b/	reach		spare	don't say /s/	pair or bear
	slump	don't say /s/	lump		plug	don't say /p/	lug
	style	don't say /s/	tile or dial		freight	don't say /f/	rate
	brook	don't say /b/	rook		cloud	don't say /k/	loud
	slung	don't say /s/	lung		spine	don't say /s/	pine or bine
	cramp	don't say /k/	ramp		pry	don't say /p/	rye
	swing	don't say /s/	wing		stung	don't say /s/	tongue or dung
	tried	don't say /t/	ride		brink	don't say /b/	rink
	still	don't say /s/	till or dill		spark	don't say /s/	park or bark

10. Say:	school	don't say /s/	cool or ghoul	11. Say:	plot	don't say /p/	lot
	groom	don't say /g/	room		black	don't say /b/	lack
	place	don't say /p/	lace		crate	don't say /k/	rate
	thread	don't say /th/	red		prose	don't say /p/	rose
	clamp	don't say /k/	lamp		flatten	don't say /f/	Latin
	friend	don't say /f/	rend		Spain	don't say /s/	pain or bain
	glean	don't say /g/	lean		broil	don't say /b/	royal
	strain	don't say /s/	train or drain		glory	don't say /g/	Lori
	fray	don't say /f/	ray		shrink	don't say /sh/	rink
	sleeve	don't say /s/	leave		blush	don't say /b/	lush

12. Say:	crime	don't say /k/	rhyme	13. Say:	sleek	don't say /s/	leak
	swore	don't say /s/	wore		froze	don't say /f/	rose
	drank	don't say /d/	rank		fruit	don't say /f/	root
	slid	don't say /s/	lid		scoop	don't say /s/	coop or goop
	plaid	don't say /p/	lad		cram	don't say /k/	ram
	sloop	don't say /s/	loop		scold	don't say /s/	cold
	thrash	don't say /th/	rash		crank	don't say /k/	rank
	flax	don't say /f/	lax		spin	don't say /s/	pin or bin
	blight	don't say /b/	light		flit	don't say /f/	lit
	stew	don't say /s/	too or do		Scott	don't say /s/	cot

Mixed Levels

14. Say:	pluck	don't say /p/	luck	(G1)	boat	instead of /b/ say /g/	goat
	stilt	don't say /s/	tilt or dilt	(F1)	soar	don't say /s/	oar
	shrank	don't say /sh/	rank	(F2)	ride	don't say /ide/	/r/
	glow	don't say /g/	low	(H1)	crust	don't say /k/	rust
	struck	don't say /s/	truck or druck	(G1)	rake	instead of /r/ say /t/	take
	freed	don't say /f/	read	(G1)	slim	don't say /s/	limb
	bring	don't say /b/	ring	(H1)	frisk	don't say /f/	risk
	slash	don't say /s/	lash	(G1)	hike	instead of /h/ say /b/	bike
	bright	don't say /b/	right	(G2)	top	instead of /op/ say /ug/	tug
	stall	don't say /s/	tall or dall	(F2)	see	don't say /s/	ee

One Minute Activities Level H1

Say: **school** Now say **school**, but don't say **/s/** → **cool**
Or: **school** without saying **/s/** → **cool**

15. Say:				16. Say:			
	graze	don't say /g/	raise		slate	don't say /s/	late
	fries	don't say /f/	rise		flow	don't say /f/	low
	scream	don't say /s/	cream or gream		slot	don't say /s/	lot
	throb	don't say /th/	rob		stray	don't say /s/	tray or dray
	glade	don't say /g/	laid		Fran	don't say /f/	ran
	crane	don't say /k/	rain		sly	don't say /s/	lie
	shred	don't say /sh/	red		blend	don't say /b/	lend
	fried	don't say /f/	ride		slide	don't say /s/	lied
	slug	don't say /s/	lug		clash	don't say /k/	lash
	gravel	don't say /g/	ravel		slab	don't say /s/	lab

17. Say:				18. Say:			
	spill	don't say /s/	pill or bill		preach	don't say /p/	reach
	thrice	don't say /th/	rice		scuff	don't say /s/	cuff or guff
	scorn	don't say /s/	corn or gorn		grade	don't say /g/	raid
	grain	don't say /g/	rain		stride	don't say /s/	tried or dried
	swim	don't say /s/	whim		brief	don't say /b/	reef
	fly	don't say /f/	lie		sleigh	don't say /s/	lay
	brunt	don't say /b/	runt		pray	don't say /p/	ray
	scar	don't say /s/	car or gar		slaw	don't say /s/	law
	try	don't say /t/	rye		prong	don't say /p/	wrong
	stone	don't say /s/	tone or doan		slump	don't say /s/	lump

Mixed Levels

19. Say:							
	dream	don't say /d/	ream	(G1)	tune	instead of /t/ say /n/	noon
	smash	don't say /s/	mash	(F2)	fight	don't say /ight/	/f/
	crow	don't say /k/	row	(F1)	cat	don't say /k/	at
	clay	don't say /k/	lay	(H1)	flight	don't say /f/	light
	snore	don't say /s/	nor	(G1)	roast	instead of /r/ say /t/	toast
	prod	don't say /p/	rod	(F1)	face	don't say /f/	ace
	spool	don't say /s/	pool or bool	(H1)	flow	don't say /f/	low
	clone	don't say /k/	lone	(F2)	lamp	don't say /amp/	/l/
	small	don't say /s/	mall	(F1)	charm	don't say /ch/	arm
	thrust	don't say /th/	rust	(G1)	made	instead of /m/ say /sh/	shade

Mixed Levels

20. Say:							
	claws	don't say /k/	laws	(H1)	bride	don't say /b/	ride
	stop	don't say /s/	top or dop	(F2)	vase	don't say /ase/	/v/
	smart	don't say /s/	mart	(G2)	cut	instead of /ut/ say /ap/	cap
	throng	don't say /th/	wrong	(G1)	road	instead of /r/ say /t/	toad
	sweet	don't say /s/	wheat	(H1)	spike	don't say /s/	pike or bike
	flock	don't say /f/	lock	(F1)	cart	don't say /k/	art
	scope	don't say /s/	cope or gope	(G1)	house	instead of /h/ say /m/	mouse
	brute	don't say /b/	root	(F1)	soak	don't say /s/	oak
	sled	don't say /s/	led	(H1)	fly	don't say /f/	lie
	trod	don't say /t/	rod	(G1)	coat	instead of /k/ say /r/	wrote

Supplemental One Minute Activities for Level H1

Say: **claw**   Now say **claw**, but don't say /k/ → **law**
Or say: **claw**   Now say it again, but don't say /k/ → **law**

S1	(c)law → law	S2	(s)tun → ton *or* done	S3	(c)reed → reed
	(s)wept → wept		(t)rip → rip		(s)cript → crypt *or* gripped
	(g)rasp → rasp		(s)kin → kin *or* gin		(c)lot → lot
	(s)tuff → tough *or* duff		(b)rag → rag		(s)nack → knack
	(b)loom → loom		(s)py → pie *or* by		(c)rag → rag
	(s)melt → melt		(b)leak → leak		(c)reep → reap
	(b)lues → lose		(s)lop → lop		(s)worn → worn
	(s)par → par *or* bar		(b)leed → lead		(b)runt → runt
	(p)latter → latter		(s)nag → nag		(s)teep → teep *or* deep
	(s)mash → mash		(b)rought → wrought		(d)ream → ream

S4	(p)lay → lay	S5	(b)raille → rail	S6	(d)rag → rag
	(s)nitch → nitch		(s)tare → tear *or* dare		(s)candal → candle *or* gandle
	(b)rash → rash		(s)pout → pout *or* bout		(b)rat → rat
	(s)core → core *or* gore		(s)well → well		(sh)rewd → rude
	(s)weat → wet		(b)link → link		(b)led → led
	(s)mack → Mac		(s)lept → lept		(s)weep → weep
	(b)ran → ran		(b)reed → read		(b)rig → rig
	(s)neer → near		(p)ressed → rest		(s)mug → mug
	(d)ries → rise		(s)worn → worn		(b)low → low
	(s)worn → worn		(d)rug → rug		(s)tub → tub *or* dub

S7	(s)nob → knob	S8	(p)layer → layer	S9	(g)rating → rating
	(s)kim → Kim *or* gim		(c)leaner → leaner		(s)lender → lender
	(s)kirt → curt *or* gurt		(f)lying → lying		(b)luster → luster
	(s)lain → lane		(s)nicker → knicker		(c)luster → luster
	(s)lit → lit		(s)team → team *or* deem		(s)curvy → curvy *or* gurvy
	(s)mear → mere		(s)way → way		(s)mashing → mashing
	(s)mock → mock		(s)tow → tow *or* dough		(s)welter → welter
	(s)nit → knit		(t)rimmed → rimmed		(sp)lashing → lashing
	(s)crum → crumb *or* grum		(s)tuck → tuck *or* duck		(s)queasy → queasy
	(s)noot → newt		(s)tole → toll *or* dole		(b)lasting → lasting

One Minute Activities Level H1 – Challenge Words

For challenge words, see pages 92 and 170-171

Say: **strain** Now say **strain**, but don't say /s/ → **train (or drain)**
Or say: **strain** Now say it again, but don't say /s/ → **train (or drain)**

1. Say:
strain	don't say /s/	train *or* drain
scrape	don't say /s/	crepe *or* grape
stray	don't say /s/	tray *or* dray
spray	don't say /s/	pray *or* bray
strict	don't say /s/	tricked *or* dricked
straight	don't say /st/	rate
scrub	don't say /sc/	rub
stripe	don't say /st/	ripe
splash	don't say /sp/	lash
sprain	don't say /sp/	rain

2. Say:
strap	don't say /s/	trap *or* drap
scream	don't say /s/	cream *or* greem
street	don't say /s/	treat *or* dreat
scrum	don't say /s/	crumb *or* grumb
straight	don't say /s/	trait *or* drait
strain	don't say /st/	rain
scritch	don't say /sk/	rich
string	don't say /st/	ring
splint	don't say /sp/	lint
sprang	don't say /sp/	rang

3. Say:
stride	don't say /s/	tried *or* dried
screw	don't say /s/	crew *or* grew
strike	don't say /s/	trike *or* drike
sprint	don't say /s/	print *or* brint
stroll	don't say /s/	troll *or* droll
stride	don't say /st/	ride
screech	don't say /sk/	reach
strange	don't say /st/	range
split	don't say /sp/	lit
spread	don't say /sp/	red

4. Say:
strung	don't say /st/	rung
scream	don't say /sk/	ream
strap	don't say /st/	wrap
spring	don't say /sp/	ring
strode	don't say /st/	rode
stroll	don't say /st/	roll
spray	don't say /sp/	ray
strong	don't say /st/	wrong
script	don't say /sc/	ripped
splendid	don't say /sp/	lended

5. Say:
script	don't say /s/	crypt *or* gripped
struck	don't say /s/	truck *or* druck
scrunch	don't say /s/	crunch *or* grunch
strove	don't say /s/	trove *or* drove
sprinter	don't say /s/	printer *or* brinter
stray	don't say /st/	ray
scroll	don't say /sk/	roll
strobe	don't say /st/	robe
splendor	don't say /sp/	lender
sprinkle	don't say /sp/	wrinkle

One Minute Activities Level H2

Say: **blue** Now say **blue**, but instead of /b/ say /k/ → **clue**
Or say: **blue** Now say it again, but instead of /b/ say /k/ → **clue**

1. Say:	blue	instead of /b/ say /g/	glue	2. Say:	please	instead of /p/ say /f/	fleas
	cry	instead of /k/ say /d/	dry		cry	instead of /k/ say /f/	fry
	glow	instead of /g/ say /f/	flow		play	instead of /p/ say /k/	clay
	drew	instead of /d/ say /g/	grew		glue	instead of /g/ say /b/	blue
	free	instead of /f/ say /t/	tree		black	instead of /b/ say /p/	plaque
	grew	instead of /g/ say /t/	true		try	instead of /t/ say /f/	fry
	blank	instead of /b/ say /p/	plank		grow	instead of /g/ say /k/	crow
	blare	instead of /b/ say /f/	flare		groom	instead of /g/ say /b/	broom
	blare	instead of /b/ say /g/	glare		drip	instead of /d/ say /t/	trip
	freeze	instead of /f/ say /b/	breeze		grass	instead of /g/ say /b/	brass
3. Say:	flow	instead of /f/ say /s/	slow	4. Say:	dry	instead of /d/ say /t/	try
	cry	instead of /k/ say /t/	try		grain	instead of /g/ say /k/	crane
	plea	instead of /p/ say /f/	flee		flank	instead of /f/ say /b/	blank
	class	instead of /k/ say /g/	glass		trend	instead of /t/ say /f/	friend
	trick	instead of /t/ say /b/	brick		grab	instead of /g/ say /k/	crab
	grain	instead of /g/ say /t/	train		ply	instead of /p/ say /f/	fly
	drew	instead of /d/ say /t/	true		bright	instead of /b/ say /f/	fright
	flow	instead of /f/ say /g/	glow		tried	instead of /t/ say /f/	fried
	try	instead of /t/ say /d/	dry		flock	instead of /f/ say /b/	block
	clay	instead of /k/ say /p/	play		sled	instead of /s/ say /f/	fled
5. Say:	clue	instead of /k/ say /g/	glue	6. Say:	drip	instead of /d/ say /g/	grip
	frail	instead of /f/ say /t/	trail		dry	instead of /d/ say /k/	cry
	claim	instead of /k/ say /f/	flame		freeze	instead of /f/ say /t/	trees
	flank	instead of /f/ say /b/	blank		thread	instead of /th/ say /b/	bread
	clue	instead of /k/ say /b/	blue		brand	instead of /b/ say /g/	grand
	fly	instead of /f/ say /s/	sly		fried	instead of /f/ say /k/	cried
	glow	instead of /g/ say /s/	slow		grill	instead of /g/ say /d/	drill
	flock	instead of /f/ say /k/	clock		bleak	instead of /b/ say /s/	sleek
	slat	instead of /s/ say /f/	flat		fright	instead of /f/ say /b/	bright
	dries	instead of /d/ say /p/	prize		breeze	instead of /b/ say /f/	freeze

Mixed Levels

7. Say:	blue	instead of /b/ say /f/	flew	(H2)	blue	instead of /b/ say /g/	glue
	tree	instead of /t/ say /f/	free	(H1)	plane	don't say /p/	lane
	try	instead of /t/ say /p/	pry	(H2)	cry	instead of /k/ say /t/	try
	dries	instead of /d/ say /f/	fries	(F1)	shame	don't say /sh/	aim
	clap	instead of /k/ say /f/	flap	(H2)	tree	instead of /t/ say /f/	free
	glue	instead of /g/ say /k/	clue	(F2)	moose	don't say /oose/	/m/
	pry	instead of /p/ say /d/	dry	(H2)	slate	instead of /s/ say /p/	plate
	claw	instead of /k/ say /f/	flaw	(G1)	hair	instead of /h/ say /sh/	share
	slate	instead of /s/ say /p/	plate	(H2)	drip	instead of /d/ say /t/	trip
	crank	instead of /k/ say /d/	drank	(G2)	cub	instead of /ub/ say /at/	cat

One Minute Activities Level H2

Say: **dry** Now say **dry**, but instead of /d/ say /f/ → **fly**
Or say: **dry** Now say it again, but instead of /d/ say /f/ → **fly**

8. Say:	dry	instead of /d/ say /f/	fry	9. Say:	crew	instead of /k/ say /t/	true
	flow	instead of /f/ say /s/	slow		drove	instead of /d/ say /g/	grove
	brook	instead of /b/ say /k/	crook		drop	instead of /d/ say /p/	prop
	gray	instead of /g/ say /t/	tray		glaze	instead of /g/ say /p/	plays
	fry	instead of /f/ say /d/	dry		crane	instead of /k/ say /t/	train
	brown	instead of /b/ say /k/	crown		grand	instead of /g/ say /b/	brand
	grape	instead of /g/ say /d/	drape		grade	instead of /g/ say /b/	braid
	fled	instead of /f/ say /s/	sled		crown	instead of /k/ say /f/	frown
	groom	instead of /g/ say /b/	broom		blight	instead of /b/ say /f/	flight
	breed	instead of /b/ say /f/	freed		fries	instead of /f/ say /p/	prize
10. Say:	froze	instead of /f/ say /g/	grows	11. Say:	graze	instead of /g/ say /p/	praise
	true	instead of /t/ say /d/	drew		brag	instead of /b/ say /d/	drag
	glass	instead of /g/ say /k/	class		grail	instead of /g/ say /t/	trail
	bread	instead of /b/ say /th/	thread		flee	instead of /f/ say /g/	glee
	slight	instead of /s/ say /f/	flight		sleigh	instead of /s/ say /k/	clay
	drum	instead of /d/ say /k/	crumb		brash	instead of /b/ say /k/	crash
	creed	instead of /k/ say /f/	freed		grail	instead of /g/ say /f/	frail
	slack	instead of /s/ say /b/	black		drill	instead of /d/ say /f/	frill
	clap	instead of /k/ say /s/	slap		craze	instead of /k/ say /t/	trays
	flame	instead of /f/ say /k/	claim		black	instead of /b/ say /s/	slack
12. Say:	flee	instead of /f/ say /p/	plea	13. Say	fry	instead of /f/ say /k/	cry
	dried	instead of /d/ say /t/	tried		shrew	instead of /sh/ say /th/	threw
	craze	instead of /k/ say /g/	graze		fries	instead of /f/ say /t/	tries
	cloud	instead of /k/ say /p/	plowed		flax	instead of /f/ say /s/	slacks
	drew	instead of /d/ say /th/	threw		brute	instead of /b/ say /f/	fruit
	slam	instead of /s/ say /k/	clam		froze	instead of /f/ say /p/	prose
	freed	instead of /f/ say /k/	creed		crop	instead of /k/ say /p/	prop
	gloat	instead of /g/ say /f/	float		great	instead of /g/ say /t/	trait
	tried	instead of /t/ say /d/	dried		cramp	instead of /k/ say /g/	gramp
	praise	instead of /p/ say /f/	phrase		bloom	instead of /b/ say /g/	gloom

Mixed Levels

14. Say:	shrew	instead of /sh/ say /t/	true	(H2)	gray	instead of /g/ say /t/	tray
	grew	instead of /g/ say /th/	threw	(H1)	trail	don't say /t/	rail
	crab	instead of /k/ say /g/	grab	(H2)	claim	instead of /k/ say /f/	flame
	flight	instead of /f/ say /s/	slight	(F1)	shade	don't say /sh/	aid
	grew	instead of /g/ say /k/	crew	(H2)	flight	instead of /f/ say /s/	slight
	flank	instead of /f/ say /p/	plank	(F2)	voice	don't say /oice/	/v/
	breeze	instead of /b/ say /t/	trees	(H2)	crown	instead of /k/ say /f/	frown
	brief	instead of /b/ say /g/	grief	(G1)	wreath	instead of /wr/ say /t/	teeth
	plank	instead of /p/ say /b/	blank	(H2)	grill	instead of /g/ say /d/	drill
	crook	instead of /k/ say /b/	brook	(G2)	let	instead of /et/ say /am/	lamb

One Minute Activities Level H2

	Say:	**fry**	Now say **fry**, but instead of /f/ say /t/ → **try**
	Or say:	**fry**	Now say it again, but instead of /f/ say /t/ → **try**
	Or say:	**fry**	but instead of /f/ say /t/ → **try**

15. Say:	fry	instead of /f/ say /t/	try	16. Say:	glow	instead of /g/ say /f/	flow
	grain	instead of /g/ say /d/	drain		plaid	instead of /p/ say /g/	glad
	grade	instead of /g/ say /t/	trade		slight	instead of /s/ say /f/	flight
	slip	instead of /s/ say /k/	clip		fries	instead of /f/ say /k/	cries
	crash	instead of /k/ say /t/	trash		slip	instead of /s/ say /f/	flip
	froze	instead of /f/ say /k/	crows		crew	instead of /k/ say /d/	drew
	thread	instead of /th/ say /d/	dread		sling	instead of /s/ say /f/	fling
	phrase	instead of /ph/ say /k/	craze		cream	instead of /k/ say /d/	dream
	trip	instead of /t/ say /d/	drip		bread	instead of /b/ say /d/	dread
	brace	instead of /b/ say /g/	grace		blight	instead of /b/ say /p/	plight

17. Say	try	instead of /t/ say /k/	cry	18 Say	crime	instead of /k/ say /p/	prime
	slide	instead of /s/ say /g/	glide		crate	instead of /k/ say /f/	freight
	crown	instead of /k/ say /b/	brown		trite	instead of /t/ say /f/	fright
	brink	instead of /b/ say /d/	drink		glaze	instead of /g/ say /b/	blaze
	sleet	instead of /s/ say /f/	fleet		crouch	instead of /k/ say /g/	grouch
	flash	instead of /f/ say /k/	clash		shrill	instead of /sh/ say /d/	drill
	slick	instead of /s/ say /k/	click		club	instead of /k/ say /f/	flub
	dream	instead of /d/ say /k/	cream		blight	instead of /b/ say /s/	slight
	fried	instead of /f/ say /t/	tried		clash	instead of /k/ say /f/	flash
	praise	instead of /p/ say /t/	trays		sleigh	instead of /s/ say /p/	play

Mixed Levels

19. Say	claim	instead of /k/ say /b/	blame	(H2)	try	instead of /t/ say /k/	cry
	shred	instead of /sh/ say /b/	bread	(H1)	snail	don't say /s/	nail
	true	instead of /t/ say /g/	grew	(H2)	flash	instead of /f/ say /k/	clash
	cruise	instead of /k/ say /b/	bruise	(F1)	deer	don't say /d/	ear
	glum	instead of /g/ say /p/	plum	(H2)	slide	instead of /s/ say /g/	glide
	brush	instead of /b/ say /k/	crush	(F2)	she	don't say /E/	sh
	clam	instead of /k/ say /s/	slam	(H2)	praise	instead of /p/ say /t/	trays
	plank	instead of /p/ say /f/	flank	(G1)	like	instead of /l/ say /h/	hike
	brash	instead of /b/ say /t/	trash	(H2)	thread	instead of /th/ say /d/	dread
	thread	instead of /th/ say /d/	dread	(G2)	web	instead of /eb/ say /all/	wall

Mixed Levels

20. Say:	crave	instead of /k/ say /b/	brave	(H2)	froze	instead of /f/ say /g/	grows
	slant	instead of /s/ say /p/	plant	(H1)	climb	don't say /k/	lime
	brunt	instead of /b/ say /f/	front	(H2)	grade	instead of /g/ say /t/	trade
	grain	instead of /g/ say /b/	brain	(F1)	jar	don't say /j/	are
	slap	instead of /s/ say /k/	clap	(H2)	glass	instead of /g/ say /k/	class
	glade	instead of /g/ say /b/	blade	(F2)	zinc	don't say /ink/	z
	clock	instead of /k/ say /f/	flock	(H2)	craze	instead of /k/ say /t/	trays
	freight	instead of /f/ say /g/	great	(G1)	yawn	instead of /y/ say /g/	gone
	glide	instead of /g/ say /s/	slide	(H2)	freight	instead of /f/ say /g/	great
	brace	instead of /b/ say /t/	trace	(G2)	ball	instead of /all/ say /ox/	box

Supplemental One Minute Activities for Level H2

	Say:	**true**	Now say **true**, but instead of /t/ say /k/ → **crew**
	Or say:	**true**	Now say it again, but instead of /t/ say /k/ → **crew**
	Or say:	**true**	but instead of /t/ say /k/ → **crew**

S1	true	/t/ to /k/	crew	S2	trip	/t/ to /g/	grip	S3	phrase	/ph/ to /t/	trays
	plaid	/p/ to /k/	clad		proud	/p/ to /k/	crowd		pleat	/p/ to /f/	fleet
	slide	/s/ to /p/	plied		glean	/g/ to /k/	clean		trim	/t/ to /b/	brim
	prose	/p/ to /k/	crows		crane	/k/ to /g/	grain		sly	/s/ to /f/	fly
	slick	/s/ to /f/	flick		plea	/p/ to /g/	glee		pleat	/p/ to /s/	sleet
	brass	/b/ to /g/	grass		tried	/t/ to /p/	pride		trail	/t/ to /b/	braille
	plant	/p/ to /s/	slant		crane	/k/ to /d/	drain		prose	/p/ to /f/	froze
	crawl	/k/ to /d/	drawl		pray	/p/ to /g/	gray		slung	/s/ to /f/	flung
	slows	/s/ to /k/	close		slop	/s/ to /f/	flop		prior	/p/ to /d/	dryer
	shrank	/sh/ to /d/	drank		fruit	/f/ to /b/	brute		bright	/b/ to /t/	trite

S4	flame	/f/ to /b/	blame	S5	shriek	/sh/ to /k/	creek	S6	dryer	/d/ to /p/	prior
	blown	/b/ to /f/	flown		tried	/t/ to /k/	cried		flurry	/f/ to /b/	blurry
	slap	/s/ to /f/	flap		flinch	/f/ to /k/	clinch		fraction	/f/ to /t/	traction
	click	/k/ to /f/	flick		glue	/g/ to /f/	flew		bluster	/b/ to /k/	cluster
	group	/g/ to /t/	troop		crank	/k/ to /p/	prank		gritty	/g/ to /p/	pretty
	true	/t/ to /th/	threw		glade	/g/ to /p/	played		plaster	/p/ to /b/	blaster
	fleet	/f/ to /s/	sleet		bleat	/b/ to /s/	sleet		glimmer	/g/ to /s/	slimmer
	clank	/k/ to /b/	blank		crane	/k/ to /b/	brain		gravel	/g/ to /t/	travel
	drab	/d/ to /k/	crab		flare	/f/ to /b/	blare		platter	/p/ to /f/	flatter
	pray	/p/ to /t/	tray		crime	/k/ to /g/	grime		slender	/s/ to /b/	blender

S7	slot	/s/ to /p/	plot	S8	slow	/s/ to /f/	flow	S9	bluster	/b/ to /f/	fluster
	trail	/t/ to /f/	frail		trawl	/t/ to /k/	crawl		slipper	/s/ to /f/	flipper
	blade	/b/ to /p/	played		bring	/b/ to /sp/	spring		briar	/b/ to /d/	dryer
	drew	/d/ to /g/	grew		slump	/s/ to /p/	plump		prickle	/p/ to /t/	trickle
	fried	/f/ to /p/	pride		fray	/f/ to /g/	gray		streamer	/st/ to /sc/	screamer
	please	/p/ to /f/	fleas		trim	/t/ to /g/	grim		blender	/b/ to /sp/	splendor
	shread	/sh/ to /th/	thread		plunder	/p/ to /b/	blunder		proper	/p/ to /d/	dropper
	clone	/k/ to /f/	flown		clean	/k/ to /g/	glean		clutter	/k/ to /f/	flutter
	slack	/s/ to /p/	plaque		freed	/f/ to /g/	greed		streamer	/st/ to /k/	creamer
	cling	/k/ to /s/	sling		platter	/p/ to /k/	clatter		cluster	/k/ to /f/	fluster

LEVEL I

Basic Phoneme-level Processing
Deletion of Final Phoneme

I1   Level I1 involves deleting the final sound in a word, but the student must split a final blend in order to delete the word's final sound.

Samples: car(t) ⇢ car   gras(p) ⇢ grass

I2   Level I2 involves deleting the final sound in a word.

Samples: see(n) ⇢ see   rai(se) ⇢ ray

There are two interesting notes about Level I in relation to the other levels. First, at most levels, deleting or substituting a phoneme in the same position are of roughly equivalent difficulty. Levels H1 and H2 are of a similar level of difficulty. So are K1 and K2 as well as M1 and M2. However, deleting a final phoneme in a word is much easier than substituting a final sound. That is why Level I (deletion of a final phoneme) is here within the program while Level L (substitution of a final phoneme) is much later in the program.

Second, normally deleting a sound within a blend is more difficult than not within a blend. For example, Level F (*cat* to *at*) is much easier than Level H (*clap* to *lap*). However, this "blends are harder" phenomenon does not appear to be the case with Level I. Deleting the ending phoneme in an ending blend (*fort* to *for*), that leaves behind a CVC closed syllable is, for most students, slightly easier than deleting an ending consonant phoneme that leaves behind an open syllable (*seen* to *see*). The pattern emerged after giving the PAST (Chapter 11; Appendix C) to over 1,000 students. That is why Level I1, which splits an ending blend, comes before Level I2, which does not. There may be individual differences in performance with different children. However, in overall group results, Level I1 is easier than Level I2.

Multisyllabic/Applied Activities

The *Multisyllabic/Applied* activities are designed to help children apply the phoneme awareness skills that they have learned to two or three syllable words (see p. 91).

I2   This involves deleting the final sound of a syllable within a multisyllabic word.

Samples: pa(v)ement ⇢ payment   rece(p)tion ⇢ recession

Remember: THE FOCUS IS ON THE SOUNDS, NOT SPELLING PATTERNS.

One Minute Activities Level I1

| | Say: | **and** | Now say **and**, but don't say **/d/** | **an** |
| | Or say: | **and** | Now say it again, but don't say **/d/** | **an** |

1. Say:	and	don't say /d/	an	2. Say:	arc	don't say /k/	are
	bend	don't say /d/	been		felt	don't say /t/	fell
	art	don't say /t/	are		eyes	don't say /z/	eye
	card	don't say /d/	car		force	don't say /s/	for
	inch	don't say /ch/	in		hence	don't say /s/	hen
	farm	don't say /m/	far		arm	don't say /m/	are
	cold	don't say /d/	coal		bent	don't say /t/	been
	firm	don't say /m/	fur		grasp	don't say /p/	grass
	cart	don't say /t/	car		malt	don't say /t/	mall
	hats	don't say /s/	hat		toes	don't say /z/	toe
3. Say:	arch	don't say /ch/	are	4. Say:	lost	don't say /t/	loss
	self	don't say /f/	sell		starred	don't say /d/	star
	ant	don't say /t/	an		ford	don't say /d/	for
	band	don't say /d/	ban		joint	don't say /t/	join
	port	don't say /t/	poor		cats	don't say /s/	cat
	cars	don't say /z/	car		bench	don't say /ch/	been
	false	don't say /s/	fall		cart	don't say /t/	car
	barn	don't say /n/	bar		herd	don't say /d/	her
	mist	don't say /t/	miss		clamp	don't say /p/	clam
	fork	don't say /k/	for		shelf	don't say /f/	shell
5. Say:	dunce	don't say /s/	done	6. Say:	worm	don't say /m/	were
	cord	don't say /d/	core		sunk	don't say /k/	sung
	birth	don't say /th/	burr		slump	don't say /p/	slum
	fold	don't say /d/	foal		guilt	don't say /t/	gill
	ninth	don't say /th/	nine		sixth	don't say /th/	six
	dent	don't say /t/	den		York	don't say /k/	your
	gold	don't say /d/	goal		hilt	don't say /t/	hill
	surf	don't say /f/	sir		porch	don't say /ch/	poor
	bolt	don't say /t/	bowl		tend	don't say /d/	ten
	wilt	don't say /t/	will		storm	don't say /m/	store
7. Say:	fault	don't say /t/	fall	*Mixed Levels*	card	don't say /d/	car
	sword	don't say /d/	sore	(I2)	slope	don't say /p/	slow
	colt	don't say /t/	coal	(I1)	farm	don't say /m/	far
	bold	don't say /d/	bowl	(G1)	rhyme	instead of /r/ say /t/	time
	worn	don't say /n/	wore	(I2)	false	don't say /s/	fall
	morn	don't say /n/	more	(G2)	well	instead of /ell/ say /un/	won
	dense	don't say /s/	den	(I1)	felt	don't say /t/	fell
	fern	don't say /n/	fur	(H1)	bread	don't say /b/	red
	worse	don't say /s/	were	(I1)	stark	don't say /k/	star
	burnt	don't say /t/	burn	(H2)	grape	instead of /g/ say /d/	drape

One Minute Activities Level I1

		Say:	**belt**	Now say **belt**, but don't say /t/	**bell**	
		Or say:	**belt**	Now say it again, but don't say /t/	**bell**	

8. Say:	belt	don't say /t/	bell	9. Say:	bard	don't say /d/	bar
	dorm	don't say /m/	door		Gramp	don't say /p/	gram
	stork	don't say /k/	store		park	don't say /k/	par
	welt	don't say /t/	well		mourn	don't say /n/	more
	fund	don't say /d/	fun		pierce	don't say /s/	pier
	bask	don't say /k/	bass		think	don't say /k/	thing
	mild	don't say /d/	mile		wield	don't say /d/	wheel
	yelp	don't say /p/	yell		starve	don't say /v/	star
	past	don't say /t/	pass		paste	don't say /t/	pace
	halt	don't say /t/	hall		gulp	don't say /p/	gull

10. Say:	build	don't say /d/	bill	11. Say:	meant	don't say /t/	men
	plant	don't say /t/	plan		heard	don't say /d/	her
	course	don't say /s/	core		launch	don't say /ch/	lawn
	pinch	don't say /ch/	pin		dealt	don't say /t/	dell
	scorch	don't say /ch/	score		barge	don't say /j/	bar
	gild	don't say /d/	gill		sold	don't say /d/	sole
	baste	don't say /t/	base		least	don't say /t/	lease
	mold	don't say /d/	mole		weld	don't say /d/	well
	sort	don't say /t/	sore		fort	don't say /t/	for
	search	don't say /ch/	sir		scant	don't say /t/	scan

12. Say:	tenth	don't say /th/	ten	13. Say:	fourth	don't say /th/	four
	limp	don't say /p/	limb		quilt	don't say /t/	quill
	blest	don't say /t/	bless		word	don't say /d/	were
	bald	don't say /d/	ball		bird	don't say /d/	burr
	spilt	don't say /t/	spill		worst	don't say /t/	worse
	lined	don't say /d/	line		saint	don't say /t/	sane
	tarp	don't say /p/	tar		purse	don't say /s/	purr
	mend	don't say /d/	men		bunt	don't say /t/	bun
	brand	don't say /d/	bran		crisp	don't say /p/	Chris
	pence	don't say /s/	pen		guest	don't say /t/	guess

14. Say:	hold	don't say /d/	hole	*Mixed Levels*	hold	don't say /d/	hole
	rink	don't say /k/	ring	(H2)	trash	instead of /t/ say /k/	crash
	film	don't say /m/	fill	(I1)	sixth	don't say /th/	six
	clasp	don't say /p/	class	(G1)	moose	instead of /m/ say /g/	goose
	lamp	don't say /p/	lamb	(I1)	mild	don't say /d/	mile
	once	don't say /s/	one	(G2)	time	instead of /ime/ say /ap/	tap
	paint	don't say /t/	pain	(I1)	gold	don't say /d/	goal
	find	don't say /d/	fine	(H1)	sleep	don't say /s/	leap
	scared	don't say /d/	scare	(I1)	film	don't say /m/	fill
	board	don't say /d/	bore	(H2)	crane	instead of /k/ say /t/	train

One Minute Activities Level I1

		Say:	**serve**	Now say **serve**, but don't say **/v/**	**sir**
		Or say:	**serve**	Now say it again, but don't say **/v/**	**sir**
		Or say:	**serve**	without saying **/v/**	**sir**

15. Say:	serve	don't say /v/	sir	16. Say:	born	don't say /n/	bore
	corn	don't say /n/	core		source	don't say /s/	sore
	range	don't say /j/	rain		mark	don't say /k/	mar
	short	don't say /t/	shore		torch	don't say /ch/	tore
	bark	don't say /k/	bar		hurt	don't say /t/	her
	dance	don't say /s/	Dan		mind	don't say /d/	mine
	scarf	don't say /f/	scar		grinned	don't say /d/	grin
	tense	don't say /s/	ten		burn	don't say /n/	burr
	carve	don't say /v/	car		warmth	don't say /th/	warm
	pant	don't say /t/	pan		lest	don't say /t/	less

17. Say:	can't	don't say /t/	can	18. Say:	torn	don't say /n/	tore
	tops	don't say /s/	top		charm	don't say /m/	char
	went	don't say /t/	when		shirt	don't say /t/	sure
	stark	don't say /k/	star		branch	don't say /ch/	bran
	bunch	don't say /ch/	bun		form	don't say /m/	for
	wince	don't say /s/	win		pact	don't say /t/	pack
	fished	don't say /t/	fish		spark	don't say /k/	spar
	worth	don't say /th/	were		forge	don't say /j/	for
	built	don't say /t/	bill		spurn	don't say /n/	spur
	warm	don't say /m/	war		world	don't say /d/	whirl

19. Say:	kids	don't say /z/	kid	*Mixed Levels*	tenth	don't say /th/	ten
	work	don't say /k/	were	(I2)	troop	don't say /p/	true
	notes	don't say /s/	note	(I2)	lined	don't say /d/	line
	bears	don't say /z/	bear	(G1)	sing	instead of /s/ say /th/	thing
	starch	don't say /ch/	star	(I2)	went	don't say /t/	when
	guild	don't say /d/	gill	(G2)	head	instead of /ed/ say /ill/	hill
	lids	don't say /z/	lid	(I1)	word	don't say /d/	were
	cans	don't say /z/	can	(H1)	plot	don't say /p/	lot
	shunt	don't say /t/	shun	(I1)	mend	don't say /d/	men
	wharf	don't say /f/	war	(H2)	clue	instead of /k/ say /g/	glue

20. Say:	arch	don't say /ch/	are	*Mixed Levels*	bent	don't say /t/	been
	forth	don't say /th/	for	(I2)	grove	don't say /v/	grow
	shelve	don't say /v/	shell	(I1)	shelf	don't say /f/	shell
	part	don't say /t/	par	(G1)	pool	instead of /p/ say /t/	tool
	milk	don't say /k/	mill	(I1)	range	don't say /j/	rain
	leap	don't say /p/	Lee	(G2)	lack	instead of /ack/ say /id/	lid
	warn	don't say /n/	war	(I1)	milk	don't say /k/	mill
	silk	don't say /k/	sill	(H1)	proof	don't say /p/	roof
	mashed	don't say /t/	mash	(I1)	weld	don't say /d/	well
	norm	don't say /m/	nor	(H2)	fries	instead of /f/ say /p/	prize

Supplemental One Minute Activities for Level I1

Say:	**wealth**	Now say **wealth**, but don't say **/th/**	**well**
Or say:	**wealth**	Now say it again, but don't say **/th/**	**well**
Or say:	**wealth**	without saying **/th/**	**well**

S1	weal(th) → well	S2	glum(p) → glum	S3	ad(s) → ad
	gul(f) → gull		cor(n) → core		stin(k) → sting
	dol(t) → dole		nor(th) → nor		bas(k) → bass
	mis(t) → miss		zin(c) → zing		char(t) → char
	les(t) → less		fel(t) → fell		scar(f) → scar
	win(ch) → win		pun(t) → pun		bluffe(d) → bluff
	sin(k) → sing		smel(t) → smell		ar(f) → are
	mul(ch) → mull		owne(d) → own		spar(k) → spar
	par(ch) → par		ram(p) → ram		skim(p) → skim
	duc(t) → duck		win(c)e → win		star(t) → star

S4	pun(ch) → pun	S5	blur(p) → blur	S6	tram(p) → tram
	wan(t) → Juan		wil(t) → will		egg(s) → egg
	rif(t) → riff		char(g)e → char		mol(t) → mole
	ran(ch) → ran		dan(c)e → Dan		snor(t) → snore
	quil(t) → quill		ran(t) → ran		gas(p) → gas
	wren(ch) → wren		ben(d) → been		blur(t) → blur
	can(s) → can		por(t) → pour		four(th) → four
	mas(t) → mass		scor(n) → score		in(ch) → in
	win(k) → wing		gaun(t) → gone		war(t) → war
	ar(ch) → are		mar(t) → mar		wil(d) → while

S7	rus(t) → Russ	S8	cour(t) → core
	it(s) → it		close(d) → close
	ten(d) → ten		car(t) → car
	spar(s)e → spar		use(d) → use
	thum(p) → thumb		war(d) → war
	hul(k) → hull		nor(th) → nor
	pac(t) → pack		sur(g)e → sir
	shir(t) → sure		bir(ch) → burr
	sil(t) → sill		cam(p) → cam
	mixe(d) → mix		mas(k) → mass

One Minute Activities Level I2

        Say: **beam**   Now say **beam**, but don't say **/m/**   **bee**
        Or say: **beam**   Now say it again, but don't say **/m/**   **bee**

1. Say:	beam	don't say /m/	bee	2. Say:	rose	don't say /z/	row
	sheep	don't say /p/	she		boat	don't say /t/	bow
	time	don't say /m/	tie		safe	don't say /f/	say
	note	don't say /t/	no		tide	don't say /d/	tie
	same	don't say /m/	say		heat	don't say /t/	he
	zoom	don't say /m/	zoo		mine	don't say /n/	my
	couch	don't say /ch/	cow		hoop	don't say /p/	who
	size	don't say /z/	sigh		soak	don't say /k/	so
	meet	don't say /t/	me		youth	don't say /th/	you
	loan	don't say /n/	low		hide	don't say /d/	hi
3. Say:	seat	don't say /t/	see	4. Say:	feet	don't say /t/	fee
	house	don't say /s/	how		moon	don't say /n/	moo
	toad	don't say /d/	toe		rope	don't say /p/	row
	niece	don't say /s/	knee		guide	don't say /d/	guy
	I've	don't say /v/	I		duke	don't say /k/	do
	rhyme	don't say /m/	rye		gloom	don't say /m/	glue
	coin	don't say /n/	coy		pies	don't say /z/	pie
	shown	don't say /n/	show		seed	don't say /d/	see
	wise	don't say /z/	why		tied	don't say /d/	tie
	page	don't say /j/	pay		sown	don't say /n/	sow
5. Say:	tooth	don't say /th/	too	6. Say:	robe	don't say /b/	row
	rise	don't say /z/	rye		wheat	don't say /t/	we
	goes	don't say /z/	go		float	don't say /t/	flow
	beak	don't say /k/	bee		whose	don't say /z/	who
	rave	don't say /v/	ray		cube	don't say /b/	cue
	sought	don't say /t/	saw		sage	don't say /j/	say
	truth	don't say /th/	true		ride	don't say /d/	rye
	rate	don't say /t/	ray		dome	don't say /m/	doe
	sign	don't say /n/	sigh		bead	don't say /d/	bee
	fuse	don't say /z/	few		grape	don't say /p/	gray

Mixed Levels

7. Say:	rain	don't say /n/	ray	(I2)	beam	don't say /m/	bee
	save	don't say /v/	say	(F1)	bad	don't say /b/	add
	boot	don't say /t/	boo	(I2)	same	don't say /m/	say
	grain	don't say /n/	gray	(G1)	gum	instead of /g/ say /th/	thumb
	seen	don't say /n/	see	(I2)	shown	don't say /n/	show
	wide	don't say /d/	why	(G2)	cup	instead of /up/ say /an/	can
	soap	don't say /p/	so	(I2)	boot	don't say /t/	boo
	pine	don't say /n/	pie	(H1)	twin	don't say /t/	win
	weed	don't say /d/	we	(I2)	soap	don't say /p/	so
	race	don't say /s/	ray	(H2)	flow	instead of /f/ say /s/	slow

One Minute Activities Level I2

	Say:	**tooth**	Now say **tooth**, but don't say **/th/**	**too**
	Or say:	**tooth**	Now say it again, but don't say **/th/**	**too**

8. Say:	skies	don't say /z/	sky	9. Say:	phone	don't say /n/	foe
	teach	don't say /ch/	tee		need	don't say /d/	knee
	fluke	don't say /k/	flew		truce	don't say /s/	true
	moat	don't say /t/	mow		wake	don't say /k/	way
	paid	don't say /d/	pay		team	don't say /m/	tee
	road	don't say /d/	row		moose	don't say /s/	moo
	seek	don't say /k/	see		please	don't say /z/	plea
	weight	don't say /t/	way		quote	don't say /t/	quo
	trace	don't say /s/	tray		meek	don't say /k/	me
	news	don't say /z/	new		trade	don't say /d/	tray

10. Say	raise	don't say /z/	ray	11. Say	tribe	don't say /b/	try
	seem	don't say /m/	see		fleece	don't say /s/	flee
	tune	don't say /n/	too		prime	don't say /m/	pry
	tote	don't say /t/	toe		globe	don't say /b/	glow
	sake	don't say /k/	say		soup	don't say /p/	Sue
	teeth	don't say /th/	tee		throat	don't say /t/	throw
	bake	don't say /k/	bay		wave	don't say /v/	way
	pause	don't say /z/	paw		treat	don't say /t/	tree
	tone	don't say /n/	toe		graze	don't say /z/	gray
	you'd	don't say /d/	you		plead	don't say /d/	plea

12. Say	seize	don't say /z/	see	13. Say	drawn	don't say /n/	draw
	pain	don't say /n/	pay		rake	don't say /k/	ray
	claim	don't say /m/	clay		slide	don't say /d/	sly
	train	don't say /n/	tray		weep	don't say /p/	we
	weave	don't say /v/	we		flies	don't say /z/	fly
	ties	don't say /z/	tie		groan	don't say /n/	grow
	teen	don't say /n/	tee		bait	don't say /t/	bay
	you've	don't say /v/	you		tube	don't say /b/	too
	weak	don't say /k/	we		praise	don't say /z/	pray
	pave	don't say /v/	pay		tried	don't say /d/	try

Mixed Levels

14. Say:	sheet	don't say /t/	she	(I2)	tooth	don't say /th/	too
	wrote	don't say /t/	row	(F1)	rise	don't say /r/	eyes
	make	don't say /k/	may	(I2)	truth	don't say /th/	true
	loaf	don't say /f/	low	(G1)	wreath	instead of /r/ say /t/	teeth
	brown	don't say /n/	brow	(I2)	rain	don't say /n/	ray
	stage	don't say /j/	stay	(G2)	rack	instead of /ack/ say /ib/	rib
	nose	don't say /z/	no	(I2)	stage	don't say /j/	stay
	line	don't say /n/	lie	(H1)	speech	don't say /s/	peach or beach
	feed	don't say /d/	fee	(I2)	grape	don't say /p/	gray
	I'm	don't say /m/	I	(H2)	brown	instead of /b/ say /k/	crown

One Minute Activities Level I2

	Say:	**bloom**	Now say **bloom**, but don't say **/m/**	blue
	Or say:	**bloom**	Now say it again, but don't say **/m/**	blue
	Or say:	**bloom**	without saying **/m/**	blue

15. Say:	bloom	don't say /m/	blue	16. Say:	grace	don't say /s/	gray
	fries	don't say /z/	fry		thus	don't say /s/	the
	pace	don't say /s/	pay		browse	don't say /z/	brow
	both	don't say /th/	bow		dried	don't say /d/	dry
	stake	don't say /k/	stay		flute	don't say /t/	flew
	grove	don't say /v/	grow		those	don't say /z/	though
	freeze	don't say /z/	free		shine	don't say /n/	shy
	trees	don't say /z/	tree		growth	don't say /th/	grow
	droop	don't say /p/	drew		troop	don't say /p/	true
	cried	don't say /d/	cry		rove	don't say /v/	row
17. Say:	groom	don't say /m/	grew	18. Say:	suede	don't say /d/	sway
	fleet	don't say /t/	flee		grade	don't say /d/	gray
	plane	don't say /n/	play		Dave	don't say /v/	day
	mope	don't say /p/	mow		lime	don't say /m/	lie
	wait	don't say /t/	way		pawn	don't say /n/	paw
	neat	don't say /t/	knee		flown	don't say /n/	flow
	drive	don't say /v/	dry		skeet	don't say /t/	ski
	loss	don't say /s/	law		sane	don't say /n/	say
	wage	don't say /j/	way		keep	don't say /p/	key
	gleam	don't say /m/	glee		group	don't say /p/	grew

Mixed Levels

19. Say:	spied	don't say /d/	spy	(I2)	growth	don't say /th/	grow
	throne	don't say /n/	throw	(F1)	shown	don't say /sh/	own
	whom	don't say /m/	who	(I2)	drive	don't say /v/	dry
	sewn	don't say /n/	so	(G1)	wool	instead of /w/ say /f/	full
	freed	don't say /d/	free	(I2)	neat	don't say /t/	knee
	shoot	don't say /t/	shoe	(G2)	ring	instead of /ing/ say /est/	rest
	cruise	don't say /z/	crew	(I2)	freeze	don't say /z/	free
	fried	don't say /d/	fry	(H1)	flake	don't say /f/	lake
	clause	don't say /z/	claw	(I2)	group	don't say /p/	grew
	groove	don't say /v/	grew	(H2)	grand	instead of /g/ say /b/	brand

Mixed Levels

20. Say	slope	don't say /p/	slow	(I2)	seem	don't say /m/	see
	rage	don't say /j/	ray	(F1)	chase	don't say /ch/	ace
	thought	don't say /t/	thaw	(I2)	tune	don't say /n/	too
	roam	don't say /m/	row	(G1)	cube	instead of /k/ say /t/	tube
	keyed	don't say /d/	key	(I2)	thought	don't say /t/	thaw
	beech	don't say /ch/	bee	(G2)	pup	instead of /up/ say /in/	pin
	date	don't say /t/	day	(I2)	date	don't say /t/	day
	side	don't say /d/	sigh	(H1)	brake	don't say /b/	rake
	great	don't say /t/	gray	(I2)	treat	don't say the last /t/	tree
	doom	don't say /m/	do	(H2)	grape	instead of /g/ say /d/	drape

Supplemental One Minute Activities for Level I2

	Say:	**lawn**	Now say **lawn**, but don't say **/n/**	**law**
	Or say:	**lawn**	Now say it again, but don't say **/n/**	**law**
	Or say:	**lawn**	without saying **/n/**	**law**

S1	law(n)	→	law	S2	they('d)	→	they	S3	hee(d)	→	he
	tea(s)e	→	tee		pri(z)e	→	pry		mo(d)e	→	mow
	soo(n)	→	Sue		lie(d)	→	lie		jee(p)	→	gee
	no(t)e	→	no		staye(d)	→	stay		fu(m)e	→	few
	la(k)e	→	lay		goo(f)	→	goo		pro(n)e	→	pro
	to(m)e	→	toe		ma(d)e	→	may		stai(n)	→	stay
	crie(s)	→	cry		sui(t)	→	sue		new(t)	→	new
	la(t)e	→	lay		strai(n)	→	stray		no(d)e	→	no
	goo(s)e	→	goo		mi(n)e	→	my		la(n)e	→	lay
	kna(v)e	→	nay		do(z)e	→	dough		hi(v)e	→	hi

S4	due(s)	→	do	S5	lea(f)	→	Lee	S6	du(c)e	→	do
	roo(m)	→	rue		wa(d)e	→	way		la(t)e	→	lay
	na(m)e	→	nay		shei(k)	→	she		lea(s)e	→	Lee
	lea(n)	→	Lee		they'(v)e	→	they		hoo(f)	→	who
	no(p)e	→	no		noo(s)e	→	new		foa(m)	→	foe
	spi(n)e	→	spy		du(n)e	→	do		mo(v)e	→	moo
	moa(n)	→	mow		lea(sh)	→	Lee		staye(d)	→	stay
	glue(d)	→	glue		toa(st)	→	toe		goa(t)	→	go
	ho(p)e	→	hoe		sto(n)e	→	stow		ge(n)e	→	gee
	gra(v)e	→	gray		fra(m)e	→	fray		stewe(d)	→	stew

S7	hou(r)	→	ow	S8	lau(d)	→	law	S9	li(v)e	→	lie
	how(l)	→	how		sie(g)e	→	see		he'(s)	→	he
	I'(d)	→	I		feu(d)	→	few		hea(p)	→	he
	ma(z)e	→	may		pri(d)e	→	pry		cri(m)e	→	cry
	jo(k)e	→	Joe		glean	→	glee		sla(t)e	→	sleigh
	kee(n)	→	key		pro(b)e	→	pro		lea(g)ue	→	Lee
	moo(d)	→	moo		lie(s)	→	lie		drie(s)	→	dry
	wo(k)e	→	woe		moo(t)	→	moo		mai(d)	→	may
	pla(t)e	→	play		spie(s)	→	spy		sto(v)e	→	stow
	stoo(p)	→	stew		plea(t)	→	plea		sprai(n)	→	spray

Multisyllabic/Applied
One Minute Activities Level I2

See note about multisyllabic/applied activites on page 91 and 181

	Say:	**pavement**	Now say **pavement**, but don't say /v/	**payment**
	Or say:	**pavement**	Now say it again, but don't say /v/	**payment**

1. Say:	pavement	don't say /v/	payment	2. Say:	prosper	don't say /s/	proper
	lifter	don't say /f/	litter		pesty	don't say /s/	petty
	thirsty	don't say /s/	thirty		fisted	don't say /s/	fitted
	master	don't say /s/	matter		bunter	don't say /n/	butter
	center	don't say /n/	setter		cluster	don't say /s/	clutter
	chapter	don't say /p/	chatter		section	don't say /k/	session
	boasting	don't say /s/	boating		muster	don't say /s/	mutter
	stomping	don't say /m/	stopping		tramping	don't say /m/	trapping
	sister	don't say the 2nd /s/	sitter		wimpy	don't say /m/	whippy
	risky	don't say /s/	Ricky		toasting	don't say /s/	toting

3. Say:	fluster	don't say /s/	flutter	4. Say:	under	don't say /n/	udder
	lining	don't say /n/	lying		slender	don't say /n/	sledder
	ousting	don't say /s/	outing		factor	don't say /k/	fatter
	sifting	don't say /f/	sitting		whisker	don't say /s/	wicker
	chomping	don't say /m/	chopping		reception	don't say /p/	recession
	splinter	don't say /n/	splitter		cobbler	don't say /b/	collar
	limpy	don't say /m/	lippy		toasted	don't say /s/	toted
	paving	don't say /v/	paying		gusted	don't say /s/	gutted
	lended	don't say /n/	leaded		clomping	don't say /m/	clopping
	wasting	don't say /s/	waiting		wispy	don't say /s/	whippy

5. Say:	lonely	don't say /n/	lowly
	nesting	don't say /s/	netting
	roosting	don't say /s/	rooting
	render	don't say /n/	redder
	coasting	don't say /s/	coating
	sander	don't say /n/	sadder
	skimping	don't say /m/	skipping
	Easter	don't say /s/	eater
	jesting	don't say /s/	jetting
	faster	don't say /s/	fatter

ADVANCED PHONEME LEVELS

Levels H and I represent relatively easy phoneme-level manipulations. More advanced phoneme manipulations include 1) deleting or substituting sounds from the middle of words (called *medial* sounds); 2) substituting sounds at the end of words; and 3) reversing phonemes. To do these more challenging phoneme tasks, children must be able to locate and manipulate any possible sound in any position within a word. To be good orthographic mappers, students must be able to the match all the sounds they hear in words with the letters representing those sounds. To "map" a word to permanent memory, every sound must be accounted for, regardless of position. Thus, efficient phoneme skills are foundational to phonemic proficiency and thus for rapid, automatic sight word learning. Below are examples of the advanced phoneme manipulations:

Deletion of a medial phoneme		Substitution of a medial phoneme		Substitution of an ending phoneme	
(K1) b/r/at → bat		(J) h/a/t → h/o/t		(L1) ca/n/ → ca/t/	
(M1) la/n/d → lad		(K2) g/r/ew → g/l/ue		(L2) ben/t/ → ben/d/	
		(M2) li/s/t → li/f/t			

Levels K, L2, and M involve splitting two-phoneme blends. But some words in English have three phoneme blends, so students need to be able to develop phoneme awareness for those as well. Three phoneme blends at the beginning the words all begin with the letter *s* (e.g., *spring*, *split*, *street*).* To allow children to fine-tune their awareness of three-phoneme blends, *Challenge Words* are included at the end of K1 and K2.

Importance of the Advanced Levels
Students will not show significant reading gains until they can do all of the advanced phoneme levels (Levels J, K, L, & M) quickly and automatically. The earlier levels (especially D through G) only prepare students for *phoneme-level* skills. The goal of the program is phonemic proficiency, which is best demonstrated via quick, automatic, phoneme-level processing within manipulation tasks. From late second to third grade and following, average and above average readers can do all levels of this program quite well, even if they have had no prior phoneme awareness training. This is because phoneme awareness comes naturally to about 70% of the population. The other 30% have phoneme awareness difficulties that range from very mild to very severe. These difficulties affect reading development. Removal of their phoneme awareness difficulties directly addresses the most common cause of reading difficulty.

Acquiring phoneme skills early (grades K-2) makes for a smooth transition into reading. However, acquiring phoneme awareness skills late (grade 3 or later) does not guarantee improved reading. Older students have developed mental habits of approaching words that are inefficient. These habits need to be "unlearned" before they make progress. Chapter 6 shows how to do this.

Level N is optional. Level N involves phoneme reversal. It is included to allow you to do One Minute Activities in a small or large group setting when children are present who have mastered all the other levels. Level N can be quite difficult so it keeps those students challenged.

*This must not be confused with words like *three* and *phrase*, which contain three consonants at the beginning. The *th* and *ph* are digraphs, not blends. They each represent a single sound. All three phoneme blends begin with the letter *s*. There are also three-phoneme blends at the end of words (e.g., *first*, *worst*), but too few to create an exercise.

LEVEL J

Advanced Phoneme-level Processing
Substituting medial vowels

J   Level J involves switching the medial vowel in words.

Samples: d(a)d ⇢ d(i)d
               n(o)t ⇢ n(e)t

Multisyllabic/Applied Activities

Level J teaches students to manipulate the medial vowel in words. The *Multisyllabic/Applied* activities are designed to apply that skill two-syllable or three-syllable words. This involves switching a medial vowel for another in a multisyllabic word (see more at p. 91).

Samples: l(e)sson ⇢ l(i)sten
               n(ee)dle ⇢ n(oo)dle

Special Administration Instructions for Level J

- *Short vowels* are represented by the normal, lower case representation of that vowel:
  a as in *pat*, *e* as in *pet*, *i* as in *pit*, *o* as in *pot*, and *u* as in *putt*.
  These are five words that differ only in the short vowel: pat, pet, pit, pot, putt

- *Long vowels* are represented by the upper case representation of that vowel:
  A as in *mate*, *E* as in *meet*, *I* as in *might*, *O* as in *moat*, and *U* as in *mute* or *moot*.*
  These are five words that differ only in the long vowel: mate, meet, might, moat, mute/moot

- Note that sometimes a short vowel may be exchanged for a long vowel or vice versa:
  Say: red   instead of /e/ say /E/   read
  Say: rate   instead of /A/ say /a/   rat

*Note that there are essentially two long *u* sounds, captured in the phrase "Hey Luke! Mute that cute flute." The long *u* sound in *mute* and *cute* makes the sound of the letter's name, *u*, and is pronounced like the word *you*. The second long *u* sound as in *Luke* and *flute* is often represented by either a *u* or *oo* (*tube, duty, fruit, boot, mood*).

Remember: THE FOCUS IS ON THE SOUNDS, NOT SPELLING PATTERNS.

One Minute Activities Level J

	Say:	**dad**	Now say **dad**, but instead of **/a/** say **/i/**	**did**
	Or say:	**dad**	Now say it again, but instead of **/a/** say **/i/**	**did**

1. Say:	dad	instead of /a/ say /i/	did	2. Say:	set	instead of /e/ say /a/	sat
	bag	instead of /a/ say /i/	big		lid	instead of /i/ say /e/	led
	hat	instead of /a/ say /o/	hot		bat	instead of /a/ say /i/	bit
	map	instead of /a/ say /o/	mop		dash	instead of /a/ say /i/	dish
	get	instead of /e/ say /o/	got		his	instead of /i/ say /a/	has
	had	instead of /a/ say /i/	hid		cot	instead of /o/ say /a/	cat
	cab	instead of /a/ say /u/	cub		fan	instead of /a/ say /i/	fin
	fan	instead of /a/ say /u/	fun		mad	instead of /a/ say /u/	mud
	pat	instead of /a/ say /e/	pet		tap	instead of /a/ say /o/	top
	not	instead of /o/ say /e/	net		sat	instead of /a/ say /e/	set

3. Say:	hot	instead of /o/ say /a/	hat	4. Say:	tell	instead of /e/ say /aw/	tall
	lap	instead of /a/ say /i/	lip		sack	instead of /a/ say /i/	sick
	deck	instead of /e/ say /u/	duck		bed	instead of /e/ say /u/	bud
	bag	instead of /a/ say /u/	bug		den	instead of /e/ say /uh/	done
	fat	instead of /a/ say /i/	fit		cub	instead of /u/ say /a/	cab
	cap	instead of /a/ say /u/	cup		hat	instead of /a/ say /i/	hit
	rock	instead of /o/ say /a/	rack		sell	instead of /e/ say /i/	sill
	man	instead of /a/ say /e/	men		fix	instead of /i/ say /o/	fox
	run	instead of /u/ say /a/	ran		mat	instead of /a/ say /e/	met
	lad	instead of /a/ say /e/	led		hem	instead of /e/ say /i/	him

5. Say:	till	instead of /i/ say /aw/	tall	6. Say:	knack	instead of /a/ say /o/	knock
	got	instead of /o/ say /e/	get		luck	instead of /u/ say /o/	lock
	tin	instead of /i/ say /e/	ten		doll	instead of /o/ say /u/	dull
	hit	instead of /i/ say /a/	hat		hit	instead of /i/ say /u/	hut
	beg	instead of /e/ say /u/	bug		bid	instead of /i/ say /e/	bed
	dish	instead of /i/ say /a/	dash		hot	instead of /o/ say /i/	hit
	fin	instead of /i/ say /u/	fun		men	instead of /e/ say /a/	man
	met	instead of /e/ say /a/	mat		fox	instead of /o/ say /i/	fix
	lad	instead of /a/ say /i/	lid		net	instead of /e/ say /o/	not
	lack	instead of /a/ say /o/	lock		let	instead of /e/ say /i/	lit

7. Say:	pen	instead of /e/ say /a/	pan	*Mixed Levels*	hat	instead of /a/ say /o/	hot
	cat	instead of /a/ say /u/	cut	(G1)	tab	instead of /t/ say /k/	cab
	dell	instead of /e/ say /o/	doll	(J)	lap	instead of /a/ say /i/	lip
	bat	instead of /a/ say /e/	bet	(H1)	flute	don't say /f/	loot
	has	instead of /a/ say /i/	his	(J)	bat	instead of /a/ say /e/	bet
	met	instead of /e/ say /i/	mitt	(H2)	breeze	instead of /b/ say /t/	trees
	fell	instead of /e/ say /i/	fill	(J)	fell	instead of /e/ say /i/	fill
	hat	instead of /a/ say /u/	hut	(I2)	rove	don't say /v/	row
	pan	instead of /a/ say /e/	pen	(J)	pan	instead of /a/ say /e/	pen
	lid	instead of /i/ say /a/	lad	(I1)	card	don't say /d/	car

One Minute Activities Level J

	Say:	hid	Now say **hid**, but instead of /i/ say /a/	**had**
	Or say:	hid	Now say it again, but instead of /i/ say /a/	**had**

8. Say:	hid	instead of /i/ say /a/	had	9. Say:	pat	instead of /a/ say /u/	putt
	moth	instead of /aw/ say /a/	math		set	instead of /e/ say /i/	sit
	lip	instead of /i/ say /a/	lap		fad	instead of /a/ say /e/	fed
	beg	instead of /e/ say /i/	big		mop	instead of /o/ say /a/	map
	fin	instead of /i/ say /a/	fan		dug	instead of /u/ say /i/	dig
	cup	instead of /u/ say /a/	cap		big	instead of /i/ say /a/	bag
	jab	instead of /a/ say /o/	job		sing	instead of /i/ say /u/	sung
	dive	instead of /I/ say /O/	dove		sat	instead of /a/ say /i/	sit
	leg	instead of /e/ say /u/	lug		jot	instead of /o/ say /e/	jet
	sack	instead of /a/ say /o/	sock		quack	instead of /a/ say /i/	quick

10. Say:	kit	instead of /i/ say /a/	cat	11. Say:	jam	instead of /a/ say /e/	gem
	read	instead of /E/ say /O/	road		bat	instead of /a/ say /i/	bit
	lack	instead of /a/ say /u/	luck		dock	instead of /o/ say /u/	duck
	wash	instead of /aw/ say /i/	wish		fun	instead of /u/ say /a/	fan
	gate	instead of /A/ say /O/	goat		him	instead of /i/ say /u/	hum
	budge	instead of /u/ say /a/	badge		wreck	instead of /e/ say /o/	rock
	hut	instead of /u/ say /a/	hat		led	instead of /e/ say /a/	lad
	chop	instead of /o/ say /i/	chip		rack	instead of /a/ say /o/	rock
	much	instead of /u/ say /a/	match		net	instead of /e/ say /i/	knit
	sake	instead of /A/ say /a/	sack		huff	instead of /u/ say /a/	half

12. Say:	quick	instead of /i/ say /a/	quack	13. Say:	ran	instead of /a/ say /u/	run
	jog	instead of /o/ say /u/	jug		rope	instead of /O/ say /I/	ripe
	ledge	instead of /e/ say /o/	lodge		mean	instead of /E/ say /O/	moan
	hop	instead of /o/ say /i/	hip		dime	instead of /I/ say /O/	dome
	rug	instead of /u/ say /a/	rag		leg	instead of /e/ say /aw/	log
	gem	instead of /e/ say /i/	gym		seem	instead of /E/ say /u/	some
	hip	instead of /i/ say /o/	hop		tip	instead of /i/ say /o/	top
	soot	instead of /oo/ say /a/	sat		red	instead of /e/ say /i/	rid
	wet	instead of /e/ say /u/	what		hut	instead of /u/ say /i/	hit
	knack	instead of /a/ say /e/	neck		zip	instead of /i/ say /a/	zap

14. Say:	sing	instead of /i/ say /a/	sang	*Mixed Levels*	cup	instead of /u/ say /a/	cap
	pat	instead of /a/ say /i/	pit	(G1)	sun	instead of /s/ say /f/	fun
	cut	instead of /u/ say /a/	cat	(J)	hit	instead of /i/ say /u/	hut
	nip	instead of /i/ say /a/	nap	(H1)	sleep	don't say /s/	leap
	bet	instead of /e/ say /a/	bat	(J)	big	instead of /i/ say /a/	bag
	pack	instead of /a/ say /i/	pick	(H2)	cream	instead of /k/ say /d/	dream
	hem	instead of /e/ say /u/	hum	(J)	dig	instead of /i/ say /u/	dug
	dig	instead of /i/ say /u/	dug	(I2)	plane	don't say /n/	play
	fix	instead of /i/ say /a/	fax	(J)	pet	instead of /e/ say /a/	pat
	pet	instead of /e/ say /a/	pat	(I1)	inch	don't say /ch/	in

One Minute Activities Level J

	Say:	**sad**	Now say **sad**, but instead of /a/ say /e/	**said**
	Or say:	**sad**	Now say it again, but instead of /a/ say /e/	**said**
	Or say:	**sad**	but instead of /a/ say /e/	**said**

15. Say:	sad	instead of /a/ say /I/	side	16. Say:	beg	instead of /e/ say /a/	bag
	ten	instead of /e/ say /a/	tan		him	instead of /i/ say /e/	hem
	tap	instead of /a/ say /i/	tip		did	instead of /i/ say /a/	dad
	pen	instead of /e/ say /i/	pin		lot	instead of /o/ say /i/	lit
	bit	instead of /i/ say /a/	bat		fill	instead of /i/ say /e/	fell
	led	instead of /e/ say /i/	lid		gem	instead of /e/ say /a/	jam
	chip	instead of /i/ say /o/	chop		cat	instead of /a/ say /I/	kite
	bake	instead of /A/ say /E/	beak		bite	instead of /I/ say /O/	boat
	ship	instead of /i/ say /o/	shop		cheese	instead of /E/ say /O/	chose
	pet	instead of /e/ say /i/	pit		shock	instead of /o/ say /a/	shack
17. Say:	tack	instead of /a/ say /i/	tick	18. Say:	note	instead of /O/ say /I/	night
	phone	instead of /O/ say /I/	fine		rise	instead of /I/ say /A/	raise
	pin	instead of /i/ say /e/	pen		less	instead of /e/ say /E/	lease
	neck	instead of /e/ say /o/	knock		hut	instead of /u/ say /o/	hot
	lag	instead of /a/ say /e/	leg		pet	instead of /e/ say /a/	pat
	gym	instead of /i/ say /a/	jam		neat	instead of /E/ say /I/	night
	zag	instead of /a/ say /i/	zig		lane	instead of /A/ say /O/	loan
	tab	instead of /a/ say /u/	tub		jug	instead of /u/ say /o/	jog
	will	instead of /i/ say /e/	well		nice	instead of /I/ say /E/	niece
	hum	instead of /u/ say /i/	him		win	instead of /i/ say /e/	when
19. Say:	pass	instead of /a/ say /A/	pace	*Mixed Levels*	tack	instead of /a/ say /i/	tick
	kit	instead of /i/ say /u/	cut	(G1)	keep	instead of /k/ say /l/	leap
	hoax	instead of /O/ say /I/	hikes	(J)	will	instead of /i/ say /e/	well
	ten	instead of /e/ say /i/	tin	(H1)	trap	don't say /t/	rap
	shop	instead of /o/ say /i/	ship	(J)	hip	instead of /i/ say /o/	hop
	look	instead of /oo/ say /A/	lake	(H2)	froze	instead of /f/ say /g/	grows
	line	instead of /I/ say /O/	loan	(J)	seem	instead of /E/ say /u/	some
	main	instead of /A/ say /I/	mine	(I2)	fleet	don't say /t/	flee
	height	instead of /I/ say /E/	heat	(J)	main	instead of /A/ say /I/	mine
	tack	instead of /a/ say /u/	tuck	(I1)	malt	don't say /t/	mall
20. Say:	lack	instead of /a/ say /I/	like	*Mixed Levels*	sad	instead of /a/ say /I/	side
	win	instead of /i/ say /e/	when	(G1)	rain	instead of /r/ say /ch/	chain
	pan	instead of /a/ say /i/	pin	(J)	read	instead of /E/ say /O/	road
	tell	instead of /e/ say /oo/	tool	(H1)	bland	don't say /b/	land
	bug	instead of /u/ say /a/	bag	(J)	net	instead of /e/ say /i/	knit
	fuzz	instead of /u/ say /i/	fizz	(H2)	brace	instead of /b/ say /g/	grace
	dull	instead of /u/ say /o/	doll	(J)	gym	instead of /i/ say /e/	gem
	cape	instead of /A/ say /E/	keep	(I2)	moon	don't say /n/	moo
	gym	instead of /i/ say /e/	gem	(I1)	grasp	don't say /p/	grass
	wish	instead of /i/ say /aw/	wash	(J)	fill	instead of /i/ say /e/	fell

Supplemental One Minute Activities for Level J

	Say:	**same**	Now say **same**, but instead of /A/ say /E/	**seem**
	Or say:	**same**	Now say it again, but instead of /A/ say /E/	**seem**

S1	same	/A/ to /E/	seem	S2	give	/i/ to /A/	gave	S3	but	/u/ to /a/	bat
	ball	/aw/ to /e/	bell		hose	/O/ to /i/	his		then	/e/ to /a/	than
	him	/i/ to /O/	home		kit	/i/ to /I/	kite		lit	/i/ to /o/	lot
	rug	/u/ to /i/	rig		lap	/a/ to /E/	leap		myth	/i/ to /a/	math
	luck	/u/ to /o/	lock		sad	/a/ to /I/	side		room	/oo/ to /I/	rhyme
	knit	/i/ to /e/	net		sill	/i/ to /e/	sell		what	/u/ to /e/	wet
	moth	/o/ to /i/	myth		get	/e/ to /A/	gate		love	/u/ to /E/	leave
	nose	/O/ to /E/	knees		sack	/a/ to /O/	soak		time	/I/ to /E/	team
	seek	/E/ to /O/	soak		bath	/a/ to /oo/	booth		soot	/oo/ to /e/	set
	ring	/i/ to /a/	rang		leaf	/E/ to /O/	loaf		quake	/A/ to /i/	quick

S4	white	/I/ to /A/	wait	S5	lip	/i/ to /E/	leap	S6	nine	/I/ to /O/	known
	game	/A/ to /u/	gum		phone	/O/ to /a/	fan		feet	/E/ to /i/	fit
	job	/o/ to /a/	jab		leap	/E/ to /oo/	loop		lot	/o/ to /e/	let
	ring	/i/ to /aw/	wrong		knock	/o/ to /e/	neck		type	/I/ to /a/	tap
	tame	/A/ to /I/	time		loss	/aw/ to /e/	less		life	/I/ to /E/	leaf
	shape	/A/ to /E/	sheep		hoop	/oo/ to /o/	hop		dawn	/aw/ to /u/	done
	weed	/E/ to /I/	wide		these	/E/ to /O/	those		rock	/o/ to /A/	rake
	let	/e/ to /o/	lot		can	/a/ to /A/	cane		let	/e/ to /A/	late
	pick	/i/ to /a/	pack		lime	/I/ to /a/	lamb		ring	/i/ to /u/	rung
	sit	/i/ to /a/	sat		tan	/a/ to /e/	ten		moth	/aw/ to /a/	math

S7	when	/e/ to /i/	win	S8	woke	/O/ to /E/	week	S9	ride	/I/ to /E/	read
	goes	/O/ to /I/	guys		knit	/i/ to /E/	neat		laugh	/a/ to /O/	loaf
	toad	/O/ to /I/	tied		made	/A/ to /a/	mad		weed	/E/ to /I/	wide
	rid	/i/ to /e/	red		sick	/i/ to /o/	sock		kick	/i/ to /A/	cake
	knit	/i/ to /o/	not		moose	/oo/ to /I/	mice		rain	/A/ to /a/	ran
	heat	/E/ to /a/	hat		name	/A/ to /u/	numb		hide	/I/ to /i/	hid
	tone	/O/ to /a/	tan		when	/e/ to /u/	won		coach	/O/ to /a/	catch
	sick	/i/ to /a/	sack		lawn	/aw/ to /A/	lane		sit	/i/ to /e/	set
	pin	/i/ to /a/	pan		tap	/a/ to /A/	tape		lit	/i/ to /e/	let
	late	/A/ to /I/	light		soot	/oo/ to /i/	sit		wreck	/e/ to /a/	rack

Multisyllabic/Applied
One Minute Activities Level J

For multisyllabic/applied activities, see pages 91 and 192

Say: **batter** Now say **batter**, but instead of /a/ say /i/   **bitter**
Or say: **batter** Now say it again, but instead of /a/ say /i/   **bitter**

1. Say:
   - batter — instead of /a/ say /i/ — bitter
   - paddle — instead of /a/ say /e/ — pedal
   - litter — instead of /i/ say /e/ — letter
   - lesson — instead of /e/ say /i/ — listen
   - Tigger — instead of /i/ say /I/ — tiger
   - bluster — instead of /u/ say /i/ — blister
   - waiter — instead of /A/ say /aw/ — water
   - rally — instead of /a/ say /E/ — really
   - notion — instead of /O/ say /A/ — nation
   - trolley — instead of /o/ say /oo/ — truly

2. Say:
   - medal — instead of /e/ say /i/ — middle
   - paddle — instead of /a/ say /oo/ — poodle
   - weeder — instead of /E/ say /I/ — wider
   - bitter — instead of /i/ say /u/ — butter
   - fraction — instead of /a/ say /i/ — friction
   - clover — instead of /O/ say /e/ — clever
   - mansion — instead of /a/ say /e/ — mention
   - ladder — instead of /a/ say /E/ — leader
   - suffer — instead of /u/ say /A/ — safer
   - loosen — instead of /oo/ say /i/ — listen

3. Say:
   - father — instead of /o/ say /e/ — feather
   - ladder — instead of /a/ say /e/ — letter
   - waken — instead of /A/ say /E/ — weaken
   - testing — instead of /e/ say /O/ — toasting
   - needle — instead of /E/ say /oo/ — noodle
   - gable — instead of /A/ say /o/ — gobble
   - sloppy — instead of /o/ say /E/ — sleepy
   - chatter — instead of /a/ say /e/ — cheddar
   - tattle — instead of /a/ say /O/ — total
   - biker — instead of /I/ say /A/ — baker

4. Say:
   - being — instead of /E/ say /I/ — buying
   - stubble — instead of /u/ say /A/ — stable
   - noble — instead of /O/ say /i/ — nibble
   - fritter — instead of /i/ say /A/ — freighter
   - hotter — instead of /o/ say /E/ — heater
   - spatial — instead of /A/ say /e/ — special
   - hilly — instead of /i/ say /O/ — holy
   - fleeing — instead of /E/ say /I/ — flying
   - tidal — instead of /I/ say /O/ — total
   - bitter — instead of /i/ say /e/ — better

5. Say:
   - paper — instead of /A/ say /e/ — pepper
   - jolly — instead of /o/ say /e/ — jelly
   - cleaver — instead of /E/ say /e/ — clever
   - tasty — instead of /A/ say /O/ — toasty
   - wither — instead of /i/ say /e/ — weather
   - taken — instead of /A/ say /O/ — token
   - cutting — instead of /u/ say /O/ — coating
   - reader — instead of /E/ say /I/ — rider
   - haven — instead of /a/ say /e/ — heaven
   - foster — instead of /aw/ say /a/ — faster

Multisyllabic/Applied
One Minute Activities Level J

For multisyllabic/applied activities, see pages 91 and 192

Say: **shipping** Now say shipping, but instead of /i/ say /o/ **shopping**
Or say: **shipping** Now say it again, but instead of /i/ say /o/ **shopping**

6. Say: shipping   instead of /i/ say /o/   shopping
   butter   instead of /u/ say /e/   better
   puddle   instead of /u/ say /a/   paddle
   setter   instead of /e/ say /i/   sitter
   noted   instead of /O/ say /i/   knitted

   mantle   instead of /a/ say /e/   mental
   holly   instead of /o/ say /i/   hilly
   sicker   instead of /i/ say /o/   soccer
   feature   instead of /E/ say /U/   future
   simmer   instead of /i/ say /u/   summer

7. Say: become   instead of /u/ say /A/   became
   diner   instead of /I/ say /i/   dinner
   dabble   instead of /a/ say /u/   double
   compile   instead of /I/ say /e/   compel
   slander   instead of /a/ say /e/   slender

   expand   instead of /a/ say /e/   expend
   miter   instead of /I/ say /E/   meter
   constrict   instead of /i/ say /u/   construct
   budding   instead of /u/ say /i/   bidding
   affects   instead of /e/ say /i/   affix

8. Say: arise   instead of /I/ say /O/   arose
   begin   instead of /i/ say /u/   begun
   doorstep   instead of /e/ say /o/   doorstop
   forgave   instead of /A/ say /i/   forgive
   wonder   instead of /uh/ say /ah/ wander

   ghastly   instead of /A/ say /O/   ghostly
   compete   instead of /E/ say /U/   compute
   posture   instead of /o/ say /a/   pasture
   pander   instead of /a/ say /o/   ponder
   expanse   instead of /a/ say /e/   expense

9. Say: devote instead of /O/ say /ow/   devout
   rover   instead of /O/ say /i/   river
   reset   instead of /e/ say /I/   recite
   poodle   instead of /oo/ say /e/   pedal
   unlike   instead of /I/ say /o/   unlock

   weeding   instead of /E/ say /e/   wedding
   robot   instead of /o/ say /O/   rowboat
   mutter   instead of /u/ say /a/   matter
   possession   instead of /e/ say /i/   position
   sadden   instead of /a/ say /u/   sudden

10. Say: forget   instead of /e/ say /o/   forgot
    motion   instead of /o/ say /i/   mission
    began   instead of /a/ say /i/   begin
    waver   instead of /A/ say /E/   weaver
    conceal   instead of /E/ say /O/   console

    puddle   instead of /u/ say /oo/   poodle
    commit   instead of /i/ say /U/   commute
    wrapping   instead of /a/ say /i/   ripping
    connote   instead of /O/ say /o/   cannot
    meter   instead of /E/ say /a/   matter

LEVEL K

ADVANCED PHONEME-LEVEL PROCESSING
MANIPULATING THE SECOND SOUND IN INITIAL BLENDS

K1   Level K1 involves the deletion of the second sound in an initial blend. Because it involves deleting an internal sound, it is more difficult than deleting a beginning sound (Levels F1 & H1) or ending sound (Levels I1 & I2)

Samples: p(l)an → pan   b(r)ake → bake

K2   Level K2 involves the substitution of the second sound in an initial blend. Because it involves substituting an internal sound, it is more difficult than substituting a beginning sound (Levels G1 & H2) but is about as equally difficult as substituting an ending sound (Levels L1 & L2)

Samples: f(l)y → f(r)y   s(p)ill → s(k)ill

Challenge Words: Level K Activities with Three-Phoneme Blends

It is recommended that students be exposed to three-phoneme blends as well as the more common two-phoneme blends. This is the purpose of the *Challenge Words*. Students can do these *Challenge Words* after students have mastered K1 and K2 activities. Another way is to mix some of these items in while they are learning the regular K1 and K2 activities. You could keep one finger in the K1 or K2 *Challenge Words* and one finger in the regular activities. For most children, this will present no difficulty, while for others, you may need to provide additional instruction about these three phoneme blends.

    Challenge K1   This involves the deletion of the second or third sound in a three phoneme initial blend.

    Samples: s(p)lendor → slender   sp(r)out → spout

    Challenge K2   This activity involves the substitution of the second or third sound in a three phoneme initial blend.

    Samples: s(t)rain → s(p)rain   sp(l)inter → sp(r)inter

Remember: THE FOCUS IS ON THE SOUNDS, NOT SPELLING PATTERNS.

One Minute Activities Level K1

		Say:	**try**	Now say **try**, but don't say **/r/**	tie	
		Or say:	**try**	Now say it again, but don't say **/r/**	tie	

1. Say:	try	don't say /r/	tie	2. Say:	ski	don't say /k/	see
	flee	don't say /l/	fee		ply	don't say /l/	pie
	bland	don't say /l/	band		brook	don't say /r/	book
	claim	don't say /l/	came		blank	don't say /l/	bank
	grow	don't say /r/	go		clamp	don't say /l/	camp
	true	don't say /r/	too		free	don't say /r/	fee
	plan	don't say /l/	pan		skip	don't say /k/	sip
	breeze	don't say /r/	bees		break	don't say /r/	bake
	clap	don't say /l/	cap		sneak	don't say /n/	seek
	blend	don't say /l/	bend		truth	don't say /r/	tooth

3. Say:	glow	don't say /l/	go	4. Say:	stay	don't say /t/	say
	slow	don't say /l/	so		glide	don't say /l/	guide
	flat	don't say /l/	fat		speed	don't say /p/	seed
	glum	don't say /l/	gum		clash	don't say /l/	cash
	flare	don't say /l/	fair		blind	don't say /l/	bind
	trap	don't say /r/	tap		trip	don't say /r/	tip
	plain	don't say /l/	pain		drown	don't say /r/	down
	scale	don't say /k/	sale		stir	don't say /t/	sir
	fled	don't say /l/	fed		freeze	don't say /r/	fees
	sweet	don't say /w/	seat		snack	don't say /n/	sack

5. Say:	pray	don't say /r/	pay	6. Say:	brake	don't say /r/	bake
	sky	don't say /k/	sigh		plaid	don't say /l/	pad
	bright	don't say /r/	bite		crouch	don't say /r/	couch
	steal	don't say /t/	seal		bloat	don't say /l/	boat
	brag	don't say /r/	bag		proof	don't say /r/	poof
	creep	don't say /r/	keep		steam	don't say /t/	seem
	snow	don't say /n/	so		grasp	don't say /r/	gasp
	trick	don't say /r/	tick		bring	don't say /r/	bing
	fright	don't say /r/	fight		slack	don't say /l/	sack
	bread	don't say /r/	bed		trite	don't say /r/	tight

7. Say:	black	don't say /l/	back	*Mixed Levels*		claim	don't say /l/	came
	stand	don't say /t/	sand	(H1)		slack	don't say /s/	lack
	broil	don't say /r/	boil	(K1)		grow	don't say /r/	go
	crane	don't say /r/	cane	(H2)		true	instead of /t/ say /d/	drew
	brace	don't say /r/	base	(K1)		clap	don't say /l/	cap
	sport	don't say /p/	sort	(I2)		plane	don't say /n/	play
	trend	don't say /r/	tend	(K1)		clash	don't say /l/	cash
	place	don't say /l/	pace	(I2)		worse	don't say /s/	were
	grain	don't say /r/	gain	(K1)		trend	don't say /r/	tend
	skill	don't say /k/	sill	(J)		line	instead of /I/ say /O/	loan

One Minute Activities Level K1

| | Say: | **sway** | Now say **sway**, but don't say **/w/** | say |
| | Or say: | **sway** | Now say it again, but don't say **/w/** | say |

8. Say:	sway	don't say /w/	say	9. Say:	flame	don't say /l/	fame
	blade	don't say /l/	bade		snail	don't say /n/	sail
	play	don't say /l/	pay		bleak	don't say /l/	beak
	Greece	don't say /r/	geese		plow	don't say /l/	pow
	freed	don't say /r/	feed		drove	don't say /r/	dove
	crave	don't say /r/	cave		crook	don't say /r/	cook
	stick	don't say /t/	sick		flake	don't say /l/	fake
	drum	don't say /r/	dumb		swell	don't say /w/	sell
	twin	don't say /w/	tin		Fran	don't say /r/	fan
	grill	don't say /r/	gill		slang	don't say /l/	sang

10. Say:	brief	don't say /r/	beef	11. Say:	tree	don't say /r/	tee
	spell	don't say /p/	sell		swift	don't say /w/	sift
	prop	don't say /r/	pop		blight	don't say /l/	bite
	slip	don't say /l/	sip		clone	don't say /l/	cone
	blob	don't say /l/	Bob		sweat	don't say /w/	set
	flax	don't say /l/	fax		blond	don't say /l/	bond
	grab	don't say /r/	gab		crawl	don't say /r/	call
	crumb	don't say /r/	come		snore	don't say /n/	sore
	scheme	don't say /k/	seem		brass	don't say /r/	bass
	plant	don't say /l/	pant		fleet	don't say /l/	feet

12. Say:	club	don't say /l/	cub	13. Say:	glaze	don't say /l/	gaze
	speak	don't say /p/	seek		flinch	don't say /l/	finch
	pry	don't say /r/	pie		snoop	don't say /n/	soup
	sphinx	don't say /f/	sinks		please	don't say /l/	peas
	frought	don't say /r/	fought		frog	don't say /r/	fog
	stage	don't say /t/	sage		cloak	don't say /l/	Coke
	bleep	don't say /l/	beep		flight	don't say /l/	fight
	spy	don't say /p/	sigh		blare	don't say /l/	bare
	grave	don't say /r/	gave		drive	don't say /r/	dive
	sleep	don't say /l/	seep		slope	don't say /l/	soap

14. Say:	cling	don't say /l/	king	*Mixed Levels*	snow	don't say /n/	so
	blest	don't say /l/	best	(H1)	cloud	don't say /k/	loud
	spoon	don't say /p/	soon	(K1)	brake	don't say /r/	bake
	tried	don't say /r/	tied	(H2)	glass	instead of /g/ say /k/	class
	crash	don't say /r/	cash	(K1)	spoon	don't say /p/	soon
	swing	don't say /w/	sing	(I2)	wait	don't say /t/	way
	drug	don't say /r/	dug	(K1)	slight	don't say /l/	sight
	score	don't say /k/	sore	(I1)	burnt	don't say /t/	burn
	bleach	don't say /l/	beach	(K1)	snail	don't say /n/	sail
	slight	don't say /l/	sight	(J)	main	instead of /A/ say /I/	mine

One Minute Activities Level K1

| | Say: | **sling** | Now say **sling**, but don't say /l/ | sing |
| | Or say: | **sling** | Now say it again, but don't say /l/ | sing |

15. Say:	sling	don't say /l/	sing	16. Say:	swoop	don't say /w/	soup
	graze	don't say /r/	gaze		trail	don't say /r/	tail
	snake	don't say /n/	sake		slide	don't say /l/	side
	bleat	don't say /l/	beat		pluck	don't say /l/	puck
	frame	don't say /r/	fame		bled	don't say /l/	bed
	slick	don't say /l/	sick		preach	don't say /r/	peach
	drill	don't say /r/	dill		crept	don't say /r/	kept
	cruel	don't say /r/	cool		sly	don't say /l/	sigh
	stake	don't say /t/	sake		breech	don't say /r/	beach
	truck	don't say /r/	tuck		spunk	don't say /p/	sunk

17. Say:	crab	don't say /r/	cab	18. Say:	drip	don't say /r/	dip
	sleek	don't say /l/	seek		prep	don't say /r/	pep
	grew	don't say /r/	goo		blown	don't say /l/	bone
	spite	don't say /p/	site		froze	don't say /r/	foes
	braille	don't say /r/	bail		dream	don't say /r/	deem
	drawn	don't say /r/	dawn		scream	don't say /r/	scheme
	smack	don't say /m/	sack		clause	don't say /l/	cause
	bloom	don't say /l/	boom		stack	don't say /t/	sack
	flow	don't say /l/	foe		blotch	don't say /l/	botch
	spun	don't say /p/	sun		script	don't say /r/	skipped

19. Say:	scoop	don't say /k/	soup	*Mixed Levels*	great	don't say /r/	gate
	great	don't say /r/	gate	(H1)	swing	don't say /s/	wing
	skit	don't say /k/	sit	(K1)	flair	don't say /l/	fair
	flair	don't say /l/	fair	(H2)	slight	instead of /s/ say /f/	flight
	sleek	don't say /l/	seek	(K1)	sleek	don't say /l/	seek
	crate	don't say /r/	Kate	(I2)	drive	don't say /v/	dry
	blood	don't say /l/	bud	(K1)	crab	don't say /r/	cab
	scope	don't say /k/	soap	(I1)	fund	don't say /d/	fun
	brought	don't say /r/	bought	(K1)	drive	don't say /r/	dive
	prance	don't say /r/	pants	(J)	bat	instead of /a/ say /i/	bit

20. Say:	bleed	don't say /l/	bead	*Mixed Levels*	sled	don't say /l/	said
	sled	don't say /l/	said	(H1)	cries	don't say /k/	rise
	cramp	don't say /r/	camp	(K1)	slide	don't say /l/	side
	scold	don't say /k/	sold	(H2)	bread	instead of /b/ say /th/	thread
	drew	don't say /r/	do	(K1)	scheme	don't say /k/	seem
	steal	don't say /t/	seal	(I2)	flown	don't say /n/	flow
	trim	don't say /r/	Tim	(K1)	blond	don't say /l/	bond
	slaw	don't say /l/	saw	(I1)	stork	don't say /k/	store
	plump	don't say /l/	pump	(K1)	slunk	don't say /l/	sunk
	frail	don't say /r/	fail	(J)	height	instead of /I/ say /E/	heat

Supplemental One Minute Activities for Level K1

       Say: **steel**   Now say **steel**, but don't say **/t/**   seal
 Or say: **steel**   Now say it again, but don't say **/t/**   seal

S1	s(t)eel	→ seal	S2	s(t)ill	→ sill	S3	f(r)izz	→ fizz
	s(w)ung	→ sung		b(r)iar	→ buyer		s(p)ent	→ sent
	d(r)ab	→ dab		s(t)ing	→ sing		b(r)oom	→ boom
	s(t)ash	→ sash		b(r)ute	→ boot		s(qu)eeze	→ sieze
	b(r)ow	→ bow		s(t)ale	→ sale		t(r)ike	→ tike
	b(r)each	→ beach		c(l)ean	→ keen		s(t)ock	→ sock
	t(r)ot	→ tot		s(t)eep	→ seep		g(l)ut	→ gut
	s(w)eep	→ seep		f(l)og	→ fog		s(t)ole	→ sole
	t(r)oll	→ toll		sp(r)ain	→ Spain		s(l)eigh	→ say
	s(w)am	→ Sam		s(l)oop	→ soup		g(r)aph	→ gaff
S4	p(l)atter	→ patter	S5	p(l)aster	→ pastor	S6	s(w)elling	→ selling
	p(r)esent	→ peasant		t(r)opical	→ topical		t(r)apper	→ tapper
	s(l)ender	→ sender		c(l)utter	→ cutter		s(n)eakers	→ seekers
	f(l)urry	→ furry		f(r)iction	→ fiction		t(r)opics	→ topics
	s(ch)ooner	→ sooner		p(r)oper	→ popper		d(r)iver	→ diver (or drive)[1]
	p(r)etty	→ pity		c(l)eaner	→ keener		t(r)igger	→ Tigger
	s(t)ole	→ sole		b(l)ender	→ bender		b(r)eaker	→ baker
	s(l)ipper	→ sipper		c(r)ackle	→ cackle		b(r)oiler	→ boiler
	f(r)action	→ faction		t(r)ickle	→ tickle		s(t)ye	→ sigh
	s(n)icker	→ sicker		c(l)uster	→ Custer		f(l)yer	→ fire
S7	f(l)avor	→ favor	S8	f(l)orist	→ forest	S9	s(p)ider	→ cider
	s(p)eller	→ seller		p(l)easant	→ peasant		f(l)ounder	→ founder
	c(l)ove	→ cove		g(r)avel	→ gavel		st(r)eamer	→ steamer
	s(p)lendor	→ slender		s(t)oop	→ soup		g(r)oup	→ goop
	sp(l)endor	→ spender		f(r)ior	→ fire		p(l)eat	→ Pete
	s(t)irrup	→ syrup		s(c)andal	→ sandal		s(t)op	→ sop
	s(t)and	→ sand		d(r)ied	→ died		st(r)oll	→ stole
	s(p)elling	→ selling		s(t)un	→ sun		s(t)inger	→ singer
	s(w)eater	→ setter		g(l)ue	→ goo		f(l)atten	→ fatten
	f(l)avoring	→ favoring		sp(r)ead	→ sped		s(p)eaker	→ seeker

---

[1]Because there are two /r/ sounds in *driver*, both *diver* or *drive* are technically correct answers to this item. However, only the first fits a Level K1 manipulation. If the student says *drive*, acknowledge that *drive* is correct, but then repeat the item and ask him or her to delete the first /r/.

One Minute Activities Level K1 — Challenge Words

For challenge words, see pages 92 and 199

Say: **straight** Now say **straight**, but don't say **/r/** state
Or say: **straight** Now say it again, but don't say **/r/** state

Note: This involves the removal of one or two phonemes from a three phoneme onset, with a few first sounds removed to keep them focused on where the change must be.

1. Say:	straight	don't say /r/	state	2. Say:	struck	don't say /r/	stuck
	scream	don't say /cr/	seem		split	don't say /l/	spit
	strain	don't say /r/	stain		streamer	don't say /r/	steamer
	sprout	don't say /r/	spout		spray	don't say /pr/	say
	strand	don't say /tr/	sand		stroke	don't say /r/	stoke

3. Say:	stray	don't say /r/	stay	4. Say:	scrape	don't say /r/	scape
	splendor	don't say /l/	spender		split	don't say /p/	slit
	stream	don't say /r/	steam		scrum	don't say /r/	scum
	sprain	don't say /r/	Spain		strode	don't say /r/	stowed
	strove	don't say /r/	stove		script	don't say /cr/	sipped

5. Say:	stroll	don't say /r/	stole	6. Say:	strand	don't say /r/	stand
	spread	don't say /r/	sped		script	don't say /r/	skipped
	strung	don't say /r/	stung		scrum	don't say /cr/	sum
	splendor	don't say /p/	slender		split	don't say /pl/	sit
	string	don't say /r/	sting		spray	don't say /r/	spay

7. Say:	scream	don't say /r/	scheme	8. Say:	sprain	don't say /pr/	sane
	strain	don't say /tr/	sane		spread	don't say /pr/	said
	stream	don't say /r/	steam		strung	don't say /tr/	sung
	stray	don't say /tr/	say		string	don't say /tr/	sing
	splendor	don't say /pl/	sender		stroke	don't say /tr/	soak

One Minute Activities Level K2

Say: **spy**   Now say **spy**, but instead of /p/ say /k/   **sky**
Or say: **spy**   Now say it again, but instead of /p/ say /k/   **sky**

1. Say:	spy	instead of /p/ say /k/	sky	2. Say:	free	instead of /r/ say /l/	flee
	glass	instead of /l/ say /r/	grass		skim	instead of /k/ say /w/	swim
	skill	instead of /k/ say /p/	spill		blink	instead of /l/ say /r/	brink
	fly	instead of /l/ say /r/	fry		sniff	instead of /n/ say /t/	stiff
	snow	instead of /n/ say /l/	slow		frame	instead of /r/ say /l/	flame
	play	instead of /l/ say /r/	pray		spoke	instead of /p/ say /m/	smoke
	sweep	instead of /w/ say /l/	sleep		clue	instead of /l/ say /r/	crew
	clash	instead of /l/ say /r/	crash		sweep	instead of /w/ say /t/	steep
	smart	instead of /m/ say /t/	start		grew	instead of /r/ say /l/	glue
	bloom	instead of /l/ say /r/	broom		smack	instead of /m/ say /t/	stack
3. Say:	sway	instead of /w/ say /t/	stay	4. Say:	brand	instead of /r/ say /l/	bland
	glow	instead of /l/ say /r/	grow		snitch	instead of /n/ say /t/	stitch
	skin	instead of /k/ say /p/	spin		clown	instead of /l/ say /r/	crown
	flute	instead of /l/ say /r/	fruit		skate	instead of /k/ say /t/	state
	snore	instead of /n/ say /t/	store		glade	instead of /l/ say /r/	grade
	crime	instead of /r/ say /l/	climb		small	instead of /m/ say /t/	stall
	steak	instead of /t/ say /n/	snake		fry	instead of /r/ say /l/	fly
	proud	instead of /r/ say /l/	plowed		sped	instead of /p/ say /l/	sled
	slow	instead of /l/ say /n/	snow		plod	instead of /l/ say /r/	prod
	cloud	instead of /l/ say /r/	crowd		stung	instead of /t/ say /w/	swung
5. Say:	bleach	instead of /l/ say /r/	breach	6. Say:	graze	instead of /r/ say /l/	glaze
	school	instead of /k/ say /p/	spool		scout	instead of /k/ say /p/	spout
	climb	instead of /l/ say /r/	crime		cram	instead of /r/ say /l/	clam
	smell	instead of /m/ say /p/	spell		blunt	instead of /l/ say /r/	brunt
	fresh	instead of /r/ say /l/	flesh		scheme	instead of /k/ say /t/	steam
	spell	instead of /p/ say /w/	swell		sneak	instead of /n/ say /p/	speak
	grand	instead of /r/ say /l/	gland		fruit	instead of /r/ say /l/	flute
	sweet	instead of /w/ say /l/	sleet		spice	instead of /p/ say /l/	slice
	free	instead of /r/ say /l/	flee		steak	instead of /t/ say /n/	snake
	swept	instead of /w/ say /l/	slept		prod	instead of /r/ say /l/	plod
7. Say:	stale	instead of /t/ say /n/	snail	*Mixed Levels*	steak	instead of /t/ say /n/	snake
	bland	instead of /l/ say /r/	brand	(H2)	craze	instead of /k/ say /t/	trays
	sky	instead of /k/ say /l/	sly	(K2)	flute	instead of /l/ say /r/	fruit
	flee	instead of /l/ say /r/	free	(I2)	keep	don't say /p/	key
	stack	instead of /t/ say /m/	smack	(K2)	slow	instead of /l/ say /n/	snow
	glue	instead of /l/ say /r/	grew	(I1)	mourn	don't say /n/	more
	snip	instead of /n/ say /k/	skip	(K2)	clown	instead of /l/ say /r/	crown
	prank	instead of /r/ say /l/	plank	(J)	cat	instead of /a/ say /u/	cut
	spare	instead of /p/ say /k/	scare	(K2)	sped	instead of /p/ say /l/	sled
	crown	instead of /r/ say /l/	clown	(K1)	sphinx	don't say /f/	sinks

One Minute Activities Level K2

Say: **fries** Now say **fries**, but instead of **/r/** say **/l/** **flies**
Or say: **fries** Now say it again, but instead of **/r/** say **/l/** **flies**

8. Say:				9. Say:			
	fries	instead of /r/ say /l/	flies		grass	instead of /r/ say /l/	glass
	sky	instead of /k/ say /l/	sly		score	instead of /k/ say /t/	store
	scuff	instead of /k/ say /t/	stuff		flight	instead of /l/ say /r/	fright
	close	instead of /l/ say /r/	crows		snack	instead of /n/ say /t/	stack
	smack	instead of /m/ say /n/	snack		brunt	instead of /r/ say /l/	blunt
	braid	instead of /r/ say /l/	blade		stall	instead of /t/ say /m/	small
	sneeze	instead of /n/ say /k/	skis		pry	instead of /r/ say /l/	ply
	glump	instead of /l/ say /r/	grump		sphere	instead of /f/ say /p/	spear
	spill	instead of /p/ say /k/	skill		cramp	instead of /r/ say /l/	clamp
	skate	instead of /k/ say /l/	slate		sway	instead of /w/ say /t/	stay

10. Say:				11. Say:			
	stale	instead of /t/ say /k/	scale		skid	instead of /k/ say /l/	slid
	clamp	instead of /l/ say /r/	cramp		snore	instead of /n/ say /k/	score
	skill	instead of /k/ say /t/	still		claw	instead of /l/ say /r/	craw
	blush	instead of /l/ say /r/	brush		smell	instead of /m/ say /w/	swell
	snip	instead of /n/ say /l/	slip		braid	instead of /r/ say /l/	blade
	flog	instead of /l/ say /r/	frog		snap	instead of /n/ say /l/	slap
	stomp	instead of /t/ say /w/	swamp		glad	instead of /l/ say /r/	grad
	green	instead of /r/ say /l/	glean		smack	instead of /m/ say /l/	slack
	spied	instead of /p/ say /l/	slide		flock	instead of /l/ say /r/	frock
	skate	instead of /k/ say /l/	slate		stoop	instead of /t/ say /k/	scoop

12. Say:				13. Say:			
	spur	instead of /p/ say /t/	stir		spiff	instead of /p/ say /t/	stiff
	clock	instead of /l/ say /r/	crock		swept	instead of /w/ say /t/	stepped
	skip	instead of /k/ say /l/	slip		smear	instead of /m/ say /n/	sneer
	swung	instead of /w/ say /t/	stung		crowd	instead of /r/ say /l/	cloud
	bloke	instead of /l/ say /r/	broke		scout	instead of /k/ say /n/	snout
	snack	instead of /n/ say /l/	slack		pray	instead of /r/ say /l/	play
	switch	instead of /w/ say /t/	stitch		Spain	instead of /p/ say /t/	stain
	storm	instead of /t/ say /w/	swarm		flow	instead of /l/ say /r/	fro
	flesh	instead of /l/ say /r/	fresh		snit	instead of /n/ say /k/	skit
	snuff	instead of /n/ say /t/	stuff		store	instead of /t/ say /n/	snore

14. Say:				*Mixed Levels*			
	flame	instead of /l/ say /r/	frame		state	instead of /t/ say /k/	skate
	scare	instead of /k/ say /t/	stair	(H2)	slant	instead of /s/ say /p/	plant
	smoke	instead of /m/ say /p/	spoke	(K2)	free	instead of /r/ say /l/	flee
	crash	instead of /r/ say /l/	clash	(I2)	drive	don't say /v/	dry
	speed	instead of /p/ say /k/	skied	(K2)	grass	instead of /r/ say /l/	glass
	glean	instead of /l/ say /r/	green	(I1)	stork	don't say /k/	store
	stay	instead of /t/ say /w/	sway	(K2)	sphere	instead of /f/ say /t/	steer
	swell	instead of /w/ say /p/	spell	(J)	bat	instead of /a/ say /e/	bet
	groom	instead of /r/ say /l/	gloom	(K2)	sneak	instead of /n/ say /p/	speak
	snap	instead of /n/ say /l/	slap	(K1)	pry	don't say /r/	pie

One Minute Activities Level K2

Say: **slate**　　Now say **slate**, but instead of /l/ say /k/　skate
Or say: **slate**　　Now say it again, but instead of /l/ say /k/　skate
Or say: **slate**　　but instead of /l/ say /k/　skate

15. Say:	slate	instead of /l/ say /k/	skate	16. Say:	class	instead of /l/ say /r/	crass
	grow	instead of /r/ say /l/	glow		scorn	instead of /k/ say /w/	sworn
	skim	instead of /k/ say /l/	slim		pride	instead of /r/ say /l/	plied
	clank	instead of /l/ say /r/	crank		stark	instead of /t/ say /p/	spark
	snide	instead of /n/ say /l/	slide		grade	instead of /r/ say /l/	glade
	flies	instead of /l/ say /r/	fries		star	instead of /t/ say /p/	spar
	smear	instead of /m/ say /t/	steer		bled	instead of /l/ say /r/	bread
	blight	instead of /l/ say /r/	bright		spin	instead of /p/ say /k/	skin
	spill	instead of /p/ say /t/	still		ply	instead of /l/ say /r/	pry
	plank	instead of /l/ say /r/	prank		swim	instead of /w/ say /k/	skim
17. Say:	skies	instead of /k/ say /p/	spies	18. Say:	swam	instead of /w/ say /k/	scam
	prance	instead of /r/ say /l/	plants		spare	instead of /p/ say /t/	stare
	smear	instead of /m/ say /f/	sphere		clutch	instead of /l/ say /r/	crutch
	fro	instead of /r/ say /l/	flow		skit	instead of /k/ say /n/	snit
	swing	instead of /w/ say /t/	sting		score	instead of /k/ say /w/	swore
	clam	instead of /l/ say /r/	cram		crank	instead of /r/ say /l/	clank
	scan	instead of /k/ say /p/	span		star	instead of /t/ say /k/	scar
	brink	instead of /r/ say /l/	blink		brush	instead of /r/ say /l/	blush
	stake	instead of /t/ say /n/	snake		snail	instead of /n/ say /t/	stale
	swim	instead of /w/ say /l/	slim		crass	instead of /r/ say /l/	class
19. Say:	sky	instead of /k/ say /p/	spy	*Mixed Levels*	sky	instead of /k/ say /p/	spy
	crank	instead of /r/ say /l/	clank	(H2)	fry	instead of /f/ say /k/	cry
	spear	instead of /p/ say /f/	sphere	(K2)	crowd	instead of /r/ say /l/	cloud
	cruise	instead of /r/ say /l/	clues	(I1)	throne	don't say /n/	throw
	steam	instead of /t/ say /k/	scheme	(K2)	skip	instead of /k/ say /l/	slip
	swing	instead of /w/ say /l/	sling	(I2)	rose	don't say /z/	row
	fled	instead of /l/ say /r/	Fred	(K2)	cruise	instead of /r/ say /l/	clues
	smug	instead of /m/ say /n/	snug	(J)	hid	instead of /i/ say /a/	had
	flank	instead of /l/ say /r/	Frank	(K2)	flesh	instead of /l/ say /r/	fresh
	still	instead of /t/ say /k/	skill	(K1)	club	don't say /l/	cub
20. Say:	froze	instead of /r/ say /l/	flows	*Mixed Levels*	swim	instead of /w/ say /k/	skim
	speak	instead of /p/ say /l/	sleek	(H2)	grain	instead of /g/ say /b/	brain
	scale	instead of /k/ say /n/	snail	(K2)	grow	instead of /r/ say /l/	glow
	steep	instead of /t/ say /l/	sleep	(I2)	wage	don't say /j/	way
	crock	instead of /r/ say /l/	clock	(K2)	skate	instead of /k/ say /l/	slate
	snake	instead of /n/ say /t/	stake	(I1)	pierce	don't say /s/	pier
	swoop	instead of /w/ say /n/	snoop	(K2)	flies	instead of /l/ say /r/	fries
	glaze	instead of /l/ say /r/	graze	(J)	fell	instead of /e/ say /i/	fill
	slop	instead of /l/ say /t/	stop	(K2)	snake	instead of /n/ say /t/	stake
	crank	instead of /r/ say /l/	clank	(K1)	scoop	don't say /k/	soup

Supplemental One Minute Activities for Level K2

Say: **snare** Now say **snare**, but instead of **/n/** say **/k/** **scare**
Or say: **snare** Now say it again, but instead of **/n/** say **/k/** **scare**

S1	snare	/n/ to /k/	scare	S2	spar	/p/ to /k/	scar	S3	scar	/k/ to /p/	spar
	spam	/p/ to /w/	swam		snack	/n/ to /m/	smack		spell	/p/ to /m/	smell
	spool	/p/ to /k/	school		spam	/p/ to /l/	slam		scare	/k/ to /n/	snare
	spar	/p/ to /t/	star		stab	/t/ to /l/	slab		snitch	/n/ to /w/	switch
	sneer	/n/ to /t/	steer		spark	/p/ to /t/	stark		span	/p/ to /k/	scan
	spare	/p/ to /n/	snare		scoop	/k/ to /t/	stoop		swam	/w/ to /l/	slam
	steep	/t/ to /w/	sweep		spear	/p/ to /t/	steer		stair	/t/ to /k/	scare
	smock	/m/ to /t/	stock		swoop	/w/ to /t/	stoop		switch	/w/ to /n/	snitch
	speak	/p/ to /n/	sneak		snub	/n/ to /t/	stub		spiff	/p/ to /n/	sniff
	skip	/k/ to /n/	snip		sneak	/n/ to /l/	sleek		spout	/p/ to /t/	stout

S4	snoop	/n/ to /k/	scoop	S5	spot	/p/ to /l/	slot	S6	swoop	/w/ to /k/	scoop
	sneeze	/n/ to /koo/	squeeze		steer	/t/ to /m/	smear		spot	/p/ to /w/	swat
	swift	/w/ to /n/	sniffed		spout	/p/ to /n/	snout		snare	/n/ to /p/	spare
	stop	/t/ to /w/	swap		sting	/t/ to /l/	sling		stair	/t/ to /p/	spare
	scope	/k/ to /l/	slope		spun	/p/ to /t/	stun		scoop	/k/ to /w/	swoop
	stick	/t/ to /l/	slick		scoop	/k/ to /n/	snoop		swelling	/w/ to /p/	spelling
	sneer	/n/ to /p/	spear		stammer	/t/ to /p/	spammer		stallion	/t/ to /k/	scallion
	spoon	/p/ to /w/	swoon		flier	/l/ to /r/	fryer		snoop	/n/ to /l/	sloop
	still	/t/ to /p/	spill		steamer	/t/ to /k/	schemer		steamer	/t/ to /k/	schemer
	smile	/m/ to /t/	style		sneakers	/n/ to /koo/	squeakers		snicker	/n/ to /t/	sticker

S7	flight	/l/ to /r/	fright	S8	spindle	/p/ to /w/	swindle	S9	stamper	/t/ to /k/	scamper
	scarlet	/k/ to /t/	starlet		sputter	/p/ to /t/	stutter		grammar	/r/ to /l/	glamour
	sneakers	/n/ to /p/	speakers		grassy	/r/ to /l/	glassy		scatter	/k/ to /m/	smatter
	spelling	/p/ to /m/	smelling		pleasant	/l/ to /r/	present		smuggle	/m/ to /n/	snuggle
	spatter	/p/ to /k/	scatter		speaker	/p/ to /n/	sneaker		sputter	/p/ to /t/	stutter
	stolen	/t/ to /w/	swollen		style	/t/ to /m/	smile		fragrant	/r/ to /l/	flagrant
	present	/r/ to /l/	pleasant		fragrance	/r/ to /l/	flagrance		spelling	/p/ to /w/	swelling
	flying	/l/ to /r/	frying		speller	/p/ to /t/	stellar		swindle	/w/ to /p/	spindle
	speaker	/p/ to /koo/	squeaker		glimmer	/l/ to /r/	grimmer		swollen	/w/ to /t/	stolen
	glamour	/l/ to /r/	grammar		crack	/r/ to /l/	clack		scurvy	/k/ to /w/	swearvy

One Minute Activities Level K2—Challenge Words

For challenge words, see pages 92 and 199

	Say:	**strain**	Now say **strain**, but instead of /t/ say /p/	**sprain**
	Or say:	**strain**	Now say it again, but instead of /t/ say /p/	**sprain**

1. Say:
strain	instead of /t/ say /p/	sprain
sprint	instead of /r/ say /l/	splint
strap	instead of /t/ say /k/	scrap
spring	instead of /p/ say /t/	string

2. Say:
spray	instead of /p/ say /t/	stray
streamer	instead of /t/ say /k/	screamer
splinter	instead of /l/ say /r/	sprinter
scrap	instead of /k/ say /t/	strap

3. Say:
stray	instead of /t/ say /p/	spray
sprain	instead of /p/ say /t/	strain
script	instead of /k/ say /t/	stripped
stream	instead of /t/ say /k/	scream

4. Say:
sprung	instead of /p/ say /t/	strung
strung	instead of /t/ say /p/	sprung
scroll	instead of /k/ say /t/	stroll
splint	instead of /l/ say /r/	sprint

5. Say:
stroll	instead of /t/ say /k/	scroll
sprint	instead of /r/ say /l/	splint
string	instead of /t/ say /p/	spring
scream	instead of /k/ say /t/	stream

LEVEL L

ADVANCED PHONEME-LEVEL PROCESSING
SUBSTITUTING ENDING CONSONANT SOUNDS

L1   Level L1 involves the substitution of the final consonant sound in a single syllable word.

       Samples: see(d) → sea(t)   hi(d)e → hi(v)e

L2   Level L2 involves the substitution of the final consonant sound in a final consonant blend.

       Samples: war(m) → war(n)   for(c)e → for(k)

Multisyllabic/Applied Activities

The *Multisyllabic/Applied* activities are designed to help children apply the phoneme awareness skills that they have learned to two or three syllable words (see p. 91).

L1 & L2   This involves substituting the last sound of the first syllable of a two syllable word. Because it is not always clear in this multisyllabic/applied activity whether an item best fits L1 or L2, these levels are combined for this activity.

       Samples: ci(n)der → si(s)ter   ar(t)ful → ar(m)ful

Level L is much more difficult than Level I, which also involves ending sounds. Children can more easily delete ending sounds (Level I) than substitute ending sounds (Level L).

Remember: THE FOCUS IS ON THE SOUNDS, NOT SPELLING PATTERNS.

One Minute Activities Level L1

Say: **add** Now say **add**, but instead of **/d/** say **/n/** **an**
Or say: **add** Now say it again, but instead of **/d/** say **/n/** **an**

1. Say:
add	instead of /d/ say /n/	an
as	instead of /z/ say /n/	an
if	instead of /f/ say /n/	in
ash	instead of /sh/ say /t/	at
each	instead of /ch/ say /t/	eat
I'd	instead of /d/ say /m/	I'm
aid	instead of /d/ say /j/	age
odd	instead of /d/ say /n/	on
in	instead of /n/ say /t/	it
us	instead of /s/ say /p/	up

2. Say:
in	instead of /n/ say /f/	if
aim	instead of /m/ say /j/	age
ash	instead of /sh/ say /m/	am
sub	instead of /b/ say /n/	sun
eve	instead of /v/ say /t/	eat
that	instead of /t/ say /n/	than
am	instead of /m/ say /d/	add
seed	instead of /d/ say /t/	seat
I'd	instead of /d/ say /v/	I've
hive	instead of /v/ say /d/	hide

3. Say:
an	instead of /n/ say /m/	am
if	instead of /f/ say /t/	it
on	instead of /n/ say /d/	odd
at	instead of /t/ say /m/	am
oath	instead of /th/ say /k/	oak
eat	instead of /t/ say /v/	eve
pet	instead of /t/ say /n/	pen
is	instead of /z/ say /t/	it
up	instead of /p/ say /v/	of
fade	instead of /d/ say /s/	face

4. Say:
at	instead of /t/ say /n/	an
cub	instead of /b/ say /p/	cup
net	instead of /t/ say /k/	neck
at	instead of /t/ say /d/	add
mouse	instead of /s/ say /th/	mouth
aim	instead of /m/ say /t/	ate
hope	instead of /p/ say /m/	home
gain	instead of /n/ say /t/	gate
I'll	instead of /l/ say /d/	I'd
hem	instead of /m/ say /n/	hen

5. Say:
cheap	instead of /p/ say /k/	cheek
make	instead of /k/ say /d/	made
teen	instead of /n/ say /th/	teeth
dive	instead of /v/ say /m/	dime
hid	instead of /d/ say /m/	him
shook	instead of /k/ say /d/	should
job	instead of /b/ say /g/	jog
late	instead of /t/ say /k/	lake
yet	instead of /t/ say /s/	yes
cough	instead of /f/ say /t/	caught

6. Say:
had	instead of /d/ say /f/	half
neat	instead of /t/ say /d/	need
sheep	instead of /p/ say /t/	sheet
rhyme	instead of /m/ say /d/	ride
bat	instead of /t/ say /j/	badge
fish	instead of /sh/ say /t/	fit
math	instead of /th/ say /n/	man
can	instead of /n/ say /p/	cap
mice	instead of /s/ say /t/	might
goal	instead of /l/ say /t/	goat

7. Say:
an	instead of /n/ say /t/	at
it	instead of /t/ say /f/	if
dish	instead of /sh/ say /d/	did
am	instead of /m/ say /n/	an
out	instead of /t/ say /ch/	ouch
map	instead of /p/ say /n/	man
ate	instead of /t/ say /p/	ape
has	instead of /z/ say /d/	had
us	instead of /s/ say /v/	of
fix	instead of /ks/ say /t/	fit

Mixed Levels
(H2)	dish	instead of /sh/ say /d/	did
	dried	instead of the 1st /d/ say /t/	tried
(L1)	has	instead of /z/ say /d/	had
(I1)	mild	don't say /d/	mile
(L1)	fix	instead of /ks/ say /t/	fit
(J)	moth	instead of /aw/ say /a/	math
(L1)	sub	instead of /b/ say /n/	sun
(K1)	snoop	don't say /n/	soup
(L1)	net	instead of /t/ say /k/	neck
(K1)	spare	instead of /p/ say /t/	stare

One Minute Activities Level L1

Say: **sad**   Now say **sad**, but instead of **/d/** say **/t/**   **sat**
Or say: **sad**   Now say it again, but instead of **/d/** say **/t/**   **sat**

8. Say:	sad	instead of /d/ say /t/	sat	9. Say:	safe	instead of /f/ say /v/	save
	run	instead of /n/ say /sh/	rush		rise	instead of /z/ say /m/	rhyme
	hat	instead of /t/ say /d/	had		tube	instead of /b/ say /th/	tooth
	get	instead of /t/ say /s/	guess		sick	instead of /k/ say /t/	sit
	soup	instead of /p/ say /t/	suit		room	instead of /m/ say /f/	roof
	tide	instead of /d/ say /m/	time		won	instead of /n/ say /t/	what
	tax	instead of /ks/ say /p/	tap		foam	instead of /m/ say /n/	phone
	bathe	instead of /th/ say /k/	bake		wrote	instead of /t/ say /p/	rope
	lime	instead of /m/ say /n/	line		tape	instead of /p/ say /m/	tame
	hot	instead of /t/ say /p/	hop		coach	instead of /ch/ say /t/	coat
10. Say:	fit	instead of /t/ say /n/	fin	11. Say:	whose	instead of /z/ say /m/	whom
	load	instead of /d/ say /f/	loaf		nice	instead of /s/ say /t/	night
	numb	instead of /m/ say /n/	none		men	instead of /n/ say /t/	met
	pave	instead of /v/ say /n/	pain		chin	instead of /n/ say /p/	chip
	reach	instead of /ch/ say /d/	read		bat	instead of /t/ say /th/	bath
	cab	instead of /b/ say /t/	cat		deep	instead of /p/ say /d/	deed
	head	instead of /d/ say /n/	hen		his	instead of /z/ say /d/	hid
	miss	instead of /s/ say /ks/	mix		lock	instead of /k/ say /t/	lot
	seem	instead of /m/ say /n/	seen		moon	instead of /n/ say /s/	moose
	gave	instead of /v/ say /m/	game		gem	instead of /m/ say /t/	jet
12. Say:	sought	instead of /t/ say /s/	sauce	13 Say:	goat	instead of /t/ say /z/	goes
	teeth	instead of /th/ say /ch/	teach		coat	instead of /t/ say /d/	code
	weep	instead of /p/ say /k/	week		hose	instead of /z/ say /p/	hope
	tab	instead of /b/ say /k/	tack		let	instead of /t/ say /d/	led
	pat	instead of /t/ say /th/	path		them	instead of /m/ say /n/	then
	beach	instead of /ch/ say /k/	beak		wash	instead of /sh/ say /k/	walk
	cage	instead of /j/ say /k/	cake		seen	instead of /n/ say /t/	seat
	need	instead of /d/ say /s/	neice		mop	instead of /p/ say /m/	mom
	rush	instead of /sh/ say /g/	rug		six	instead of /ks/ say /t/	sit
	save	instead of /v/ say /m/	same		jug	instead of /g/ say /j/	judge
14. Say:	ban	instead of /n/ say /k/	back	*Mixed Levels*	sad	instead of /d/ say /t/	sat
	hub	instead of /b/ say /t/	hut	(H2)	cloud	instead of /k/ say /p/	plowed
	mood	instead of /d/ say /n/	moon	(L1)	hat	instead of /t/ say /d/	had
	sip	instead of /p/ say /t/	sit	(I1)	yelp	don't say /p/	yell
	road	instead of /d/ say /m/	roam	(L1)	late	instead of /t/ say /k/	lake
	phase	instead of /z/ say /d/	fade	(J)	lip	instead of /i/ say /a/	lap
	come	instead of /m/ say /p/	cup	(L1)	mood	instead of /d/ say /n/	moon
	quiz	instead of /z/ say /t/	quit	(K1)	spy	don't say /p/	sigh
	peace	instead of /s/ say /ch/	peach	(L1)	mouth	instead of /th/ say /s/	mouse
	guess	instead of /s/ say /t/	get	(K2)	swing	instead of /w/ say /t/	sting

One Minute Activities Level L1

	Say:	**seek**	Now say **seek**, but instead of **/k/** say **/t/**	seat
	Or say:	**seek**	Now say it again, but instead of **/k/** say **/t/**	seat
	Or say:	**seek**	but instead of **/k/** say **/t/**	seat

15. Say:	seek	instead of /k/ say /t/	seat	16. Say:	hush	instead of /sh/ say /m/	hum
	rove	instead of /v/ say /d/	road		seam	instead of /m/ say /t/	seat
	tide	instead of /d/ say /m/	time		move	instead of /v/ say /n/	moon
	shed	instead of /d/ say /l/	shell		knife	instead of /f/ say /t/	night
	lake	instead of /k/ say /n/	lane		sat	instead of /t/ say /k/	sack
	rave	instead of /v/ say /n/	rain		was	instead of /z/ say /n/	won
	sun	instead of /n/ say /ch/	such		root	instead of /t/ say /m/	room
	zig	instead of /g/ say /p/	zip		such	instead of /ch/ say /n/	sun
	wet	instead of /t/ say /n/	when		rub	instead of /b/ say /f/	rough
	bat	instead of /t/ say /k/	back		take	instead of /k/ say /p/	tape
17. Say:	web	instead of /b/ say /n/	when	18. Say:	weave	instead of /v/ say /k/	week
	yes	instead of /s/ say /t/	yet		said	instead of /d/ say /t/	set
	wreath	instead of /th/ say /d/	read		mood	instead of /d/ say /s/	moose
	path	instead of /th/ say /k/	pack		mug	instead of /g/ say /ch/	much
	than	instead of /n/ say /t/	that		some	instead of /m/ say /n/	sun
	same	instead of /m/ say /v/	save		wait	instead of /t/ say /k/	wake
	wage	instead of /j/ say /k/	wake		toad	instead of /d/ say /n/	tone
	race	instead of /s/ say /t/	rate		robe	instead of /b/ say /d/	rode
	shave	instead of /v/ say /d/	shade		wide	instead of /d/ say /z/	wise
	roam	instead of /m/ say /b/	robe		booth	instead of /th/ say /t/	boot
19. Say:	jet	instead of /t/ say /m/	gem	*Mixed Levels*	yes	instead of /s/ say /t/	yet
	soon	instead of /n/ say /t/	suit	(H2)	slam	instead of /s/ say /k/	clam
	thin	instead of /n/ say /k/	thick	(L1)	teeth	instead of /th/ say /ch/	teach
	pouch	instead of /ch/ say /t/	pout	(I1)	word	don't say /d/	were
	ripe	instead of /p/ say /t/	right	(L1)	with	instead of /th/ say /sh/	wish
	leap	instead of /p/ say /n/	lean	(J)	beg	instead of /e/ say /i/	big
	with	instead of /th/ say /sh/	wish	(L1)	note	instead of /t/ say /z/	nose
	ball	instead of /l/ say /t/	bought	(K1)	drive	don't say /r/	dive
	note	instead of /t/ say /z/	nose	(L1)	said	instead of /d/ say /t/	set
	soon	instead of /n/ say /p/	soup	(K1)	scan	instead of /k/ say /p/	span
20. Say:	soak	instead of /k/ say /p/	soap	*Mixed Levels*	lake	instead of /k/ say /n/	lane
	cheep	instead of /p/ say /z/	cheese	(H2)	drew	instead of /d/ say /th/	threw
	main	instead of /n/ say /z/	maze	(L1)	bat	instead of /t/ say /k/	back
	rope	instead of /p/ say /t/	wrote	(I1)	halt	don't say /t/	hall
	teach	instead of /ch/ say /m/	team	(L1)	soak	instead of /k/ say /p/	soap
	leaf	instead of /f/ say /d/	lead	(J)	pat	instead of /a/ say /u/	putt
	jazz	instead of /z/ say /m/	jam	(L1)	leaf	instead of /f/ say /d/	lead
	suit	instead of /t/ say /n/	soon	(K1)	flight	don't say /l/	fight
	ran	instead of /n/ say /t/	rat	(L1)	move	instead of /v/ say /n/	moon
	lip	instead of /p/ say /d/	lid	(K2)	clutch	instead of /l/ say /r/	crutch

Supplemental One Minute Activities for Level L1

	Say:	**mat**	Now say **mat** but instead of /t/ say /n/	**man**
	Or say:	**mat**	Now say it again, but instead of /t/ say /n/	**man**

S1	mat	/t/ to /n/	man	S2	made	/d/ to /n/	main	S3	seat	/t/ to /d/	seed
	weed	/d/ to /k/	week		neck	/k/ to /t/	net		tack	/k/ to /p/	tap
	rice	/s/ to /t/	right		pace	/s/ to /d/	paid		weak	/k/ to /d/	weed
	sheet	/t/ to /p/	sheep		take	/k/ to /m/	tame		nudge	/j/ to /n/	none
	lug	/g/ to /k/	luck		soap	/p/ to /k/	soak		right	/t/ to /p/	ripe
	wish	/sh/ to /n/	win		ridge	/j/ to /m/	rim		shake	/k/ to /p/	shape
	shop	/p/ to /k/	shock		night	/t/ to /s/	nice		whose	/z/ to /p/	hoop
	wedge	/j/ to /b/	web		mitt	/t/ to /ks/	mix		shade	/d/ to /k/	shake
	shade	/d/ to /p/	shape		pass	/s/ to /th/	path		hoof	/f/ to /z/	whose
	pin	/n/ to /t/	pit		nose	/z/ to /t/	note		mob	/b/ to /m/	mom

S4	raise	/z/ to /n/	rain	S5	meek	/k/ to /n/	mean	S6	side	/d/ to /n/	sign
	wove	/v/ to /k/	woke		tube	/b/ to /n/	tune		rib	/b/ to /d/	rid
	kit	/t/ to /k/	kick		shake	/k/ to /d/	shade		miss	/s/ to /t/	mitt
	both	/th/ to /t/	boat		rug	/g/ to /n/	run		nose	/z/ to /n/	known
	cube	/b/ to /t/	cute		bike	/k/ to /t/	bite		rid	/d/ to /j/	ridge
	rose	/z/ to /p/	rope		said	/d/ to /t/	set		shape	/p/ to /k/	shake
	woke	/k/ to /v/	wove		tab	/b/ to /n/	tan		whole	/l/ to /m/	home
	rim	/m/ to /ch/	rich		wise	/z/ to /d/	wide		tool	/l/ to /n/	tune
	when	/n/ to /t/	wet		moat	/t/ to /n/	moan		pawn	/n/ to /z/	pause
	phone	/n/ to /k/	folk		luck	/k/ to /g/	lug		tip	/p/ to /k/	tick

S7	maze	/z/ to /d/	made	S8	niece	/s/ to /d/	need	S9	rich	/ch/ to /m/	rim
	gnat	/t/ to /p/	nap		keep	/p/ to /z/	keys		tan	/n/ to /ks/	tax
	pack	/k/ to /th/	path		beach	/ch/ to /z/	bees		sick	/k/ to /ks/	six
	roof	/f/ to /t/	root		mad	/d/ to /p/	map		quill	/l/ to /k/	quick
	sell	/l/ to /d/	said		not	/t/ to /b/	knob		pit	/t/ to /k/	pick
	mad	/d/ to /n/	man		peek	/k/ to /ch/	peach		mill	/l/ to /s/	miss
	keep	/p/ to /n/	keen		news	/z/ to /n/	noon		leash	/sh/ to /g/	league
	rake	/k/ to /t/	rate		phase	/z/ to /s/	face		mouth	/th/ to /s/	mouse
	pick	/k/ to /ch/	pitch		sake	/k/ to /m/	same		vibe	/b/ to /n/	vine
	wife	/f/ to /t/	white		tap	/p/ to /k/	tack		lid	/d/ to /t/	lit

One Minute Activities Level L2

		Say:	**arm**	Now say **arm**, but instead of **/m/** say **/k/**	**ark**
		Or say:	**arm**	Now say it again, but instead of **/m/** say **/k/**	**ark**

1. Say:	arm	instead of /m/ say /k/	ark	2. Say:	surf	instead of /f/ say /ch/	search
	word	instead of /d/ say /k/	work		verb	instead of /b/ say /s/	verse
	warm	instead of /m/ say /n/	warn		force	instead of /s/ say /k/	fork
	urge	instead of /j/ say /th/	earth		send	instead of /d/ say /s/	sense
	course	instead of /s/ say /t/	court		yarn	instead of /n/ say /d/	yard
	arch	instead of /ch/ say /k/	ark		norm	instead of /m/ say /th/	north
	send	instead of /d/ say /t/	sent		sharp	instead of /p/ say /k/	shark
	torn	instead of /n/ say /ch/	torch		and	instead of /d/ say /t/	ant
	earn	instead of /n/ say /j/	urge		ward	instead of /d/ say /m/	warm
	arm	instead of /m/ say /t/	art		hard	instead of /d/ say /m/	harm

3. Say:	elf	instead of /f/ say /m/	elm	4. Say:	French	instead of /ch/ say /d/	friend
	colt	instead of /t/ say /d/	cold		rant	instead of /t/ say /ch/	ranch
	stand	instead of /d/ say /s/	stance		surf	instead of /f/ say /v/	serve
	tend	instead of /d/ say /t/	tent		course	instead of /s/ say /k/	cork
	health	instead of /th/ say /p/	help		stork	instead of /k/ say /m/	storm
	cord	instead of /d/ say /s/	course		musk	instead of /k/ say /t/	must
	pulse	instead of /s/ say /p/	pulp		tend	instead of /d/ say /th/	tenth
	lurk	instead of /k/ say /n/	learn		elf	instead of /f/ say /m/	elm
	barge	instead of /j/ say /k/	bark		prince	instead of /s/ say /t/	print
	spend	instead of /d/ say /t/	spent		ark	instead of /k/ say /t/	art

5. Say:	starch	instead of /ch/ say /t/	start	6. Say:	film	instead of /m/ say /d/	filled
	rent	instead of /t/ say /ch/	wrench		hard	instead of /d/ say /t/	heart
	torque	instead of /k/ say /ch/	torch		morph	instead of /f/ say /n/	mourn
	art	instead of /t/ say /ch/	arch		harm	instead of /m/ say /t/	heart
	court	instead of /t/ say /d/	cord		fierce	instead of /s/ say /d/	feared
	whisk	instead of /k/ say /p/	whisp		lisp	instead of /p/ say /t/	list
	fend	instead of /d/ say /s/	fence		wharf	instead of /f/ say /p/	warp
	lend	instead of /d/ say /t/	lent		cord	instead of /d/ say /t/	court
	shorn	instead of /n/ say /t/	short		perch	instead of /ch/ say /s/	purse
	third	instead of /d/ say /st/	thirst		health	instead of /th/ say /d/	held

7. Say:	false	instead of /s/ say /t/	fault	*Mixed Levels*	word	instead of /d/ say /k/	work
	search	instead of /ch/ say /f/	surf	(I1)	worm	don't say /m/	were
	art	instead of /t/ say /m/	arm	(L2)	sort	instead of /t/ say /s/	source
	wand	instead of /d/ say /t/	want	(J)	mop	instead of /o/ say /a/	map
	barn	instead of /n/ say /b/	barb	(L2)	colt	instead of /t/ say /d/	cold
	silt	instead of /t/ say /k/	silk	(K1)	slope	don't say /l/	soap
	lark	instead of /k/ say /j/	large	(L2)	wand	instead of /d/ say /t/	want
	bend	instead of /d/ say /t/	bent	(K2)	brush	instead of /r/ say /l/	blush
	month	instead of /th/ say /ch/	munch	(L2)	bend	instead of /d/ say /t/	bent
	mark	instead of /k/ say /sh/	marsh	(L1)	than	instead of /n/ say /t/	that

One Minute Activities Level L2

Say: **ark**   Now say **ark**, but instead of **/k/** say **/ch/**   **arch**
Or say: **ark**   Now say it again, but instead of **/k/** say **/ch/**   **arch**

8. Say:	ark	instead of /k/ say /ch/	arch	9. Say:	arch	instead of /ch/ say /m/	arm
	bulk	instead of /k/ say /b/	bulb		card	instead of /d/ say /v/	carve
	therm	instead of /m/ say /d/	third		fork	instead of /k/ say /th/	fourth
	mart	instead of /t/ say /k/	mark		kern	instead of /n/ say /b/	curb
	elk	instead of /k/ say /s/	else		harp	instead of /p/ say /t/	heart
	earn	instead of /n/ say /th/	earth		search	instead of /ch/ say /v/	serve
	dark	instead of /k/ say /t/	dart		parch	instead of /ch/ say /k/	park
	squirm	instead of /m/ say /t/	squirt		torn	instead of /n/ say /d/	toward
	barn	instead of /n/ say /k/	bark		bunk	instead of /k/ say /ch/	bunch
	fern	instead of /n/ say /m/	firm		garb	instead of /b/ say /d/	guard
10. Say:	charm	instead of /m/ say /t/	chart	11. Say:	lunch	instead of /ch/ say /j/	lunge
	birch	instead of /ch/ say /n/	burn		hearth	instead of /th/ say /d/	hard
	ward	instead of /d/ say /n/	warn		stark	instead of /k/ say /t/	start
	stork	instead of /k/ say /d/	stored		risk	instead of /k/ say /t/	wrist
	bench	instead of /ch/ say /d/	bend		hunch	instead of /ch/ say /t/	hunt
	term	instead of /m/ say /f/	turf		coarse	instead of /s/ say /n/	corn
	monk	instead of /k/ say /th/	month		wealth	instead of /th/ say /d/	weld
	word	instead of /d/ say /th/	worth		pounce	instead of /s/ say /d/	pound
	heard	instead of /d/ say /t/	hurt		verse	instead of /s/ say /j/	verge
	torch	instead of /ch/ say /d/	toward		bark	instead of /k/ say /j/	barge
12. Say:	worse	instead of /s/ say /th/	worth	13. Say:	scorn	instead of /n/ say /ch/	scorch
	pulse	instead of /s/ say /p/	pulp		bird	instead of /d/ say /n/	burn
	bark	instead of /k/ say /b/	barb		nerve	instead of /v/ say /f/	nerf
	tarp	instead of /p/ say /t/	tart		month	instead of /th/ say /k/	monk
	sword	instead of /d/ say /s/	source		sent	instead of /t/ say /s/	sense
	firm	instead of /m/ say /n/	fern		grant	instead of /t/ say /d/	grand
	perch	instead of /ch/ say /k/	perk		worst	instead of /t/ say /d/	word
	rend	instead of /d/ say /ch/	wrench		sword	instead of /d/ say /s/	source
	force	instead of /s/ say /th/	fourth		rant	instead of /t/ say /ch/	ranch
	word	instead of /d/ say /m/	worm		lance	instead of /s/ say /d/	land
14. Say:	ant	instead of /t/ say /d/	and	*Mixed Levels*	park	instead of /k/ say /t/	part
	park	instead of /k/ say /t/	part	(I1)	sixth	don't say /th/	six
	harm	instead of /m/ say /p/	harp	(L2)	rent	instead of /t/ say /ch/	wrench
	wince	instead of /s/ say /d/	wind	(J)	dug	instead of /u/ say /i/	dig
	monk	instead of /k/ say /ch/	munch	(L2)	barn	instead of /n/ say /k/	bark
	trench	instead of /ch/ say /d/	trend	(K1)	drip	don't say /r/	dip
	elf	instead of /f/ say /s/	else	(L2)	hard	instead of /d/ say /t/	heart
	word	instead of /d/ say /s/	worse	(K2)	swim	instead of /w/ say /l/	slim
	burn	instead of /n/ say /d/	bird	(L2)	dusk	instead of /k/ say /t/	dust
	dusk	instead of /k/ say /t/	dust	(L1)	path	instead of /th/ say /k/	pack

One Minute Activities Level L2

Say: **cord** Now say **cord**, but instead of **/d/** say **/k/** **cork**
Or say: **cord** Now say it again, but instead of **/d/** say **/k/** **cork**

15. Say:	cord	instead of /d/ say /k/	cork	16. Say:	bird	instead of /d/ say /ch/	birch
	work	instead of /k/ say /d/	word		help	instead of /p/ say /d/	held
	bound	instead of /d/ say /s/	bounce		art	instead of /t/ say /k/	ark
	curd	instead of /d/ say /b/	curb		tenth	instead of /th/ say /t/	tent
	dart	instead of /t/ say /n/	darn		harp	instead of /p/ say /d/	hard
	helm	instead of /m/ say /p/	help		lend	instead of /d/ say /t/	lent
	barn	instead of /n/ say /j/	barge		ford	instead of /d/ say /m/	form
	terse	instead of /s/ say /m/	term		list	instead of /t/ say /p/	lisp
	send	instead of /d/ say /s/	sense		corn	instead of /n/ say /k/	cork
	harp	instead of /p/ say /sh/	harsh		worse	instead of /s/ say /k/	work

17 Say:	elk	instead of /k/ say /f/	elf	18. Say:	cart	instead of /t/ say /d/	card
	fort	instead of /t/ say /s/	force		held	instead of /d/ say /th/	health
	stern	instead of /n/ say /d/	stirred		warm	instead of /m/ say /f/	wharf
	board	instead of /d/ say /n/	born		birch	instead of /ch/ say /d/	bird
	tarp	instead of /p/ say /t/	tart		shard	instead of /d/ say /k/	shark
	form	instead of /m/ say /s/	force		north	instead of /th/ say /m/	norm
	chart	instead of /t/ say /m/	charm		horse	instead of /s/ say /n/	horn
	ward	instead of /d/ say /p/	warp		else	instead of /s/ say /m/	elm
	horn	instead of /n/ say /s/	horse		punch	instead of /ch/ say /k/	punk
	munch	instead of /ch/ say /th/	month		chance	instead of /s/ say /t/	chant

19. Say:	arm	instead of /m/ say /ch/	arch.	*Mixed Levels*	board	instead of /d/ say /n/	born
	font	instead of /t/ say /d/	fond	(I1)	porch	don't say /ch/	poor
	purse	instead of /s/ say /j/	purge	(L2)	horse	instead of /s/ say /n/	horn
	card	instead of /d/ say /t/	cart	(J)	quack	instead of /a/ say /i/	quick
	starch	instead of /ch/ say /d/	starred	(L2)	card	instead of /d/ say /t/	cart
	tend	instead of /d/ say /s/	tense	(K1)	blown	don't say /l/	bone
	scarce	instead of /s/ say /d/	scared	(L2)	dent	instead of /t/ say /s/	dense
	pound	instead of /d/ say /s/	pounce	(K2)	swung	instead of /w/ say /t/	stung
	dent	instead of /t/ say /s/	dense	(L2)	sword	instead of /d/ say /s/	source
	parch	instead of /ch/ say /t/	part	(L1)	shave	instead of /v/ say /d/	shade

20. Say:	welt	instead of /t/ say /th/	wealth	*Mixed Levels*	bench	instead of /ch/ say /d/	bend
	lunge	instead of /j/ say /ch/	lunch	(I1)	dent	don't say /t/	den
	barb	instead of /b/ say /k/	bark	(L2)	coarse	instead of /s/ say /t/	court
	winch	instead of /ch/ say /d/	wind	(J)	jab	instead of /a/ say /o/	job
	court	instead of /t/ say /s/	course	(L2)	tenth	instead of /th/ say /t/	tent
	search	instead of /ch/ say /j/	surge	(K1)	spite	don't say /p/	site
	nerve	instead of /v/ say /s/	nurse	(L2)	work	instead of /k/ say /s/	worse
	term	instead of /m/ say /n/	turn	(K2)	snail	instead of /n/ say /t/	stale
	bolt	instead of /t/ say /d/	bold	(L2)	charm	instead of /m/ say /t/	chart
	tense	instead of /s/ say /t/	tent	(L1)	same	instead of /m/ say /v/	save

Supplemental One Minute Activities for Level L2

Say: **bird** Now say **bird** but instead of /d/ say /th/ birth
Or say: **bird** Now say it again, but instead of /d/ say /th/ birth

S1	bird	/d/ to /th/	birth	S2	third	/d/ to/ st/	thirst	S3	ford	/d/ to /k/	fork
	worth	/th/ to /m/	worm		stunt	/t/ to /d/	stunned		print	/t/ to /s/	prince
	churn	/n/ to /p/	chirp		court	/t/ to /n/	corn		hard	/d/ to /sh/	harsh
	worm	/m/ to /d/	word		wharf	/f/ to /m/	warm		stark	/k/ to /ch/	starch
	porch	/ch/ to /t/	port		birth	/th/ to /ch/	birch		wrist	/t/ to /k/	risk
	stand	/d/ to /s/	stance		plunk	/k/ to /j/	plunge		curve	/v/ to /b/	curb
	carve	/v/ to /d/	card		turf	/f/ to /s/	terse		larch	/ch/ to /d/	lard
	built	/t/ to /d/	build		mast	/t/ to /k/	mask		mince	/s/ to /t/	mint
	held	/d/ to /p/	help		surf	/f/ to /j/	surge		pinch	/ch/ to /d/	pinned
	perk	/k/ to /ch/	perch		range	/j/ to /d/	rained		storm	/m/ to /d/	stored
S4	warn	/n/ to /p/	warp	S5	warn	/n/ to /t/	wart	S6	form	/m/ to /th/	fourth
	silk	/k/ to /t/	silt		blurb	/b/ to /t/	blurt		hard	/d/ to /p/	harp
	charge	/j/ to /t/	chart		corn	/n/ to /s/	course		land	/d/ to /s/	lance
	bench	/ch/ to /t/	bent		force	/s/ to /t/	fort		morn	/n/ to /f/	morph
	plant	/t/ to /d/	planned		grand	/d/ to /t/	grant		park	/k/ to /s/	parse
	squirt	/t/ to /m/	squirm		synth	/th/ to /s/	since		forge	/j/ to /s/	force
	force	/s/ to /m/	form		worse	/s/ to /k/	work		toward	/d/ to /n/	torn
	wisk	/k/ to /p/	wisp		park	/k/ to /ch/	parch		sparse	/s/ to /k/	spark
	elk	/k/ to /m/	elm		barge	/j/ to /n/	barn		hint	/t/ to /j/	hinge
	verb	/b/ to /j/	verge		meant	/t/ to /d/	mend		torch	/ch/ to /k/	torque
S7	dart	/t/ to /k/	dark	S8	pierce	/s/ to /d/	peered	S9	mend	/d/ to /t/	meant
	worse	/s/ to /d/	word		spent	/t/ to /d/	spend		shark	/k/ to /p/	sharp
	guard	/d/ to /b/	garb		church	/ch/ to /n/	churn		tinge	/j/ to /t/	tint
	churn	/n/ to /ch/	church		sort	/t/ to /d/	sword		storm	/m/ to /k/	stork
	worn	/n/ to /m/	warm		cold	/d/ to /t/	colt		fork	/k/ to /t/	fort
	turn	/n/ to /m/	term		worth	/th/ to /k/	work		wrench	/ch/ to /t/	rent
	since	/s/ to /j/	singe		brand	/d/ to /ch/	branch		since	/s/ to /ch/	cinch
	guild	/d/ to /t/	guilt		sort	/t/ to /s/	source		port	/t/ to /ch/	porch
	perk	/k/ to /s/	purse		course	/s/ to /n/	corn		kiln	/n/ to /t/	kilt
	must	/t/ to /k/	musk		nurse	/s/ to /v/	nerve		word	/d/ to /st/	worst

Multisyllabic/Applied
One Minute Activities for Levels L1 and L2

For multisyllabic/applied words, see pages 91 and 210

	Say:	**listing**	Now say **listing**, but instead of /s/ say /f/	**lifting**
	Or say:	**listing**	Now say it again, but instead of /s/ say /f/	**lifting**

1. Say:
artful	instead of /t/ say /m/	armful
bustle	instead of /s/ say /b/	bubble
pasting	instead of /s/ say /n/	painting
cushy	instead of /sh/ say /k/	cookie
listing	instead of /s/ say /f/	lifting
roasting	instead of /st/ say /p/	roping
hasn't	instead of /z/ say /v/	haven't
shuffle	instead of /f/ say /v/	shovel
Casper	instead of /s/ say /m/	camper
actor	instead of /k/ say /f/	after

2. Say:
muskie	instead of /s/ say /n/	monkey
sifter	instead of /f/ say /s/	sister
hadn't	instead of /d/ say /z/	hasn't
planter	instead of /n/ say /s/	plaster
crimpy	instead of /m/ say /s/	crispy
ranted	instead of /n/ say /f/	rafted
cepter	instead of /p/ say /n/	center
whimper	instead of /m/ say /s/	whisper
clasping	instead of /s/ say /m/	clamping
factor	instead of /k/ say /s/	faster

3. Say:
lightness	instead of /t/ say /k/	likeness
chiefly	instead of /f/ say /p/	cheaply
tainted	instead of /n/ say /s/	tasted
cinder	instead of /n/ say /s/	sister
tilted	instead of /l/ say /n/	tinted
clumsy	instead of /m/ say /t/	clutzy
grateful	instead of /t/ say /s/	graceful
tinting	instead of /n/ say /l/	tilting
mulching	instead of /l/ say /n/	munching
resting	instead of /s/ say /n/	renting

4. Say:
mobster	instead of /b/ say /n/	monster
haven't	instead of /v/ say /d/	hadn't
auger	instead of /g/ say /th/	author
tenting	instead of /n/ say /s/	testing
cancel	instead of /n/ say /p/	capsule
faithful	instead of /th/ say /s/	faceful
rinky	instead of /ng/ say /s/	risky
conception	instead of /p/ say /s/	concession
abcess	instead of /b/ say /k/	access
busted	instead of /s/ say /n/	bunted

5. Say:
axle	instead of /ks/ say /p/	apple
wispy	instead of /s/ say /m/	wimpy
hulking	instead of /l/ say /s/	husking
fateful	instead of /t/ say /th/	faithful
rooting	instead of /t/ say /f/	roofing
cinder	instead of /n/ say /f/	sifter
useful	instead of /s/ say /th/	youthful
minty	instead of /n/ say /s/	misty
melding	instead of /l/ say /n/	mending
anvil	instead of /n/ say /d/	Advil

LEVEL M

Advanced Phoneme-level Activities
Deleting and Substituting Internal Phonemes
in Ending blends

M1 Level M1 involves deletion of the second from last sound in an ending blend in a single syllable word. This requires splitting an ending blend.

Samples: coa(s)t → coat   de(s)k → deck

M2 Level M2 involves substitution of the second from last sound in a word, which requires splitting an ending blend.

Samples: li(f)t → li(s)t   pai(n)t → pa(s)te

Remember: THE FOCUS IS ON THE SOUNDS, NOT SPELLING PATTERNS.

One Minute Activities Level M1

| | | Say: | **hand** | Now say **hand**, but don't say **/n/** | **had** |
| | | Or say: | **hand** | Now say it again, but don't say **/n/** | **had** |

1. Say:	ant	don't say /n/	at	2. Say:	grand	don't say /n/	grad
	send	don't say /n/	said		soft	don't say /f/	sought
	camp	don't say /m/	cap		bent	don't say /n/	bet
	and	don't say /n/	ad		end	don't say /n/	Ed
	fend	don't say /n/	fed		desk	don't say /s/	deck
	baste	don't say /s/	bait		beast	don't say /s/	beat
	spend	don't say /n/	sped		bunt	don't say /n/	but
	beeped	don't say /p/	beat		boast	don't say /s/	boat
	blend	don't say /n/	bled		friend	don't say /n/	Fred
	gland	don't say /n/	glad		backed	don't say /k/	bat

3. Say:	sand	don't say /n/	sad	4. Say:	pond	don't say /n/	pod
	hind	don't say /n/	hide		went	don't say /n/	wet
	mask	don't say /s/	Mac		dusk	don't say /s/	duck
	boast	don't say /s/	boat		sent	don't say /n/	set
	want	don't say /n/	watt		feast	don't say /s/	feet
	bend	don't say /n/	bed		vest	don't say /s/	vet
	moved	don't say /v/	mood		dent	don't say /n/	debt
	cast	don't say /s/	cat		blocked	don't say /k/	blot
	boost	don't say /s/	boot		vent	don't say /n/	vet
	shocked	don't say /k/	shot		must	don't say /s/	mutt

5. Say:	pest	don't say /s/	pet	6. Say:	past	don't say /s/	pat
	bust	don't say /s/	but		hint	don't say /n/	hit
	clamp	don't say /m/	clap		capped	don't say /p/	cat
	waste	don't say /s/	wait		sect	don't say /k/	set
	ghost	don't say /s/	goat		rant	don't say /n/	rat
	braved	don't say /v/	braid		chapped	don't say /p/	chat
	gust	don't say /s/	gut		sift	don't say /f/	sit
	fringe	don't say /n/	fridge		hound	don't say /n/	how'd
	rasp	don't say /s/	rap		flapped	don't say /p/	flat
	fact	don't say /k/	fat		mend	don't say /n/	med

7. Say:	lend	don't say /n/	led	*Mixed Levels*	hand	don't say /n/	had
	band	don't say /n/	bad	(J)	leg	instead of /e/ say /u/	lug
	tend	don't say /n/	Ted	(M1)	cast	don't say /s/	cat
	taunt	don't say /n/	taught	(K1)	dream	don't say /r/	deem
	locked	don't say /k/	lot	(M1)	dusk	don't say /s/	duck
	coast	don't say /s/	coat	(K2)	Spain	instead of /p/ say /t/	stain
	fiend	don't say /n/	feed	(M1)	sand	don't say /n/	sad
	east	don't say /s/	eat	(L1)	robe	instead of /b/ say /d/	rode
	clocked	don't say /k/	clot	(M1)	locked	don't say /k/	lot
	west	don't say /s/	wet	(L2)	verb	instead of /b/ say /s/	verse

One Minute Activities Level M1

		Say:	**land**		Now say **land**, but don't say **/n/**	**lad**
		Or say:	**land**		Now say it again, but don't say **/n/**	**lad**

8. Say:	land	don't say /n/	lad	9. Say:	rend	don't say /n/	red
	chant	don't say /n/	chat		swept	don't say /p/	sweat
	wept	don't say /p/	wet		guest	don't say /s/	get
	best	don't say /s/	bet		task	don't say /s/	tack
	risk	don't say /s/	Rick		next	don't say /ks/	net
	bound	don't say /n/	bowed		heaped	don't say /p/	heat
	coped	don't say /p/	coat		bind	don't say /n/	bide
	fast	don't say /s/	fat		kicked	don't say /k/	kid
	sipped	don't say /p/	sit		mint	don't say /n/	mit
	brand	don't say /n/	Brad		rind	don't say /n/	ride

10. Say:	cost	don't say /s/	caught	11. Say:	pump	don't say /m/	pup
	waved	don't say /v/	wade		flask	don't say /s/	flack
	gasp	don't say /s/	gap		just	don't say /s/	jut
	stomp	don't say /m/	stop		apt	don't say /p/	at
	pact	don't say /k/	pat		six	don't say /k/	Sis
	hunt	don't say /n/	hut		grieved	don't say /v/	greed
	topped	don't say /p/	tot		deft	don't say /f/	debt
	raft	don't say /f/	rat		hacked	don't say /k/	hat
	looped	don't say /p/	loot		pomp	don't say /m/	pop
	skipped	don't say /p/	skit		scant	don't say /n/	scat

12. Say:	act	don't say /k/	at	13. Say:	chomp	don't say /m/	chop
	wand	don't say /n/	wad		strived	don't say /v/	stride
	mix	don't say /k/	miss		shunt	don't say /n/	shut
	raved	don't say /v/	raid		chimp	don't say /m/	chip
	clomp	don't say /m/	clop		prompt	don't say /p/	propped
	grist	don't say /s/	grit		lest	don't say /s/	let
	locked	don't say /k/	lot		roped	don't say /p/	wrote
	champ	don't say /m/	chap		mixed	don't say /k/	mist
	toast	don't say /s/	tote		wound	don't say /n/	wooed
	paved	don't say /v/	paid		splint	don't say /n/	split

14. Say:	roost	don't say /s/	root	*Mixed Levels*	land	don't say /n/	lad
	meant	don't say /n/	met	(J)	till	instead of /i/ say /aw/	tall
	knelt	don't say /l/	net	(M1)	ghost	don't say /s/	goat
	hunt	don't say /n/	hut	(K1)	prep	don't say /r/	pep
	tisk	don't say /s/	tick	(M1)	hunt	don't say /n/	hut
	silt	don't say /l/	sit	(K2)	store	instead of /t/ say /n/	snore
	knocked	don't say /k/	knot	(M1)	past	don't say /s/	pat
	burst	don't say /s/	Bert	(L1)	wide	instead of /d/ say /z/	wise
	mapped	don't say /p/	mat	(M1)	guest	don't say /s/	get
	flint	don't say /n/	flit	(L2)	urge	instead of /j/ say /th/	earth

One Minute Activities Level M1

Say: **jest**   Now say **jest**, but don't say /s/   **jet**
Or say: **jest**   Now say it again, but don't say /s/   **jet**

15. Say:	jest	don't say /s/	jet	16. Say:	list	don't say /s/	lit
	most	don't say /s/	moat		waist	don't say /s/	wait
	swamp	don't say /m/	swap		blimp	don't say /m/	blip
	lisp	don't say /s/	lip		clasp	don't say /s/	clap
	looped	don't say /p/	loot		wimp	don't say /m/	whip
	wrecked	don't say /k/	red		cusp	don't say /s/	cup
	faint	don't say /n/	fate		wiped	don't say /p/	white
	swept	don't say /p/	sweat		draft	don't say /f/	drat
	slant	don't say /n/	slat		scooped	don't say /p/	scoot
	mast	don't say /s/	mat		fist	don't say /s/	fit
17. Say:	mist	don't say /s/	mitt	18. Say:	nest	don't say /s/	net
	limp	don't say /m/	lip		camp	don't say /m/	cap
	pulp	don't say /l/	pup		wrapped	don't say /p/	rat
	whisk	don't say /s/	wick		rust	don't say /s/	rut
	cupped	don't say /p/	cut		heaved	don't say /v/	heed
	bask	don't say /s/	back		lopped	don't say /p/	lot
	lamp	don't say /m/	lap		tusk	don't say /s/	tuck
	sepped	don't say /p/	seat		skimp	don't say /m/	skip
	runt	don't say /n/	rut		aft	don't say /f/	at
	wisp	don't say /s/	whip		burnt	don't say /n/	Bert
19. Say:	pecked	don't say /k/	pet	*Mixed Levels*	limp	don't say /m/	lip
	frost	don't say /s/	frought	(J)	luck	instead of /u/ say /o/	lock
	sapped	don't say /p/	sat	(M1)	lest	don't say /s/	let
	nicked	don't say /k/	knit	(K1)	scream	don't say /r/	scheme
	brisk	don't say /s/	brick	(M1)	skimp	don't say /m/	skip
	hopped	don't say /p/	hot	(K2)	swarm	instead of /w/ say /t/	storm
	shaved	don't say /v/	shade	(M1)	rust	don't say /s/	rut
	musk	don't say /s/	muck	(L1)	race	instead of /s/ say /t/	rate
	weaved	don't say /v/	weed	(M1)	act	don't say /k/	at
	leapt	don't say /p/	let	(L2)	surf	instead of /f/ say /ch/	search
20. Say:	roast	don't say /s/	wrote	*Mixed Levels*	jest	don't say /s/	jet
	nipped	don't say /p/	knit	(J)	sack	instead of /a/ say /o/	sock
	punt	don't say /n/	putt	(M1)	gasp	don't say /s/	gap
	lift	don't say /f/	lit	(K1)	sleek	don't say /l/	seek
	moped	don't say /p/	moat	(M1)	left	don't say /f/	let
	docked	don't say /k/	dot	(K2)	switch	instead of /w/ say /t/	stitch
	trend	don't say /n/	tred	(M1)	clasp	don't say /s/	clap
	left	don't say /f/	let	(L1)	wage	instead of /g/ say /k/	wake
	ramp	don't say /m/	rap	(M1)	mast	don't say /s/	mat
	pant	don't say /n/	pat	(L2)	arm	instead of /m/ say /k/	ark

One Minute Activities Level M2

Say: **act**   Now say **act**, but instead of /k/ say /n/   ant
Or say: **act**   Now say it again, but instead of /k/ say /n/   ant

1. Say:	act	instead of /k/ say /n/	ant	2. Say:	clasp	instead of /s/ say /m/	clamp
	fact	instead of /k/ say /s/	fast		aft	instead of /f/ say /k/	act
	rent	instead of /n/ say /s/	rest		bent	instead of /n/ say /s/	best
	clicks	instead of /k/ say /p/	clips		left	instead of /f/ say /n/	lent
	fast	instead of /s/ say /ks/	faxed		flips	instead of /p/ say /k/	flicks
	wimp	instead of /m/ say /s/	wisp		nest	instead of /s/ say /ks/	next
	shocked	instead of /k/ say /p/	shopped		burnt	instead of /n/ say /s/	burst
	lapse	instead of /p/ say /k/	lacks		left	instead of /f/ say /s/	lest
	left	instead of /f/ say /n/	lent		stacked	instead of /k/ say /sh/	stashed
	duct	instead of /k/ say /s/	dust		knocks	instead of /k/ say /t/	knots
3. Say:	act	instead of /k/ say /p/	apt	4. Say:	aft	instead of /f/ say /n/	ant
	fact	instead of /k/ say /ks/	faxed		drift	instead of /f/ say /p/	dripped
	hoax	instead of /k/ say /p/	hopes		Gramp	instead of /m/ say /s/	grasp
	went	instead of /n/ say /s/	west		snacks	instead of /k/ say /p/	snaps
	left	instead of /f/ say /p/	leapt		lost	instead of /s/ say /f/	loft
	clamp	instead of /m/ say /s/	clasp		fist	instead of /s/ say /sh/	fished
	flocks	instead of /k/ say /p/	flops		text	instead of /ks/ say /s/	test
	last	instead of /s/ say /f/	laughed		grant	instead of /n/ say /f/	graft
	raft	instead of /f/ say /n/	rant		ramp	instead of /m/ say /s/	rasp
	cast	instead of /s/ say /n/	can't		sops	instead of /p/ say /k/	socks
5. Say:	loft	instead of /f/ say /s/	lost	6. Say:	deft	instead of /f/ say /n/	dent
	limp	instead of /m/ say /s/	lisp		lest	instead of /s/ say /n/	lent
	sips	instead of /p/ say /k/	six		taunt	instead of /n/ say /s/	tossed
	lift	instead of /f/ say /k/	licked		mast	instead of /s/ say /p/	mapped
	rent	instead of /n/ say /k/	wrecked		crest	instead of /s/ say /p/	crept
	rust	instead of /s/ say /sh/	rushed		rift	instead of /f/ say /s/	wrist
	rift	instead of /f/ say /p/	ripped		ant	instead of /n/ say /k/	act
	paint	instead of /n/ say /s/	paste		stunt	instead of /n/ say /f/	stuffed
	tricks	instead of /k/ say /p/	trips		tact	instead of /k/ say /ks/	taxed
	taint	instead of /n/ say /s/	taste		whipped	instead of /p/ say /s/	wished
7. Say:	lift	instead of /f/ say /s/	list	Mixed Levels	fact	instead of /k/ say /s/	fast
	pact	instead of /k/ say /s/	past	(J)	beg	instead of /e/ say /u/	bug
	crimp	instead of /m/ say /s/	crisp	(M2)	lift	instead of /f/ say /s/	list
	lashed	instead of /sh/ say /f/	laughed	(K2)	flesh	instead of /l/ say /r/	fresh
	sits	instead of /t/ say /p/	sips	(M2)	went	instead of /n/ say /s/	west
	tent	instead of /n/ say /s/	test	(L1)	shave	instead of /v/ say /d/	shade
	rats	instead of /t/ say /p/	wraps	(M2)	left	instead of /f/ say /s/	lest
	trucked	instead of /k/ say /s/	trust	(L2)	source	instead of /s/ say /t/	sort
	blushed	instead of /sh/ say /n/	blunt	(M2)	bent	instead of /n/ say /s/	best
	next	instead of /ks/ say /s/	nest	(M1)	whisk	don't say /s/	wick

One Minute Activities Level M2

	Say:	**fast**	Now say **fast**, but instead of /s/ say /k/ **fact**
	Or say:	**fast**	Now say it again, but instead of /s/ say /k/ **fact**

8. Say:	fast	instead of /s/ say /k/	fact	9. Say:	beeped	instead of /p/ say /s/	beast
	lest	instead of /s/ say /f/	left		best	instead of /s/ say /n/	bent
	crisp	instead of /s/ say /m/	crimp		flocks	instead of /k/ say /p/	flops
	hushed	instead of /sh/ say /f/	huffed		past	instead of /s/ say /k/	pact
	tract	instead of /k/ say /p/	trapped		gushed	instead of /sh/ say /s/	gust
	craft	instead of /f/ say /k/	cracked		six	instead of /k/ say /t/	sits
	shaved	instead of /v/ say /p/	shaped		worst	instead of /s/ say /n/	weren't
	ant	instead of /n/ say /p/	apt		rest	instead of /s/ say /k/	wrecked
	chant	instead of /n/ say /p/	chapped		bluffed	instead of /f/ say /sh/	blushed
	tent	instead of /n/ say /ks/	text		racks	instead of /k/ say /p/	wraps

10. Say:	fist	instead of /s/ say /ks/	fixed	11. Say:	list	instead of /s/ say /f/	lift
	runt	instead of /n/ say /s/	rust		west	instead of /s/ say /p/	wept
	tent	instead of /n/ say /s/	test		taint	instead of /n/ say /p/	taped
	flax	instead of /k/ say /p/	flaps		mist	instead of /s/ say /ks/	mixed
	mint	instead of /n/ say /s/	mist		vest	instead of /s/ say /n/	vent
	quaint	instead of /n/ say /k/	quaked		flicked	instead of /k/ say /p/	flipped
	roast	instead of /s/ say /p/	roped		roped	instead of /p/ say /t/	wrote
	crept	instead of /p/ say /s/	crest		coast	instead of /s/ say /ks/	coaxed
	shift	instead of /f/ say /p/	shipped		vent	instead of /n/ say /s/	vest
	mint	instead of /n/ say /ks/	mixed		faint	instead of /n/ say /s/	faced

12. Say:	coast	instead of /s/ say /p/	coped	13. Say:	leashed	instead of /sh/ say /f/	leafed
	slant	instead of /n/ say /p/	slapped		flats	instead of /t/ say /k/	flax
	blunt	instead of /n/ say /f/	bluffed		wished	instead of /sh/ say /f/	wiffed
	ax	instead of /k/ say /p/	apps		fits	instead of /t/ say /k/	fix
	host	instead of /s/ say /p/	hoped		lisp	instead of /s/ say /m/	limp
	vent	instead of /n/ say /ks/	vexed		pact	instead of /k/ say /n/	pant
	test	instead of /s/ say /n/	tent		chicks	instead of /k/ say /p/	chips
	dust	instead of /s/ say /k/	duct		clamp	instead of /m/ say /s/	clasp
	crust	instead of /s/ say /sh/	crushed		dished	instead of /st/ say /p/	dipped
	wept	instead of /p/ say /s/	west		shocks	instead of /k/ say /p/	shops

14. Say:	went	instead of /n/ say /p/	wept	*Mixed Levels*	crisp	instead of /s/ say /m/	crimp
	graft	instead of /f/ say /n/	grant	(J)	hit	instead of /i/ say /a/	hat
	tact	instead of /k/ say /p/	tapped	(M2)	mast	instead of /s/ say /p/	mapped
	crops	instead of /p/ say /k/	crocks	(K2)	snack	instead of /n/ say /l/	slack
	lift	instead of /f/ say /n/	lint	(M2)	paint	instead of /n/ say /s/	paste
	faint	instead of /n/ say /k/	faked	(L1)	roam	instead of /m/ say /b/	robe
	spoofed	instead of /f/ say /k/	spooked	(M2)	crocks	instead of /k/ say /p/	crops
	dots	instead of /t/ say /k/	docks	(L2)	yarn	instead of /n/ say /d/	yard
	kicks	instead of /k/ say /t/	kits	(M2)	tact	instead of /k/ say /p/	tapped
	nix	instead of /k/ say /t/	knits	(M1)	tusk	don't say /s/	tuck

One Minute Activities Level M2

Say: **act** Now say **act**, but instead of /k/ say /f/ aft
Or say: **act** Now say it again, but instead of /k/ say /f/ aft

15. Say:	act	instead of /k/ say /f/	aft	16. Say:	text	instead of /ks/ say /n/	tent
	clashed	instead of /sh/ say /p/	clapped		knacks	instead of /k/ say /p/	naps
	flaps	instead of /p/ say /t/	flats		crashed	instead of /sh/ say /k/	cracked
	rant	instead of /n/ say /f/	raft		wrapped	instead of /p/ say /k/	racked
	blunt	instead of /n/ say /f/	bluffed		apt	instead of /p/ say /n/	ant
	worst	instead of /s/ say /k/	worked		lips	instead of /p/ say /k/	licks
	wrist	instead of /s/ say /f/	rift		cashed	instead of /sh/ say /p/	capped
	burst	instead of /s/ say /n/	burnt		wrist	instead of /s/ say /p/	ripped
	rust	instead of /s/ say /f/	roughed		mint	instead of /n/ say /f/	miffed
	tint	instead of /n/ say /p/	tipped		punt	instead of /n/ say /f/	puffed

17. Say:	aft	instead of /f/ say /p/	apt	18. Say:	west	instead of /s/ say /n/	went
	grasp	instead of /s/ say /m/	Gramp		coax	instead of /k/ say /t/	coats
	nips	instead of /p/ say /k/	nicks		heaped	instead of /p/ say /v/	heaved
	mist	instead of /s/ say /n/	mint		roost	instead of /s/ say /f/	roofed
	wraps	instead of /p/ say /t/	rats		stacks	instead of /k/ say /t/	stats
	cast	instead of /s/ say /p/	capped		joint	instead of /n/ say /s/	joist
	raved	instead of /v/ say /n/	rained		rest	instead of /s/ say /n/	rent
	rant	instead of /n/ say /p/	wrapped		sift	instead of /f/ say /p/	sipped
	lots	instead of /t/ say /k/	locks		tips	instead of /p/ say /k/	ticks
	apt	instead of /p/ say /k/	act		past	instead of /s/ say /n/	pant

19. Say:	mops	instead of /p/ say /k/	mocks	*Mixed Levels*	mist	instead of /s/ say /n/	mint	
	must	instead of /s/ say /f/	muffed	(J)	fox	instead of /o/ say /i/	fix	
	rasp	instead of /s/ say /m/	ramp	(M2)	test	instead of /s/ say /n/	tent	
	locked	instead of /k/ say /p/	lopped	(K2)	cruise	instead of /r/ say /l/	clues	
	wisp	instead of /s/ say /m/	wimp	(M2)	past	instead of /s/ say /k/	packed	
	stops	instead of /p/ say /k/	stocks	(L1)	booth	instead of /th/ say /t/	boot	
	sent	instead of /n/ say /k/	sect	(M2)	lamp	instead of /m/ say /s/	lasp	
	roast	instead of /s/ say /p/	roped	(L2)	send	instead of /d/ say /s/	sense	
	mint	instead of /n/ say /f/	miffed	(M2)	muffed	instead of /f/ say /s/	must	
	waved	instead of /v/ say /n/	waned	(M1)	tusk	don't say /s/	tuck	

20. Say:	wept	instead of /p/ say /n/	went	*Mixed Levels*	flicked	instead of /k/ say /p/	flipped	
	least	instead of /s/ say /p/	leaped	(J)	men	instead of /e/ say /a/	man	
	flint	instead of /n/ say /k/	flicked	(M2)	test	instead of /s/ say /ks/	text	
	list	instead of /s/ say /n/	lint	(K2)	sky	instead of /k/ say /p/	spy	
	rent	instead of /n/ say /k/	wrecked	(M2)	vent	instead of /n/ say /s/	vest	
	mix	instead of /k/ say /t/	mitts	(L1)	wide	instead of /d/ say /z/	wise	
	knits	instead of /t/ say /p/	nips	(M2)	mint	instead of /n/ say /ks/	mixed	
	bunt	instead of /n/ say /f/	buffed	(L2)	force	instead of /s/ say /k/	fork	
	flaunt	instead of /n/ say /s/	flossed	(M2)	list	instead of /s/ say /n/	lint	
	slapped	instead of /p/ say /sh/	slashed	(M1)	skimp	don't say /m/	skip	

LEVEL N

Optional Advanced Phoneme-level Processing
Phoneme Reversal

N1 Level N1 involves reversing the sounds in a single syllable word.

Samples: keep → peek   tap → pat
niece → seen   ape → pay

N2 Level N2 involves reversing the sounds in a two or three syllable word.

Samples: midnight → tine dim   city → ee tiss
aid num → Monday   tin gam → magnet

As mentioned previously, *this is an optional level, not necessary for the successful completion of the program*. It can be used for students in a small or large group who are very skilled at the other levels. Phoneme reversal can be difficult and keep the students interested and challenged. You want to keep these students challenged while you help the other students who require phoneme awareness training. You would have to flip back and forth between Level N and the level at which the others are working. This way, students of differing ability levels can participate in the activity, an example of what is called *differentiated instruction*.

Special Administration Instructions for Level N

- The most important thing to remember is that Level N is not a reversal of spelling patterns. It is a reversal of *sounds*. In the first two examples for N1 above, reversing the sounds and spelling patterns yield the same result. However, in the second two examples, reversing the letters, then trying to pronounce the resulting spelling does not yield the correct answer. Another example is with N2. We do nit say "MAG-net," because in most two syllable words, the vowel in the unstressed syllable gets reduced. We really say something closer to "MAG-nit" (the pronunciation guide for *magnet* at dictionary.com is "mag-nit"). So the phonetic spellings provided as answers to items are designed to reflect what we say, regardless of the spelling pattern.

- You will notice that the reversal of sounds in N1 words always results in another, real word. However, there are not many two syllable words that, when reversed, form real word. So N2 uses nonsense words. Sometimes you go from a real word to a nonsense word. Other times you present a nonsense word and when the sounds are reversed, it becomes a real word.

- While there are only eight one minute activities for N2, remember that reversing any two syllable word will do, so long as you focus on the sound not the spelling pattern. Feel free to make up your own One Minute Activities to supplement the limited N2 activities (avoid words with *r* in them, as they do not reverse well).

Remember: THE FOCUS IS ON THE SOUNDS, NOT SPELLING PATTERNS.

One Minute Activities Level N1

Say: **I'm** Now say **I'm** backwards ⟶ **my**
Or say: Say **I'm** backwards ⟶ **my**

1. Say:	I'm	⟶	my	2. Say:	ace	⟶	say	3. Say:	ape	⟶	pay
	tee	⟶	eat		zone	⟶	nose		doom	⟶	mood
	tack	⟶	cat		nut	⟶	ton		dose	⟶	sowed
	oat	⟶	toe		cook	⟶	cook		mom	⟶	mom
	net	⟶	ten		zoo	⟶	ooze		sub	⟶	bus
	till	⟶	lit		jab	⟶	badge		tube	⟶	boot
	pat	⟶	tap		did	⟶	did		vase	⟶	save
	dad	⟶	dad		pitch	⟶	chip		knack	⟶	can
	face	⟶	safe		meet	⟶	team		Pam	⟶	map
	law	⟶	all		nip	⟶	pin		cab	⟶	back

4. Say:	aid	⟶	day	5. Say:	own	⟶	no	6. Say:	tips	⟶	spit
	note	⟶	tone		tuck	⟶	cut		stab	⟶	bats
	bib	⟶	bib		gut	⟶	tug		knit	⟶	tin
	dim	⟶	mid		tot	⟶	tot		bomb	⟶	mob
	pack	⟶	cap		mitt	⟶	Tim		kick	⟶	kick
	pop	⟶	pop		shack	⟶	cash		Don	⟶	nod
	buck	⟶	cub		cake	⟶	cake		tote	⟶	tote
	lean	⟶	kneel		Jake	⟶	cage		keep	⟶	peak
	neat	⟶	teen		Midge	⟶	Jim		keel	⟶	leak
	lace	⟶	sail		con	⟶	knock		pal	⟶	lap

Mixed Levels

7. Say:	Kay	⟶	ache	8. Say:	babe	⟶	babe	(N1)	zone	now say it backwards	nose
	muss	⟶	some		veal	⟶	leave	(M2)	rent	instead of /n/ say /s/	rest
	taught	⟶	taught		pope	⟶	pope	(L1)	soon	instead of /n/ say /t/	suit
	kiss	⟶	sick		steam	⟶	meets	(N1)	eek!	now say it backwards	key
	judge	⟶	judge		Deb	⟶	bed	(L2)	card	instead of /d/ say /t/	cart
	Jay	⟶	age		foal	⟶	loaf	(J)	knock	instead of /o/ say /e/	neck
	step	⟶	pets		niece	⟶	seen	(N)	neat	now say it backwards	teen
	bay	⟶	Abe		gnat	⟶	tan	(M1)	raft	don't say /f/	rat
	spite	⟶	types		dote	⟶	toad	(N)	cheap	now say it backwards	peach
	teach	⟶	cheat		duce	⟶	sued	(K2)	stake	instead of /t/ say /n/	snake

Mixed Levels:

9. Say:	copes	⟶	spoke	10. Say:	scat	⟶	tax	(N1)	make	say it backwards	came
	tike	⟶	kite		make	⟶	came	(K2)	stare	instead of /t/ say /p/	spare
	save	⟶	vase		sake	⟶	case	(L1)	leaf	instead of /f/ say /d/	lead
	spam	⟶	maps		tip	⟶	pit	(L2)	form	instead of /m/ say /s/	force
	sauce	⟶	sauce		bat	⟶	tab	(M1)	whisk	don't say /s/	wick
	kits	⟶	stick		noon	⟶	noon	(J)	pin	instead of /i/ say /e/	pen
	tight	⟶	tight		mug	⟶	gum	(N)	mug	now say it backwards	gum
	stiff	⟶	fits		nap	⟶	pan	(M2)	wrist	instead of /s/ say /f/	rift
	dame	⟶	made		none	⟶	none	(L1)	net	instead of /t/ say /k/	neck
	Bob	⟶	Bob		fine	⟶	knife	(N)	pack	now say it backwards	cap

One Minute Activities Level N1

Say: **eat** Now say **eat** backwards → **tea**
Or say: Say **eat** backwards → **tea**

11. Say:	eat	→	tea	12. Say:	aim	→	may	13. Say: tine	→ night
	mop	→	palm		ooze	→	zoo	dean	→ need
	nine	→	nine		deed	→	deed	vie	→ I've
	cheap	→	peach		seep	→	peace	choke	→ coach
	poke	→	cope		Lee	→	eel	stop	→ pots
	pup	→	pup		stock	→	cots	votes	→ stove
	chow	→	ouch		cuts	→	stuck	dill	→ lid
	Ken	→	neck		deed	→	deed	feel	→ leaf
	fife	→	fife		mode	→	dome	snout	→ towns
	sub	→	bus		combs	→	smoke	caught	→ talk

14. Say:	roar	→	roar	15. Say:	gag	→	gag	16. Say: tell	→ let
	eek!	→	key		fins	→	sniff	spin	→ nips
	mile	→	lime		Ned	→	den	known	→ known
	spat	→	taps		gnome	→	moan	chap	→ patch
	leap	→	peel		lease	→	seal	Mets	→ stem
	tile	→	light		dell	→	led	staff	→ fats
	ice	→	sigh		stayed	→	dates	bad	→ dab
	chum	→	much		loot	→	tool	snit	→ tins
	name	→	main		mill	→	limb	Coke	→ Coke
	cud	→	duck		spate	→	tapes	dough	→ owed

Mixed Levels

17. Say:	stone	→	notes	18. Say:	oat	→	toe	(N1) votes	now say it backwards	stove
	gull	→	lug		none	→	none	(M1) nest	don't say /s/	net
	loop	→	pool		gel	→	ledge	(L1) soak	instead of /k/ say /p/	soap
	noun	→	noun		ban	→	nab	(L2) card	instead of /d/ say /t/	cart
	deal	→	lead		spot	→	tops	(N) seep	now say it backwards	peace
	dote	→	toad		kit	→	tick	(J) rise	instead of /I/ say /A/	raise
	vague	→	gave		puck	→	cup	(N) ledge	now say it backwards	gel
	Todd	→	dot		nick	→	kin	(K2) swing	instead of /w/ say /t/	sting
	lull	→	lull		chance	→	snatch	(N) tops	now say it backwards	spot
	span	→	naps		mock	→	calm	(M2) tent	instead of /n/ say /s/	test

Mixed Levels

19. Say:	ooze	→	zoo	20. Say:	cats	→	stack	(N1) case	now say it backwards	sake
	might	→	time		mime	→	mime	(M2) least	instead of /s/ say /p/	leaped
	skate	→	takes		ticks	→	skit	(L1) jazz	instead of /z/ say /m/	jam
	keeps	→	speak		lip	→	pill	(N) snoot	now say it backwards	tunes
	snip	→	pins		sap	→	pass	(L2) arm	instead of /m/ say /ch/	arch
	picks	→	skip		skim	→	mix	(J) lease	instead of /E/ say /e/	less
	germ	→	merge		cod	→	dock	(N) skim	now say it backwards	mix
	though	→	oath		snoot	→	tunes	(M1) hunt	don't say /n/	hut
	main	→	name		cease	→	cease	(N) name	now say it backwards	main
	nicks	→	skin		stoke	→	coats	(K2) clam	instead of /l/ say /r/	cram

One Minute Activities Level N2

Say: **candy** Now say **candy** backwards → **eed nack**
Or say: Say **candy** backwards → **eed nack**

1. Say:	candy	→	eed nack	2. Say:	midnight	→	tine dim
	pets toof	→	footstep		ten gam	→	magnet
	city	→	ee tiss		Monday	→	aid num
	make eeb	→	became		aid zoot	→	Tuesday
	college	→	gel lock		baseball	→	laub sabe
	eef awk	→	coffee		uh boot	→	tuba
	cotton	→	nut tock		collie	→	ee lock
	cake puck	→	cupcake		oat pit	→	tiptoe
	doughnut	→	tun owed		downtown	→	nowt nowd
	ee pug	→	guppy		neesh um	→	machine
3. Say:	funny	→	enough	4. Say:	tepee	→	eep eat
	ee dad	→	daddy		tack bob	→	bobcat
	dolphin	→	niff lod		notice	→	sit own
	towboat	→	towboat		nick ate	→	taken
	magic	→	kij am		oval	→	love oh
	oss ees	→	seesaw		luh bate	→	table
	maybe	→	eeb aim		daytime	→	might aid
	jack cap	→	package		aid nuss	→	Sunday
	pancake	→	cake nap		open	→	nep oh
	ease cat	→	taxi		un oot	→	tuna
5. Say:	menu	→	you nem	6. Say:	mongoose	→	soog nom
	ticket	→	ticket		dice deb	→	bedside
	panda	→	ud nap		season	→	nuz ees
	noops eat	→	teaspoon		lope dat	→	tadpole
	pocket	→	tick op		valley	→	eel av
	knit pack	→	captain		eeg ash	→	shaggy
	soda	→	uh dose		pony	→	een ope
	shiff tack	→	catfish		tiz iv	→	visit
	donkey	→	eek nawd		vanish	→	shin av
	uh fose	→	sofa		nobe cab	→	backbone
7. Say:	tess nuss	→	sunset	8. Say:	oat oaf	→	photo
	police	→	seal ope		touchdown	→	nowd chud
	tiv lev	→	velvet		toab meets	→	steamboat
	puppet	→	tep up		total	→	luh tote
	eep up	→	puppy		oad ash	→	shadow
	stagecoach	→	choke jates		tonsil	→	luss not
	toab lace	→	sailboat		oal ip	→	pillow
	someday	→	aid muss		toothpick	→	kip thoot
	dufe ees	→	seafood		luff sue	→	useful
	navy	→	ee vane		seashell	→	lesh ees

One Minute Activities Level N2

Say: **bagpipe** Now say **bagpipe** backwards → **pipe gab**
Or say: Say **bagpipe** backwards → **pipe gab**

9. Say:	bagpipe	→	pipe gab	10. Say:	shellfish	→	shiff lesh
	luss nep	→	pencil		eat nelp	→	plenty
	postage	→	jit soap		suitcase	→	sake toose
	faw kate	→	takeoff		jay neat	→	teenage
	toolbox	→	skob loot		jackpot	→	top kadge
	gaz giz	→	zig zag		lub muff	→	fumble
	snapshot	→	tosh pans		mustache	→	shat sum
	toab file	→	lifeboat		cat muth	→	thumbtack
	mansion	→	nush nam		roadside	→	dies door
	pets toof	→	footstep		nush kiff	→	fiction
11. Say:	mailbox	→	skob laim	12. Say:	snowman	→	nam owns
	leem toe	→	oatmeal		chow pots	→	stopwatch
	speechless	→	sell cheeps		mascot	→	tock sam
	niff row	→	orphan		main kin	→	nickname
	mischief	→	fich sim		necktie	→	ite ken
	rub ane	→	neighbor		pish meets	→	steamship
	icebox	→	skob sigh		noot pen	→	Neptune
	lub rom	→	marble		monkey	→	eek num
	smokestack	→	cats combs		neat nine	→	nineteen
	lun giss	→	signal		jumbo	→	oab mudge
13. Say:	napkin	→	nick pan	14. Say:	banjo	→	nab
	kin kip	→	picnic		eek nod	→	donkey
	cactus	→	sut cack		census	→	sus ness
	might deb	→	bedtime		ketch tame	→	checkmate
	lazy	→	eez ale		falcon	→	nick laugh
	oss gidge	→	jigsaw		laub mug	→	gumball
	goblet	→	tell bog		lub bake	→	cable
	sell deece	→	seedless		notes mile	→	limestone
	gentle	→	lut nedge		begun	→	nug eeb
	soob buck	→	caboose		eece naf	→	fancy
15. Say:	market	→	teck rom	16. Say:	misty	→	eat sim
	eel kyle	→	likely		lud nack	→	candle
	skyline	→	nile ikes		locksmith	→	thims kol
	ud nap	→	panda		lauf tine	→	nightfall
	padlock	→	kol dap		sample	→	lup mass
	lud nas	→	sandal		nish oh	→	ocean
	needless	→	sell deen		sometime	→	might muss
	let oam	→	motel		snesh ape	→	patience
	safeguard	→	drog face		simple	→	lup miss
	neg rob	→	bargain		lim oss	→	sawmil

– 231 –

APPENDICES

Appendix A
PHONOLOGICAL AWARENESS DEVELOPMENT CHART
(SEE CHAPTER 8 FOR MORE DETAILS)

Student Name _____   School Year or Semester _____

Degree of Proficiency

SYLLABLE LEVEL PROCESSING

Basic Syllable Levels (Pre-K to late kindergarten)*

		Multisensory Stage				Knowledge Stage	Automatic Stage
		L/S	VSp	VSeq	Oral		
D1	Delete: (cow)boy → boy						
D2	Delete: (un)der → der						
E1	Delete: (pine)apple → apple						
E2	Delete: (de)liver → liver						

Advanced Syllable Levels (mid kindergarten to late first grade and older, struggling readers)*

E3	Delete: (tri)angle → angle						
E4	Delete: (an)imal → imal						
E5	Delete: ele(phant) → ele						

ONSET-RIME LEVEL PROCESSING *(mid kindergarten to early first grade and some older, struggling readers)**

F1	Delete: (c)at → at						
F2	Delete: m(an) → m						
G1	Substitute: (n)ot → (h)ot						
G2	Substitute: t(an) → t(oy)						

PHONEME-LEVEL PROCESSING

Basic Phoneme Levels (late kindergarten to late first grade and older, struggling readers)*

H1	Delete: (p)lane → lane						
H2	Substitute: (c)lass → (g)lass						
I1	Delete: car(t) → car						
I2	Delete: shee(p) → she						

Advanced Phoneme Levels (late first grade to early third and older, struggling readers)*

J	Substitute: b(a)g → b(i)g						
K1	Delete: c(l)ub → cub						
K2	Substitute: g(r)ow → g(l)ow						
L1	Substitute: pe(t) → pe(n)						
L2	Substitute: sen(t) → sen(d)						
M1	Delete: be(s)t → bet						
M2	Substitute: li(f)t → li(s)t						

*Grade estimates represent when most students become competent in the respective level. When students are trained with this program, the lower estimates are the better guidelines. Individual rates of development will vary.

Prepared by David A. Kilpatrick, Ph.D.

Appendix B
PROGRAM COMPARISON CHART

	Equipped for Reading Success	McInnis/ARL (1999)	Rosner Program (1973)
	–	A	–
	–	B	A
	–	–	B
	–	C1	C
	–	C2	C
Syllable Levels	D1	D1	D
	D2	D2	D
	E1	E1	E
	E2	E2	E
	E3	E3	E
	E4	E4	E
	E5	I	E
Onset-Rime Levels	F1	F	F
	F2	–	–
	G1	G	G
	G2	–	–
Phoneme Levels	H1	–	H
	H2	H	G
	I1	–	H
	I2	–	–
	J	J	H
	K1	–	–
	K2	K	H
	L1	L	G
	L2	–	–
	M1	–	H
	M2	–	–
	N1	–	–
	N2	–	–

This chart provides information on the differences between three historically-related programs. The phonological awareness training aspect of *Equipped for Reading Success* can be viewed as the third generation of the original Rosner program, updated based upon 40 years of additional research and field testing. The Rosner and McInnis programs had levels A, B, and C, which essentially examined one-to-one counting and basic working memory (e.g., "Say *red, green, blue*" "Now say *red, blue*" "What color did I forget?").

Appendix C
PHONOLOGICAL AWARENESS
SCREENING TEST (PAST)

The following pages contain four versions of the *Phonological Awareness Screening Test* (PAST), Forms A, B, C, and D. These multiple versions are designed for periodic updates throughout the school year.

For instructions on administering the PAST, see Chapter 11. Also visit www.thepasttest.com to get free PDF versions of the PAST in order to print them out to get a better looking copy than you would get from this book due to the spiral binding (see copyright fair-use statement below). Also, that website contains some video demonstrations of the PAST and provides documents with data on the PAST's reliability and validity.

Copyright notice Appendix C: The owner of this manual is free to photocopy the PAST (Forms A-D) for individual classroom use or use in a resource room, special class, or private tutoring. There is no limit to the number of copies that can be made for individual classroom use. However, owner's of this manual are not authorized to provide other teachers with this assessment or copies of any other pages from this manual. Direct interested parties to www.thepasttest.com.

Also note: No one should administer the PAST unless he or she has thoroughly read the instructions in Chapter 11 and practiced it multiple times on students for whom the results are not consequential. It is also recommended that the user seek feedback from a school psychologist, speech pathologist, or another professional trained in individualized assessments.

There is no value in giving the PAST if the results are invalid due to improper administration.

PHONOLOGICAL AWARENESS SCREENING TEST (PAST) FORM A

David A. Kilpatrick, Ph.D. © 2003, 2010, 2019
Adapted from the levels used in McInnis (1999) & Rosner (1973)

Name: _____ Date: _____ Grade _____ Age _____
Teacher: _____ D.O.B.: _____ Evaluator: _____

INSTRUCTIONS: See *Equipped for Reading Success* Chapter 11: "Assessment of Phonological Awareness" for how to administer the PAST.

RESULTS:

	Correct	Automatic		
Basic Syllable	___/12	___/12	Highest Correct Level:	___
Initial Phoneme/Onset-Rime	___/10	___/10	(Levels not passed below the highest correct level)	___
Basic Phoneme	___/10	___/10		
Advanced Phoneme	___/20	___/20	Highest Automatic Level:	
Test Total	___/52	___/52	(Non-automatic levels below highest automatic level)	___

Approximate Grade Level:	*PreK/K*	*K*	*late K/early 1st*	*1st*	*late 1st/early 2nd*	*2nd*	*late 2nd to adult*

Note: The grade levels listed throughout the *PAST* are estimates based on various research studies and clinical experience. They are not formalized norms.

I. SYLLABLE LEVELS

Basic Syllable Levels (D, E2 - preschool to mid kindergarten; E3 - mid to late kindergarten)

LEVEL D Say *bookcase*. Now say *bookcase* but don't say *book*.
FEEDBACK: "If you say *bookcase* without saying *book*, you get *case*."

D1 (book)case ____   (sun)set ____   space(ship) ____   ___/3 A: ___/3
D2 (sil)ver ____   (mar)ket ____   gen(tle) ____   ___/3 A: ___/3

LEVEL E Say *umbrella*. Now say *umbrella* but don't say *um*.
FEEDBACK: "If you say *umbrella* without saying *um*, you get *brella*."

E2 (um)brella___   (fan)tastic ___   (Oc)tober ___   ___/3 A: ___/3
E3 (al)phabet___   (Sat)urday___   (tri)cycle___   ___/3 A: ___/3

Basic Syllable Total: ___/12 A:___/12

II. INITIAL PHONEME / ONSET-RIME LEVELS

Onset-Rime Levels (kindergarten to mid first grade)

LEVEL F Say *feet*. Now say *feet* but don't say /f/.
FEEDBACK: "If you say *feet* without the /f/, you get *eat*; *feet-eat*."

(f)eet → eat ___   (c)ough → off ___
(t)ame → aim ___   (t)ime → I'm ___   (c)one → own ___   ___/5 A: ___/5

LEVEL G Say *guide*. Now say *guide* but instead of /g/ say /r/.
FEEDBACK: "If you say *guide*, and change the /g/ to /r/, you get *ride*; *guide-ride*."

(g)uide /r/ → ride ___   (m)ore /d/ → door ___
(g)um /th/ → thumb ___   (l)ed /s/ → said ___   (f)eel /s/ → seal ___   ___/5 A: ___/5

Onset-Rime Total: ___/10 A:___/10

PAST Form A
III. PHONEME LEVELS

Basic Phoneme Levels (early to late first grade)

LEVEL H

H1 (Deletion) Say *sleep.* Now say *sleep* but don't say /s/.
FEEDBACK: "If you say *sleep* without the /s/, you get *leap*; *sleep-leap*."

(s)leep → leap ___   (c)rane → rain ___

H2   Say *grew.* Now say *grew* but instead of /g/ say /t/.
FEEDBACK: "If you say *grew*, and change the /g/ to /t/, you get *true*; *grew-true*."

(g)rew → (t)rue ___   (c)rane → (b)rain ___   (f)lows → (c)lose ___   ___/5 A: ___/5

LEVEL I Say *went.* Now say *went* but don't say /t/.
FEEDBACK: "If you say *went* without the /t/, you get *when*; *went-when*."

I1 wen(t) → when ___   ran(g)e → rain ___

I2 whea(t) → we ___   nie(c)e → knee ___   dri(v)e → dry ___   ___/5 A: ___/5

Basic Phoneme Total: ___/10 A: ___/10

Advanced Phoneme Levels (early to late second grade; Level M is early third grade to adult)

LEVEL J Say *ran.* Now say *ran* but instead of /a/ say /u/.
FEEDBACK: "If you say *ran*, and change the /a/ to /u/, you get *run*; *ran-run*."

(*Short sound* of vowel)   r(a)n /u/ → run ___   k(i)t /u/ → cut ___   d(e)n /u/ → done ___

(*Long sound* of vowel)   b(ea)k /A/ → bake ___   f(i)ne /O/ → phone ___   ___/5 A: ___/5

LEVEL K

K1 (Deletion) Say *bread.* Now say *bread* but don't say /r/.
FEEDBACK: "If you say *bread* without the /r/, you get *bed*; *bread-bed*."

b(r)ead → bed ___   s(n)eak → seek ___

K2 (Substitution) Say *crew.* Now say *crew* but instead of /r/ say /l/.
FEEDBACK: "If you say *crew*, and change the /r/ to /l/, you get *clue*; *crew-clue*."

c(r)ew → c(l)ue ___   s(c)ale → s(n)ail ___   s(n)eeze → s(k)is ___   ___/5 A: ___/5

LEVEL L Say *some.* Say *some* but instead of /m/ say /n/.
FEEDBACK: "If you say *some*, and change the /m/ to /n/, you get *sun*; *some-sun*."

so(m)e /n/ → sun ___   rhy(m)e /d/ → ride ___

nigh(t) /s/ → nice ___   see(m) /t/ → sea(t) ___   kee(p) /z/ → keys ___   ___/5 A: ___/5

LEVEL M

M1 (Deletion) Say *ghost.* Now say *ghost* but don't say /s/.
FEEDBACK: "If you say *ghost* without the /s/, you get *goat*; *ghost-goat*."

gho(s)t → goat ___   roa(s)t → wrote ___

M2 (Substitution) Say *sift.* Now say *sift* but instead of /f/ say /p/.
FEEDBACK: "If you say *sift*, and change the /f/ to /p/, you get *sipped*; *sift-sipped*."

si(f)t → si(pp)ed ___   tru(s)t → tru(ck)ed ___   de(f)t → de(ck)ed ___   ___/5 A: ___/5

Advanced Phoneme Total: ___/20 A: ___/20

Correct   Automatic

PHONOLOGICAL AWARENESS SCREENING TEST (PAST) FORM B

David A. Kilpatrick, Ph.D. © 2003, 2010, 2019
Adapted from the levels used in McInnis (1999) & Rosner (1973)

Name: _____ Date: _____ Grade _____ Age _____
Teacher: _____ D.O.B.: _____ Evaluator: _____

INSTRUCTIONS: See *Equipped for Reading Success* Chapter 11: "Assessment of Phonological Awareness" for how to administer the PAST.

RESULTS:

	Correct	Automatic		
Basic Syllable	___/12	___/12	Highest Correct Level:	_____
Initial Phoneme/Onset-Rime	___/10	___/10	(Levels not passed below the highest correct level)	_____
Basic Phoneme	___/10	___/10		
Advanced Phoneme	___/20	___/20	Highest Automatic Level:	
Test Total	___/52	___/52	(Non-automatic levels below highest automatic level)	_____

Approximate Grade Level:	PreK/K	K	late K/early 1st	1st	late 1st/early 2nd	2nd	late 2nd to adult

Note: The grade levels listed throughout the *PAST* are estimates based on various research studies and clinical experience. They are not formalized norms.

I. SYLLABLE LEVELS

Basic Syllable Levels (D, E2 - preschool to mid kindergarten; E3 - mid to late kindergarten)

LEVEL D Say *leapfrog*. Now say *leapfrog* but don't say *leap*.
FEEDBACK: "If you say *leapfrog* without saying *leap*, you get *frog*."

Correct   Automatic

D1 (leap)frog ____   (door)bell ____   mail(box) ____   ___/3 A: ___/3
D2 (cor)ner ____   (mem)ber ____   mar(ble) ____   ___/3 A: ___/3

LEVEL E Say *carnation*. Now say *carnation* but don't say *car*.
FEEDBACK: "If you say *carnation* without saying *car*, you get *nation*."

E2 (car)nation ____   (gym)nastics ____ (Sep)tember ____   ___/3 A: ___/3
E3 (or)nament ____   (at)mosphere ____ (Af)rica ____   ___/3 A: ___/3

Basic Syllable Total: ___/12 A: ___/12

II. INITIAL PHONEME / ONSET-RIME LEVELS

Onset-Rime Levels (kindergarten to mid first grade)
LEVEL F Say *far*. Now say *far* but don't say /f/.
FEEDBACK: "If you say *far* without the /f/, you get *are*; *far-are*."

(f)ar → are ____   (n)ame → aim ____
(f)ive → I've ____ (c)ore → oar ____   (l)oan → own ____   ___/5 A: ___/5

LEVEL G Say *kite*. Now say *kite* but instead of /k/ say /r/.
FEEDBACK: "If you say *kite*, and change the /k/ to /r/, you get *right*; *kite-right*."

(k)ite /r/ → right ____   (c)ane /r/ → rain ____   ___/5 A: ___/5
(t)ime /r/ → rhyme ____   (s)oup /h/ → hoop ____   (sh)are /h/ → hair ____

Onset-Rime Total: ___/10 A: ___/10

PAST Form B
III. PHONEME LEVELS

Basic Phoneme Levels (early to late first grade)

LEVEL H

H1 (Deletion) **Say *sleeve*. Now say *sleeve* but don't say /s/.**
FEEDBACK: "If you say *sleeve* without the /s/, you get *leave*; *sleeve-leave*."

(s)leeve → leave ___ (g)reat → rate ___

H2 (Substitution) **Say *freeze*. Now say *freeze* but instead of /f/ say of /t/.**
FEEDBACK: "If you say *freeze*, and change the /f/ to /t/, you get *trees*; *freeze-trees*."

(f)reeze → (t)rees ___ (c)rew → (t)rue ___ (p)roud → (c)rowd ___   ___/5 A: ___/5

LEVEL I Say *sword*. Now say *sword* but don't say /d/.
FEEDBACK: "If you say *sword* without the /d/, you get *sore*; *sword-sore*."

I1 swor(d) → sore ___ mean(t) → men ___

I2 sea(t) → see ___ grou(p) → grew ___ wi(d)e → why ___   ___/5 A: ___/5

Basic Phoneme Total: ___/10 A: ___/10

Advanced Phoneme Levels (early to late second grade; Level M is early third grade to adult)

LEVEL J Say *man*. Now say *man* but instead of /a/ say /e/.
FEEDBACK: "If you say *man*, and change the /a/ to /e/, you get *man*; *man-men*."

(*Short sound* of vowel) m(a)n /e/ → men ___ n(e)ck /o/ → knock ___ d(o)t /e/ → debt ___
(*Long sound* of vowel) l(oa)n /I/ → line ___ s(i)de /E/ → seed ___   ___/5 A: ___/5

LEVEL K

K1 (Deletion) **Say *spy*. Now say *spy* but don't say /p/.**
FEEDBACK: "If you say *spy* without the /p/, you get *sigh*; *spy-sigh*."

s(p)y → sigh ___ c(l)aim → came ___

K2 (Substitution) **Say *crime*. Now say *crime* but instead of /r/ say /l/.**
FEEDBACK: "If you say *crime*, and change the /r/ to /l/, you get *climb*; *crime-climb*."

c(r)ime → c(l)imb ___ g(r)ew → g(l)ue ___ c(l)oud → c(r)owd ___   ___/5 A: ___/5

LEVEL L Say *set*. Now say *set* but instead of /t/ say /d/.
FEEDBACK: "If you say *set*, and change the /t/ to /d/, you get *said*; *set-said*."

se(t) /d/ → said ___ whe(n) /t/ → wet ___

sou(p) /n/ → soon ___ to(n)e /d/ → toad ___ kni(f)e /t/ → night ___   ___/5 A: ___/5

LEVEL M

M1 (Deletion) **Say *dusk*. Now say *dusk* but don't say /s/.**
FEEDBACK: "If you say *dusk* without the /s/, you get *duck*; *dusk-duck*."

du(s)k → duck ___ she(l)f → chef ___

M2 (Substitution) **Say *rift*. Now say *rift* but instead of /f/ say /s/.**
FEEDBACK: "If you say *rift*, and change the /f/ to /s/, you get *wrist*; *rift-wrist*."

ri(f)t → wri(s)t ___ te(s)t → te(n)t ___ le(f)t → lea(p)t ___   ___/5 A: ___/5

Advanced Phoneme Total: ___/20 A: ___/20

Correct Automatic

PHONOLOGICAL AWARENESS SCREENING TEST (PAST) FORM C

David A. Kilpatrick, Ph.D. © 2003, 2010, 2019
Adapted from the levels used in McInnis (1999) & Rosner (1973)

Name: _____ Date: _____ Grade _____ Age _____
Teacher: _____ D.O.B.: _____ Evaluator: _____

INSTRUCTIONS: See *Equipped for Reading Success* Chapter 11: "Assessment of Phonological Awareness" for how to administer the PAST.

RESULTS:

	Correct	Automatic		
Basic Syllable	___/12	___/12	Highest Correct Level:	___
Initial Phoneme/Onset-Rime	___/10	___/10	(Levels not passed below the highest correct level)	___
Basic Phoneme	___/10	___/10		
Advanced Phoneme	___/20	___/20	Highest Automatic Level:	___
Test Total	___/52	___/52	(Non-automatic levels below highest automatic level)	___

Approximate Grade Level:	PreK/K	K	late K/early 1st	1st	late 1st/early 2nd	2nd	late 2nd to adult

Note: The grade levels listed throughout the *PAST* are estimates based on various research studies and clinical experience. They are not formalized norms.

I. SYLLABLE LEVELS

Basic Syllable Levels (D, E2 - preschool to mid kindergarten; E3 - mid to late kindergarten)

LEVEL D Say *footprint*. Now say *footprint* but don't say *foot*.
FEEDBACK: "If you say <u>footprint</u> without saying <u>foot</u>, you get <u>print</u>."

				Correct	Automatic
D1	(foot)print ___	(row)boat ___	mid(night) ___	___/3	A: ___/3
D2	(ta)ble ___	(o)ver ___	pan(da) ___	___/3	A: ___/3

LEVEL E Say *invention*. Now say *invention* but don't say *in*.
FEEDBACK: "If you say <u>invention</u> without saying <u>in</u>, you get <u>vention</u>."

E2	(in)vention ___	(ma)gician ___	(me)chanic ___	___/3 A: ___/3
E3	(at)mosphere ___	(cu)cumber ___	(car)penter ___	___/3 A: ___/3

Basic Syllable Total: ___/12 A: ___/12

II. INITIAL PHONEME / ONSET-RIME LEVELS

Onset-Rime Levels (kindergarten to mid first grade)

LEVEL F Say *sheet*. Now say *sheet* but don't say /sh/.
FEEDBACK: "If you say <u>sheet</u> without the /sh/, you get <u>eat</u>; <u>sheet-eat</u>."

(sh)eet → eat ___   (ph)one → own ___
(n)ame → aim ___   (r)ide → I'd ___   (w)ar → or ___

___/5 A: ___/5

LEVEL G Say *loop*. Now say *loop* but instead of /l/ say /s/.
FEEDBACK: "If you say <u>loop</u>, and change the /l/ to /s/, you get <u>soup</u>; <u>loop-soup</u>."

(l)oop /s/ → soup ___   (p)ut /f/ → foot ___
(p)ool /r/ → rule ___   (c)are /ch/ → chair ___   (b)owl /g/ → goal ___

___/5 A: ___/5

Onset-Rime Total: ___/10 A: ___/10

PAST Form C

III. PHONEME LEVELS

Basic Phoneme Levels (early to late first grade)

LEVEL H
H1 (Deletion/ **Say *sweet*. Now say *sweet* but don't say /s/.**
FEEDBACK: "If you say *sweet* without the /s/, you get *wheat*; *sweet-wheat*."

(s)weet → wheat ___   (ph)rase → raise ___

H2 (Substitution) **Say *true*. Now say *true* but instead of /t/ say /g/.**
FEEDBACK: "If you say *true*, and change the /t/ to /g/, you get *grew*; *true-grew*."

(t)rue → (g)rew ___   (c)laim → (b)lame ___   (t)roop → (g)roup ___   ___/5 A: ___/5

LEVEL I Say *word*. Now say *word* but don't say /d/.
FEEDBACK: "If you say *word* without the /d/, you get *were*; *word-were*."

I1 wor(d) → were ___   lam(p) → lamb ___

I2 boa(t) → bow ___   toa(d) → toe ___   hou(se) → how ___   ___/5 A: ___/5

Basic Phoneme Total: ___/10 A: ___/10

Advanced Phoneme Levels (early to late second grade; Level M is early third grade to adult)

LEVEL J Say *bat*. Now say *bat* but instead of /a/ say /i/.
FEEDBACK: "If you say *bat*, and change the /a/ to /i/, you get *bit*; *bat-bit*."

(*Short sound* of vowel)   b(a)t /i/ → bit ___   g(e)m /a/ → jam ___   m(a)tch /u/ → much ___

(*Long sound* of vowel)   sh(ee)p /A/ → shape ___   ch(o)se /E/ → cheese ___   ___/5 A: ___/5

LEVEL K
K1 (Deletion) **Say *sled*. Now say *sled* but don't say /l/.**
FEEDBACK: "If you say *sled* without the /l/, you get *said*; *sled-said*."

s(l)ed → said ___   b(r)eeze → bees ___

K2 (Substitution) **Say *crows*. Now say *crows* but instead of /r/ say /l/.**
FEEDBACK: "If you say *crows*, and change the /r/ to /l/, you get *close*; *crows-close*."

c(r)ows → c(l)ose ___   b(r)aid → b(l)ade ___   c(r)uise → c(l)ues ___   ___/5 A: ___/5

LEVEL L Say *hen*. Now say *hen* but instead of /n/ say /d/.
FEEDBACK: "If you say *hen*, and change the /n/ to /d/, you get *head*; *hen-head*."

he(n) /d/ → head ___   ri(s)e /m/ → rhyme ___

migh(t) /s/ → mice ___   tu(b)e /th/ → tooth ___   sou(p) /t/ → suit ___   ___/5 A: ___/5

LEVEL M
M1 (Deletion) **Say *swept*. Now say *swept* but don't say /p/.**
FEEDBACK: "If you say *swept* without the /p/, you get *sweat*; *swept-sweat*."

swe(p)t → sweat ___   fri(n)ge → fridge ___

M2 (Substitution) **Say *rent*. Now say *rent* but instead of /n/ say /k/.**
FEEDBACK: "If you say *rent*, and change the /n/ to /k/, you get *wrecked*; *rent-wrecked*."

re(n)t → wre(ck)ed ___   ro(p)ed → roa(s)t ___   lea(s)t → lea(p)ed ___   ___/5 A: ___/5

Advanced Phoneme Total: ___/20 A: ___/20

Correct   Automatic

PHONOLOGICAL AWARENESS SCREENING TEST (PAST) FORM D

David A. Kilpatrick, Ph.D. © 2003, 2010, 2019
Adapted from the levels used in McInnis (1999) & Rosner (1973)

Name: _____ Date: _____ Grade _____ Age _____
Teacher: _____ D.O.B.: _____ Evaluator: _____

INSTRUCTIONS: See *Equipped for Reading Success* Chapter 11: "Assessment of Phonological Awareness" for how to administer the PAST.

RESULTS:

	Correct	Automatic		
Basic Syllable	___/12	___/12	Highest Correct Level:	_____
Initial Phoneme/Onset-Rime	___/10	___/10	(Levels not passed below the highest correct level)	_____
Basic Phoneme	___/10	___/10		
Advanced Phoneme	___/20	___/20	Highest Automatic Level:	_____
Test Total	___/52	___/52	(Non-automatic levels below highest automatic level)	_____

Approximate Grade Level:	PreK/K	K	late K/early 1st	1st	late 1st/early 2nd	2nd	late 2nd to adult

Note: The grade levels listed throughout the *PAST* are estimates based on various research studies and clinical experience. They are not formalized norms.

I. SYLLABLE LEVELS

Basic Syllable Levels (D, E2 - preschool to mid kindergarten; E3 - mid to late kindergarten)

Correct   Automatic

LEVEL D   Say *sidewalk*. Now say *sidewalk* but don't say *side*.
FEEDBACK: "If you say *sidewalk* without saying *side*, you get *walk*."

D1   (sail)boat ____   (door)way ____   week(end) ____   ___/3 A: ___/3
D2   (dol)phin ____   (car)pet ____   mor(ning) ____   ___/3 A: ___/3

LEVEL E   Say *tornado*. Now say *tornado* but don't say *tor*.
FEEDBACK: "If you say *tornado* without saying *tor*, you get *nado*."

E2   (tor)nado ____   (per)mission ____   (de)partment ____   ___/3 A: ___/3
E3   (in)strument ____ (con)centrate ____ (wil)derness ____   ___/3 A: ___/3

Basic Syllable Total: ___/12 A: ___/12

II. INITIAL PHONEME / ONSET-RIME LEVELS

Onset-Rime Levels (kindergarten to mid first grade)

LEVEL F   Say *joke*. Now say *joke* but don't say /j/.
FEEDBACK: "If you say *joke* without the /j/, you get *oak*; *joke-oak*."

(j)oke → oak ____   (r)ise → eyes ____
(j)ar → are ____   (f)ake → ache ____   (l)ake → ache ____   ___/5 A: ___/5

LEVEL G   Say *read*. Now say *read* but instead of /r/ say /n/.
FEEDBACK: "If you say *read*, and change the /r/ to /n/, you get *need*; *read-need*."

(r)ead /n/ → need ____   (h)er /f/ → fur ____
(c)ode /t/ → toad ____   (l)ed /s/ → said ____   (th)ese /ch/ → cheese ____   ___/5 A: ___/5

Onset-Rime Total: ___/10 A: ___/10

PAST Form D

III. PHONEME LEVELS

Basic Phoneme Levels (early to late first grade)

LEVEL H
H1 (Deletion) **Say *tried*. Now say *tried* but don't say /t/.**
FEEDBACK: "If you say *tried* without the /t/, you get *ride*; *tried-ride*."

(t)ried → ride ___   (s)lam → lamb ___

H2 (Substitution) **Say *froze*. Now say *froze* but instead of /f/ say of /g/.**
FEEDBACK: "If you say *froze*, and change the /f/ to /g/, you get *grows*; *froze-grows*."

(f)roze → (g)rows ___   (t)rees → (f)reeze ___   (f)ries → (p)rize ___   ___/5 A: ___/5

LEVEL I Say *port*. Now say *port* without the /t/.
FEEDBACK: "If you say *port* without the /t/, you get *poor*; *port-poor*."

I1 por(t) → poor ___   sur(f) → sir ___

I2 sa(m)e → say ___   pla(c)e → play ___   nee(d) → knee ___   ___/5 A: ___/5

Basic Phoneme Total: ___/10 A: ___/10

Advanced Phoneme Levels (early to late second grade; Level M is early third grade to adult)

LEVEL J Say *hit*. Now say *hit* but instead of /i/ say /a/.
FEEDBACK: "If you say *hit*, and change the /i/ to /a/, you get *hat*; *hit-hat*."

(*Short sound* of vowel)   h(i)t /a/ → hat ___   wh(e)n /i/ → win ___   t(oo)l /e/ → tell ___

(*Long sound* of vowel)   g(a)te /O/ → goat ___   c(a)pe /E/ → keep ___   ___/5 A: ___/5

LEVEL K
K1 (Deletion) **Say *try*. Now say *try* but don't say /r/.**
FEEDBACK: "If you say *try* without the /r/, you get *tie*; *try-tie*."

t(r)y → tie ___   s(l)ope → soap ___

K2 (Substitution) **Say *snail*. Now say *snail* but instead of /n/ say /t/.**
FEEDBACK: "If you say *snail*, and change the /n/ to /t/, you get *stale*; *snail-stale*."

s(n)ail → s(t)ale ___   f(l)ows → f(r)oze ___   g(l)ean → g(r)een ___   ___/5 A: ___/5

LEVEL L Say *foam*. Now say *foam* but instead of /m/ say /n/.
FEEDBACK: "If you say *foam*, and change the /m/ to /n/, you get *phone*; *foam-phone*."

foa(m) /n/ → phone ___   je(t) /m/ → gem ___

bo(th) /t/ → boat ___   wro(t)e /p/ → rope ___   tee(th) /ch/ → teach ___   ___/5 A: ___/5

LEVEL M
M1 (Deletion) **Say *wisp*. Now say *wisp* but don't say /s/.**
FEEDBACK: "If you say *wisp* without the /s/, you get *whip*; *wisp-whip*."

wi(s)p → whip ___   toa(s)t → tote ___

M2 (Substitution) **Say *ripped*. Now say *ripped* but instead of /p/ say /s/.**
FEEDBACK: "If you say *ripped*, and change the /p/ to /s/, you get *wrist*; *ripped-wrist*."

ri(pp)ed → wri(s)t ___   so(f)t → sa(l)t ___   ta(s)te → tai(n)t ___   ___/5 A: ___/5

Advanced Phoneme Total: ___/20 A: ___/20

Correct   Automatic

Appendix D
ACTIVITIES THAT PROMOTE MAPPING THROUGH WORD STUDY

The strategies below are explained in Chapter 6. Use this page as a quick reference for lesson planning.

1) Teach students the vocabulary of mapping

Develop the students' instructional vocabulary (e.g., *syllable, onset, phoneme, rime unit, blend, digraph*).

2) Phoneme-to-grapheme mapping technique

Students point to the letters/graphemes that represents sounds called out by the teacher.

3) Teach students to map rime units

Teach the rime units and other word parts. Also, do phoneme awareness activities on rime units.

4) Introduce words orally first

Before introducing a new word, discuss its oral properties to prepare them to "map" the oral sounds in the word to the letter string that forms the printed word.

5) Use look-alike words

Use look-alike words (e.g., *black, block, brick, brink, break, blink*) when you do flash cards, word searches, etc. This forces students to attend to every letter in the word, which promotes mapping.

6) Mapping irregular words

Always point out and reinforce the regular elements in words. Make special note of the irregular part(s).

7) Direct mapping technique

Have a student orally segment a word before looking at its printed form. Ask questions about which letter or letters make certain sounds in the oral word. For example: "In *clap*, which letter says /l/?"

8) Backward decoding technique

Have students sound out words, back to front, one rime unit or onset at a time.

9) Highlight rime units in words

Underline or otherwise highlight rime units in words (s<u>ent</u>, st<u>art</u>, c<u>ar</u>p<u>ent</u>er).

10) Use oral spelling to reinforce mapping

This reinforces phoneme awareness of a given word, and helps make the word a familiar letter string.

11) Oral decoding

Orally spell words and have students recognize the word(s) based on the oral spelling.

12) Invented spelling

When spelling previously untaught words, encourage invented spelling. Then correct as needed.

13) Reading nonsense words

Have children read 5-10 nonsense words per lesson (e.g., *blat, splank*).

14) Spelling nonsense words

Have children spell 3-5 nonsense words per lesson (e.g., *ap, blim, freep, coaf*).

15) Spelling irregular words

Have children spell irregular words (Appendix I).

16) Word structure analysis

Have students mark up words by underlining rime units and circling onsets.

17) Making/Breaking Words

Provide students with the letters of a big word. Have them record how many words they can make from those letters.

18) Words Their Way

Use this program to promote spelling, phonics, and word study.

19) Reversed sentence reading technique

Have students read a sentence going from the last word back to the first to avoid guessing based on context.

20) Use all capitals and other forms of presenting words

Present words in ways that disrupt their normal "look" including all capitals, mixed case (e.g., SePteMbEr; rEAsON), or print words vertically.

21) Reading sideways and upside-down

Have students read sometimes with the text rotated sideways (left and/or right) and sometimes upside down.

22) Multiple font and mixed case reading

Use different and unusual fonts to throw off the visual "look" of words.

23) Spaced out letters technique

Have words printed with large spaces between (e.g., w a l k   h a m m e r).

24) Linked words technique

Use connected text with no spacing to force students to use phonetic decoding. Perhaps vary the look of the words by using all lowercase or all uppercase or mixed cases (i.e., pRiNTwORdSLikEtHiSwiTHoUtSpACeEs).

Appendix E

LETTER-SOUND HELPS: ALPHABET, DIGRAPHS, AND BLENDS

See Chapter 12 for additional helps with the alphabet, digraphs, diphthongs, and blends below. Use these to reinforce reading, spelling, and phoneme awareness (see Glossary for use of terms).

ALPHABET – LETTERS & SOUNDS

Consonants (see Chapter 12 for help in pronouncing consonants in isolation)

Consistently pronounced consonants:

The letters *d, j, m, n, t, v,* and *z* all produce fairly consistent sounds and require no further comment.

Inconsistently pronounced consonants:

- **b** Usually consistent except when silent (e.g., *comb;* see *Silent Consonant Combinations*, below).

- **c** Makes a "hard *c*" (i.e., /k/) when followed by *a, o,* and *u* (e.g., *cake, come, cut*) and a "soft *c*" (i.e., /s/) when followed by *e, i,* or *y* (*center, city, cycle*). Rarely it makes other sounds (e.g., *cello, suspicion*). When followed by *h* it forms the *ch* digraph.

- **f** Almost always makes the /f/ sound (e.g., *friend*), except in one of the most common words (*of*).

- **g** Usually a "hard *g*" when followed by the vowels *a, o,* and *u* (e.g., *gate, got, gum*), and when the g is doubled (e.g., *foggy, piggy*) and a "soft *g*" (i.e., /j/) when followed by *e, i* or *y* (*gentle, giant, gym*). There are some exceptions (e.g., *get, gift*).

- **h** Fairly consistent but occasionally silent (e.g., *ghost*). It combines with other consonants to form digraphs (i.e., *ch, gh, ph, sh, th*).

- **k** Fairly consistent but sometimes silent in the *kn* combination (see next page). Combines with the letter *c* at the end of many words so that the *c* and *k* combine to form one /k/ sound (*back, sock*).

- **l** Generally consistent but silent in *-alk* and *–olk* words (e.g., *walk, talk; folk, yolk*), yet is pronounced in *-elk, -ilk,* and *-ulk* words (*elk, milk, bulk*).

- **p** Consistently /p/, however, when followed by the letter *h* becomes the *ph* diagraph. Very rarely, the *p* followed by *h* splits between two syllables and is not a diagraph (e.g., *shepherd, upholster*).

- **qu** The letter *q* is always followed by the vowel *u* so they should be taught together. The only exceptions I know of are proper names: *Iraq* and the short form of Shaquille O'Neal (*Shaq*).

- **r** This is consistent but vowels preceding it typically change their sound (see more under "vowels").

- **s** This says /s/ most of the time, but at the end of many common words it makes the /z/ sound (e.g., *is, was, hers, his, has, nose, these, those, wins, runs*), especially on possessives and plurals (*Tom's, theirs, hers, mom's, kids, wins, tables, toys*). Rarely, *s* can make the /sh/ sound (e.g., *sure, sugar*) or be silent (*island, aisle*).

- **w** Functions as a consonant at the beginning of a syllable (*west, want*) and as a vowel at the end of a syllable (*sow, law, new*) and is silent when followed by the letter *r* (*write, wrist, wrong, wrap*) or in words related to *who* (*who, whose, who's, whom, who'd*).

- **x** This is the only letter of the alphabet whose standard sound is made up of two phonemes. It combines the sounds /k/ and /s/ (thus, the *Boston Red Sox* and *Chicago White Sox* baseball teams spell their team name as a phonetically accurate equivalent to *socks*). Pronounce *x* as /ks/. In the beginning of words, it makes a /z/ sound (xylophone, Xavier). In x-ray, the x functions as the end of the first syllable with the /e/ not written (i.e., ex-ray).

- **y** Functions as a consonant at the beginning of a syllable (*yes, yellow*) and as vowel at the end of a syllable (*say, any, boy, sky*); as a vowel, it can make a long *e* sound /E/ (*busy, cloudy*), a long *i* sound /I/ (*sly, why*) or can be part of a vowel diphthong (*boy, hey*).

– 247 –

Vowels

Each vowel can make sounds in addition to usual "long" and "short" sounds. They all make a *schwa* sound, which is like a very quick, short /u/ sound (e.g., the *a* in *about* or *i* in *holiday*). This occurs most commonly in unstressed syllables of multisyllabic words (see examples). *R-controlled* means that the vowel sounds are different before an *r*. Notice that *er*, *ir*, and *ur* all make the same sound. In R-controlled syllables, the o functions like a long o /O/ (*for*), and the *a* sounds like a short *o* /o/ (e.g., *car*).

Short Vowel Sounds		Long Vowel Sounds		Schwa sound	R-controlled vowel sounds	
/a/	pat, had, ran	/A/	cake, save, paid	*a*bout	/ar/	car, artist
/e/	pet, red, pen	/E/	be, need, theme	tel*e*scope	/er/	her, after
/i/	pit, win, flip	/I/	ride, crime, fried	an*i*mal	/ir/	girl, circle
/o/	pot, job, stop	/O/	loan, note, goal	daff*o*dil	/or/	for, order
/u/	putt, up, fun	/U/	flute, cute, rude	*u*pon	/ur/	burn, urgent

Vowel combinations

These are too numerous and have too many exceptions to review here. Some vowel combinations are generally quite consistent (e.g., *ee* and *oa*), while others are very inconsistent (e.g., *ea* can be long *e* [*bead*], short *e* [*head*], long *a* [*steak*]).

Digraphs

ch   Normally the /ch/ sound (e.g., *church, chicken, cheese, latch*), sometimes /k/ (*chorus, character, anchor, echo*), rarely /sh/ (*chef, chute, charades, machine*), and at least once, silent (*yacht*)

gh   Makes the /f/ sound (e.g., *laugh, rough, cough, enough*) or is silent (*though, daughter, light*) at the end of words. It rarely begins a word; when it does it uses the hard /g/ (primarily *ghost, ghastly, ghetto,* and *ghoul*)

ph   Makes the /f/ sound (e.g., *phone, graph, alphabet*)

sh   Typically makes the /sh/ sound as in (*she, fish, ship, cash*)

th   Voiced sound as in (*the, these, that, there, them*) (see Chapter 12)

th   Unvoiced sound as in (*think, thank, teeth, south*) (see Chapter 12)

Silent Consonant Combinations

kn–   The *k* is silent (e.g., *know, knew, knife, knee, knight*)

wh–   The *h* is silent (e.g., *what, where, when, why, which*) except in the word *who* and its derivatives (*whose, whom*) where the *w* is silent and the *h* is pronounced.

–mb   Found at the end of words, the *b* is silent (e.g., *comb, tomb, bomb, climb, crumb, plumb*)

Common Blends

Beginning blends

bl	blue, black	fr	free, fry	sk	ski, skate	squ	square, squeak
br	bring, bright	gl	glass, glue	sl	sled, sleep	st	stand, stay
cl	clown, clean	gr	great, grade	sm	smile, smart	sw	sweet, swing
cr	crash, crack	pl	place, play	sn	snow, snap	tr	tree, train
dr	drink, drum	pr	price, prove	sp	spot, space	tw	twice, twist
fl	fly, flat	sc	score, scan				

Beginning Three phoneme blends

scr	screen, scrub	spr	spring, spray
spl	split, splash	str	string, straw

Beginning Blend-Digraph combinations

phr	phrase
shr	shred, shrub, shrug
thr	three, throw, thread

Ending blends

There are many ending blends (e.g., *band, left*). Some are the same as beginning blends (e.g., *list, stop*) while others are only ending blends (*send, wept*). Rather than teach ending blends as isolated units, it may be useful to teach them within the context of *rime units* (see Appendix F).

Appendix F

COMMON RIME UNITS, PREFIXES, AND SUFFIXES

Below is a list of select rime units and *affixes* (i.e., prefixes and suffixes). Teachers can use these to reinforce reading, spelling, and phoneme awareness. Students should learn these word parts as familiar letter sequences, storing them like they store a word. Thus, mapping techniques that apply to words also apply to these word parts. Doing phoneme awareness activities on these word parts is the best way to help students anchor these word parts in memory (see Chapter 6).

Prefixes

Some common prefixes are also rime units. Some prefixes are also words, yet many are *only* prefixes. The list below separates them into these categories.

Prefix only			Prefix *and* rime unit		Prefix, rime unit, and word	
de	**mis**	**pro**	**ab**	**im**	**an**	**ad**
dis	**pre**	**re**	**un**		**in**	

Suffixes

Suffixes vs. rime units: Many common letter strings that form suffixes also form rime units. Suffixes are *added* to a root word to change the word while rime units are *built into the root* of the word. For example, the *ed* in *red* is a rime unit. But when *ed* is added to a word, it changes the word. Adding *ed* to *stop* changes the word to a past tense *stopped*. When *ance* is in the word *dance,* it is part of the root and therefore a rime unit. But when *ance* is added to the word *accept*, it changes the verb to the noun *acceptance*. The pronunciation may differ between the rime form and suffix form. With few exceptions (e.g., *advance*) in the suffix form, the vowel reduces to a schwa (consider *ance* in *dance* vs. *attendance*). Some suffixes and rime units, like *able,* are questionable as true rime units because they have two syllables. However, for practical, instructional purposes, they are included among the rime units.

Suffix only			Suffix *and* rime unit			Suffix, rime unit, *and* word	
ful	**ness**	**tion**	**ance**	**ence**	**ing**	**able**	**ant**
ment	**ous**		**ed**	**ent**	**er**		

Rime units

Rime units are the building blocks of syllables. As students store rime units for automatic, effortless recognition, they increase their potential for expanding their sight vocabulary and simplifying the storage of multisyllabic words. Teach these rime units and give examples, also, do phoneme awareness activities with them (see Chapter 6).

Only a limited number of rime units are listed. There are an overwhelming number of them, when one considers all of the possible combinations[1] that can make up a rime unit, there are hundreds of rime units. Listed the most common rime units that tend to follow the simplest patterns. Hundreds of words can be built from these simple rime units.

---

[1] Combinations include: vowel-consonant (e.g., *-ip*); vowel-consonant-*e* (e.g., *-ake*) diphthong-consonant (e.g., *-oup*), diphthong-consonant-*e* (e.g., *-ouse*), vowel-consonant blend (e.g., *-isk*); vowel-consonant blend-*e* (e.g., *-ence*), diphthong-consonant blend-*e* (e.g., *-ounce*), to name a few.

PARTIAL LIST OF RIME UNITS

Items with an asterisk (*) represent rime units with more that one pronunciation. A sample of each pronunciation is given alphabetically. The asterisk follows the more common pronunciation.
See pages 55-56 for one way to efficiently use the rimes in this list.

A		**E**		**I**		**O**		**U**	
ab	cab, tab	ead	bead,* head	ib	fib, rib	oach	broach, coach	ub	club, tub
ace	face, race	eak	break, speak*	ibe	scribe, tribe	oad	road,* broad	ube	cube, tube
ack	back, rack	eal	real, seal	ice	dice, nice	oak	cloak, soak	uch	much, such
ad	bad, mad	eam	dream, team	ich	rich, which	oar	roar, soar	uck	duck, truck
ag	bag, tag	ear	bear, fear*	ick	brick, thick	oat	coat, float	ud	bud, mud
age	page, stage	ease	grease, please*	id	hid, kid	ob	job, rob	ug	hug, rug
aid	afraid, paid	each	reach, teach	ide	ride, side	ock	clock, sock	ull	dull,* pull
ail	fail, nail	eat	great, heat*	ife	life, wife	od	nod, rod	ule	mule, rule
ain	pain, rain	eck	check, neck	ig	big, wig	ode	code, rode	um	drum, gum
air	hair, stair	ed	bed, red	ight	bright, light	og	dog, jog*	un	fun, run
aise	raise, praise	eed	feed, need	ike	bike, like	oke	broke, joke	une	June, tune
ake	bake, rake	eek	creek, week	ile	file, mile	ole	pole, role	up	cup, pup
ale	pale, sale	eel	feel, wheel	ill	bill, will	oll	doll, roll*	ur	blur, fur
all	ball, tall	een	been, seen*	im	him, rim	om	from, mom,* whom	ure	pure, sure
am	clam, jam	eep	deep, sleep	ime	dime, time	ome	home, some*	us	bus, plus
ame	came, tame	eer	cheer, deer	in	chin, win	on	con,* son	use	amuse, fuse
an	pan, tan	eet	feet, meet	ine	mine, pine	one	bone,* done, gone	ush	brush,* push
ane	cane, plane	eeze	breeze, sneeze	int	mint,* pint	oom	broom, room	ut	cut,* put
ap	map, tap	eg	leg, peg	ip	lip, sip	op	hop, top	ute	cute, flute
ape	cape, tape	ell	sell, tell	ipe	pipe, ripe	ope	hope, rope		
ar	car,* war	em	stem, them	ire	fire, tire	or	for, nor		
are	care, scare	en	pen, ten	is	his,* this	ore	before, score		
arm	farm,* warm	ench	bench, wrench	ish	dish, wish	ose	dose, hose,* lose		
arn	barn,* warn	er	after, her	it	bit, sit	ot	got, hot		
ase	case,* phase	ere	here,* where, were	itch	ditch, pitch	ote	note, vote		
ash	cash,* wash	ess	dress, guess	ite	kite, white	ouch	couch,* touch		
ass	glass, pass	et	get, set	ive	dive,* give	ould	could, should		
at	cat, sat	ew	few, grew	ix	fix, six	our	hour,* pour, tour		
atch	batch, match	ey	they,* key	ize	prize, size	ove	drove,* love, move		
ate	gate, rate					ox	box, fox		
ath	bath, math								
ave	have, save*								
ax	relax, tax								
ay	day, stay								

Appendix G

Look–Alike Words to Promote Word Study

See Chapter 6 for an explanation of the use of look-alike words. The following are just samples. You can create your own. You can generate lists or flashcards.

again, about, able, away, along, around, after, another, against, almost, always

and, an, a, am, ask, at, as, ant, aunt, any, all, ago, also

be, bee, by, buy, but, bay, been, beep, bin, bit, bite, bike, bat, but, bug, bag, bow

before, below, belong, being, believe, because, became, better, bitter, batter, butter, between

black, block, blink, bloke, brick, brink, brisk, blunt, brand, broad, bread, bland, bleed, bled, blade, break, brake, bike, blast, blaze, bake, bound, bloat, blight, bright, bring, bride, boast

bond, band, bind, bone, bane, bird, both, bore, bout, boat, bank, bunk, bark, back

boar, board, bored, boat, bound, bond

bottom, bottle, brittle, bubble

can, cap, cat, car, card, carp, cart, cast, case, cab, crab, cash, can't

come, came, cane, cape, comb, corn

course, cause, coarse, cord, corn, cost

deck, duck, disk, desk

do, don't does, down, day, did

during, doing, daring, dying, didn't

each, east, eat, eaten, earn, enough, enter, end, edge, even, every, eyes

for, far, few, form, fort, four, forty, fourteen, fortieth, force, fork

fact, fat, fast, first, frank, fad, far

from, form, front, fright, fry, free, freedom, fresh, friend, find, found

got, get, gut, gum, go, good, God

great, green, greed, grade, greet

government, governor, grocer, gardener, graduate, general

hand, had, hard, hide, hear, heard, head, have, here

he, his, her, him, has, how, have

hit, hat, hut, hot, had, ham, has, his, hey, hid, hip, hog, hop, how, hub, hug, huge, hum, high, nigh

hound, house, horse, how, home, hope, howl, bowl

himself, herself, however

if, of, I've, I'm, in, it, its, is, ink

into, inside, intend, indeed, instead

just, jest, judge, juice, joy,

know, knew, knot, knee, knife, knight, knack, kneed

last, lamb, late, lake, laid, lame, list, limp, link, left, like, long, look

left, let, lit, lead, led, less, list, last, link, lid, link, life, live

little, level, light, ladder, latter, later

lunch, launch, laugh, least, league

may, my, me, many, made, make, mine, must, more, might, men, met, man

much, must, mud, most

no, on, not, new, now

next, nest, need, nice, mice, night

number, nothing, never, newer

of, if, off, on, or

old, oat, oar, out, one, own, our, hour, odd, or, once, only

often, offer, open, only, own, other, order, over

put, pat, pet, pit, part

public, people, please, pencil, place, plank, plastic, paper

right, ride, risk, rode

should, shout, shed, she'd, shield, shut, sheet, send, sent, slide, slid, slice

so, sew, sow, show, snow, saw, was, set, sit, sat, see, say, she

something, someone, somewhere, sometime, summer, somehow

since, says, said, send, some, same, sent, such, seen, seed, seep, sane

small, smell, smile, stall, style

split, spilt, spilled, stilt, spell, spill

state, stay, stray, style, stand, sand

take, tack, tap, tape, top, tip, tick, tin, thin, tint, task, tan, tab, trap, track, truck, truck,

trade, train, tide, time, tied, tie, tidy, tiny, tire, tiger, tired, timed, tight, told, toss, turn

think, thick, three, tree, the, they, them, this, the, then, than, that, thus, these, those, time, there, their, theirs, they're, theft, thief, theme, they'd, they'll, they've, thin, thing, third, thirst, thumb, thud, thug

though, thought, through, throughout, thorough, throw, trough, tough, thigh, tongue, touch, tight, therefore, theory, theater, thimble, thrift, tooth

to, two, too, ton, toy, tow, toe, toad, toast, tone, tote, twin, twice, took, take, told, tell, tilt, toll, tool, tomb, tube, took, tooth, torn, toss, tour, toad, tuck, tuna, tune, tile, title, type

toward, towed, twice, twin, tweed, twist, twirl, twine, tower, towel, town, twelve, twenty, twig, twinkle

torch, touch, today, total

trace, tray, trap, try, tree, track, trick, truck, train, trade, tram, trail, trash, treat, trend, trial, tribe, trim, trip, true, trunk, truth

together, tomorrow, therefore, tonight, thermometer, treasure, torpedo, tradition, traffic, triangle, triple, troop, trophy, trumpet, tumble, thimble, turkey, turtle

tickle, tackle, tattle, tassel, ticket, tissue, travel, twinkle

us, use, up, as, used

until, united, untied, under, upon

water, washer, waiter, wait, waited, walk, walker, whether, weather

will, well, world, word

who, what, where, when, why, was, with, were, we, while, will, whom, wheat, would, which, work, weak, week went

with, wish, wind, white, write

without, within, witness, winter, winner, winning

was, saw, war, wash, we

year, years, yes, yield, your, you, yet

Appendix H
Nonsense Words for Word Study

Chapter 6 describes two word-study activities that use nonsense words; spelling and reading (see Chapter 6 for details). This appendix provides over 3,000 nonsense words so teachers can make immediate use of these strategies and minimize time spent lesson planning. Select words from these pages that meet the needs of a given lesson.

These words are true nonsense words. I avoided misspellings of real words (e.g., *gote* is not included because it is pronounced like *goat*). Also, any words that remotely sounded like inappropriate words were not included (if you catch anything I missed, e-mail me!).

Teachers can expand this list by adding endings to the words. For example, *frib* becomes *fribbing, fribber, fribbed, fribble, fribation* by adding common endings. This helps students learn simple spelling rules regarding adding endings to words. For example, *mip* would become *mipping, mipper,* and *mipped*, while *mipe* becomes *miping, miper,* and *miped*. The latter example is a long vowel with a silent *e*, and there is no doubling of the final consonant. However, long vowel words without a silent *e* just have the endings added directly, so *cload* becomes *cloading, cloader,* and *cloaded*. Short vowel words with a consonant blend at the end do not double the final consonant, thus *yend* becomes, *yending, yender,* and *yended*. Other endings can be added as students progress (e.g., -ence, -iment, -able, -est, -ist, -ent, -ly, -ful, etc.). Another way to create good nonsense words is take any existing multisyllable word and change a key letter, often the first one. Thus, *careful* becomes *pareful*, *deliver* becomes *teliver*, and *saving* becomes *siving*. Given the possibilities described here, the 3,000+ nonsense words below can easily become over 10,000 nonsense words.

The list is organized by rime units. It closely parallels the rime unit list in Appendix F. The words are alphabetized within rime unit. If you want to focus on words with a certain beginning, you can quickly generate a list based on looking through each rime unit list to find words that begin with the blend you are teaching. For example, if you are working on the beginning blend *br*, you can skim through each rime unit list and take any *br* nonsense words you find. If you only want five words for your lesson, you scan the first several rime unit lists to get *brab, brack, brage, brame,* and *brap*.

TIP: Photocopy this list (personal use only by owners of this book). Then, on the photocopied list, you can check off the words as you use them from year to year, or reading group to reading group. As described in Chapter 6, have your students read 5-10 nonsense words and spell 3-5 nonsense words per lesson. The reading part should take 30 seconds and the spelling part would take another 90 seconds. *Remember, reading nonsense words promotes letter-sound skills and oral blending while spelling nonsense words promotes letter-sound skills and phoneme awareness.* Also, orally spell a nonsense word to see if they can correctly say it, or ask them to spell a nonsense word you say. These activities force kids to track though words and help them break the habit of guessing based on the first letter and the length of the word.

LIST OF NONSENSE WORDS

bab	phab	twab	crace	sprace	frack	nad	slad	yag
hab	plab	whab	drace	squace	glack	pad	smad	blag
mab	prab		dwace	stace	grack	rad	snad	clag
pab	scrab	bace	flace	swace	prack	vad	spad	chag
rab	shab	dace	frace	thace	scrack	yad	splad	glag
sab	shrab	hace	glace	thrace	spack	zad	sprad	grag
vab	smab	jace	knace	twace	splack	blad	stad	plag
wab	snab	nace	prace	whace	sprack	crad	strad	prag
yab	spab	quace	scrace		strack	drad	thad	scrag
zab	splab	sace	shace	cack	swack	flad	trad	smag
brab	sprab	tace	shrace	dack	thack	frad	twad	spag
clab	squab	wace	skace	gack	thrack	knad		splag
chab	strab	yace	slace	vack	twack	prad	cag	sprag
dwab	thab	zace	smace	brack		scad	mag	squag
frab	thrab	blace	snace	chack	jad	scrad	pag	strag
glab	trab	clace	splace	drack	kad	shad	quag	trag

– 252 –

twag	splail	squake	stran	knape	zarm	shase	shrate	plave
	sprail	swake	thran	phape	blarm	slase	smate	prave
bage	squail	thake		plape	clarm	smase	snate	scave
dage	strail	thrake	hane	prape	flarm	snase	splate	scrave
hage	swail	trake	nane	scape	glarm	splase	sprate	smave
jage	thail		quane	shrape	knarm	sprase	squate	snave
lage		rale	tane	slape	plarm	squase	swate	spave
mage	dain	zale	yane	smape	scarm	stase	thate	splave
nage	hain	chale	blane	snape	sharm	strase	thrate	sprave
quage	nain	crale	clane	squape	skarm	thrase	twate	squave
tage	quain	drale	flane	stape	slarm	twase		strave
vage	tain	prale	frane	strape	smarm		cath	thave
yage	yain	scrale	glane	swape	snarm	fash	dath	thrave
zage	zain	smale	prane	thape	sparm	jash	fath	trave
blage	clain	spale	scane	thrape	splarm	pash	gath	twave
brage	flain	sprale	scrane	trape	tharm	tash	jath	
clage	frain	squale	shrane	twape	wharm	vash	nath	bax
crage	glain	strale	smane			yash	quath	cax
drage	knain	thale	splane	dar	carn	zash	sath	dax
flage	prain		squane	har	farn	blash	tath	gax
knage	scain	bame	stane	lar	harn	chash	vath	hax
plage	scrain	hame	strane	nar	jarn	drash	wath	kax
prage	shain	jame	swane	sar	karn	frash	yath	nax
scrage	shrain	pame	thrane	var	larn	glash	zath	pax
shage	skain	quame	twane	yar	marn	grash	blath	quax
slage	smain	rame		zar	narn	phash	brath	rax
smage	snain	vame	bap	blar	parn	prash	clath	zax
snage	splain	wame	fap	clar	quarn	scash	chath	blax
spage	squain	yame	quap	flar	rarn	scrash	crath	brax
splage	thain	zame	vap	glar	sarn	shash	drath	clax
sprage	thrain	brame	wap	plar	varn	snash	flath	chax
strage		chame	blap	shar	zarn	spash	frath	drax
thage	caise	crame	brap	slar	blarn	sprash	glath	frax
trage	jaise	drame	drap	smar	clarn	strash	grath	glax
	kaise	glame	glap	snar	charn	thash	knath	grax
daid	laise	grame	grap	splar	flarn		phath	prax
haid	naise	plame	phap	thar	glarn	dat	plath	scax
jaid	yaise	prame	plap	twar	knarn	jat	prath	scrax
naid	zaise	scame	prap		plarn	yat	scath	spax
quaid	claise	scrame	scap	gare	scarn	zat	scrath	splax
taid	draise	shrame	shap	jare	sharn	blat	shath	sprax
vaid	knaise	skame	shrap	lare	slarn	clat	shrath	strax
yaid	scraise	slame	skap	nare	smarn	crat	slath	
zaid	shraise	sname	smap	quare	snarn	glat	smath	tay
blaid	smaise	spame	squap	sare	sparn	grat	snath	vay
claid	snaise	splame	stap	vare	splarn	prat	spath	yay
chaid	splaise	sprame	thap	zare	squarn	scrat	splath	zay
craid	swaise	squame	thrap	dware	starn	smat	sprath	blay
draid	thaise	stame	twap	knare	swarn	snat	squath	scray
knaid	twaise	strame		plare	tharn	strat	stath	smay
scaid		swame	bape	slare	twarn	thrat	strath	snay
scraid	dake	thame	dape	smare		trat	trath	squay
smaid	gake	thrame	fape	splare	dase		twath	thray
snaid	pake	trame	hape	sprare	fase	jate		
splaid	vake	twame	lape	thrare	gase	quate	bave	geal
thaid	yake		mape	tware	hase	vate	fave	jeal
twaid	zake	gan	pape		jase	yate	jave	queal
	clake	lan	quape	barm	nase	zate	mave	yeal
cail	chake	yan	sape	darm	quase	blate	quave	bleal
dail	frake	zan	vape	garm	sase	brate	tave	breal
kail	glake	blan	wape	jarm	tase	clate	vave	cheal
yail	grake	cran	yape	larm	wase	chate	yave	creal
zail	knake	dran	zape	marm	yase	drate	zave	dreal
chail	plake	glan	blape	narm	zase	flate	blave	freal
crail	prake	pran	brape	parm	clase	frate	chave	greal
drail	scake	scran	clape	rarm	crase	glate	drave	preal
prail	scrake	slan	chape	sarm	drase	knate	flave	sceal
scrail	smake	sman	flape	tarm	flase	phate	frave	screal
smail	splake	splan	frape	varm	knase	scrate	glave	sheal
spail	sprake	spran	glape	yarm	scrase	shate	phave	shreal

skeal	sleck	queek	sleen	reat	fleg	crem	ver	shet
smeal	smeck	teek	smeen	veat	freg	drem	yer	shret
sneal	sneck	veek	sneen	yeat	gleg	frem	zer	sket
spreal	spleck	yeek	speen	zeat	kneg	glem	cler	slet
streal	spreck	zeek	spreen	breat	pleg	grem	fler	smet
sweal	squeck	breek	squeen	creat	sceg	knem	gler	snet
theal	steck	cleek	streen	dreat	screg	plem	kner	spet
threal	streck	dreek	sween	freat	sheg	prem	pler	splet
treal	sweck	fleek	theen	gleat	shreg	scem	scer	spret
tweal	theck	gleek	threen	preat	skeg	screm	sker	squet
	threck	kneek	treen	sceat	sleg	shem	smer	stret
feam	tweck	pheek		screat	smeg	shrem	sner	swet
geam		pleek	feep	shreat	sneg	skem	spler	thet
heam	ged	preek	geep	skeat	speg	slem	squer	tret
jeam	ped	sceek	meep	smeat	spleg	smem	swer	twet
keam	qued	screek	neep	sneat	spreg	snem	twer	
leam	ved	skeek	queep	speat	squeg	spem		cib
meam	yed	smeek	veep	spleat	steg	splem	cess	gib
neam	cled	spleek	yeep	spreat	streg	sprem	dess	hib
peam	ched	spreek	zeep	squeat	sweg	squem	kess	kib
queam	cred	sweek	breep	theat	theg	strem	pess	mib
veam	gled	theek	cleep		threg	swem	quess	pib
weam	gred	threek	dreep	deeze	treg	threm	ress	quib
yeam	kned	treek	fleep	feeze	tweg	trem	sess	tib
zeam	phed		freep	geeze	wheg	twem	tess	vib
bleam	pred	beel	gleep	jeeze		whem	vess	wib
cleam	sced	geel	greep	leeze	kell		wess	yib
fleam	scred	jeel	kneep	meeze	lell	cen	zess	zib
fream	sked	leel	pheep	reeze	mell	nen	bress	blib
gream	smed	queel	pleep	seeze	rell	quen	cless	brib
kneam	sned	yeel	preep	veeze	vell	ren	fless	clib
pheam	spled	breel	sceep	yeeze	zell	sen	fress	chib
pleam	squed	cheel	screep	zeeze	brell	ven	gless	flib
pream	sted	dreel	shreep	bleeze	chell	blen	gress	frib
sheam	stred	freel	skeep	cleeze	crell	bren	kness	grib
sleam	swed	greel	smeep	creeze	drell	clen	phess	knib
sneam	thed	preel	sneep	dreeze	frell	cren	pless	phib
speam	twed	sceel	speep	fleeze	grell	dren	scess	plib
spleam		screel	spleep	gleeze	prell	flen	scress	prib
spream	beed	sheel	spreep	greeze	scell	fren	sless	scib
sweam	ceed	shreel	squeep	pheeze	screll	gren	smess	scrib
thream	jeed	skeel	streep	preeze	shrell	phen	sness	shrib
tream	keed	smeel	theep	sceeze	skell	plen	spess	skib
tweam	meed	sneel	threep	screeze	sprell	pren	spless	slib
	queed	spreel	treep	shreeze	squell	scren	spress	smib
geck	veed	streel	tweep	smeeze	stell	shen	squess	snib
jeck	yeed	sweel		speeze	strell	shren	stess	spib
leck	zeed	threel	keer	spleeze	thell	sken	swess	splib
meck	cleed	treel	meer	spreeze	threll	slen	thess	sprib
queck	cheed	tweel	zeer	steeze	trell	smen	thress	stib
seck	dreed		bleer	streeze	twell	snen	twess	strib
veck	gleed	feen	breer	sweeze		spen		swib
weck	preed	geen	creer		bem	splen	det	thib
yeck	sceed	heen	dreer	geg	cem	spren	het	thrib
zeck	shreed	neen	fleer	heg	jem	squen	ket	trib
bleck	sleed	reen	gleer	jeg	kem	sten	quet	twib
breck	smeed	veen	pleer	neg	lem	stren	zet	whib
cleck	spleed	yeen	sceer	queg	mem	swen	blet	
creck	spreed	zeen	screer	reg	nem	thren	bret	cibe
dreck	squeed	bleen	skeer	seg	pem	tren	clet	dibe
freck	streed	cheen	sleer	teg	quem	twen	cret	fibe
gleck	sweed	creen	spleer	veg	rem		dret	hibe
greck	theed	dreen	streer	weg	sem	ber	flet	kibe
kneck	threed	fleen		yeg	vem	der	glet	libe
pheck		freen	deat	zeg	wem	jer	gret	mibe
pleck	deek	kneen	geat	bleg	yem	ker	phet	nibe
preck	heek	pheen	jeat	breg	zem	ler	plet	pibe
sceck	jeek	pleen	keat	cleg	blem	mer	pret	quibe
sheck	keek	shreen	leat	cheg	brem	ner	scet	ribe
shreck	neek	skeen	queat	creg	chem	ter	scret	sibe

− 254 −

tibe	swick	hife	swig	whike	strim	snimp	fint	quipe
wibe	thrick	jife	thig		thim	squimp	gint	sipe
yibe	twick	kife	thrig	cile	thrim	stimp	jint	vipe
zibe		mife	trig	quile	twim	swimp	kint	yipe
blibe	gid	pife		sile		thimp	nint	zipe
clibe	jid	quife	dight	yile	bime	thrimp	quint	blipe
chibe	nid	sife	jight	zile	cime	trimp	rint	bripe
cribe	pid	tife	pight	brile	fime		sint	clipe
dribe	tid	vife	quight	crile	gime	din	vint	chipe
flibe	vid	yife	vight	drile	jime	hin	wint	dripe
fribe	wid	zife	yight	frile	kime	min	yint	flipe
glibe	zid	blife	zight	grile	nime	nin	zint	fripe
gribe	blid	brife	clight	prile	pime	rin	blint	glipe
knibe	brid	clife	chight	scile	quime	vin	brint	knipe
phibe	clid	chife	cright	scrile	sime	yin	chint	phipe
plibe	chid	crife	dright	snile	vime	zin	crint	plipe
pribe	crid	drife	glight	spile	wime	blin	drint	pripe
scibe	drid	flife	gright	sprile	yime	brin	frint	scipe
shibe	flid	frife	pright	squile	zime	crin	grint	scripe
shribe	frid	glife	scight	strile	blime	drin	knint	shipe
skibe	knid	grife	scright	swile	brime	flin	phint	shripe
slibe	phid	plife	shight	thile	drime	frin	plint	skipe
smibe	plid	prife	shright	thrile	flime	glin	scint	slipe
snibe	prid	scife	skight	twile	frime	knin	scrint	smipe
spibe	scrid	scrife	snight		glime	plin	shrint	squipe
splibe	smid	skife	splight	lill	knime	prin	skint	stipe
spribe	snid	slife	squight	rill	phime	scrin	slint	thipe
squibe	spid	smife	stight	vill	plime	shrin	smint	thripe
stibe	splid	snife	stright	yill	scime	slin	spint	tripe
stribe	sprid	spife	swight	zill	scrime	smin	strint	twipe
swibe	stid	splife	thight	brill	shime	splin	swint	
thribe	strid	sprife	thright	crill	shrime	sprin	thint	bire
twibe	swid	squife	twight	prill	skime	squin	thrint	gire
	thid	stife		scrill	snime	stin	trint	jire
bice	thrid	swife	fike	small	spime	strin	twint	kire
gice	trid	thrife	gike	snill	sprime	swin	whint	nire
hice	twid	trife	jike	sprill	squime	thrin		quire
jice		twife	quike	squill	stime	trin	bip	vire
kice			rike	strill	strime		fip	yire
wice	jide	hig	sike	thill	thime	bine	gip	zire
yice	kide	kig	vike	trill	thrime	gine	kip	blire
zice	mide	lig	wike	twill	trime	hine	mip	clire
blice	nide	quig	yike		twime	jine	vip	chire
clice	pide	sig	zike	bim		kine	brip	glire
chice	quide	tig	blike	cim	cimp	quine	frip	knire
drice	yide	vig	brike	fim	dimp	yine	glip	scrire
flice	zide	yig	clike	gim	fimp	zine	phip	skire
frice	blide	blig	chike	mim	gimp	bline	plip	slire
glice	clide	brig	crike	nim	himp	chine	prip	smire
phice	gride	clig	flike	pim	jimp	crine	scip	snire
plice	knide	chig	frike	quim	kimp	drine	scrip	splire
scrice	phide	crig	glike	yim	mimp	fline	shrip	sprire
shice	plide	drig	grike	zim	quimp	frine	smip	stire
smice	scide	flig	knike	blim	rimp	gline	squip	swire
snice	scride	frig	phike	clim	simp	grine	stip	thire
sprice	shride	glig	plike	chim	timp	pline	swip	twire
strice	skide	grig	prike	crim	vimp	prine	thip	
thice	smide	plig	scike	drim	yimp	scrine	thrip	bish
	splide	scig	scrike	flim	zimp	sline	twip	gish
gick	spride	scrig	slike	frim	brimp	smine		kish
yick	squide	shrig	smike	knim	climp	spline	bipe	lish
zick	stide	skig	snike	phim	drimp	sprine	cipe	mish
blick	swide	slig	splike	plim	flimp	squine	dipe	nish
grick	thide	smig	sprike	scim	frimp	strine	fipe	pish
phick	thride	snig	stike	snim	glimp	thrine	gipe	quish
plick	twide	splig	squike	spim	grimp	trine	jipe	rish
scrick		sprig	swike	splim	knimp		kipe	vish
smick	bife	stig	thike	sprim	phimp	bint	lipe	yish
squick	cife	strig	thrike	squim	plimp	cint	mipe	zish
strick	dife		twike	stim	slimp	dint	nipe	blish
	gife							

– 255 –

brish	thrite	quize	scroak	fob	brod	plog	sprole	strome
clish	twite	yize	shoak	hob	chod	prog	squole	thome
chish		zize	shroak	pob	crod	scog	swole	throme
crish	bive	blize	sloak	quob	drod	scrog	thole	trome
drish	kive	brize	snoak	tob	flod	shog	throle	
flish	mive	clize	sploak	vob	frod	shrog	twole	bon
frish	nive	chize	sproak	wob	glod	skog		fon
glish	pive	frize	squoak	yob	grod	slog	fom	hon
grish	quive	glize	swoak	zob	phod	snog	gom	lon
knish	rive	grize	thoak	brob	smod	spog	jom	mon
plish	sive	knize	throak	clob	snod	splog	lom	pon
prish	tive	phize	troak	chob	spod	sprog	nom	yon
scish	yive	plize	twoak	crob	splod	squog	quom	zon
scrish	zive	scrize		drob	sprod	stog	som	blon
shrish	blive	shize	joar	flob	stod	strog	vom	bron
skish	brive	slize	loar	frob	strod	swog	wom	clon
slish	clive	smize	voar	glob	thod	thog	yom	chon
smish	crive	snize	zoar	grob	throd	throg	zom	cron
snish	flive	splize	bloar	phob	twod	trog	blom	dron
spish	frive	squize	broar	plob		twog	brom	flon
splish	glive	strize	cloar	prob	dode		clom	fron
sprish	grive	swize	croar	scob	fode	boke	chom	phon
stish	plive	thrize	froar	scrob	jode	doke	crom	plon
strish	prive	twize	gloar	shob	pode	goke	drom	pron
thish	scive		groar	skob	quode	hoke	flom	scon
thrish	scrive	doad	ploar	smob	vode	loke	glom	shon
trish	shive	foad	proar	spob	wode	moke	grom	shron
twish	shrive	joad	sloar	splob	yode	noke	knom	skon
	skive	poad	smoar	sprob	zode	quoke	phom	slon
dit	slive	quoad	spoar	squob	blode	roke	plom	smon
git	smive	voad	sploar	stob	brode	voke	shom	snon
jit	snive	woad	squoar	strob	clode	zoke	shrom	spon
rit	spive	yoad	stroar	thob	chode	droke	slom	splon
vit	splive	zoad	thoar	trob	drode	floke	snom	spron
yit	sprive	bload	throar	twob	frode	froke	spom	squon
blit	squive	cload	troar		phode	gloke	splom	ston
drit	stive	choad		bock	plode	groke	sprom	stron
glit	swive	droad	doat	gock	prode	knoke	squom	swon
plit	thive	fload	foat	quock	scode	ploke	stom	thon
prit	trive	gload	hoat	vock	scrode	proke	strom	thron
scrit	twive	phoad	joat	yock	shrode	scoke	throm	tron
sprit		pload	loat	zock	skode	shoke	trom	twon
squit	bix	scoad	poat	brock	smode	shroke	twom	
swit	lix	scroad	soat	drock	spode	sloke		jone
thrit	quix	smoad	woat	glock	splode	snoke	bome	pone
trit	rix	spoad	yoat	grock	sprode	sploke	gome	quone
	vix	sproad	zoat	plock	squode	sproke	jome	rone
dite	wix	sproad	broat	prock	swode	squoke	lome	vone
gite	yix	troad	cloat	scrock	thode	swoke	vome	wone
jite	zix	twoad	choat	shrock	trode	thoke	wome	yone
pite	blix		croat	slock	twode	troke	yome	blone
vite	crix	boak	droat	snock		twoke	zome	brone
yite	drix	doak	froat	splock	cog		blome	chone
zite	frix	goak	groat	sprock	gog	nole	brome	frone
blite	glix	hoak	phoat	squock	kog	quole	clome	glone
chite	grix	loak	ploat	strock	mog	vole	chome	plone
crite	plix	moak	proat	swock	quog	wole	flome	smone
drite	scrix	noak	shoat	thock	rog	yole	glome	spone
glite	smix	quoak	spoat	throck	tog	zole	grome	splone
grite	snix	roak	sploat	trock	vog	brole	plome	sprone
prite	swix	voak	sproat	twock	wog	chole	prome	squone
scite	thix	zoak	stoat		yog	crole	shome	strone
scrite	thrix	droak	stroat	dod	zog	frole	slome	swone
skite		floak	swoat	fod	brog	grole	smome	trone
snite	fize	froak	thoat	hod	chog	knole	snome	
splite	hize	gloak	troat	jod	crog	prole	spome	foom
squite	jize	knoak	twoat	vod	drog	shole	splome	goom
strite	kize	ploak		yod	glog	smole	sprome	noom
swite	mize	proak	dob	zod	grog	snole	squome	poom
thite	nize	scoak		blod	phog	spole	stome	soom

voom	shrope	prot	dox	gube	shud	thrull	crun	skur
yoom	smope	splot	hox	hube	shrud	trull	drun	smur
cloom	snope	sprot	lox	jube	snud	twull	flun	snur
choom	squope	throt	mox	mube	splud	whull	frun	splur
croom	stope		nox	pube	sprud		glun	thur
droom	strope	bote	tox	rube	swud	bule	grun	twur
floom	swope	dote	vox	sube	thrud	cule	plun	
froom	thope	fote	wox	vube	trud	dule	prun	cush
knoom	thrope	hote	yox	wube		hule	slun	dush
proom	trope	jote	zox	yube	gug	kule	smun	gush
scoom		lote	brox	zube	kug	nule	snun	hush
shoom	jor	pote	chox	blube	nug	sule	splun	jush
skoom	kor	sote	drox	brube	sug	vule	sprun	kush
sloom	vor	wote	flox	clube	vug	wule	strun	nush
smoom	zor	yote	frox	chube	wug	zule	swun	sush
spoom	blor	zote	glox	crube	yug	brule	trun	vush
sploom	clor	brote	grox	drube	zug	chule	twun	wush
sproom	glor	clote	plox	flube	blug	frule		yush
squoom	plor	chote	prox	frube	brug	knule	fune	zush
stoom	slor	drote	scox	glube	clug	prule	hune	clush
stroom	splor	frote	scrox	grube	crug	scrule	pune	chush
troom	thor	grote	slox	knube	flug	shule	vune	drush
		phote	snox	phube	frug	smule	wune	frush
dop	jore	plote	splox	plube	glug	snule	yune	glush
fop	vore	prote	sprox	prube	grug	spule	zune	grush
gop	zore	scrote	strox	shube	knug	sprule	blune	knush
nop	blore	slote	swox	slube	prug	strule	brune	prush
quop	clore	snote	thox	smube	scrug	thule	clune	scush
rop	glore	spote	throx	snube	shug	trule	chune	scrush
vop	plore	splote	trox	spube	snug		crune	shrush
yop	slore	sprote		splube	spug	fum	drune	skush
zop	splore	stote	bub	sprube	splug	jum	flune	smush
blop		strote	dub	stube	sprug	lum	frune	snush
brop	bose	thote	fub	strube	strug	pum	glune	spush
frop	cose	trote	gub	swube	swug	tum	grune	splush
knop	fose		jub	thube	thrug	vum	plune	sprush
phop	mose	bove	lub	thrube	trug	wum	shune	stush
scop	vose	fove	mub	trube	twug	zum	shrune	strush
scrop	yose	gove	vub	twube	whug	blum	slune	swush
skop	zose	hove	wub	whube		brum	smune	thush
smop	blose	jove	yub		cull	clum	splune	trush
snop	brose	nove	zub	fud	jull	flum	stune	
squop	drose	pove	brub	gud	kull	frum	thune	dut
strop	plose	sove	crub	hud	rull	grum	thrune	lut
thop	smose	tove	drub	jud	sull	phum	trune	vut
throp	snose	yove	frub	lud	tull	prum		yut
trop	sprose	zove	glub	nud	vull	shum	cur	zut
twop	strose	blove	knub	pud	wull	snum	dur	blut
	trose	brove	phub	rud	yull	spum	gur	brut
bope		chove	plub	sud	zull	splum	jur	chut
fope	bot	crove	prub	tud	brull	sprum	kur	crut
jope	fot	flove	shub	vud	chull	stum	lur	drut
lope	mot	frove	slub	wud	crull	trum	mur	frut
vope	sot	knove	smub	yud	drull	whum	nur	grut
wope	vot	phove	spub	zud	frull		rur	phut
yope	wot	plove	splub	brud	grull	hun	tur	prut
zope	yot	scove	sprub	clud	prull	jun	vur	sput
blope	zot	smove	strub	chud	shull	lun	zur	thut
brope	brot	snove	thub	drud	smull	mun	brur	trut
clope	chot	spove	thrub	frud	snull	vun	clur	
chope	drot	splove	trub	glud	spull	yun	chur	
flope	flot	sprove	twub	grud	sprull	zun	flur	
frope	frot	swove	whub	knud	stull	blun	glur	
glope	glot	thove		phud	strull	brun	knur	
prope	grot	throve	dube	plud	swull	clun	plur	
shope	phot		fube	prud	thull	chun	scur	

Appendix I
IRREGULAR WORDS FOR WORD STUDY

See Chapter 6 for more information. Words with an asterisk (*) are Dolch words.

above	buoyant	debris	floor	height	knead
ache	bureau	debt	foreign	heighten	*know
acne	bury	deny	fought	heir	koala
acre	busy	depot	four	herb	labor
acreage	buy	diamond	friend	herbivorous	larynx
actual	calf	dingy	*from	hilarity	laser
again	canoe	do	fuselage	hind	leopard
aisle	care	*does	future	his	leapt
algae	cello	done	gallant	honest	learn
alibi	certain	door	geyser	honk	lecture
align	chassis	doubt	give	honor	leisure
alley	chauffeur	dough	gnat	hour	length
*almost	chef	drought	goes	hue	lengthen
amateur	chord	dwarf	gone	hustle	license
among	chorus	early	gourmet	hygiene	lichen
anchor	cleanse	earth	guarantee	hymn	licorice
ancient	climb	echo	guess	hyperbole	lieutenant
*are	clothes	eighth	guest	hypocrisy	limb
*been	collision	*enough	guide	indict	linear
beige	colonel	epoch	guild	into	lingerie
beret	color	equal	guitar	intrigue	listen
biscuit	*come	equity	hackneyed	iron	liter
blind	conscience	ether	half	irony	lose
both	corps	etiquette	halt	is	love
bough	cough	etymology	has	island	luxurious
bouquet	country	*eyes	hasten	isle	maneuver
break	course	facial	*have	islet	*many
breathe	courteous	fasten	head	jealous	margarine
broad	creative	feign	headache	jealousy	matinee
brought	crepe	feint	health	kayak	meadow
buffet	crochet	few	healthy	khaki	meant
build	deaf	fiancé	heard	kind	measure
built	dealt	fiend	heart	kiosk	measurement
buoy	death	*find	heifer	knack	mechanic

menial	opaque	pleasure	rendezvous	spatula	ukulele
menu	opinion	plumage	resent	squander	unconscious
mild	oppress	plumb	reservoir	stomach	vague
module	oral	plumber	result	strange	veins
morale	orange	plumbing	resume	subtle	vicious
most	orchard	pneumonia	reveille	suede	waffle
mother	organ	preface	revenue	sugar	wand
move	oriole	premier	rhythm	sundae	*war
muscle	other	prestige	rind	superfluous	warm
mutual	ought	pretty	rogue	sure	warn
narrate	oval	pristine	rouge	surely	was
nasal	oven	proprietor	rouse	surgeon	*water
natural	owe	prove	*said	swamp	watt
neutral	pagan	proven	salmon	swap	weigh
niche	pageant	psalm	salve	swarm	*were
niece	palm	pudding	scene	swat	what
ninth	papyrus	puddle	scenery	sweat	*where
none	paralysis	pull	scent	sweater	*who
nose	patient	pulley	scepter	sword	whom
novice	pear	punctual	schedule	syrup	whose
nuclear	pearl	punctuate	schwa	talk	wild
oblige	people	purchase	senior	taste	wolf
oboe	peril	push	sergeant	terrace	woman
ocean	period	*put	sew	*the	women
octave	periodical	qualm	sewing	thought	wood
odor	perish	quart	sewn	*through	word
*of	perishable	quarter	shoe	thwart	world
*off	peso	quarter	siege	thyme	worm
often	pewter	quartz	sieve	to	worth
oh	piece	radii	sigh	tomb	would
*old	pier	ratio	sign	tongue	wounded
oleo	pierce	react	silhouette	torque	writhe
olive	pigeon	receipt	siphon	tortoise	wrong
*once	pint	recipe	social	tough	yacht
*one	piracy	rehearse	solder	treacherous	yield
onion	plague	rehearsal	son	trough	yolk
*only	plaid	reign	source	truth	
opal	plateau	rely	sovereign	two	

Appendix J
GLOSSARY OF TERMS

This glossary contains many of the terms used in this manual. It also includes other common terms related to reading instruction. **Bold** words or phrases within the definitions indicate that there is an entry for that term elsewhere in this glossary.

AIS This stands for Academic Intervention Services in some locations (e.g., my home state of NY) and refers to services provided to general educational students for extra help in reading, writing, and math. This same service in the past was referred as **Title 1**.

Alliteration Word play that involves using many words sharing the same beginning sounds (e.g., the big black bug bit the big brown bear).

Alphabetic principle The insight that the oral sounds (phonemes) in spoken words are represented by letters in print. Once children develop the alphabetic principle, their ability to read improves.

Analogy Reading unfamiliar words based on similar patterns in familiar words. The student takes parts of words he knows (e.g., rime units, blends, digraphs) and applies them to decoding, this is sometimes called reading by analogy.

ARL Acronym for **Assured Readiness for Learning**.

Assured Readiness for Learning A learning program developed by Dr. Philip McInnis and first used in the 1972-73 school year. The program developed the readiness skills necessary for reading, math, and written expression. For reading, the Assured Readiness for Learning (ARL) program make use of **phonological awareness, letter-sound learning** (including multisensory training of letters), **rime units** (called **Decoding Keys**), the Directed Reading Lesson, the Assured Reading Assignment, among other elements.

Auditory analysis skill An older term used for **phonological awareness**.

Automaticity This refers to the state of being able to do something instantly, effortlessly, and without conscious thought.

Balanced instruction A viewpoint in reading that says that we should teach students using a combination of traditional phonics, whole word, and Whole Language approaches. The problem with this view is that 1) different teachers will mix and match differently resulting in very different instruction; 2) there is no evidence that merely mixing and matching will produce better reading; 3) all of the traditional approaches to reading (phonics, whole word, Whole Language) are "pre-scientific." They were developed before the last 30-40 years worth of research on the reading process; and 4) All of the traditional approaches produce a 20% - 30% failure rate. Why should we expect a mixture of flawed approaches to produce good results? A better way to make use of these traditional approaches is highlighted in Chapter 5.

Basal reader A reading textbook or reading series. The orientation of a reading series can be **phonics, whole word, literature based**, or a combined approach. Because basal readers have traditionally used the whole word method, another term for the whole word method is **basal reading approach**.

Basal reading approach Another term for the **whole word** reading method.

Blend A combination of two consonants in which the sounds of the two letters are pronounced together, and each sound can be distinctly heard. Examples of beginning blends include: *bl, br, cl, gr, pl,* and *str*. Examples of ending blends include: *rt, st, ld, rd, nd,* and *sk*. Compare with **digraph**. A way to remember the meaning of this term is that the word *blend* begins and ends with blends (i.e., *bl, nd*).

Blending The process of combining sounds to make a word. This could mean phonemic blending, which involves sounding out a printed word and blending those sounds together. It could also mean oral blending, where a student is presented with oral sounds that they blend to make a word. It is necessary to have sufficient oral blending in order to do phonemic blending. See also **oral blending**.

Bonding One of the descriptive terms used by researcher Linnea Ehri for **orthographic mapping**.

Consonant In oral language, consonants represent various types of restrictions of airflow when producing words, ranging from fully stopping the airflow (/t/) to very limited restriction (e.g., /r/). In written English, the consonants are *b, c, d, f, g, h, j, k, l, m, n, p, q, r, s, t, v, x, z*, but also *w* and *y* when they begin a syllable or word (e.g., *way, yes,* but not *cow, any,* where they function as vowels). There are more spoken consonant sounds than there are written consonants. As examples, the sound at the beginning of the third syllable of *collision* does not have an English letter, and the written digraph *th* is used to represent two spoken consonants (note the different *th* sounds between in *think* vs. *then*).

Consonant digraph See **Digraph**.

Controlled vocabulary A reading concept in which children are exposed to the same words they are learning over and over so that they can presumably learn those words more easily. This assumes that repetition alone will help children permanently store words. Controlled vocabularies are often used in **whole word** and **phonics** instruction.

Decoding A term used for word recognition in reading. The term can be used in the broad sense of translating text into meaning. In this sense, decoding refers to word identification regardless of whether it is immediate and spontaneous or whether it involves sounding out unfamiliar words. In a narrow sense, decoding refers to the process used when a person approaches an unfamiliar word. Strategies for decoding include sounding out the word and using contextual and linguistic clues.

Decoding key A term used in ARL for a **rime unit**.

– 260 –

Glossary

Digraph A combination of two letters designed to represent a single sound. There are both consonant digraphs and vowel digraphs. For the most common consonant digraphs (*ch*, *ph*, *sh*, *th*, and *gh*), neither of sounds normally associated with those consonants are heard. For example, notice how the normal sounds of *c* or *h* are not heard in *ch*. A more broad definition of consonant digraph includes less common consonant combinations which preserve the sound of one of the consonants while the other is silent, such as *gn–*, *kn–*, *wh–*, and *–mb*. Compare with **blend**. An easy way to remember the meaning of this term is that the word *digraph* contains a digraph (i.e., *ph*). A *vowel digraph* is when two vowels come together to form a single sound (e.g., *ou, ee, oa, ai*).

Diphthong When two vowels together each provide some contribution to the resulting sound. For example, in *oil*, and *boy* (with the letter y functioning as a vowel), each letter contributes to the vowel sound produced.

Direct mapping A term used in the 1990s by some researchers for what is now called **orthographic mapping.** The term is being re-used in this program in a different way as a word-study technique (Chapter 6).

Dolch words These represent a list of words developed by Dolch in the 1930s that includes the 220 most common words used in written English. These words make up 50% of all the words in print. They include words like *it, is, in, him, her, was, the, and, a, who, what*, etc. Because they are so common, the whole word approach emphasizes them to get students "up and running" with reading. This seems logical until we consider that 40% or more of them are not phonetically regular (e.g., *of, the, one, said, two*). Because of this, at the earliest stages of reading development (late kindergarten to mid first grade, or later for weaker readers), teachers should only select Dolch words that are phonetically regular (*on, it, in, at, not, can, men, see*, etc.). This will decrease the chances that students will resort to compensating strategies to remember them. When students are good mappers, then Dolch words are highly recommended because of their strategic significance in reading.

Dyslexia A reading and spelling disorder in which an individual struggles with word-level reading, despite adequate learning opportunities and effort. Different people use the term differently. Most researchers define the disorder to include individuals who are weak word-level readers but there is no standard for how low a person needs to be to be considered to have dyslexia. Studies of dyslexia range in their cut offs for defining dyslexia from those in the bottom 2% of readers all the way to the bottom 40%! Most studies make a cut off as the bottom 10% to 20%. Webster's College Dictionary simply defines dyslexia as a reading difficulty. Dyslexia in most cases is caused by either severe **phonological awareness** difficulties, or a combination of difficulties with phonological awareness and other lower-level linguistic difficulties, such as poor **rapid automatized naming**, and/or **working memory**. The common belief that dyslexia is defined by reversing or transposing letters is incorrect. Reversals and transpositions are caused by 1) a small subset of individuals with dyslexia who also have visual-spatial perceptual deficits in addition to their reading problems and 2) developmentally normal reading and spelling errors. It is common for first and even early second graders to reverse and transpose letters in their reading and spelling. Those with dyslexia make similar mistakes because they are often reading at a first or second grade reading level. Thus, these mistakes are typical for their reading level and are not the result of visual-spatial-perceptual deficits. Because individuals with dyslexia may spend a few years at the first grade reading level, some of these reversals and transpositions become a habit. As they move to a higher reading level, these reversals and transpositions become ingrained habits.

The term *dyslexia* has historically been a medical and psychological term, not an educational one. However, based upon recent federal and state legislation, the term is coming into use in schools.

Exception word See **Irregular word**.

Glass Analysis A remedial reading method developed by Gerald Glass which had children focus on what he called "clusters," meaning **blends**, **digraphs**, and **rime units**.

Grapheme A single or multiple letter unit of print that corresponds to a single **phoneme**. Most graphemes are a single letter (e.g., t = /t/ and r = /r/). However, some graphemes that represent a single phoneme can involve two or more letters. For example, consonant and vowel **digraphs** are multi-letter units that represent a single phoneme (e.g., *sh, th, oo, oa*). Other multi-letter graphemes occur as well. For example, the *–igh* in *high* and *–ough* in *though* are multi-letter graphemes. They are graphemes because they represent a single phoneme.

Hyperlexia Is a condition in which a student is proficient at word-level reading but, due to weak language skills, displays poor reading comprehension. The term hyperlexia derives from the fact that such students' word reading is above (i.e., hyper) their comprehension. Hyperlexia is essentially the opposite pattern from **dyslexia**. Those with dyslexia have difficulty reading words, but generally display good comprehension if the passage is read to them. Sometimes, hyperlexics have been referred to as "word callers."

Invented spelling If a student is writing and does not know the correct spelling of a word, invented spelling encourages students to spell words the way they sound. This keeps them from losing their train of thought while looking a word up in a dictionary. Invented spelling promotes the use of a wider range of vocabulary in children's writing because they are not restricted to including only words they can spell. Invented spelling developed a bad reputation because some teachers using this approach did not insist on having students learn the proper spelling of words. However, when a student first tries to write a word, invented spelling forces the student to use phoneme awareness ("What sounds do I hear in this word?") and letter-sound skills ("What letters make those sounds?"). While a great idea for writing new words, teachers should expect that students quickly transition to the correct spellings.

Irregular word Also called an exception word, an irregular word does not conform to traditional phonetic spelling patterns. For example, if pronounced via standard English grapho-phoneme pronunciation, *put*, *island*, and *colonel* would not be correctly pronounced based on their spellings.

Glossary

Language processing 1) An older term for **phonological awareness** made popular in the **ARL** program. 2) Abilities with higher language skills like oral comprehension, vocabulary, grammar, etc.

LD Learning Disability.

Letter-sound knowledge or **letter-sound skills** The ability to correctly identify letter names and sounds. This also includes accurate knowledge of **blends, digraphs,** and **diphthongs**. Letter-sound knowledge, along with phonological blending, allow students to do **phonetic decoding**. Phonics instruction typically goes beyond basic letter-sound knowledge to make explicit many of the patterns of printed language along with a variety of rules to assist in sounding out words. The more developed form of these skills is **letter-sound proficiency.**

Letter-sound skills The ability to immediately recognize the phonetic attributes of the consonants, vowels, **blends**, **digraphs**, and vowel combinations.

Letter-sound proficiency This goes beyond simply knowing the **letter-sound knowledge** to being skilled enough that sounds associated with letters are instantly and unconsciously activated upon seeing letters. This level of proficiency with letters and sounds results in more efficient phonetic decoding. Also, when combined with **phonemic proficiency**, it is central to remembering words via **orthographic mapping**.

Letter strings This is another way of referring to written words that focuses on the fact that the letters in printed words are designed to line up with the phoneme sequence (or "string") in spoken words.

Lexical tuning hypothesis One term researchers use for orthographic mapping.

Lexicon This is another word for *dictionary* and is used by researchers to refer to the pool of words a student knows (i.e., their mental dictionary, so to speak). The **orthographic lexicon** refers to all the words a student can instantly and effortlessly identify (i.e., words in the student's sight vocabulary). The **phonological lexicon** refers to words that are orally familiar to the students, whether or not the student knows the meaning of those words. The **semantic lexicon** is a subset of the phonological lexicon that includes only words that a student has partial or full understanding of the meaning.

Lindamood Phoneme Sequencing Program (LiPS) Previously called *Auditory Discrimination in Depth, this* was one of the first formal **phonological awareness** training programs. Many studies have shown it to be effective. This must not be confused with the more recent Lindamood *Seeing Stars Program*, which studies show has limited effectiveness.

Linguistic reading approach A method of reading that relies heavily on **word families**. The original linguistic program was Bloomfield and Barnhart's *Let's Read* (1961). Other linguistic readers include the **ARL** *First Grade Stories* and *Decoding Keys Stories, Merrill Linguistics,* and *SRA Linguistics*. Many **phonics** programs also have incorporated some linguistics into their materials. Linguistic readers are appropriate for students who can do **onset-rime** level of **phonological awareness** (Levels F & G), but are not skilled at the **phoneme** levels.

Literature-based approach This approach became popular with the advent of the **whole language** movement. It advocates using children's literature to teach reading rather than basal readers or phonetically decodable readers.

Look-Say method Another term for the **whole word** reading approach.

Map See **orthographic mapping**.

Metalinguistic awareness Another term used by researchers to refer to **phonological awareness**.

Multisyllabic words Refers to words with more than one syllable.

Neighbors A British term for members of a **word family**.

Nonsense words Pronounceable letter patterns that are not real words (e.g., *blamp, vit, torg*). Tests that assess nonsense word reading are likely to be the best way to evaluate a student's phonetic decoding skills, because the student has no prior exposure to these "words." Spelling nonsense words assesses letter-sound skills and phoneme awareness.

Onset The consonant or consonants within a syllable that precede the vowel. In the words *hand, street,* and *tie,* the *h, st,* and *t,* are the onsets, respectively. Not all syllables have onsets (e.g., *in, at, on*) because many syllables begin with a vowel.

Onset-rime A level of **phonological awareness** development that is typically more difficult than (basic) syllable-level awareness (D1 through E2) but less difficult than **phoneme-level** awareness. First articulated in the 1980s by Rebecca Treiman and others, the onset-rime level involves separating syllables into two elements, the onset and the rime. The **onset** refers to the portion of the syllable that precedes the vowel. The rime refers to the portion of the syllable that includes the vowel and any consonants following the vowel within the syllable (see also **Rime**).

Oral blending The process of taking individual parts of oral words and blending them together to make a word. For example, if a student is presented with the oral phonemes /s/ /a/ /t/ and student recognizes that these sounds make up the word *sat*. Oral blending is required for many of the **One Minute Activities** and is also required for **phonetic decoding**.

Orthographic lexicon This is a term researchers use for a **sight word vocabulary**. It refers to all the written words that are familiar to the student and are instantly and effortlessly recognized.

Orthographic mapping The mental process we use to store words for immediate, effortless, retrieval. It requires **phoneme proficiency** and **letter-sound proficiency**, as well as the ability to unconsciously or consciously make connections between the oral sounds in spoken words and the letters in written words.

Orthography From ancient Greek words meaning "straight writing," this refers to the correct spellings of words. Children need orthographic skills to read and spell words correctly. Orthographic knowledge allows us to distinguish between words like *stair* and *stare* or *made* and *maid*.

Orton-Gillingham method A phonetic reading method based on the work of Samuel Orton. In addition to teaching the **letter-sound skills**, Orton-Gillingham also teaches phonics rules to assist in the identification of unfamiliar words. This approach has been very popular in tutoring with children with severe reading disabilities. There is little or no direct **phoneme awareness** built into this program, except phoneme skills that are incidental to learning phonics skills. At most, they teach phoneme segmentation, which does not represent enough phonemic awareness to be a skilled reader (see chapter 7).

Paired-associate learning (PAL) PAL is the skill of being able to associate two items with each other, so that when one item is present, it instantly activates a memory or association with the other. We learn other peoples' names via PAL. It is also the basis for learning letter names and letter sounds. In years past, it was assumed that PAL was the main mechanism for remembering words, that is, you simply associate a verbal word with the visual form of the word. However, we know that is not the case (see Chapter 4).

Penultimate Second from last. The penultimate sound is the second sound from the end of the word.

Phoneme The smallest unit of sound within oral words. For example, *sat* has three phonemes (/s/ /a/ /t/), while *shoe* has two (/sh/ /oo/), and *stake* has four (/s/ /t/ /A/ /k/). Phonemes often match up to letters but many times do not, as these examples illustrate.

Phoneme awareness Being aware of individual phonemes within words, this is a subcategory of **phonological awareness**. It represents a more difficult type of phonological awareness than other levels of phonological awareness (i.e., rhyming, alliteration, syllable skills or onset-rime skills). Phoneme awareness, particularly **phonemic proficiency**, is necessary for efficient storage of written words in long-term memory.

Phoneme discrimination The ability to distinguish between two words that differ only by one phoneme (e.g., the words *had* and *hat* differ by only one phoneme). Phoneme discrimination is required to tell these two words apart. Most children develop this skill before their first birthday. By contrast, **phoneme awareness** is developed at about age six or seven.

Phoneme sensitivity This is another term used by researchers for **phoneme awareness.**

Phonemic proficiency The ability to instantly and unconsciously access the phonemes in spoken words. It is a more developed phonemic skill beyond **phoneme awareness** and is central for **orthographic mapping**.

Phonetic decoding The process of combining letter-sound knowledge and **oral blending** to sound out unfamiliar written words.

Phonics A system for approaching reading that focuses on the relationship between the printed forms and oral forms of words. Phonics provides assistance in sounding out words that are unfamiliar to the reader. Letter sounds, **blends**, **digraphs**, and vowel combinations are learned and then applied to reading. Also, rules for likely pronunciations are learned. More elaborate forms of instruction in phonics may involve the use of extensive rules designed to guide **decoding** and pronunciation.

Phonogram A phonogram is a written symbol that stands for a letter, word, or word part (*phono* means *sound* and *gram* means *something written*). Teachers have commonly used the term to refer to **rime units**.

Phonological Having to do with the sound properties of oral language.

Phonological awareness Having an awareness of sound properties of words. This includes rhyming and **alliteration**. It also involves the skill of manipulating sounds within words, whether those sounds are **syllables**, **onsets**, **rimes**, or individual **phonemes**.

Phonological lexicon This refers to: 1) All the words that are stored in a person's oral long-term memory. For example, a student may have heard the word *integrity* before, but not know what it means. Because it is orally familiar, it is in his phonological long-term memory. It should be noted that all words in a students' oral vocabulary (words the student knows the meaning of) are a subcategory of words in the child's phonological lexicon; and 2) All of the parts of words that are familiar because they are in phonologically familiar words (e.g., the *ip* in *lip*, *dip*, *chip*, the *oap* in *soap*, etc.).

Phonological long-term memory see **Phonological lexicon.**

Phonological sensitivity This is another term used by researchers to denote **phonological awareness.**

Rapid automatized naming Sometimes referred to as simply *rapid naming* or RAN, rapid automatized naming refers to how quickly one can name presumably automatic information (numbers, letters, colors, or objects). Students with slow naming speed typically struggle with reading. Currently, there is no research on intervention with RAN. However, some data suggests that children with RAN problems who are efficient with **phoneme awareness**, **letter-sound skills**, phonological working memory, and **oral blending**, develop a pattern of slow, accurate reading with good comprehension. Several studies showed spontaneous improvement in RAN following improvements in phoneme awareness and word-level reading.

Reading styles The assumption that children learn to read in different ways, visually or auditorily. Some educators distinguish between visual learners and auditory learners. However, research over the last 40 years has failed to demonstrate the validity of that distinction.

Rhyming Juxtaposing two or more words that have a similar sounding oral rime unit (e.g., *bat, hat, sat*). Rhyming is oral, so words with different spelling patterns may rhyme (i.e., *right, white, height*).

Representation hypothesis A term used by researcher Charles Perfetti for **orthographic mapping**.

Resource A special educational service. Resource is available for reading, math, or written expression.

Response to Intervention (RTI) A service delivery framework for academic difficulties and/or for diagnosing learning disabilities. Tier 1 of RTI represents general educational instruction provided to all students and is supposed to be "best practice" (though it seems best practice rarely occurs in reading in U.S. schools). For students unsuccessful in reading with Tier 1 instruction, Tiers 2 and 3 represent more individualized and intensive help using intervention techniques demonstrated by research to be effective. There is little evidence "best practice" is occurring here also. Intervention practices shown by research to be ineffective appear to be the norm at Tier 2 and Tier 3. Further, students must demonstrate failure in Tiers 1 and 2 (and possibly 3 in some versions of RTI) before being considered to have a learning disability.

Rime An alternative spelling of rhyme. However, reading researchers have taken this obscure spelling of rhyme and given it a slightly altered definition. Rime refers to that part of a syllable that contains the vowel sound and any consonant sounds in that syllable that follow the vowel. It is similar to the printed **phonogram**. The term is often used to refer to both oral or written forms.

Glossary

Rime unit Another term for **rime**, oral or written. However, in this manual the term *rime unit* it is used for written form.

Rosner Auditory Motor Program One of the first formal **phonological awareness** training programs.

RTI See **Response to Intervention**

Schwa A very short vowel sound, almost like a brief short *u* sound (or less commonly a short *i*) that appears in words, typically in a non-stressed syllable of a multisyllabic word. For example, the *a* in the word *about* is neither a short *a* or long *a* but rather is a schwa. Notice how the second *e* in *elephant* is pronounced differently from the first because it is in a non-stressed syllable (see **vowel reduction**). The first *e* is the short *e* the second is the schwa. The schwa is typically represented in print as an upside down (and sometimes italicized) letter *e* (e.g., ə or *ə*).

Self-teaching hypothesis The self-teaching hypothesis points out that very few of the 30,000 to 70,000 written words familiar to skilled adult readers were directly taught to them by their teachers or parents. Thus, the rest of the words we learn on their own via self-teaching. Self-teaching is based on phonetically decoding newly encountered words while reading. This helps create an orthographic memory.

Semantic lexicon This refers to all the words for which a student fully or partially understands the meaning.

Sight words 1) words not phonetically regular and assumed to be learned "by sight" (i.e., can't be sounded out); 2) high frequency words typically taught as whole word units in kindergarten and first grade; and 3) *any* word that is immediately recognized "by sight," that is, any previously learned words that are part of a person's sight vocabulary, regardless of whether they are "regular" or "irregular." It is only this third definition that was used in this book (and is also the definition used by researchers).

Sight word reading method Another term for the **whole word** reading method.

Sight word vocabulary or **sight vocabulary** The pool of words that a person can identify immediately and effortlessly, without the need to sound out the word or use context clues. Researchers also call this the **orthographic lexicon**.

Stress The part of a multisyllabic word that receives more emphasis. Sometimes the term accent is used (e.g., in the word *table*, one might say the accent is on the first syllable). Unstressed syllables often have a **vowel reduction**.

Syllable A word or part of a word that involves one voicing (movement of air through the vocal cords). It can be explained to children as one opening and closing of one's mouth while speaking. With the use of a puppet, they can see the puppet's mouth open and close, once for each syllable.

Title I A federally funded general educational service providing extra help in reading, writing and math.

Vowel In oral language, a vowel refers to sounds we make within words when air goes through our vocal cords without much restriction (compared to **consonants** which involve restriction of the air flow). In written language, the vowels in English are the letters *a, e, i, o, u,* and *y* (when it is not at the beginning of a word or syllable, e.g., *my, sky, flying, analyze*). There are far more oral vowels than written vowels. Teachers routine speak of "short" and "long" vowels which combined represent 10 vowel sounds. But there are others, such as the **schwa** and those represented by various vowel combinations (e.g., *oo* in *good* or *au* in *autumn*).

Vowel digraph See **digraph**.

Vowel reduction This refers to the situation when vowels in non-stressed syllables in multisyllabic words are reduced to either a schwa sound (such as the *i* in *holiday* or *marigold*), or to the short *i* sound (as the letter *e* in *market* or *magnet*). See also **schwa**.

Whole language A reading philosophy which emphasizes, among other things 1) integration of all aspects of language: reading, writing, speaking, and listening rather than teaching these as separate subjects; 2) use of authentic reading and writing activities as opposed to drill and rote memory; 3) use of children's literature to teach reading rather than basal readers; 4) avoiding breaking the language down into small parts as is done in **phonics**, the **linguistic approach**, and **phoneme awareness** training. This is not to be confused with the **whole word** reading method.

Whole word reading method This is a traditional reading method that also goes by terms like the *look-say method*, **basal reading approach**, and the **sight word method**. The whole word method seeks to have children learn words as whole visual units, without breaking the word down into parts as is commonly done in **phonics** and **linguistic reading** approaches. Many whole word readers use a **controlled vocabulary** to be sure that children get to see the words they are learning over and over. This is not to be confused with **whole language**.

Wilson reading method A **phonics**-based reading method based on the **Orton-Gillingham** approach. In addition to teaching the **letter-sound skills**, Wilson teaches rather extensive phonics rules. There is not much emphasis placed on **phoneme awareness** beyond the phoneme skills that are incidental to learning phonics and simple segmentation. Most competent readers read fluently without knowing the extensive rules taught in this program. The more basic aspects of the program related to letter acquisition and basic letter-sound skills are very consistent with research in reading.

Word families A group of words that share the same **rime unit** and which rhyme with each other. For example, *tan, van, can, man,* and *ran* are all part of the same word family. The **linguistic reading approach** relies heavily on word families.

Word mapping This is the term that was used for **orthographic mapping** in the original, 2002 edition of this manual.

Word study Defined in this manual as the unconscious or conscious process of making connections between the oral structure of spoken words and the printed letter sequences used to represent those words.

Working memory Working memory refers to the temporary memory buffer that holds the information you are thinking about right now. As your thoughts or attention shifts, that buffer gets emptied of the information you were just thinking about to make room for what your attention has shifted to. A common test of working memory is to have students repeat back a series of numbers. Students with stronger working memories can repeat back more numbers than those with weaker working memories. Working memory is commonly associated with difficulties in reading decoding, reading comprehension, math, and written expression. When students guess at words using context or sound words out phonetically, they use their working memory resources to do so. However, this draws the limited working memory resources away from reading comprehension. By contrast, when student instantly recognize words, they require little or no working memory resources to do so, and this allows their working memory to focus on reading comprehension.

Appendix K
REFERENCES

The following references represent most of the research studies or research summaries I read while preparing the original (2002) and current (2016) program. To make this manual more readable, the APA format of providing in-text citations for each of the facts mentioned was not used. Instead, this list of bibliographic references is presented to make explicit the sources behind this program.

Free resources are available which summarize the research I've presented in this book. They are available from the US Government at www.nichd.nih.gov, and do a search on "reading resources." Also, the publication "Teaching Reading IS Rocket Science" and "Where We Stand: K-12 Literacy" are available in PDF format from the American Federation of Teachers at www.aft.org. Finally, the Florida Center for Reading Research www.fcrr.org is a good source of research-based information.

Books, Booklets, Tests, Popular Articles, & Programs:

Adams, M. J., & Bruck, M. (1995). Resolving the "Great Debate." *American Educator, 19(2)*, 7, 10-20.
Adams, M. J., Foorman, B. R., Lundberg, I., & Beeler, T. (1998). The elusive phoneme. *American Educator, 22(1/2)*, 18-22.
American Federation for Teachers (1999). *Teaching reading IS rocket science*. Washington, D.C.: AFT.
American Federation for Teachers (2007). *Where we stand: K-12 literacy*. Washington, D.C.: AFT.
Beck, I. L., & Juel, C. (1995). The role of decoding in learning to read. *American Educator, 19(2)*, 8, 21-24, 39-42.
Beck, I. L., McKeown, M. G., Hamilton, R. L., & Kucan, L. (1998). Getting at the meaning: How to help students unlock difficult text. *American Educator, 22(1/2)*, 66-71, 85.
Gaskins, I.W., Ehri, L.C., Cress, C. O'Hara, C., & Donnelly, K. (1996/1997). Procedures for word learning: Making discoveries about words. *The Reading Teacher, 50*, 312-327.
Glass, G. G. & Glass, E. W. (1978). *Glass-Analysis for Decoding Only: Teacher's Guide*. Garden City, NY: Easier to Learn.
Hall, S. L. & Moats, L. C. (2000). Why reading to children is important. *American Educator, Spr.*, 26-33.
Greene, J. F. (1998). Another chance: Help for older students with limited literacy. *American Educator, 22(1/2)*, 74-79.
Johnson, F. R. (1998). The reader, the text, and the task: Learning words in first grade. *The Reading Teacher, 51*, 666-675.
Johnston, F. R. (1999). The timing and teaching of word families. *The Reading Teacher, 53(1)*, 64-75.
Joyce, B., Hrycauk, M. & Calhoun, E. (2001). A second chance for struggling readers. *Educational Leadership, March*, 42-46.
Kilpatrick, D. A. (2015). *Essentials of assessing, preventing, and overcoming reading difficulties*. Hoboken, NJ: Wiley & Sons.
Lyon, G. R. (1998). Why learning to read is not a natural process. *Educational Leadership, March*, 14-18.
Moats, L. C. (1995). The missing foundation in teacher preparation. *American Educator, 19(2)*, 9, 43-51.
Moats, L. C. (1998). Teaching decoding. *American Educator, 22(1/2)*, 42-49, 95-96.
Moats, L. C. (2001). When older students can't read. *Educational Leadership, March*, 36-40.
Walsh, K., Glaser, D., & Wilcox, D. D. (2006). *What education schools aren't teaching about reading and what elementary teachers aren't learning*. Washington, D. C.: National Council for Teacher Quality.
National Reading Panel. (2000). *Teaching children to read. The summary of the report of the National Reading Panel*. Washington, D.C.: US Government Printing Office.
Rosner, J. (1973). *The perceptual skills curriculum, Program II: Auditory-motor skills*. New York: Walker Educational.
Stanovich, K. E. (1993/1994). Romance and reality. *The Reading Teacher, 47(4)*, 280-291.
Torgesen, J. K. (1998). Catch them before they fall: Identification and assessment to prevent reading failure in young children. *American Educator, 22(1/2)*, 32-39.
Wagner, R. K., Torgesen, J. K., & Rashotte, C. A. (1999). *The Comprehensive Test of Phonological Processing (CTOPP)*. Austin, TX: Pro-ED.
Wagner, R. K., Torgesen, J. K., Rashotte, C. A., & Pearson, N. (2013). *The Comprehensive Test of Phonological Processing–Second Edition (CTOPP-2)*. Austin, TX: Pro-ED.
Wagstaff, J. M. (1997/1998). Building practical knowledge of letter-sound correspondences: A beginner's word wall and beyond. *The Reading Teacher, 51(4)*, 298-304.
Yopp, H. K. (1992). Developing phoneme awareness in young children. *The Reading Teacher, 45(9)*, 696-703.

Research Articles and Books:

Aarnoutse, C., Leeuwe, J. V., Voeten, M. & Oud, H. (2001). Development of decoding, reading comprehension, vocabulary, and spelling during the elementary school years. *Reading and Writing: An Interdisciplinary Journal, 14(1-2)*, 61-68.

Aaron, P. G. (1995). Recent advances in reading instruction and remediation: Introduction to mini-series. *School Psychology Review, 24(3)*, 327-330.

Aaron, P. G. & Joshi, R. M. (1992). *Reading problems: Consultation and remediation*. New York: Guilford Press.

References

Aaron, P. G., Joshi, R. M., Gooden, R., & Bentum, K. E. (2008). Diagnosis and treatment of reading disabilities based on the component model of reading: An alternative to the discrepancy model of LD. *Journal of Learning Disabilities, 41(1)*, 67-84.

Adams, M. J. (1979). Models of word recognition. *Cognitive Psychology, 11*, 133-176.

Adams, M. J. (1990). *Beginning to read: Thinking and learning about print*. Cambridge, MA: MIT Press.

Adams, M. J. & Henry, M. K. (1997). Myths and realities about words and literacy. *School Psychology Review, 26(3)*, 427-437.

Adams, M. J. & Huggins, A. W. F. (1985). The growth of children's sight vocabulary: A quick test with educational and theoretical implications. *Reading Research Quarterly, 20(3)*, 262-281.

Adelman, J. S., & Brown, G. D. A. (2007). Phonographic neighbors, not orthographic neighbors, determine word naming latencies. *Psychonomic Bulletin & Review, 14*, 455-459.

Ahmed, Y., Wagner, R. K., & Kantor, P. T. (2012). How visual word recognition is affected by developmental dyslexia. In J. S. Adelman (Ed.), *Visual word recognition (Vol. 2): Meaning and context, individuals and development* (pp. 196-215). New York: Psychology Press.

Alario, F.X., De Cara, B., & Zieglar, J. C. (2007). Automatic activation of phonology in silent reading is parallel: Evidence from beginning and skilled readers. *Journal of Experimental Child Psychology, 97*, 205-219.

Alegria, J. & Morais, J. (1991). Segmental analysis and reading acquisition. In Rieben, L. & Perfetti, C. A. (Eds.) *Learning to read: Basic research and its implications* (pp. 135-148). Hillsdale, NJ: Erlbaum.

Allington, R. L. (1998). Pedagogy in early reading. Paper presented at the New York State Reading Symposium, February 11, 1998, Albany, NY.

Allington, R. L. (1978). Effects of contextual constraints upon rate and accuracy. *Perceptual and Motor Skills, 46*, 1318.

Allington, R. L. & Woodside-Hiron, H. (1999). The politics of literacy teaching: How "research" shaped educational policy. *Educational Researcher, 28(8)*, 4-13.

American Speech-Language-Hearing Association (2001). Roles and responsibilities of speech-language pathologists with respect to reading and writing in children and adolescents (position statement, executive summary of guidelines, technical report). *ASHA Supplement, 21*, 17-27. Rockville, MD: Author.

Anderson, M. & Reid, C. (2009). Don't forget about levels of explanation. *Cortex, 45*, 560–561.

Anderson, R. C., Hiebert, E. H., Scott, J.A., & Wilkinson, I. A. G. (1985). *Becoming a nation of readers: The report of the Commission on Reading*. Pittsburgh, PA: National Academy of Education.

Andrews, S. (1992). Frequency and neighborhood effects on lexical access: Lexical similarity or orthographic redundancy? *Journal of Experimental Psychology: Learning, Memory, and Cognition, 18*, 234-254.

Andrews, S. (2012). Individual differences in skilled visual word recognition and reading. In J. S. Adelman (Ed.), *Visual word recognition (Vol. 2): Meaning and context, individuals and development* (pp. 151-172). New York: Psychology Press.

Anthony, J. L., Lonigan, C. J., Burgess, S. R., Driscoll, K., Philips, B. M., & Cantor, B. G. (2002). Structure of preschool phonological sensitivity: Overlapping sensitivity to rhyme, words, syllables, and phonemes. *Journal of Experimental Child Psychology, 82*, 65-92.

Anthony, J. L., Lonigan, C. J., Driscoll, K., Phillips, B. M., and Burgess, S. R. (2003). Phonological sensitivity: A quasi-parallel progression of word structure units and cognitive operations. *Reading Research Quarterly, 38*, 470-487.

Apel, K. (2009). The acquisition of mental orthographic representations for reading and spelling development. *Communication Disorders Quarterly 31(1)*, 42-52.

Apel, K., Wolter, J. A., & Masterson, J. J. (2006). Effects of phonotactic and orthotactic probabilities during fast mapping on 5-year-olds' learning to spell, *Developmental Neuropsychology, 29(1)*, 21–42.

Archer, N., & Bryant, P. (2001). Investigating the role of context in learning to read: A direct test of Goodman's model. *British Journal of Psychology, 92*, 579-591.

Backman, J. (1983). The role of psycholinguistic skills in reading acquisition: A look at early readers. *Reading Research Quarterly, 18*, 466-479.

Baker, S. K., Kameenui, E. K., Simmons, D. C., & Stahl, S. (1994). Beginning reading: Educational tools for diverse learners. *School Psychology Review, 23(3)*, pp. 372-391.

Ball, E. & Blachman, B. (1991). Does phoneme awareness training in kindergarten make a difference in early word recognition and developmental spelling? *Reading Research Quarterly, 26*, 49-66.

Balota, D., Yap, M., Cortese, M. J., Hutchison, K. A., Kessler... Treiman, R. (2007). The English Language Project. *Behavior Research Methods, 39*, 445-459.

Barker, T., & Torgesen, J. (1995). An evaluation of computer-assisted instruction in phonological awareness with below average readers. *Journal of Educational Computing Research, 13*, 89-103.

Barker, T. A., Torgesen, J. K., Wagner, R. K. (1992). The role of orthographic processing skills on five different reading tasks. *Reading Research Quarterly, 27(4)*, 335-345.

Baron, J. & McKillop, B. J. (1975). Individual differences in speed of phonemic analysis, visual analysis, and reading. *Acta Psychologica, 39*, 91-96.

Bentin, S., Hammer, R., & Cahan, S. (1991). The effects of aging and first grade schooling on the development of phonological awareness. *Psychological Science, 2(4)*, 271-274.

Bentin, S., & Leshem, H. (1993). On the interaction between phonological awareness and reading acquisition: It's a two-way street. *Annals of Dyslexia, 43*, 125-148.

Berninger, V. W., Thalberg, S. P., Debruyn, I., Smith, R. (1987). Preventing reading disabilities by assessing and remediating phonemic skills. *School Psychology Review, 16(4)*, 554-565.

Bertelson, P. Morais, J. Alegria, J., & Content, A. (1985). Phonetic analysis capacity and learning to read. *Nature, 313*, 73-74.

Blachman, B.A. (1984). Relationship of rapid naming ability and language analysis skills to kindergarten and first-grade reading achievement. *Journal of Educational Psychology, 76(4)*, 610-622.

Blachman, B. A. (1991). Phonological awareness: Implications for prereading and early reading instruction In Brady, S. A. & Shankweiler, D. P. (Eds.) *Phonological processes in literacy: A tribute to Isabelle Y. Liberman* (pp. 29-45). Hillsdale, NJ: Erlbaum.

Blachman, B. A. (1997) (Ed.) *Foundations of reading acquisition and dyslexia*. Mahwah, NJ: Erlbaum.

Blachman, B. A. (1997). Early intervention and phonological awareness: A cautionary tale. In B. A. Blachman, (Ed.) *Foundations of reading acquisition and dyslexia* (pp. 409-430). Mahwah, NJ: Erlbaum.

Blachman, B., Ball, E., Black, R., & Tangel, D. (1994). Kindergarten teachers develop phoneme awareness in low-income, inner-city classrooms: Does it make a difference? *Reading and Writing: An Interdisciplinary Journal, 6*, 1-18.

Blachman, B. A., Schatschneider, C., Fletcher, J. M., & Clonan, S., M. (2002). Early reading intervention: A classroom prevention study and a remediation study. In B. R. Foorman, (Ed.), *Preventing and remediating reading difficulties: Bringing science to scale* (pp. 253-271). Baltimore, MD: York Press.

Blachman, B. A., Tangel, D. M., Ball, E. W., Black, R., & McGraw, C. K. (1999). Developing phonological awareness and word recognition skills: A two-year intervention with low-income, inner city children. *Reading and Writing: An Interdisciplinary Journal, 11(3)*, 239-273.

Bloomfield, L., & Barnhart, C. L. (1961). *Let's read*. Detroit, MI: Wayne State University Press.

Boada, R., & Pennington, B. F. (2006). Deficient implicit phonological representations in children with dyslexia. *Journal of Experimental Child Psychology, 95*, 153-193.

Booth, J. R. & Perfetti, C. A. (2002). Onset and rime structure influences naming but not early word identification in children and adults. *Scientific Studies of Reading, 6(2)*, 1-23.

Bowers, P. & Newby-Clark, E. (2002). The role of naming speed within a model of reading acquisition. *Reading and Writing: An Interdisciplinary Journal, 15(1-2)*, 109-126.

Bowers, J. S., Davis, C. J., & Hanley, D. A. (2005). Automatic semantic activation of embedded words: Is there a "hat" in "that"? *Journal of Memory & Language, 52*, 131-143.

Bowers, P. G., Sunseth, K., & Golden, J. (1999). The route between rapid naming and reading progress. *Scientific Studies of Reading, 3(1)*, 31-53.

References

Bowey, J. A. (2002). Reflections on onset-rime and phoneme sensitivity as predictors of beginning word reading. *Journal of Experimental Child Psychology, 82*, 29-40.

Bowey, J. A. (2008). Is a "Phoenician" reading style superior to a "Chinese" reading style? Evidence from fourth graders. *Journal of Experimental Child Psychology, 100*, 186-214.

Bowey, J. A., & Hansen, J. (1994). The development of orthographic rimes as units of word recognition. *Journal of Experimental Child Psychology, 58*, 465-488.

Bowey, J. A. & Muller, D. (2005). Phonological recoding and rapid orthographic learning in third graders' silent reading: A critical test of the self-teaching hypothesis. *Journal of Experimental Child Psychology, 92*, 203-219.

Bowey, J. A. & Rutherford, J. (2007). Imbalanced word-reading profiles in eighth-graders. *Journal of Experimental Child Psychology, 96*, 169-196.

Bowey, J. A. & Underwood, N. (1996). Further evidence that orthographic rime usage in nonwords reading increases with word-level reading proficiency. *Journal of Experimental Child Psychology, 63*, 526-562.

Bradley, L. & Bryant, P.E. (1983). Categorizing sounds and learning to read–A causal connection. *Nature, 301*, 419-421.

Bradley, L. & Bryant, P.E. (1991). Phonological skills before and after learning to read. In Brady, S. A. & Shankweiler, D. P. (Eds.) *Phonological processes in literacy: A tribute to Isabelle Y. Liberman* (pp. 37-45). Hillsdale, NJ: Erlbaum.

Brady, S. A. (1991). The role of working memory in reading disability. In Brady, S. A. & Shankweiler, D. P. (Eds.) *Phonological processes in literacy: A tribute to Isabelle Y. Liberman* (pp. 129-151). Hillsdale, NJ: Erlbaum.

Brady, S. A. (1997). Ability to encode phonological representations: An underlying difficulty in poor readers. In B. A. Blachman, (Ed.) *Foundations of reading acquisition and dyslexia* (pp. 21-47). Mahwah, NJ: Erlbaum.

Brady, S. A. (2011). Efficacy of phonics teaching for reading outcomes: Indications from post-NRP research. In S. A. Brady, D. Braze, & C. A. Fowler (Eds.), *Explaining individual differences in reading: Theory and evidence*. (pp. 69-96). New York, NY: Psychology Press.

Brady, S., Fowler, A., Stone, B., & Winbury, N. (1994). Training phonological awareness: A study with inner-city kindergarten children. *Annals of Dyslexia, 44*, 26-59.

Brady, S. A. & Shankweiler, D. P. (1991). *Phonological processes in literacy: A tribute to Isabelle Y. Liberman*. Hillsdale, NJ: Erlbaum.

Braze, D., McRoberts, G. W., & McDonough, C. (2011). Early precursors of reading-relevant phonological skills. In S. A. Brady, D. Braze, & C. A. Fowler (Eds.), *Explaining individual differences in reading: Theory and evidence*. (pp. 23-43). New York, NY: Psychology Press.

Brennan, F., & Ireson, J. (1997). Training phonological awareness: A study to evaluate the effects of a program of metalinguistic games in kindergarten. *Reading and Writing: An Interdisciplinary Journal, 9*, 241-263.

Breznitz, Z. (2002). Asynchrony of visual-orthographic and auditory-phonological word recognition processes: An underlying factor in dyslexia. *Reading and Writing: An Interdisciplinary Journal, 15(1-2)*, 15-42.

Breznitz, Z. & Share, D. (2002). Introduction on timing and phonology. *Reading and Writing: An Interdisciplinary Journal, 15(1-2)*, 1-3.

Brown, G. D. A., & Devers, R. P. (1999). Units of analysis in nonword reading: Evidence from children and adults. *Journal of Experimental Child Psychology, 73*, 208-242.

Bruck, M. (1990). Word-recognition skills of adults with childhood diagnosis of dyslexia. *Developmental Psychology, 26*, 439-454.

Bruck, M. (1992). Persistence of dyslexics' phonological awareness deficits. *Developmental Psychology, 28*, 874-886.

Bruck, M., Genesee, F., & Caravolas, M. (1997). A cross-linguistic study of early literacy acquisition. In B. A. Blachman, (Ed.) *Foundations of reading acquisition and dyslexia* (pp. 145-162). Mahwah, NJ: Erlbaum.

Bruck, M. & Treiman, R. (1992). Learning to pronounce words: The limitations of analogies. *Reading Research Quarterly, 27*, 374-388.

Bruce, D. J. (1964). The analysis of word sounds by young children. *British Journal of Educational Psychology, 34*, 158-170.

Bruno, J. L., Manis, F. R., Keating, P., Sperling, A. J., Nakamoto, J. & Seidenberg, M. (2007). Auditory word identification in dyslexic and normally achieving readers. *Journal of Experimental Child Psychology, 97*, 183-204.

Bryant, P. (2002). It doesn't matter whether onset and rime predicts reading better than phoneme awareness does or vice versa. *Journal of Experimental Child Psychology, 82*, 41-46.

Bryant, P. E., Nunes, T. & Bindman, M. (1997). Children's understanding of the connection between grammar and spelling. In B. A. Blachman, (Ed.) *Foundations of reading acquisition and dyslexia* (pp. 219-240). Mahwah, NJ: Erlbaum.

Burani, C. Marcolini, S., De Luca, M., & Zoccolotti, P. (2008). Morpheme-based reading aloud: Evidence from dyslexic and skilled Italian readers. *Cognition, 108*, 243-262.

Bus, A. G. & van IJzendoorn, M. H. (1999). Phonological awareness and early reading: A meta-analysis of experimental training studies. *Journal of Educational Psychology, 91(3)*, 403-414.

Byrne, B. (1991). Experimental analysis of the child's discovery of the alphabetic principle. In Rieben, L. & Perfetti, C. A. (Eds.) *Learning to read: Basic research and its implications* (pp. 75-84). Hillsdale, NJ: Erlbaum.

Byrne, B. & Fielding-Barnsley, R. (1989). Phoneme awareness and letter knowledge in the child's acquisition of the alphabetic principle. *Journal of Educational Psychology, 81(3)*, 313-321.

Byrne, B. & Fielding-Barnsley, R. (1990). Acquiring the alphabetic principle: A case for teaching recognition of phoneme identity. *Journal of Educational Psychology, 82(4)*, 805-812.

Byrne, B. & Fielding-Barnsley, R. (1991). Evaluation of a program to teach phoneme awareness to young children. *Journal of Educational Psychology, 83(4)*, 451-455.

Byrne, B., & Fielding-Barnsley, R. (1995). Evaluation of a program to teach phoneme awareness to young children: A two- and three-year follow-up and a new preschool trial. *Journal of Educational Psychology, 87*, 488-503.

Byrne, B. Fielding-Barnsley, R, Ashley, L., & Larsen, K. (1997). Assessing the child's and the environment's contribution to reading acquisition: What we know and what we don't know. In B. A. Blachman, (Ed.) *Foundations of reading acquisition and dyslexia* (pp. 265-285). Mahwah, NJ: Erlbaum.

Byrne, B., & Ledez, J. (1983). Phonological awareness in reading-disabled adults. *Australian Journal of Psychology, 35(2)*, 185-197.

Cain, K., Oakhill, J., & Bryant, P. (2000). Phonological skills and comprehension failure: A test of the phonological processing deficit hypothesis. *Reading and Writing: An Interdisciplinary Journal, 13*, 31-56.

Calfee, R. (1991). Decoding and spelling. What to teach, when to teach it, how to teach it. *Psychological Science, 2*, 83-85.

Caplan, D. (2004). Functional neuroimaging studies of written sentence comprehension. *Scientific Studies of Reading, 8(3)*, 225-240.

Caravolas, M., Volín, J., & Hulme, C. (2005). Phoneme awareness is a key component of alphabetic literacy skills in consistent and inconsistent orthographies: Evidence from Czech and English children. *Journal of Experimental Child Psychology, 92*, 107–139.

Cardoso-Martins, C., Mamede Resende, S., & Assunção Rodrigues, L. (2002). Letter name knowledge and the ability to learn to read by processing letter-phoneme relations in words: Evidence from Brazilian Portuguese-speaking children. *Reading and Writing: An Interdisciplinary Journal, 15(3-4)*, 409-432.

Carlisle, J. F. (1991). Questioning the psychological reality of onset-rime as a level of phonological awareness. In Brady, S. A. & Shankweiler, D. P. (Eds.) *Phonological processes in literacy: A tribute to Isabelle Y. Liberman* (pp. 85-95). Hillsdale, NJ: Erlbaum.

Carroll, J. B. (1956). The case of Dr. Flesch (critique of *Why Johnny Can't Read*). *American Psychologist, 111 (3)*, 158-163.

Cassar, M., & Treiman, R. (1997). The beginnings of orthographic knowledge: Children's knowledge of double letters in words. *Journal of Educational Psychology, 89*, 632-644.

Castles, A., Davis, C., Cavalot, P., & Forster, K. (2007). Tracking the acquisition of orthographic skills in developing readers: Masked priming effects. *Journal of Experimental Child Psychology, 97*, 165-182.

Castles, A. & Nation, K. (2006). How does orthographic learning happen? In S. Andrews, (Ed.), *From inkmarks to ideas: Challenges and controversies about word recognition and reading* (pp. 151-179). London, UK: Psychology Press.

Carroll, D. (2008). *The psychology of language, (5th Ed)*. Belmont, CA: Thompson/Wadsworth.

References

Carroll, J. B. (1956). The case of Dr. Flesch. *American Psychologist, 11*(3), 158-163.

Cattell, J. M. (1886). The time taken up by cerebral operations. *Mind, 44,* 524-538.

Catts, H. W. (2009). The Narrow View of Reading promotes a broad view of comprehension. *Language, Speech and Hearing Services in Schools, 40,* 178-183.

Catts, H. W., Alolf, S. M., & Weismer, S. E. (2006). Language deficits in poor comprehenders: A case for the Simple View of Reading. *Journal of Speech, Language, and Hearing Research, 49,* 278-293.

Catts, H. W., Fey, M. E., Zhang, X., & Tomblin, J. B. (1999). Language basis of reading and reading disabilities: Evidence from a longitudinal investigation. *Scientific Studies of Reading, 3*(4), 331-361.

Chafouleas, S. M., Lewandowski, L. J., Smith, C. R. & Blachman, B. A. (1997). Phonological awareness skills in children: Examining performance across tasks and ages. *Journal of Psychoeducational Assessment, 19,* 216-226.

Chafouleas, S. M. & Martens, B. K. (2002). Accuracy-based phonological awareness tasks: Are they reliable, efficient, and sensitive to growth? *School Psychology Quarterly, 17*(2), 128-147.

Chafouleas, S. M., VanAuken, T. L. & Dunham, K. (2001). Not all phonemes are created equal: The effects of linguistic manipulations on phonological awareness tasks. *Journal of Psychoeducational Assessment, 19,* 216-226.

Chall, J. S. (1999). Some thoughts on reading research: Revisiting the first-grade studies. *Reading Research Quarterly, 34*(1), 8-10.

Chall, J., Roswell, F. G. & Blumenthal, S. H. (1963). Auditory blending ability: A factor in success in beginning reading. *The Reading Teacher, 17,* 113-118.

Chiappe, P., Stringer, R., Siegel, L. S. & Stanovich, K. E. (2002). Why the timing deficit hypothesis does not explain reading disability in adults. *Reading and Writing: An Interdisciplinary Journal, 15*(1-2), 73-107.

Christiansen, C. A. & Bowey, J. A. (2005). The efficacy of orthographic rime, grapheme–phoneme correspondence, and implicit phonics approaches to teaching decoding skills. *Scientific Studies of Reading, 9*(4), 327-349.

Cole, P., Mangan, A., & Grainger, J. (1999). Syllable-sized units in visual word recognition: Evidence from skilled and beginning readers of French. *Applied Psycholinguistics, 20,* 507-532.

Coltheart, M. (2005). Modeling reading: The dual-route approach. In M. J. Snowling & C. Hulme (Eds.), *The science of reading: A handbook* (pp. 6-23). Malden, MA: Blackwell.

Coltheart, M. (2012). Dual-route theories of reading aloud. In J. S. Adelman (Ed.), *Visual word recognition (Vol. 1): Models and methods, orthography and phonology* (pp. 3-27). New York: Psychology Press.

Coltheart, M. Curtis, B., Atkins, P. & Haller, M. (1993). Models of reading aloud: Dual-route and parallel-distributed-processing approaches. *Psychological Review, 100*(4), 589-608.

Coltheart, V., & Leahy, J. (1992). Children's and adults' reading of nonwords: Effects of regularity and consistency. *Journal of Experimental Psychology: Learning, Memory, and Cognition, 18,* 718-729.

Compton, D. L., Miller, A. C., Elleman, A. M., & Steacy, L. M. (2014) Have we forsaken reading theory in the name of "quick fix" interventions for children with reading disability? *Scientific Studies of Reading, 18*(1), 55-73.

Crowder, R. (1982). *The psychology of reading: An introduction.* New York: Oxford University Press.

Crowder, R. G. & Wagoner, R. K. (1992). *The psychology of reading: An introduction.* New York: Oxford University Press.

Cunningham, A. (1990). Explicit versus implicit instruction in phoneme awareness. *Journal of Experimental Child Psychology, 50,* 429-444.

Cunningham, A. (2006). Accounting for children's orthographic learning while reading text: Do children self-teach? *Journal of Experimental Child Psychology, 95,* 56-77.

Cunningham, A., Perry, K. E. & Stanovich, K. E. (2001). Converging evidence for the concept of orthographic processing. *Reading and Writing: An Interdisciplinary Journal, 14*(5-6), 549-568.

Cunningham, A. E., Perry, K. E., Stanovich, K. E., & Share, D. L. (2002). Orthographic learning during reading: Examining the role of self-teaching. *Journal of Experimental Child Psychology, 82,* 185-199.

Cunningham, A. E., & Stanovich, K. E. (1990). Assessing print exposure and orthographic processing skill in children: A quick measure of reading experience. *Journal of Educational Psychology, 82,* 733-740.

Davis, J. M. & Spring, C. (1990). The Digit Naming Speed Test: Its power and incremental validity in identifying children with specific reading disabilities. *Psychology in the Schools, 27,* 15-22.

Deacon, S. H., Conrad, N., & Pacton, S. (2008). A statistical learning perspective on children's learning about graphotactic and morphological regularities in spelling. *Canadian Psychology, 49*(2) 118-124.

Dehaene, S. & Cohen, L. (2011). The unique role of the visual word form area in reading. *Trends in Cognitive Sciences, 15*(6), 254-262.

de Jong, P. F. (2007). Phonological awareness and the use of phonological similarity in letter–sound learning. *Journal of Experimental Child Psychology, 98,* 131-152.

de Jong, P. F. (2011). What discrete and serial rapid automatized naming can reveal about reading. *Scientific Studies of Reading, 15*(4), 314-337.

de Jong, P. F., Sevke, M-J. & van Veen, M. (2000). Phonological sensitivity and the acquisition of new words in children. *Journal of Experimental Child Psychology, 76,* 275-301.

de Jong, P. F. & Share, D. L. (2007). Orthographic learning during oral and silent reading. *Scientific Studies of Reading, 11*(1), 55-70.

Dixon, M., Stuart, M. & Masterson, J. (2002). The relationship between phonological awareness and the development of orthographic representations. *Reading and Writing: An Interdisciplinary Journal, 15*(3-4), 295-316.

Dolch, E. W. (1936). A basic sight vocabulary. *Elementary School Journal, February,* 456-460.

Duffy, G. G. & Hoffmann, J. V. (1999). In pursuit of an illusion: The flawed search for a perfect method. *The Reading Teacher, 53*(1), 10-16.

Durand, M. Hulme, C. Larkin, R., & Snowling, M. (2005). The cognitive foundations of reading and arithmetic skills in 7- to 10-year-olds. *Journal of Experimental Child Psychology, 91,* 113-136.

Durgunoglu, A. Y. & Oney, B. (1999). A cross-linguistic comparison of phonological awareness and word recognition. *Reading and Writing: An Interdisciplinary Journal, 11*(4), 281-299.

Ehri, L. C. (1991). Learning to read and spell words. In Rieben, L. & Perfetti, C. A. (Eds.) *Learning to read: Basic research and its implications* (pp. 57-73). Hillsdale, NJ: Erlbaum.

Ehri, L. C. (1992). Reconceptualizing the development of sight word reading and its relationship to recoding. In Gough, P. B., Ehri, L. C., & Treiman, R. (Eds.) *Reading Acquisition.* Hillsdale, NJ: Lawrence Erlbaum Associates.

Ehri, L. C. (1997). Sight word learning in normal readers and dyslexics. In B. A. Blachman, (Ed.) *Foundations of reading acquisition and dyslexia* (pp. 163-189). Mahwah, NJ: Erlbaum.

Ehri, L. C. (1998a). Grapheme-phoneme knowledge is essential for learning to read words in English. In Metsala, J. L. & Ehri, L. C. (Eds.) *Word recognition in beginning literacy.* (pp. 3-40). Mahwah, NJ: Erlbaum.

Ehri, L. C. (1998b). Research on learning to read and spell: A personal-historical perspective. *Scientific Studies of Reading, 2*(2), 97-114.

Ehri, L. C. (2005a). Learning to read words: Theory, findings, and issues. *Scientific Studies of Reading, 9*(2), 167-188.

Ehri, L. C. (2005b). Development of sight word reading: Phases and findings. In M. J. Snowling & C. Hulme (Eds.), *The science of reading: A handbook* (pp. 135-154). Malden, MA: Blackwell.

Ehri, L. C. (2014). Orthographic Mapping in the acquisition of sight word reading, spelling memory, and vocabulary learning, *Scientific Studies of Reading,* 18(1), 5-21.

Ehri, L. C. & Robbins, C. (1992). Beginners need some decoding skill to read words by analogy. *Reading Research Quarterly, 27*(1), 13-26.

Ehri, L. C., & Saltmarsh, J. (1995). Beginning readers outperform older disabled readers in learning to read words by sight. *Reading and Writing: An Interdisciplinary Journal, 7,* 295-326.

Ehri, L. C., & Soffer, A. G. (1999). Graphophoneme awareness: Development in elementary students. *Scientific Studies of Reading, 3*(1), 1-30.

Ehri, L. C., & Wilce, L. S. (1985). Movement into reading: Is the first stage of printed word learning visual or phonetic? *Reading Research Quarterly, 20,* 163-179.

References

Ehri, L. C., & Wilce, L. S. (1987a). Cipher versus cue reading: An experiment in decoding acquisition. *Journal of Educational Psychology, 79*, 3-13.

Ehri, L. C., & Wilce, L. S. (1987b). Does learning to spell help beginners learn to read words? *Reading Research Quarterly, 22*, 47-65.

Ehri, L. C., Wilce, L. S. & Taylor, B. B. (1987). Children's categorization of short vowels in words and the influence of spellings. *Merrill-Palmer Quarterly, 33(3)*, 393-421.

Elbro, C., Borstrøm, I., & Peterson, D. K. (1998). Predicting dyslexia from kindergarten: The importance of distinctness of phonological representations of lexical items. *Reading Research Quarterly, 33(1)*, 36-60.

Elbro, C. & Jensen, M. N. (2005). Quality of phonological representations, verbal learning, and phoneme awareness in dyslexic and normal readers. *Scandinavian Journal of Psychology, 46*, 375-384.

Engen, L. & Høien, T. (2002). Phonological skills and reading comprehension. *Reading and Writing: An Interdisciplinary Journal, 15(7-8)*, 613-631.

Evans, J. J., Floyd, R. G., McGrew, K. S., & Leforgee, M. H. (2001). The relations between measures of Cattell-Horn-Carroll (CHC) cognitive abilities and reading achievement during childhood and adolescence. *School Psychology Review, 31(2)*, 246-262.

Fawcett, A. J. & Nicolson, R. I. (1995). Persistence of phonological awareness deficits in older children with dyslexia. *Reading and Writing: An Interdisciplinary Journal, 7*, 361-376.

Felton, R. H. & Pepper, P. P. (1995). Early identification of phonological deficits in kindergarten and early elementary children at risk for reading disability. *School Psychology Review, 24(3)*, 405-414.

Fitzgerald, J. (1999). What is this thing called "balance?" *Reading Teacher, 53(2)*, 100-107.

Fletcher, J. M., Shaywitz, S. E., Shankweiler, D. P., Katz, L., Liberman, I. Y., Steubing, K. K., Francis, D. J., Fowler, A. E., & Shaywitz, B. A. (1994). Cognitive profiles of reading disability: Comparisons of discrepancy and low achievement definitions. *Journal of Educational Psychology, 86*, 6-23.

Fletcher, J. M., Morris, R., Lyon, G. R., Steubing, K. K., Shaywitz, S. E., Shankweiler, D. P., Katz, & Shaywitz, B. A. (1997). Subtypes of dyslexia: An old problem revisited. In B. A. Blachman, (Ed.) *Foundations of reading acquisition and dyslexia* (pp. 95-114). Mahwah, NJ: Erlbaum.

Flynn, L. J., Zheng, X., & Swanson, H. L. (2012). Instructing struggling older readers: A selective meta-analysis of intervention research. *Learning Disabilities Research and Practice, 27*, 21–32.

Foorman, B. R. (1995). Research on "The Great Debate": Code-oriented versus whole language approaches to reading instruction. *School Psychology Review, 24(3)*, 376-392.

Foorman, B., & Al Otaiba, S. (2009). Reading remediation: State of the art. In K. Pugh & P. McCardle (Eds.), *How children learn to read: Current issues and new directions in the integration of cognition, neurobiology and genetics of reading and dyslexia research and practice* (pp. 257-274). New York: Psychology Press.

Foorman, B., Francis, D. J., Fletcher, J. M., Schatschneider, C., & Mehta, P. (1998). The role of instruction in learning to read: Preventing reading failure in at-risk children. *Journal of Educational Psychology, 90(1)*, 37-55.

Foorman, B. R., Francis, D. J., Novy, D.M, & Liberman, D. (1991). How letter-sound instruction mediates progress in first-grade reading and spelling. *Journal of Educational Psychology, 83(4)*, 456-469.

Foorman, B. R., Francis, D.J., Winikates, D., Mehta, P., Schatschneider, C., & Fletcher, J. (1997). Early interventions for children with reading disabilities. *Scientific Studies of Reading, 1(3)*, 255-276.

Foorman, B. R., & Torgesen, J. K. (2001). Critical elements of classroom and small-group instruction promote reading success in all children. *Learning Disabilities Research & Practice, 16*(4), 203–212.

Foorman, B. R., Francis, D. J., Shaywitz, S. E., Shaywitz, B. A., & Fletcher, J. M. (1997). The case for early reading intervention. In B. A. Blachman, (Ed.) *Foundations of reading acquisition and dyslexia* (pp. 243-264). Mahwah, NJ: Erlbaum.

Forster, K. I. (2012). A parallel activation model with a sequential twist. In J. S. Adelman (Ed.), *Visual word recognition (Vol. 1): Models and methods, orthography and phonology* (pp. 52-69). New York: Psychology Press.

Fowler, A. E. (1991). How early phonological development might set the stage for phoneme awareness. In Brady, S. A. & Shankweiler, D. P. (Eds.) *Phonological processes in literacy: A tribute to Isabelle Y. Liberman* (pp. 97-117). Hillsdale, NJ: Erlbaum.

Fowler, C. A. (2011). How theories of phonology may enhance understanding of the role of phonology in reading development and reading disability. In S. A. Brady, D. Braze, & C. A. Fowler (Eds.), *Explaining individual differences in reading: Theory and evidence.* (pp. 3-19). New York: Psychology Press.

Fox, B. & Routh, D. K. (1976). Phonemic analysis and synthesis as word attack skills. *Journal of Educational Psychology, 68*, 70-74.

Fox and Routh (1984). Phonemic analysis and synthesis as word attack skills: Revisited. *Journal of Educational Psychology, 76*, 1059-1064.

Freppon, P. A. & Dahl, K. L. (1998). Balanced instruction: Insights and considerations. *Reading Research Quarterly, 33,(2)*, 240-251.

Frost, R. (1998). Toward a strong phonological theory of visual word recognition: True issues and false trails. *Psychological Bulletin, 123(1)*, 71-99.

Frost, R. (2005). Orthographic systems and skilled word recognition processes in reading. In M. J. Snowling & C. Hulme (Eds.), *The science of reading: A handbook* (pp. 272-295). Malden, MA: Blackwell.

Fuchs, L. S., Fuchs, D., Hosp, M. K., & Jenkins, J. R. (2001). Oral reading fluency as an indicator of reading competence: A theoretical, empirical, and historical analysis. *Scientific Studies of Reading, 5(3)*, 239-256.

Fuchs, D., Hale, J. B., & Kearns, D. M. (2011). On the importance of a cognitive processing perspective: An introduction. *Journal of Learning Disabilities 44(2)*, 99–104.

Gaddes, W. H. (1985). *Learning disabilities and brain function: A neuropsychological approach* (2nd ed.). New York: Springer-Verlag.

Gambrell, L. B., & Jawitz, P. B. (1993). Mental imagery, text illustrations, and children's story comprehension and recall. *Reading Research Quarterly, 28(3)*, 265-276.

Gersons-Wolfensberger, D. C. M. & Ruijssenaars, W. A. J. J. M. (1997). Definition and treatment of dyslexia: A report by the Committee on Dyslexia of the Health Council of the Netherlands. *Journal of Learning Disabilities, 30(2)*, 209-213.

Geva, E. (1999). Introduction: Linguistic process in reading across orthographies. *Reading & Writing: An Interdisciplinary Journal, 11(4)*, 275-280.

Glezer, L. S., Kim, J., Rule, J., Jiang, X., & Riesenhuber, M. (2015). Adding words to the brain's visual dictionary: Novel word learning selectively sharpens orthographic representations in the VWFA. *Journal of Neuroscience, 35(12)*, 4965-4972.

Goff, D. A., Pratt, C. & Ong, B. (2005). The relations between children's reading comprehension, working memory, language skills and components of reading decoding in a normal sample. *Reading and Writing: An Interdisciplinary Journal, 18*, 583–616.

Goldstein, D. M. (1976). Cognitive-linguistic functioning and learning to read in preschoolers. *Journal of Educational Psychology, 68(6)*, 680-688.

Good, R. H., Simmons, D. C. & Smith, S. (1998). Effective academic interventions in the United States: Evaluating and enhancing the acquisition of early reading skills. *School Psychology Review, 27(1)*, pp. 45-56.

Goodman, K. S. (1965). A linguistic study of cues and miscues in reading. *Elementary English*, 639-643.

Goodman, K. S. (1976). Behind the eye: What happens in reading. In Singer, H. & Ruddell, R. B. (Eds.) *Theoretical models and processes of reading* (2nd ed.), (pp. 470-496), Newark, DE: International Reading Association.

Goodman, K. S. (1976). Reading: A psycholinguistic guessing game. In Singer, H., & Ruddell, R. B. (Eds.), *Theoretical Models and Processes of Reading* (2nd ed., pp. 497–508). Newark, DE: International Reading Association.

Goodman, K. S. (1981). Response to Stanovich. *Reading Research Quarterly, 16*(3), 477-478.

Goodman, K. S. (2005). Making sense of written language: A lifelong journey. *Journal of Literacy Research, 37*, 1-24.

Goswami, U. (1988). Orthographic analogies and reading development. *Quarterly Journal of Experimental Psychology, 40A(2)*, 239-268.

Goswami, U. (1993). Toward an interactive analogy model of reading development: Decoding vowel graphemes in beginning reading. *Journal of Experimental Child Psychology, 56*, 443-475.

Goswami, U. (1998). The role of analogies in the development of word recognition. In Metsala, J. L. & Ehri, L. C. (Eds.) *Word recognition in beginning literacy*. (pp. 41-63). Mahwah, NJ: Erlbaum.

Goswami, U., & Mead, F. (1992). Onset and rime awareness and analogies in reading. *Reading Research Quarterly, 27(2),* 153-162.

Gough, P. B. (1993). The beginning of decoding. *Reading & Writing: An Interdisciplinary Journal, 5,* 181-192.

Gough, P. B., & Juel, C. (1991). The first stages of word reading. In Rieben, L. & Perfetti, C. A. (Eds.) *Learning to read: Basic research and its implications* (pp. 47-56). Mahwah, NJ: Erlbaum.

Gough, P. B., Juel, C., & Griffith, P. L. (1992). Reading, spelling, and the orthographic cipher. In Gough, P.B., Ehri, L. C. & Treiman, R. (Eds.) *Reading Acquisition*. (pp. 35-47). Hillsdale, NJ: Erlbaum.

Gough, P. B., & Tunmer, W. E. (1986). Decoding, reading, and reading disability. *Remedial and Special Education, 7,* 6-10.

Gough, P. B., & Walsh, M. A. (1991). Chinese, Phoenicians, and the orthographic cipher of English. In Brady, S. A. & Shankweiler, D. P. (Eds.) *Phonological processes in literacy: A tribute to Isabelle Y. Liberman* (pp. 199-209). Hillsdale, NJ: Erlbaum.

Grainger, J. & Whitney, C. (2004). ☐Does the huamn mnid raed wrods as a wlohe? *Trends in Cognitive Sciences, 8(2),* 58-59.

Graves, M. F., & Dykstra, R. (1997). Contextualizing the First-Grade Studies: What is the best way to teach children to read? *Reading Research Quarterly, 32(4),* 342-344.

Greaney, K. T., Tunmer, W. E., & Chapman, J. W. (1997). The use of rime-based orthographic analogy training as an intervention strategy for reading-disabled children. In B. A. Blachman, (Ed.) *Foundations of reading acquisition and dyslexia* (pp. 327-345). Mahwah, NJ: Erlbaum.

Griffiths, Y. M., & Snowling, M. J. (2002). Predictors of exception word and nonword reading in dyslexia children: The severity hypothesis. *Journal of Educational Psychology, 94,* 34-43.

Grossen, B. & Carnine, D. (1991). Strategies for maximizing reading success in the regular classroom. In G. Stoner, M. R. Shinn, & H. M. Walker, H. M. (Eds.), *Interventions for achievement and behavior problems* (pp. 333-355). Silver Spring, MD: National Association of School Psychologists.

Halderman, L. K., Ashby, J., & Perfetti, C. A. (2012). Phonology: An early and integral role in identifying words. In J. S. Adelman (Ed.), *Visual word recognition (Vol. 1): Models and methods, orthography and phonology* (pp. 207-228). New York: Psychology Press.

Hammill, D. D. (2004). What we know about correlates of reading. *Exceptional Children, 70(4),* 453-468.

Hanson, V. L. (1991). Phonological processing without sound. In Brady, S. A. & Shankweiler, D. P. (Eds.) *Phonological processes in literacy: A tribute to Isabelle Y. Liberman* (pp. 153-161). Hillsdale, NJ: Erlbaum.

Harn, B. A., Stoolmiller, M., & Chard, D. J. (2008). Measuring the dimensions of alphabetic principle on the reading development of first graders: The role of automaticity and unitization. *Journal of Learning Disabilities, 41,* 143-157.

Hart, T. M., Berninger, V. M., & Abbott, R. D. (1997). Comparison of teaching single or multiple orthographic-phonological connections for word recognition and spelling: Implications for instructional consultation. *School Psychological Review, 26(2),* 279-297.

Hatcher, P. J. & Hulme, C. (1999). Phonemes, rhymes, and intelligence as predictors of children's responsiveness to remedial reading instruction: Evidence from a longitudinal intervention study. *Journal of Experimental Child Psychology, 72,* 130-153.

Hayes, H., Treiman, R., & Kessler, B. (2006). Children use vowels to help them spell consonants. *Journal of Experimental Child Psychology, 94,* 27-42.

Helfgott, J. (1976). Phoneme segmentation and blending skills of kindergarten children: Implications for beginning reading acquisition. *Contemporary Educational Psychology, 1,* 157-169.

Hempenstall, K. (2002). The Three-Cuing System: Help or hindrance? *Direct Instruction News, 2(2),* 42-51.

Herman, P.A. (1985). The effect of repeated readings on reading rate, speech pauses, and word recognition accuracy. *Reading Research Quarterly, 20,* 553-565.

Ho, C. S.-H., & Bryant, P. (1997). Learning to read Chinese beyond the logographic phase. *Reading Research Quarterly, 32(3),* 276-289.

Høien, T. Lundberg, I., Stanovich, K. E., & Bjaalid, I-K. (1995). Components of phonological awareness. *Reading and Writing: An Interdisciplinary Journal, 7,* 171-188.

Hoover, W. A. & Gough, P. B. (1990). The simple view of reading. *Reading and Writing: An Interdisciplinary Journal, 2,* 127-160.

Hulme, C., Bowyer-Crane, C., Carroll, J. M., Duff, F. J., Snowling, M. J. (2012). The causal role of phoneme awareness and letter-sound knowledge in learning to read: Combining intervention studies with mediation analyses. *Psychological Science, 23(6),* 572–577.

Hulme, C., Goetz, K. Gooch, D. Adams, J. & Snowling, M. J. (2007). Paired-associate learning, phoneme awareness, and learning to read. *Journal of Experimental Child Psychology, 96,* 150-166.

Hulme, C., Hatcher, P. J. Nation, K., Brown, A., Adams, J. & Stuart, G. (2002). Phoneme awareness is a better predictor of early reading skill than onset-rime awareness. *Journal of Experimental Child Psychology, 82,* 2-28.

Hulme, C. & Snowling, M. J. (2011). Children's reading comprehension difficulties: Nature, causes, and treatments. *Current Directions in Psychological Science, 20(3),* 139-142.

Hulme, C., Snowling, M., Caravolas, M. & Carroll, J. (2005). Phonological skills are (probably) one cause of success in learning to read: A comment on Castles and Coltheart. *Scientific Studies of Reading, 9(4),* 351-365.

Hurford, D. P. (1990). Training phonemic segmentation ability with a phonemic discrimination intervention in second and third grade children with reading disabilities. *Journal of Learning Disabilities, 23(9),* 564-569.

Iaquinta, A. (2006). Guided reading: A research-based response to the challenges of early reading instruction. *Early Childhood Education Journal, 33(6),* 413-418.

Invernizzi, M., Abouzeid, M., & Gill, J. T. (1994). Using students' invented spellings as a guide for spelling instruction that emphasizes word study. *The Elementary School Journal, 95(2),* 155-167.

Iversen, S., & Tunmer, W.E. (1993). Phonological processing skills and the Reading Recovery program. *Journal of Educational Psychology, 85,* 112-126.

Jackson, N. E., Chen, H. Goldsberry, L, Kim, A., & Vanderwerff, C. (1999). Effects of variations in orthographic information on Asian and American readers' English text reading. *Reading & Writing: An Interdisciplinary Journal, 11,* 345-379.

Jenkins, J. R., Hudson, R. F., & Johnson, E. S. (2007). Screening for at-risk readers in a response to intervention framework. *School Psychology Review, 36(4),* 582-600.

Johnson, E. S., Jenkins, J. R., & Jewell, M. (2005). Analyzing components of reading on performance assessments: An Expanded Simple View. *Reading Psychology, 26,* 267-283.

Jones, D., & Christensen, C. A. (1999). Relationship between automaticity in handwriting and students' ability to generate written text. *Journal of Educational Psychology, 91(1),* 44-49.

Jorm, A. F. (1977). Children's reading processes revealed by pronunciation latencies and errors. *Journal of Educational Psychology, 69(2),* 166-171.

Jorm, A. & Share, D. (1983). Phonological recoding and reading acquisition. Applied Psycholinguistics, 4, 103-147.

Joshi, R. M. (1995). Assessing reading and spelling skills. *School Psychology Review, 24(3),* 361-375.

Joshi, R. M., Binks, E., Hougen, M., Dahlgren, M. E., Ocker-Dean, & Smith, D. L. (2009). Why elementary teachers might be inadequately prepared to teach reading. *Journal of Learning Disabilities, 42(5),* 392-402.

Juel, C. (1988). Learning to read and write: A longitudinal study of 54 children from first through fourth grades. *Journal of Educational Psychology, 80,* 437-447.

Juel, C., Griffith, P.L., & Gough, P.B. (1986). Acquisition of literacy: A longitudinal study of children in first and second grade. *Journal of Educational Psychology, 78,* 243-255.

Kame'enui, E. J., & Simmons, D. C. (2001). Introduction to this special issue: The DNA of Reading Fluency. *Scientific Studies of Reading, 5(3),* 203-210.

Kamhi, A. G. (2009). The case for the Narrow View of Reading. *Language, Speech, and Hearing Services in the Schools, 40,* 174-177.

Katz, L., & Frost, S. J. (2001). Phonology constrains the internal orthographic representation. *Reading & Writing: An Interdisciplinary Journal, 14,* 297-332.

References

Kilpatrick, D. A. (2012a). Phonological segmentation assessment is not enough: A comparison of three phonological awareness tests with first and second graders. *Canadian Journal of School Psychology, 27(2)*, 150-165.

Kilpatrick, D. A. (2012b). Not all phonological awareness tests are created equal: Considering the practical validity of phonological manipulation vs. segmentation. *Communiqué: Newspaper of the National Association of School Psychologists, 40(6)*, 31-33.

Kilpatrick, D. A. (2014). Tailoring interventions in reading based on emerging research on the development of word recognition skills. In Mascolo, J. T., Flanagan, D. P., & Alfonso, V. C. (Eds.) *Essentials of planning, selecting and tailoring intervention: Addressing the needs of the unique learner.* (pp. 123-150). Hoboken, NJ: Wiley.

Kilpatrick, D. A. (2015). *Essentials of assessing, preventing, and overcoming reading difficulties.* Hoboken, NJ: Wiley.

Kilpatrick, D. A., & Cole, L. A. (2015). Exploring the development of sight-word learning in second and fifth graders using rimes, pseudorimes, and real-word rimes. (manuscript under review).

Kim (Yoon), Y. H., & Goetz, E. T. (1994). Context effects on word recognition and reading comprehension of poor and good readers: A test of the interactive-compensatory hypothesis. *Reading Research Quarterly, 29(1)*, 179-188.

Kinder, D. & Carnine, D. (1991). Direct Instruction: What it is and what it is becoming. *Journal of Behavioral Education, 1(2)*, 193-213.

Kirby, J. R., Parrila, R. K., & Pfeiffer, S. L. (2003). Naming speed and phonological awareness as predictors of reading development. *Journal of Educational Psychology, 95(3)*, 453-464.

Kjeldsen, A-C., Kärnä, A., Niemi, P., Olofsson, A., & Witting, K. (2014) Gains from training in phonological awareness in kindergarten predict reading comprehension in grade 9. *Scientific Studies of Reading, 18(6)*, 452-467.

Kroese, J. M., Hynd, G. E., Knight, D. F., Hiemenz, J. R., & Hall, J. (2000). Clinical appraisal of spelling ability and its relationship to phoneme awareness (blending, segmenting, elision, and reversal), phonological memory, and reading in reading disabled, ADHD, and normal children. *Reading & Writing: An Interdisciplinary Journal, 13*, 105-131.

Kyte, C. S. & Johnson, C. J. (2006). The role of phonological recoding in orthographic learning. *Journal of Experimental Child Psychology, 93*, 166-185.

Laing, E. & Hulme, C. (1999). Phonological and semantic processes influence beginning readers' ability to learn to read words. *Journal of Experimental Child Psychology, 73*, 183-207.

Landi, N., Perfetti, C. A., Bolger, D. J. Dunlap, S., & Foorman, B. R. (2006). The role of discourse context in developing word form representations: A paradoxical relation between reading and learning. *Journal of Experimental Child Psychology, 94*, 114-133.

Lee, J., & Yoon, S. Y. (2016 in press). The effects of repeated reading on reading fluency for students with reading disabilities: A meta-analysis. *Journal of Learning Disabilities.*

Lenchner, O., Gerber, M. M., & Routh, D. K. (1990). Phonological awareness tasks as predictors of decoding ability: Beyond segmentation. *Journal of Learning Disabilities, 23(4)*, 240-247.

Lennon, J. E. & Slesinski, C. (1999). Early intervention in reading: Results of a screening and intervention program for kindergarten students. *School Psychology Review, 28(3)*, 353-364.

Lervag, A. & Hulme, C. (2009). Rapid Automatized Naming (RAN) taps a mechanism that places constraints on the development of early reading fluency. *Psychological Science, 20(8)*, 1040-1047.

Lesiak, J. L. (1997). Research based answers to questions about emergent literacy in kindergarten. *Psychology in the Schools, 34(2)*, 143-160.

Levin, J.R. (1991). Editor's introduction to three studies on reading acquisition. *Journal of Educational Psychology, 83(4)*, 435-436.

Levy, B. A. & Lysynchuk, L. (1997). Beginning word recognition: Benefits of training by segmentation and whole word methods. *Scientific Studies of Reading, 1(4)*, 359-387.

Lewkowicz, N. K. (1980). Phoneme awareness training: What to teach and how to teach it. *Journal of Educational Psychology, 72(5)*, 686-700.

Liberman, A. M. (1997). How theories of speech affect research in reading and writing. In B. A. Blachman, (Ed.) *Foundations of reading acquisition and dyslexia* (pp. 3-19). Mahwah, NJ: Erlbaum.

Liberman, I. (1973). Segmentation of the spoken word on reading acquisition. *Bulletin of the Orton Society, 23*, 65-77.

Liberman, I. Y., Shankweiler, D., Fischer, F. W. & Carter, B. (1974). Explicit syllable and phoneme segmentation in the young child. *Journal of Experimental Child Psychology, 18*, 201-212.

Liberman, I. Y., & Shankweiler, D. (1991). Phonology and beginning reading: A Tutorial. In Rieben, L. & Perfetti, C. A. (Eds.) *Learning to read: Basic research and its implications* (pp. 3-17). Mahwah, NJ: Erlbaum.

Lonigan, C. J. (2002). Development and promotion of emergent literacy skills in children at-risk of reading difficulties. In B. R. Foorman, (Ed.), *Preventing and remediating reading difficulties: Bringing science to scale* (pp. 23-50). Baltimore, MD: York Press.

Lonigan, C. J., Anthony, J. L., Phillips, B. M., & Purpura, D. J. (2009). The nature of preschool phonological processing abilities and their relations to vocabulary, general cognitive abilities, and print knowledge. *Journal of Educational Psychology, 101(2)*, 345-358.

Lovett, B., J. (2011). On the diagnosis of learning disabilities in gifted students: Reply to Assouline et al. (2010). *Gifted Child Quarterly, 55(2)*, 149-151.

Lovett, M. W., & Steinbach, K. A. (1997). The effectiveness of remedial programs for reading disabled children of different ages: Does the benefit decrease for older children? *Learning Disability Quarterly, 20*, 189-210.

Lundberg, I. (1991). Phoneme awareness can be developed without reading instruction. In Brady, S. A. & Shankweiler, D. P. (Eds.) *Phonological processes in literacy: A tribute to Isabelle Y. Liberman* (pp. 47-53). Hillsdale, NJ: Erlbaum.

Lupker, S. J. (2005). Visual word recognition: Theories and findings. In M. J. Snowling & C. Hulme (Eds.), *The science of reading: A handbook* (pp. 39-60). Malden, MA: Blackwell.

Lyster, S.-A.H. (2002). The effects of morphological versus phonological awareness training in kindergarten on reading development. *Reading and Writing: An Interdisciplinary Journal, 15(3-4)*, 261-295.

MacDonald, G. W. & Cornwall, A. (1995). The relationship between phonological awareness and reading and spelling achievement eleven years later. *Journal of Learning Disabilities, 28*, 523-527.

Maclean, M., Bryant, P. E., & Bradley, L. (1987). Rhymes, nursery rhymes and reading in early childhood. *Merrill-Palmer Quarterly, 33*, 255-282.

Manis, F. R., Custodio, R., & Szeszulski, P. A. (1993). Development of phonological and orthographic skill: A 2-year longitudinal study of dyslexic children. *Journal of Experimental Child Psychology, 56*, 64-86.

Mann, V. A. (1991a). Are we taking too narrow a view of the conditions for development of phonological awareness? In Brady, S. A. & Shankweiler, D. P. (Eds.) *Phonological processes in literacy: A tribute to Isabelle Y. Liberman* (pp. 55-64). Hillsdale, NJ: Erlbaum.

Mann, V. A. (1991b). Phonological abilities: Effective predictors of future reading ability. In Rieben, L. & Perfetti, C. A. (Eds.) *Learning to read: Basic research and its implications* (pp. 121-133). Hillsdale, NJ: Erlbaum.

Mann, V. A., Tobin, P., & Wilson, R. (1987). Measuring phonological awareness through the invented spellings of kindergarten children. *Merrill-Palmer Quarterly, 33(3)*, 365-391.

Marsh, G. & Mineo, R. J. (1977). Training preschool children to recognize phonemes in words. *Journal of Educational Psychology, 69(6)*, 748-753.

Marinus, E. & de Jong, P. F. (2008). The use of sublexical clusters in normal and dyslexic readers. *Scientific Studies of Reading, 12(3)*, 253-280.

Marsh, G., & Mineo, R. J. (1977). Training preschool children to recognize phonemes in words. *Journal of Educational Psychology, 69(6)*, 748-753.

Martens, V. E. G., & de Jong, P. F. (2006). The effect of visual word features on the acquisition of orthographic knowledge. *Journal of Experimental Child Psychology, 93*, 337-356.

Martin-Chang, S. L., Levy, B. A., & O'Neil, S. (2007). Word acquisition, retention, and transfer: Findings from contextual and isolated word training. *Journal of Experimental Child Psychology, 96*, 37-56.

Masonheimer, P., Drum, P., & Ehri, L. (1984). Does environmental print identification lead children into word reading? *Journal of Reading Behavior, 16*, 257-272.

Mattingly, I. G. (1991). Modularity, working memory, and reading disability. In Brady, S. A. & Shankweiler, D. P. (Eds.) *Phonological processes in literacy: A tribute to Isabelle Y. Liberman* (pp. 163-171). Hillsdale, NJ: Erlbaum.

McBride-Chang, C. (1995). What is phonological awareness? *Journal of Educational Psychology, 87*(2), 179-192.

McClung, N. A., O'Donnell, C. R., & Cuningham, A. E. (2012). Orthographic learning and the development of visual word recognition. In J. S. Adelman (Ed.), *Visual word recognition (Vol. 2): Meaning and context, individuals and development* (pp. 173-195). New York: Psychology Press.

McDougall, S. J. P. & Donohoe, R. (2002). Reading ability and memory span: Long-term memory contributions to span for good and poor readers. *Reading and Writing: An Interdisciplinary Journal, 15*(3-4), 359-387.

McDougall, S., Hulme, C., Ellis, A. & Monk, A. (1994). Learning to read: The role of short-term memory and phonological skills. *Journal of Experimental Child Psychology, 58*, 112-133.

McGeown, S. P., Medford, E., & Moxon, G. (2013). Individual differences in children's reading and spelling strategies and the skills supporting strategy use. *Learning and Individual Differences, 28*, 75–81.

McGuiness, D., McGuiness, C., & Donohue, J. (1995). Phonological training and the alphabet principle: Evidence for reciprocal causality. *Reading Research Quarterly, 30*, 830-852.

McInnis, P. J. (1981). *Decoding keys for reading success*. New York NY: Walker Educational.

McInnis, P. J. (1999). *A guide to readiness and reading: Phoneme awareness and blending* (3rd ed.). Penn Yan, NY: ARL.

McNeil, J. D. & Stone, J. (1965). Note on teaching children to hear separate sounds in spoken words. *Journal of Educational Psychology, 56*(1), 13-15.

Mehta, P. D., Foorman, B. R., Branum-Martin, L. & Taylor, W. P. (2005). Literacy as a unidimensional multilevel construct: Validation, sources of influence, and implications in a longitudinal study in grades 1 to 4. *Scientific Studies of Reading, 9*(2), 85-116.

Messbauer, V. C. S. & de Jong, P. F. (2003). Word, nonword, and visual paired associate learning in Dutch dyslexic children. *Journal of Experimental Child Psychology, 84*, 77-96.

Metsala, J. L. (2011). Lexical reorganization and the emergence of phonological awareness. In S. B. Neuman & D. K. Dickinson (Eds.), *Handbook of early literacy research, Vol. 3*. (pp. 66-82). New York: Guilford.

Metsala, J. L. & Ehri, L. C. (1998) (Eds.) *Word recognition in beginning literacy*. Mahwah, NJ: Erlbaum.

Metsala, J. L., Stanovich, K. E., & Brown, G. D. A. (1998). Regularity effects and the phonological deficit model of reading disabilities: A meta-analytic review. *Journal of Educational Psychology, 90*(2), 279-293.

Meyer, B. J. G., Talbot, A. P., & Florencio, D. (1999). Reading rate and prose retrieval. *Scientific Studies of Reading, 3*(4), 303-329.

Moats, L. (2009). Still wanted: Teachers with knowledge of language. *Journal of Learning Disabilities, 42, (5)*, 387-391.

Moats, L. C., & Foorman, B. R. (1997). Introduction to special issue of SSR: Components of Effective Reading Instruction. *Scientific Studies of Reading, 1*(3), 187-189.

Moll, K., Fussenegger, B., Willburger, E., & Landerl, K. (2009). RAN is not a measure of orthographic processing: Evidence from the asymmetric German orthography. *Scientific Studies of Reading, 13*(1), 1–25. DOI: 10.1080/10888430802631684

Morais, J. (1991). Constraints on the development of phoneme awareness. In Brady, S. A. & Shankweiler, D. P. (Eds.) *Phonological processes in literacy: A tribute to Isabelle Y. Liberman* (pp. 5-27). Hillsdale, NJ: Erlbaum.

Morais, J., Carey, L., Alegria, J., & Bertelson, P. (1979). Does awareness of speech as a sequence of phones arise spontaneously? *Cognition, 7*, 323, 331.

Morris, R. D., Stuebing, K. K., Fletcher, J. M., Shaywitz, S. E., Lyon, G. R., Shankweiler, D. P., Katz, L., Francis, D. J., & Shaywitz, B. A. (1998). Subtypes of reading disability: Variability around a phonological core. *Journal of Educational Psychology, 90*(3), 347-373.

Morrison, F. J. (1991). Learning (and not learning) to read: A developmental framework. In Rieben, L. & Perfetti, C. A. (Eds.) *Learning to read: Basic research and its implications* (pp. 163-174). Hillsdale, NJ: Erlbaum.

Misra, M, Katzir, T., Wolf, M., & Poldrak, R. A. (2004). Neural systems for rapid automatized naming in skilled readers: Unraveling the RAN–reading relationship. *Scientific Studies of Reading, 8*(3), 241-256.

Monaghan, J. & Ellis, A. W. (2002). Age of acquisition and the completeness of phonological representations. *Reading and Writing: An Interdisciplinary Journal, 15*(7-8), 759-788.

Moustafa, M. (1995). Children's productive phonological recoding. *Reading Research Quarterly, 30*, 464-476.

Murry, B. A. (1998). Gaining alphabetic insight: Is phoneme manipulation skill or identify knowledge causal? *Journal of Educational Psychology, 90*(3), 461-475.

Muter, V. & Snowling, M. (1998). Concurrent and longitudinal predictors of reading: The role of metalinguistic and short-term memory skills. *Reading Research Quarterly, 33*(3), 320-337.

Nation, K. (2005). Children's reading comprehension difficulties. In M. J. Snowling & C. Hulme (Eds.), *The science of reading: A handbook* (pp. 248-265). Malden, MA: Blackwell.

Nation, K., Allen, R. & Hulme, C. (2001). The limitation of orthographic analogy in early reading development: Performance on the Clue-Word Task depends on phonological priming and elementary decoding skills, not the use of orthographic analogy. *Journal of Experimental Child Psychology, 80*, 75-94.

Nation, K., Angell, P., & Castles, A. (2007). Orthographic learning via self-teaching in children learning to read English: Effects of exposure, durability, and context. *Journal of Experimental Child Psychology, 96*, 71-84.

Nation, K., & Cocksey, J. (2009). Beginning readers activate semantics from sub-word orthography. *Cognition, 110*, 273-278.

National Reading Panel. (2000). Teaching children to read. The report of *the National Reading Panel: Reports of the* subgroups. Washington, D.C.: US Government Printing Office.

Nelson, J. M. & Machek, G. R. (2007). A survey of training, practice, and competence in reading assessment and intervention. *School Psychology Review, 36*(2), 311-327.

Nicholson, T. (1991). Do children read words better in context or in lists? A classic study revisited. *Journal of Educational Psychology, 83*(4), 444-450.

Nicholson, T. (1997). Closing the gap on reading failure: Social background, phoneme awareness, and learning to read. In B. A. Blachman, (Ed.) *Foundations of reading acquisition and dyslexia* (pp. 381-407). Mahwah, NJ: Erlbaum.

Nikolopoulos, D., Goulandris, N., Hulme, C. & Snowling, M. J. (2006). The cognitive bases of learning to read and spell in Greek: Evidence from a longitudinal study. *Journal of Experimental Child Psychology, 94*, 1-17.

O'Connor, R. E. & Padeliadu, S. (2000). Blending versus whole word approaches in first grade remedial reading: Short-term and delayed effects on reading and spelling words. *Reading and Writing: An Interdisciplinary Journal, 13*, 159-182.

Oakhill, J. & Kyle, F. (2000). The relation between phonological awareness and working memory. *Journal of Experimental Child Psychology, 75*, 152-164.

Oakhill, J., Cain, K., & Bryant, P. E. (2003). The dissociation of word reading and text comprehension: Evidence from component skills. *Language and Cognitive Processes, 18*(4), 443-468.

Olson, R. & Datta, H. (2002). Visual-temporal processing in reading-disabled and normal twins. *Reading and Writing: An Interdisciplinary Journal, 15*(1-2), 127-149.

Olson, R. K., Wise, B., Johnson, M., & Ring, J. (1997). The etiology and remediation of phonologically based word recognition and spelling disabilities: Are phonological deficits the "hole" story? In B. A. Blachman, (Ed.) *Foundations of reading acquisition and dyslexia* (pp. 305-326). Mahwah, NJ: Erlbaum.

Olson, R. K., Wise, B., Ring, J., & Johnson, M. (1997). Computer-based remedial training in phoneme awareness and phonological decoding: Effects on the posttraining development of word recognition. *Scientific Studies of Reading, 1*(3), 235-253.

Oney, B. Peter, M. & Katz, L. (1997). Phonological processing in printed word recognition: Effects of age and writing system. *Scientific Studies of Reading, 1*(1), 65-83.

Pacton, S., Fayol, M., & Perruchet, P. (2005). Children's implicit learning of graphotactic and morphological regularities. *Child Development, 76*, 324-339.

References

Pammer, K. & Kevan, A. (2007). The contribution of visual sensitivity, phonological processing, and Nonverbal IQ to children's reading. *Scientific Studies of Reading, 11(1)*, 33-53.

Padget, S. Y., Knight, D. F., & Sawyer, D. J. (1996). Tennessee meets the challenge of dyslexia. *Annals of Dyslexia, 46*, 51-72.

Palmer, E. D., Brown, T. T., Petersen, S. E., & Schlaggar, B. L. (2004). Investigation of the functional neuroanatomy of single word reading and its development. *Scientific Studies of Reading, 8(3)*, 203-223.

Papalewis, R. (2004). Struggling middle school readers: Successful, accelerating intervention. *Reading Improvement, 41(1)*, 24-37.

Papanicolaou, A. C., Simos, P. G., Fletcher, J. M., Francis, D. J., Foorman, B. R., Castillo, E. M., & Sarkari, S. (2002). Early development and plasticity of neurophysiological processes involved in reading. In B. R. Foorman, (Ed.), *Preventing and remediating reading difficulties: Bringing science to scale* (pp. 3-21). Baltimore, MD: York Press.

Patel, T. K., Snowling, M. J., & de Jong, P. F. (2004). A cross-linguistic comparison of children learning to read in English and Dutch. *Journal of Educational Psychology, 96(4)*, 785-797.

Pearson, P. D. (1998). Final report/Executive summary. New York State Reading Symposium, February 11, 1998, Albany, NY.

Pennington, B. F., Van Orden, G., Kirson, D. & Haith, M. (1991). What is the causal relationship between verbal STM problems and dyslexia? In Brady, S. A. & Shankweiler, D. P. (Eds.) *Phonological processes in literacy: A tribute to Isabelle Y. Liberman* (pp. 173-186). Hillsdale, NJ: Erlbaum.

Perfetti, C. A. (1986). Continuities in reading acquisition, reading skill, and reading disability. *Remedial & Special Education, 7(1)*, 11-21.

Perfetti, C. A. (1991a). On the value of simple ideas in reading instruction. In Brady, S. A. & Shankweiler, D. P. (Eds.) *Phonological processes in literacy: A tribute to Isabelle Y. Liberman* (pp. 211-218). Hillsdale, NJ: Erlbaum.

Perfetti, C. A. (1991b). Representations and awareness in the acquisition of reading competence. In Rieben, L. & Perfetti, C. A. (Eds.) *Learning to read: Basic research and its implications* (pp. 33-44). Hillsdale, NJ: Erlbaum.

Perfetti, C. A., Beck, I., Bell, L., & Hughes, C. (1987). Phonemic knowledge and learning to read are reciprocal: A longitudinal study of first grade children. *Merrill-Palmer Quarterly, 33*, 283-319.

Perfetti, C. & Bolger, D. J. (2004). The brain might read that way. *Scientific Studies of Reading, 8(3)*, 293-304.

Petrill, S. A., Deater-Deckard, K., Thompson, L., DeThorne, L. S. & Schatschneider, C. (2006). Reading skills and early readers: Genetic and shared environmental influences. *Journal of Learning Disabilities, 39(7)*, 48-55.

Piasta, S. B., Conner, C. M., Fishman, B. J., & Morrison, F. J. (2009). Teachers' knowledge of literacy concepts, classroom practice, and student reading growth. *Scientific Studies of Reading, 13(3)*, 224-248.

Piasta, S. B., & Wagner, R. K. (2010). Developing early literacy skills: A meta-analysis of alphabet learning and instruction. *Reading Research Quarterly, 45(1)*, 8–38.

Plaut, D. C. (2005). Connectionist approaches to reading. In M. J. Snowling & C. Hulme (Eds.), *The science of reading: A handbook* (pp. 24-38). Malden, MA: Blackwell.

Poldrack, R. A. & Sandak, R. (2004). Introduction to this special issue: The cognitive neuroscience of reading. *Scientific Studies of Reading, 8(3)*, 199-202.

Post, Y. V. & Carreker, S. (2002). Orthographic similarity and phonological transparency in spelling. *Reading and Writing: An Interdisciplinary Journal, 15(3-4)*, 317-340.

Pratt, A. C., & Brady, S. (1988). Relation of phonological awareness to reading disability in children and adults. *Journal of Educational Psychology, 80*, 319-323.

Rack, J., Hulme, C., Snowling, M., & Wightman, J. (1994). The role of phonology in young children's learning of sight words: The direct mapping hypothesis. *Journal of Experimental Child Psychology, 57*, 42-71.

Rack, J. P., Snowling, M. J. & Olsen, R. K. (1992). The nonword reading deficit in developmental dyslexia: A review. *Reading Research Quarterly, 27*, 28-53.

Ramus, F. & Szenkovits, G. (2009). Understanding the nature of the phonological deficit. In K. Pugh & P. McCardle (Eds.), *How children learn to read: Current issues and new directions in the integration of cognition, neurobiology and genetics of reading and dyslexia research and practice.* (pp. 153-169). New York: Psychology Press.

Rankhorn, B., England, G., Collins, S. M., Lockavitch, J. F., & Algozzine, B. (1998). Effects of the failure free reading program on students with severe reading disabilities. *Journal of Learning Disabilities, 31(3)*, 307-312.

Rapp, D. N., van den Broek, P., McMaster, K. L., Kendeou, P., & Espin, C. A. (2007). Higher-order comprehension processes in struggling readers: A perspective for research and intervention. *Scientific Studies of Reading, 11(4)*, 289–312.

Rashotte, C. A., MacPhee, K. & Torgesen, J. K. (2001). The effectiveness of a group reading instruction program with poor readers in multiple grades. *Learning Disabilities Quarterly, 24(2)*, 119-134.

Rayner, K., Juhasz, B. J., & Pollatsek, A. (2005). Eye movements during reading. In M. J. Snowling & C. Hulme (Eds.), *The science of reading: A handbook* (pp. 79-97). Malden, MA: Blackwell.

Rayner, K., & Pollatsek, A. (1989). *The psychology of reading.* Hillsdale, NJ: Erlbaum.

Rayner, K., Sereno, S. C., Lesch, M. F., & Pollatsek, A. (1995). Phonological codes are automatically activated during reading: Evidence from an eye movement priming paradigm. *Psychological Science, 6(1)*, 26-32.

Read, C. (1991). Access to syllable structure in language and learning. In Brady, S. A. & Shankweiler, D. P. (Eds.) *Phonological processes in literacy: A tribute to Isabelle Y. Liberman* (pp. 119-124). Hillsdale, NJ: Erlbaum.

Readence, J. E., & Barone, D. M. (1997). Revisiting the First-Grade Studies: The importance of literacy history. *Reading Research Quarterly, 32(2)*, 340-341.

Reason, R. (1998). Effective academic interventions in the United Kingdom: Does the "specific" in specific learning difficulties (disabilities) now make a difference to the way we teach? *School Psychology Review, 27(1)*, 57-65.

Reynolds, C. R., & Shaywitz, S. E. (2009). Response to Intervention: Ready or not? or, From wait-to-fail to watch-them-fail. *School Psychology Quarterly, 24(2)*, 130–145.

Rieben, L., Meyer, A., & Perregaux, C. (1991). Individual differences and lexical representations: How five 6-year-old children search for and copy words. In Rieben, L. & Perfetti, C. A. (Eds.) *Learning to read: Basic research and its implications* (pp. 85-101). Hillsdale, NJ: Erlbaum.

Rieben, L. & Perfetti, C. A. (1991) (Eds.) *Learning to read: Basic research and its implications.* Hillsdale, NJ: Erlbaum.

Reitsma, P. (1983). Printed word learning in beginning readers. *Journal of Experimental Child Psychology, 36*, 321-339.

Riccio, C. A. & Hynd, G. W. (1995). Contributions of neuropsychology to our understanding of developmental reading problems. *School Psychology Review, 24(3)*, 415-425.

Rosner, J. & Simon, D. P. (1971). The Auditory Analysis Test: An initial report. *Journal of Learning Disabilities, 4(7)*, 384-392.

Sadoski, M., McTigue, E. M, & Paivio, A. (2012). A Dual Coding Theoretical Model of decoding in reading: Subsuming the LaBerge and Samuels Model. *Reading Psychology, 33(5)*, 465-496.

Salmein, R. & Helenius, P. (2004). Functional neuroanatomy of impaired reading in dyslexia. *Scientific Studies of Reading, 8(3)*, 257-272.

Sandak, R., Mencl, W. E., Frost, S. J., & Pugh, K. R. (2004). The neurobiological basis of skilled and impaired reading: Recent findings and new directions. *Scientific Studies of Reading, 8(3)*, 273-292.

Santa, C. M. & Høien, T. (1999). An assessment of Early Steps: A program for early intervention of reading problems. *Reading Research Quarterly, 34(1)*, 54-79.

Savage, R. (2006). Reading comprehension is not always the product of nonsense word decoding and linguistic comprehension: Evidence from teenagers who are extremely poor readers. *Scientific Studies of Reading, 10(2)*, 143-164.

Savage, R., Blair, R., & Rvachew, S. (2006). Rimes are not necessarily favored by prereaders: Evidence from meta- and epilinguistic phonological tasks. *Journal of Experimental Child Psychology, 94*, 183-205.

Scanlon, D. M. & Vellutino, F. R. (1997). A comparison of the instructional backgrounds and cognitive profiles of poor, average, and good readers who were initially identified as at risk for reading failure. *Scientific Studies of Reading, 1(3)*, 191-215.

References

Scanlon, D. M. & Vellutino, F. R., Small, S. G., Fanuele, D. P., & Sweeney, J. (2005). Severe reading difficulties: Can they be prevented? *Exceptionality, 13*, 209-227.

Scarborough, H. S. & Brady, S. A. (2002). Toward a common terminology for talking about speech and reading: A glossary of the "phon" words and some related terms. *Journal of Literacy Research, 34(3)*, 299-336.

Schatschneider, C., Fletcher, J. M., Francis, D. J., Carlson, C. D., & Foorman, B. R. (2004). Kindergarten prediction of reading skills: A longitudinal comparative analysis. *Journal of Educational Psychology, 96(2)*, 265-282.

Schatschneider, C., Francis, D. J., Foorman, B. R., Fletcher, J. M., & Mehta, P. (1999). The dimensionality of phonological awareness: An application of item response theory. *Journal of Educational Psychology, 91(3)*, 439-449.

Scholes, R. J. (1993). In search of phonemic consciousness: A follow-up on Ehri (pp. 45-53). In R. J. Scholes (Ed.). *Literacy and language analysis*. Hillsdale, NJ: Lawrence Erlbaum.

Schotter, E. R., & Rayner, K. (2012). Eye movements in word recognition and reading. In J. S. Adelman (Ed.), *Visual word recognition (Vol. 2): Meaning and context, individuals and development* (pp. 73-101). New York: Psychology Press.

Schwanenflugel, P. J., Morris, R. D., Kuhn, M. R., Strauss, G. P., & Sieczko, J. M. (2008). The influence of reading unit size on the development of Stroop interference in early word decoding. *Reading and Writing: An Interdisciplinary Journal, 21*, 177-203.

Scott, J. & Ehri, L. (1990). Sight word reading in prereaders: Use of logographic vs. alphabetic access routes. *Journal of Reading Behavior, 22*, 149-166.

Seidenberg, M. S. (2002). Connectionist models of reading. *Current Directions in Psychological Science, 14(5)*, 238-242.

Sears, N. C. & Johnson, D. M. (1986). The effects of visual imagery on spelling performance and retention among elementary students. *Journal of Educational Research 79(4)*, 230-233.

Seymour, P. H. K., & Evans, H. M. (1994). Levels of phonological awareness and learning to read. *Reading and Writing: An Interdisciplinary Journal, 6*, 221-250.

Shankweiler, D. (1999). Words to meanings. *Scientific Studies of Reading, 3(2)*, 113-127.

Shankweiler, D., Lundquist, E., Katz, L. Stuebing, K. K., Fletcher, J. M., Brady, S., Fowler, A., Dreyer, L. G., Marchione, K. E., Shaywitz, S. E., & Shaywitz, B. A. (1999). Comprehension and decoding: Patterns of association in children with reading difficulties. *Scientific Studies of Reading, 3(1)*, 69-94.

Share, D.L. (1995). Phonological recoding and self-teaching: Sine qua non of reading acquisition. *Cognition, 55*, 151-218.

Share, D. L. (1999). Phonological recoding and orthographic learning: A direct test of the Self-Teaching Hypothesis. *Journal of Experimental Child Psychology 72*, 95–129

Share, D. (2011). On the role of phonology in reading acquisition: The Self-Teaching Hypothesis. In S. A. Brady, D. Braze, & C. A. Fowler (Eds.), *Explaining individual differences in reading: Theory and evidence*. (pp. 45-68). New York, NY: Psychology Press.

Share, D., Jorm, A. F., MacLean, R. & Matthews, R. (2002). Temporal processing and reading disability. *Reading and Writing: An Interdisciplinary Journal, 15(1-2)*, 151-178.

Shimron, J. (1999). The role of vowel signs in Hebrew: Beyond word recognition. *Reading and Writing: An Interdisciplinary Journal, 11*, 301-319.

Sibley, D. E. & Kello, C. T. (2012). Learned orthographic representations facilitates large-scale modeling of word recognition. In J. S. Adelman (Ed.), *Visual word recognition (Vol. 1): Models and methods, orthography and phonology* (pp. 28-51). New York: Psychology Press.

Simos, P.G., Fletcher, J.M., Bergman, E., Breier, J.I., Foorman, B.R., Castillo, E.M., Fitzgerald, M., & Papanicolau, A.C. (2002). Dyslexia-specific brain activation profile becomes normal following successful remedial training. *Neurology, 58*, 1203–1213.

Simos, P. G., Rezaie, R., Fletcher, J. M., & Papanicolaou, A. C. (2013). Time-constrained functional connectivity analysis of cortical networks underlying phonological decoding in typically developing school-aged children: A magneto-encephalography study. *Brain & Language 125*, 156–164.

Skinner, C. H., Logan, P., Robinson, S. L., & Robinson, D. H. (1997). Demonstration as a reading intervention for exceptional learners: Beyond acquisition. *School Psychology Review, 26(3)*, 437-447.

Smith, F. (1999). Why systematic phonics and phoneme awareness instruction constitute an educational hazard. *Language Arts, 77(2)*, 150-155.

Smith, F. & Goodman, K. S. (1971). On the psycholinguistic method of teaching reading. *Elementary School Journal, 71*, 177-181.

Snider, V. E. (1995). A primer on phoneme awareness: What it is, why it's important, and how to teach it. *School Psychology Review, 24(3)*, 393-404.

Snow, C. E., Burns, M. S., & Griffin, P. (1998). *Preventing reading difficulties in young children*. Washington, D.C.: National Academy Press.

Snowling, M. J. (2006). Acceptance speech of Samuel Torrey Orton Award. *Annals of Dyslexia, 56(2)*, 199-204.

Snowling, M. J. (2011). Beyond phonological deficits: Sources of individual differences in reading disability. In S. A. Brady, D. Braze, & C. A. Fowler (Eds.), *Explaining individual differences in reading: Theory and evidence*. (pp. 121-136). New York: Psychology Press.

Snowling, M., Nation, K., Moxham, P., Gallagher, A., & Frith, U. (1997). Phonological processing skills of dyslexic students in higher education: A preliminary report. *Journal of Research in Reading, 20(1)*, 31-41.

Speece, D. L., & Case, L. P. (2001). Classification in context: An alternative to identifying early reading disability. *Journal of Educational Psychology, 93(4)*, 735-749.

Speece, D. L., Mills, C., Ritchey, K. D., & Hillman, E. (2003). Initial evidence that letter fluency tasks are valid indicators of early reading skill. *Journal of Special Education, 36(4)*, 223-233.

Sprenger-Charolles, L. (1991). Word-identification strategies in a picture context: Comparisons between "good" and "poor" readers. In Rieben, L. & Perfetti, C. A. (Eds.) *Learning to read: Basic research and its implications* (pp. 175-187). Hillsdale, NJ: Erlbaum.

Sprenger-Charolles, L. Siegel, L. S., Bechennec, D. & Serniclaes, W. (2003). Development of phonological and orthographic processing in reading aloud, in silent reading, and in spelling: A four-year longitudinal study. *Journal of Experimental Child Psychology, 84*, 184-217.

Sprenger-Charolles, L. Siegel, L. S., & Bonnet, P. (1998). Reading and spelling acquisition in French: The role of phonological mediation and orthographic factors. *Journal of Experimental Child Psychology, 68*, 134-165.

Stahl, S. A. (1999). Why innovations come and go (and mostly go): The case of Whole Language. *Educational Researcher, 28(8)*, 13-22.

Stahl, S. A., Duffy-Hester, A. M., & Stahl, K. A. D. (1998). Everything you wanted to know about phonics (but were afraid to ask). *Reading Research Quarterly, 33(3)*, 338-355.

Stahl, S. A. & Kuhn, M. R. (1995). Does Whole Language or instruction matched to learning styles help children learn to read? *School Psychology Review, 24(3)*, 393-404.

Stahl, S. A. & Murray, B. A. (1994). Defining phonological awareness and its relationship to early reading. *Journal of Educational Psychology, 86(2)*, 221-234.

Stanovich, K. E. (1981). Response to Goodman's critique. *Reading Research Quarterly, 17(1)*, 157-159.

Stanovich, K. E. (1991a). Discrepancy definitions of reading disability: Has intelligence led us astray? *Reading Research Quarterly, 26*, 7-29.

Stanovich, K. E. (1991b). Changing models of reading and reading acquisition. In Rieben, L. & Perfetti, C. A. (Eds.) *Learning to read: Basic research and its implications* (pp. 19-31). Hillsdale, NJ: Erlbaum.

Stanovich, K. E., Cunningham, A. E., & Cramer, B. B. (1984). Assessing phonological awareness in kindergarten children: Issues of task comparability. *Journal of Experimental Child Psychology, 38*, 175-190.

Stanovich, K. E., & Siegel, L. S. (1994). Phenotypic performance profile of children with reading disabilities: A regression-based test of the phonological-core variable-difference model. *Journal of Educational Psychology, 86(1)*, 24-53.

Stanovich, K. E., Siegel, L. S. Gottardo, A. Chiappe, P. & Sidhu, R. (1997). Subtypes of developmental dyslexia: Differences in phonological and orthographic coding. In B. A. Blachman, (Ed.) *Foundations of reading acquisition and dyslexia* (pp. 115-141). Mahwah, NJ: Erlbaum.

Stanovich, K. E., West, R. F., & Cunningham, A. (1991). Beyond phonological processes: Print exposure and orthographic processing. In Brady, S. A. & Shankweiler, D. P. (Eds.) *Phonological processes in*

References

literacy: *A tribute to Isabelle Y. Liberman* (pp. 219-235). Hillsdale, NJ: Erlbaum.

Stein, J. F. (2012). Biological-level account of developmental dyslexia. In J. S. Adelman (Ed.), *Visual word recognition (Vol. 2): Meaning and context, individuals and development* (pp. 216-243). New York: Psychology Press.

Stuart, M., Masterson, J., & Dixon, M. (2000). Spongelike acquisition of sight vocabulary in beginning readers? *Journal of Research in Reading, 23*, 12–27.

Stuart, M., Stainthorp, R., & Snowling, M. (2008). Literacy as a complex activity: Deconstructing the Simple View of Reading. *Literacy, 42(2)*, 59-66.

Studdert-Kennedy, M. (2002). Deficits in phoneme awareness do not arise from failures in rapid auditory processing.. *Reading and Writing: An Interdisciplinary Journal, 15(1-2)*, 5-14.

Suggate, S. P. (2016). A meta-analysis of the long-term effects of phoneme awareness, phonics, fluency, and reading comprehension interventions. *Journal of Learning Disabilities, 49(1)* 77–96.

Swan, D. & Goswami, U. (1997). Phonological awareness deficits in developmental dyslexia and the phonological representations hypothesis. *Journal of Experimental Child Psychology, 66*, 18-41.

Swank, L. K. & Catts, H. W. (1994). Phonological awareness and written word decoding. *Language, Speech, and Hearing Services in Schools, 25*, 9-14.

Tallal, P., Miller, S. L., Jenkins, W. M., & Merzenich, M. M. (1997). The role of temporal processing in developmental language-based learning disorders: Research and clinical implications. In B. A. Blachman, (Ed.) *Foundations of reading acquisition and dyslexia* (pp. 49-66). Mahwah, NJ: Erlbaum.

Terry, N. P. & Scarborough, H. S. (2011). The phonological hypothesis as a valuable framework for studying the relation of dialect variation to early reading skills. In S. A. Brady, D. Braze, & C. A. Fowler (Eds.), *Explaining individual differences in reading: Theory and evidence.* (pp. 97-117). New York: Psychology Press.

Torgesen, J. K. (1977). Memorization processes in reading-disabled children. *Journal of Educational Psychology, 69(5)*, 571-578.

Torgesen, J. K. (1991). Cross-age consistency in phonological processing. In Brady, S. A. & Shankweiler, D. P. (Eds.) *Phonological processes in literacy: A tribute to Isabelle Y. Liberman* (pp. 187-193). Hillsdale, NJ: Erlbaum.

Torgesen, J. K., Alexander, A. W., Wagner, R. K., Rashotte,, C. A., Voeller, K. K. S., & Conway, T. (2001). Intensive remedial instruction for children with severe reading, disabilities: Immediate and long-term outcomes from two instructional approaches. *Journal of Learning Disabilities, 34(1)*, 33-58, 78.

Torgesen, J. K., Rashotte, C. A.., Alexander, A., Alexander, J., & MacPhee, K. (2003). Progress toward understanding the instructional conditions necessary for remediating reading difficulties in older children. In B. R. Foorman, (Ed.), *Preventing and remediating reading difficulties: Bringing science to scale* (pp. 275-297). Baltimore, MD: York Press.

Torgesen, J. K., Wagner, R. K., & Rashotte, C. (1997). Prevention and remediation of severe reading difficulties: Keeping the end in mind. *Scientific Studies of Reading, 1(3)*, 217-234.

Torgesen, J. K., Wagner, R. K., Rashotte, C. A., Herron, J., & Lindamood, P., (2010). Computer-assisted instruction to prevent early reading difficulties in students at risk for dyslexia: Outcomes from two instructional approaches. *Annals of Dyslexia, 60*, 40–56.

Treiman, R. (1991). The role of intrasyllabic units in learning to read. In Rieben, L. & Perfetti, C. A. (Eds.) *Learning to read: Basic research and its implications* (pp. 149-160). Hillsdale, NJ: Erlbaum.

Treiman, R. (1997). Spelling in normal children and dyslexics. In B. A. Blachman, (Ed.) *Foundations of reading acquisition and dyslexia* (pp. 191-218). Mahwah, NJ: Erlbaum.

Treiman, R., Broderick, V. Tincoff, R. & Rodriguez, K. (1998). Children's phonological awareness: Confusions between phonemes that differ only in voicing. *Journal of Experimental Child Psychology, 68*, 3-21.

Treiman, R., Goswami, U. & Bruck, M. (1990). Not all nonwords are alike: Implications for reading development and theory. *Memory and Cognition, 18*, 559-567.

Treiman, R. & Kessler, B. (2006). Spelling as statistical learning: Using consonantal context to spell vowels. *Journal of Educational Psychology, 98(3)*, 642–652.

Treiman, R., Kessler, B., Zevin, J. D., Bick, S., & Davis, M. (2006). Influence of consonantal context on the reading of vowels: Evidence from children. *Journal of Experimental Child Psychology, 93*, 1-24.

Treiman, R., Mullennix, J., Bijeljac-Babic, R., & Richmond-Welty, E. D. (1995). The special role of rimes in the description, use, and acquisition of English orthography. *Journal of Experimental Psychology: General, 124*, 107-136.

Treiman, R., Sotak, L. & Bowman, M. (2001). The roles of letter names and letter sounds in connecting print to speech. *Memory & Cognition, 29(6)*, 860-873.

Treiman, R. & Zukowski, A. (1991). Children's awareness of rhymes, syllables, and phonemes. In Brady, S. A. & Shankweiler, D. P. (Eds.) *Phonological processes in literacy: A tribute to Isabelle Y. Liberman* (pp. 67-83). Hillsdale, NJ: Erlbaum.

Troia, G. A. (1999). Phonological awareness intervention research: A critical review of the experimental methodology. *Reading Research Quarterly, 34(1)*, 28-52.

Tunmer, W. E. (1991). Phonological awareness and literacy acquisition. In Rieben, L. & Perfetti, C. A. (Eds.) *Learning to read: Basic research and its implications* (pp. 105-119). Hillsdale, NJ: Erlbaum.

Tunmer, W. (2011). Forward. In S. A. Brady, D. Braze, & C. A. Fowler (Eds.), *Explaining individual differences in reading: Theory and evidence.* (pp. ix-xiv). New York, NY: Psychology Press.

Tunmer, W. E. & Chapman, J. W. (2002). The relation of beginning readers' reported word identification strategies to reading achievement, reading-related skills, and academic self-perceptions. *Reading and Writing: An Interdisciplinary Journal, 15(3-4)*, 341-358.

Tunmer, W. E., & Chapman, J. W., & Prochnow, J. E. (2002). Preventing negative Matthew Effects in at-risk readers: A retrospective study. In B. R. Foorman, (Ed.), *Preventing and remediating reading difficulties: Bringing science to scale* (pp. 121-163). Baltimore, MD: York Press.

Tunmer, W. E., Herriman, M.L. & Nesdale, A.R. (1988). Metalinguistic abilities and beginning reading. *Reading Research Quarterly, 23*, 134-158.

Tunmer, W. E. & Nesdale, A. R. (1985). Phonemic segmentation skill and beginning reading. *Journal of Educational Psychology, 77(4)*, 417-427.

Vaessen, A., Gerretsen, P., & Blomert, L. (2009). Naming problems do not reflect a second independent core deficit in dyslexia: Double deficits explored. *Journal of Experimental Child Psychology 103*, 202–221.

Van den Broeck, W. & Geudens, A. (2012). Old and new ways to study characteristics of reading disability: The case of the nonword-reading deficit. *Cognitive Psychology, 65*, 414–456.

Van den Broeck, W., Geudens, A., & van den Bos, K. P. (2010). The Nonword-Reading Deficit of disabled readers: A developmental interpretation. *Developmental Psychology. 46(3)*, 717–734.

Van Orden, G. C. & Kloos, H. (2005). The question of phonology and reading. In M. J. Snowling & C. Hulme (Eds.), *The science of reading: A handbook* (pp. 61-78). Malden, MA: Blackwell.

Varnhagen, C. K., Boechler, P. M. & Steffler, D. J. (1999). Phonological and orthographic influences on children's vowel spelling. *Scientific Studies of Reading, 3(4)*, 363-379.

Vaughn, S., Cirino, P. T. Wanzek, J., Wexler, J., Fletcher, J. M., Denton, C. D., Barth, A., Romain, M., & Francis, D. J. (2010). Response to intervention for middle school students with reading difficulties: Effects of a primary and secondary intervention. *School Psychology Review, 39(1)*, 3–21.

Vaughn, S. & Fletcher, J. (2012). Response to intervention with secondary school students with reading disabilities. *Journal of Learning Disabilities, 45(3)*, 244-256.

Vaughn, S., Wexler, J., Leroux, A., Roberts, G., Denton, C., Barth, A., & Fletcher, J. (2012). Effects of intensive reading intervention for eighth-grade students with persistently inadequate response to intervention. *Journal of Learning Disabilities, 45(6)*, 515-525.

Vellutino, F. R. (1991). Introduction to three studies on reading acquisition: Convergent findings on theoretical foundations of code-oriented versus whole-language approaches to reading instruction. *Journal of Educational Psychology, 83(4)*, 437-443.

Vellutino, F. R., Fletcher, J. M. Snowling, M. J., & Scanlon, D. M. (2004). Specific reading disability (dyslexia): What have we learned in the past four decades? *Journal of Child Psychology and Psychiatry 45(1)*, 2–40.

Vellutino, F. R., & Scanlon, D. M. (1987). Phonological coding, phonological awareness, and reading ability: Evidence from a longitudinal and experimental study. *Merrill-Palmer Quarterly, 33,* 321-363.

Vellutino, F. R., & Scanlon, D. (1991a). The preeminence of phonologically based skills in learning to read. In Brady, S. A. & Shankweiler, D. P. (Eds.) *Phonological processes in literacy: A tribute to Isabelle Y. Liberman* (pp. 219-235). Hillsdale, NJ: Erlbaum.

Vellutino, F. R., & Scanlon, D. (1991b). The effects of instructional bias on word identification. In Rieben, L. & Perfetti, C. A. (Eds.) *Learning to read: Basic research and its implications* (pp. 189-203). Mahwah, NJ: Erlbaum.

Vellutino, F. R., Scanlon, D. M., & Jaccard, J. J. (2003). Toward distinguishing between cognitive and experiential deficits as primary sources of difficulty in learning to read: A two year follow-up of difficult to remediate and readily remediated poor readers. In B. R. Foorman, (Ed.), *Preventing and remediating reading difficulties: Bringing science to scale* (pp. 73-120). Baltimore, MD: York Press.

Vellutino, F. R., Scanlon, D. M., Sipay, E. R., Small, S. G., Pratt, A., Chen, R., & Denkla, M. B. (1996). Cognitive profiles of difficult-to-remediate and readily remediated poor readers: Early intervention as a vehicle for distinguishing between cognitive and experiential deficits as basic causes of specific reading disability. *Journal of Educational Psychology, 88,* 601-638.

Vellutino, F. R., Scanlon, D. M., & Sipay, E. R. (1997). Toward distinguishing between cognitive and experiential deficits as primary sources of difficulty in learning to read: The importance of early intervention in diagnosing specific reading disability. In B. A. Blachman, (Ed.) *Foundations of reading acquisition and dyslexia* (pp. 347-379). Mahwah, NJ: Erlbaum.

Vellutino, F. R., Tunmer, W. E., Jaccard, J. J., & Chen, R. (2007). Components of reading ability: Multivariate evidence for a Convergent Skills Model of reading development. *Scientific Studies of Reading, 11(1),* 3-32.

Verhoeven, L., Schreuder, R., Baayen, R. H. (2006). Learnability of graphotactic rules in visual word identification. *Learning and Instruction, 16,* 538-548.

Vukovic, R. K. & Siegel, L. S. (2006). The Double-Deficit Hypothesis: A comprehensive analysis of the evidence. *Journal of Learning Disabilities, 39(1),* 25-47.

Wagner, R. K., Muse, A. E., Stein, T. L., Cukrowicz, K. C., Harrell, E. R., Rashotte, C. A., & Samwel, C. S. (2002). How to assess reading-related phonological abilities. In B. R. Foorman, (Ed.), *Preventing and remediating reading difficulties: Bringing science to scale* (pp. 51-70). Baltimore, MD: York Press.

Wagner, R. K., & Torgesen, J. K. (1987). The nature of phonological processing and its causal role in the acquisition of reading skills. *Psychological Bulletin, 101,* 192-212.

Wagner, R. K., Torgesen, J. K., Laughon, P., Simmons, K., & Rashotte, C. A. (1993). Development of young readers' phonological processing abilities. *Journal of Educational Psychology, 85(1),* 83-103.

Wagner, R. K., Torgesen, J. K., & Rashotte, C. A. (1994). Development of reading-related phonological abilities: New evidence of bidirectional causality from a latent variable longitudinal study. *Developmental Psychology, 30(1),* 73-87.

Wagner, R. K., Torgesen, J. K., Rashotte, C. A., Hecht, S. A., Barker, T. A., Burgess, S. R., Donahue, J., & Garon, T. (1997). Changing relations between phonological abilities and word-level reading as children develop from beginning to skilled readers: A 5-year longitudinal study. *Developmental Psychology, 33(3),* 468-479.

Walsh, K., Glaser, D., & Dunne-Wilcox, D. (2006). *What elementary teachers don't know about reading and what teacher preparation programs aren't teaching.* Washington, DC: National Council for Teacher Quality.

Wallach, L., Wallach, M. A., Dozier, M. G., & Kaplan, N. E. (1977). Poor children learning to read do not have trouble with auditory discrimination but do have trouble with phoneme recognition. *Journal of Educational Psychology, 69(1),* 36-39.

Wanzek, J., & Vaughn, S. (2007). Research-based implications from extensive early reading interventions. *School Psychology Review, 36,* 541–561.

Wanzek, J., Vaughn, S., Scammacca, N. K., Metz, K., Murray, C. S., Roberts, G., & Danielson, L. (2013). Extensive reading interventions for students with reading difficulties after grade 3. *Review of Educational Research, 83(2),* 163–195.

Watkins, M. W., Glutting, J. J., Lei, P. (2007). Validity of the full-scale IQ when there is significant variability among WISC-III and WISC-IV factor scores. *Applied Neuropsychology, 14(1),* 13–20.

Weaver, P. A. & Resnick, L. B. (1979). The theory and practice of early reading: An introduction. In Resnick, L. B. & Weaver, P. A. (Eds.) *Theory and practice of early reading,* Volume 3. Hillsdale, NJ: Erlbaum.

Whalley, K. & Hansen, J. (2006). The role of prosodic sensitivity in children's reading development. *Journal of Research in Reading, 29(3),* 288–303.

Williams, J. P. (1980). Teaching decoding with an emphasis on phoneme analysis and phoneme blending. *Journal of Educational Psychology, 72,* 1-15.

Windfuhr, K. & Snowling, M. J. (2001). The relationship between paired associate learning and phonological skills in normally developing readers. *Journal of Experimental Child Psychology, 80,* 160-173.

Wolf, M. (1991). The word-retrieval deficit hypothesis and developmental dyslexia. *Learning and Individual Differences, 3(3),* 205-223.

Wolf, M. (1991). Naming speed and reading: The contribution of the cognitive neurosciences. *Reading Research Quarterly, 26(2),* 123-141.

Wolf, M. (1997). A provisional, integrative account of phonological and naming-speed deficits in dyslexia: Implications for diagnosis and intervention. In B. A. Blachman, (Ed.) *Foundations of reading acquisition and dyslexia* (pp. 67-92). Mahwah, NJ: Erlbaum.

Wolf, M. & Katzir-Cohen, T. (2001). Reading fluency and its intervention. *Scientific Studies of Reading, 5(3),* 211-238.

Wolf, M., O'Rourke, A. G., Gidney, C., Lovett, M., Cirino, & Morris, R. (2002). The second deficit: An investigation of the independence of phonological and naming-speed deficits in developmental dyslexia. *Reading and Writing: An Interdisciplinary Journal, 15(1-2),* 43-72

Wolff, P. H. (2002). Timing precision and rhythm in developmental dyslexia. *Reading and Writing: An Interdisciplinary Journal, 15(1-2),* 179-206.

Wylie, R. E., & Durrell, D. D. (1970). Teaching vowels through phonograms. *Elementary English, 47,* 787-791.

Yopp, H. K. (1988). The validity and reliability of phoneme awareness tests. *Reading Research Quarterly, 23(3),* 159-177.

Zemelman, S. Daniels, H. & Bizar, M. (1999). Sixty years of reading research–But who's listening? *Phi Delta Kappan,* March, 513-517.

Zhurova, L. E. (1963). The development of analysis of words into their sounds by preschool children. *Soviet Psychology and Psychiatry, 2(2),* 17-27.

Ziegler, J. C. & Goswami, U. (2005). Reading acquisition, developmental dyslexia, and skilled reading across languages: A psycholinguistic grain size theory. *Psychological Bulletin, 131(1),* 3–29.

Zifcak, M. (1981). Phonological awareness and reading acquisition. *Contemporary Educational Psychology, 6,* 117-126.

Index

Alliteration, 17, 19, 74, 260
Alphabet, 30, 105, 106, 247
    in relation to phonemes, 14, 34, 37
Alphabetic principle, 36, 103, 260
American Federation of Teachers, 2, 266
Assessment, 12, 75
Assured Readiness for Learning, v, vi, 22, 42, 86, 105, 120, 236, 260, 262, 273

Backward decoding technique, 60, 61, 66, 69, 70, 246
Behavior, impact of poor reading, 1, 112, 113
Bonding. *See* Orthographic mapping

Compensating, 3, 48, 52, *See* also Chapter 13
    common signs of, 113
    due to developmentally inappropriate reading materials, 48
    the most common strategies, 57
    what to do about it, 116
Comprehensive Test of Phonological Processing, 93, 266
Consolidated alphabetic phase, 50
Consolidated Alphabetic Phase, 47

Deaf readers, 30
Developmental Reading Approach, 12, 46
Direct mapping. *See* Orthographic mapping
Dolch words, 103, 110, 261, 269
Dyslexia, 118, 121, 123, 261

Ehri's theory of sight word acquisition, 46, 47, 48
Eye movement research, 37, 40

Familiar letter strings. *See* Letter strings
Flash cards
    use of, 109
Fluency, 3, 5, 9, 12, 21, 31
    influence of orthographic mapping on, 31
Full alphabetic phase, 49, 50
Full Alphabetic Phase, 47

Guessing words
    as a compensating strategy, 52, 57, 61
    as word identification, 6, 52

Hyperlexia, 7, 261

Independent work time, 70
Intelligence
    and compensating, 113, 115
    and phonemic awareness, 17, 84
    and reading, 1
Invented spelling, 70, 246
Invented Spelling, 63
Irregular words, 34, 103, 246
    and compensators, 114
    and mapping, 58, 69
    and phonics, 103

kindergarten
    importance of early phonological awareness training in, 17
Kindergarten, 12, 19, 48
    importance of early phonological awareness training in, 13

Lesson plan samples, 71
Letter sounds, 36, 101, *See* also Letter-sound skills
    in irregular words, 58
    teaching, 106
Letter strings, 32
    familiar, 32, 35, 36, 37, 39

Index

meaningful, 32, 33, 34
Letter-sound skills, 7, **12**, 36, 45, 262, *See* also
    Chapter 12
    additional helps, 247
    how to develop, 104
    their role in orthographic mapping, 41
Lindamood, 2, 262
Linguistic reading approach, 49, 50, 262
    and Response to Intervention, 124
    vs. phonics, 50
Listening comprehension, 115
Look-alike words, 57, 251

Making/Breaking Words, 65
McInnis, v, vi, 22, 42, 77, 86, 94, 99, 236, 260, 273
Meaningful letter strings. *See* Letter strings
Mixed-case research, 28, 29
Multisensory learning
    of phonological awareness skills, 78

National Reading Panel, 68, 266, 273
nonsense words, 71
Nonsense words, 63, 262
    for assessing phonics skills, 115
    for phoneme reversal, 227
    for word study activities, 252
    reading, 64, 120, 246
    spelling, 64, 71, 246

One Minute Activities, 56, 78, 83, 86, See also
    Chapter 10
    as a type of phonological manipulation, 76
    effectiveness, 87
    how to use, 89
    use in small and large groups, 87
Onset-Rime. *See* Phonological awareness, Levels of
Oral blending, 7, 73, 122, 262
    built into One Minute Activities, 78
    role in phonic decoding, 101, 106
Orthographic mapping, 4, 6, 27, 34
    defined, 262

    impact on fluency, 31
    impact on reading comprehension, 31
    three components of, 41
    vs. phonics, 39
Orthography, 7, 66, 121, 262
Orton-Gillingham reading approach, 102, 262

Paired-associate learning, 7, 104, 263
Partial alphabetic phase, 50
Partial Alphabetic phase
    and the linguistic reading approach, 49
Partial Alphabetic Phase, 46
PAST. *See Phonological Awareness Screening Test*
Phoneme, what is a, 14
phonemic awareness
    importance for orthographic mapping, 34
    vs. phonemic discrimination, 16
    word storage, 37
Phonemic awareness, 7, **12**, 13, 45, 263, *See* also
    Phonological awareness
    and word storage, 34, 43
    importance for orthographic mapping, 37,
        41, 50
    not an isolated skill, 45
    relationship with intelligence, 17
    vs. phonics, 15
    vs. phonological awareness, 13, 27
Phonemic awareness problems, 35
    early identification, 17
    failure to recognize, 21
Phonemic awareness training. *See* Phonological
    awareness training
Phonemic *discrimination*, 263
    vs. awareness, 16
Phonetic decoding. *See* Sounding out words
Phonics, 6, 29, 42, 46, 263
    developmental appropriateness of, 51
    no guarantee of later retrieval, 70
    phonetic approximation, 103
    phonological awareness requirements for,
        49, 50

Index

vs. orthographic mapping, 37
vs. the linguistic approach to reading, 50
Phonogram, 263
Phonological awareness. *See* also Phonemic awareness
   becoming proficient
      Automatic Stage, 83
      Knowledge Stage, 83
   Becoming proficient
      Multisensory Stage, 77
   development of, 48, 235
   how much needed for proficient reading, 21
   levels of
      level at which weak readers "get stuck", 21
      phoneme level, 21
   Levels of, 19, 22, 23
      onset-rime level, 19, 23, 24, 49, 262
      phoneme level, 19, 23, 25, 27
      syllable level, 19, 23, 24
   nature of "awareness", 15
   segmentation vs. manipulation, 75
   Types of
      isolation, 74
      Isolation, 78
      manipulation, 21, 74
         deletion, 22
         reversal, 227
         substitution, 22
      most efficient type, 75
      segmentation, 21, 74, 78
   vs. phonemic awareness, 13, 27
Phonological Awareness, 263
   levels of
      onset-rime level, 20
Phonological awareness assessment. *See* Assessment
Phonological Awareness Screening Test, 93, 237
Phonological awareness training, 17, 21, 85
   age & grade considerations, 17
   with typical readers, 17

Pre-alphabetic phase, 49
Pre-alphabetic Phase, 46
Prevention of reading problems, 13, 17, 116, 123

Rapid automatized naming, 7, 93, 122, 123
Rapid Automatized Naming, 263
Reading approaches, 47, 48, 50, *See* also Whole word reading approach; Whole Language; Linguistic reading approach; Phonics
Reading comprehension, 3, 6, 7, 9, 12, 17, 31, 72
   impact of working memory, 115
   importance of fluency for, 3
   influence of orthographic mapping on, 31
   of a compensator, 112, 113, 114, 115
Reading disabilities, 41, 102, 118
   a new perspective on, 123
   A new perspective on, 121
Rebus reading method, 49
Remediation, 3, 12, 42, 46, 118, 123
   prevention better than, 116
Response to Intervention, 263
Reversal of phonemes. *See* Phonological awareness, Types of, manipulation, reversal
Reversals of letters, 118, 119, 120, 261
Rhyming, 13, 17, 19, 74
Rime, 20, 21
   definition of, 20, 263
Rime Unit, 20, 50, 55, 61, 249
   importance in orthographic mapping, 36
Rosner, v, vi, 2, 22, 94, 236, 264
RTI. *See* Response to Intervention

Self-teaching hypothesis, 102
Self-Teaching Hypothesis, 264
Sight vocabulary, 6, 12, 36, 39, 264
   development of, 46, 48
      Pre-alphabetic phase, 46
   impact of orthographic mapping, 31
   meaning of term, 27
   role of phonemic awareness in development

of, 27
Sight word
  meaning of term, 27, 264
Silent reading, 36, 68
Simple View of Reading, 7, 8, 9
Sounding out words, 3
  in phonic decoding, 6, 15, 36, 260
  no guarantee of later retrieval, 70
  proper pronunciation of sounds, 106, 109
  rime units helpful in, 55, 56
  role of oral blending in, 260
  vs. instant recognition, 6, 27, 36, 37
  vs. orthographic mapping, 6, 29, 39
Spelling, 56, 63, 66, 88
  and compensators, 114
  impact of difficulties, 112
  invented, 63, 70, 246, 261
  nonsense words, 64, 71
  oral, 62
  reversals and transpositions in, 119

Transpositions of letters. *See* Reversals of letters

Visual memory
  and deaf readers, 30
  and poor readers, 29
  correlation with sight vocabulary, 29
  importance for reading, 30
  inefficiency of, 30
  used in compensating, 57

Visual memory theory
  assumed in word recognition, 3, 27
  disproved, 29
  may promote weak reading, 29
Vocabulary, 7
  and reading comprehension, 7
  controlled, 260
  instructional terms for reading, 54

Whole Language, 6, 41, 42, 46, 264
Whole word reading approach, 6, 41, 46, 51, 52, 62, 264
Wilson reading approach, 102, 264
Word family approach, 264, *See* Linguistic reading approach
Word identification, 6
  skills needed for, 6
  types of, 6
  via guessing, 6
  via phonics, 6
  vs. word recognition, 5, 50
Word recognition, 3, 6
  vs. word identification, 5, 37, 50
Word study, 12, 41, 45, 264, *See* also Chapter 6
  defined, 41
  techniques, 246
Words Their Way, 66
Working memory, 7, 122, 264
  impact on reading comprehension, 115

NOTES